"The church today needs men—men wh[...] Word and can translate truth into life, [...] *seling Men* is a work that can help transfo[...] Street has served Christ well with this collection of essays. What a delight to read the words of men who believe that a sufficient Christ, revealed in His sufficient Word, can thoroughly equip men for every good work. May God use it for His glory and the strengthening of His church."

Tim Pasma, Pastor, LaRue Baptist Church,
Fellow in the National Association of Nouthetic Counselors

—⚏—

"*Men Counseling Men* is an important book. We live in a Christian culture in great need of godly men to shepherd one another and their families. This book is a rich resource to help meet this need. I am happy to commend it."

Dr. Heath Lambert, Professor and Department Coordinator
for Biblical Counseling, Boyce College

—⚏—

"A monumental achievement! *Men Counseling Men* is a biblical, Christ-centered resource that will further equip men to engage in authentic discipleship ministries within the context of the local church and for the purpose of helping other men grow in God's transforming grace. John Street has pulled together the collective wisdom of highly qualified men throughout this book, which should be valued by all who want to develop dynamic men's ministries for the glory of God."

Rick Wilson, Pastor of Grace Covenant Church,
Beavercreek, Ohio and Director of Titus School for Leadership Development

—⚏—

"Men in today's church face two significant challenges: finding the courage and wisdom needed to shepherd men through the issues of temptation and struggle pervasive in our society, and the total lack of sound biblical resources that equip them to address these issues from a biblical perspective. *Men Counseling Men* offers sure counsel from those who have been refined by the realities of pastoral ministry and will enable men to move toward their spiritual brothers with confidence. The topics covered in this book will help godly fathers, brothers, and husbands encourage and exhort the men in their lives with both truth and love."

Dr. Mark Tatlock, Executive Vice President and Provost,
The Master's College

"*Men Counseling Men* is a good book that has, as its practical working methodology, the need to disciple men with the deepest roots within the richest soil of all: Holy Scripture. I rejoice that each of the authors of this volume believe in the total sufficiency of the Bible for the vital ministry of showing men their sins and the only lasting solutions for them. May this helpful manual equip many for the goal of seeing our Savior, Jesus Christ, as the one true image to which Christians must conform their lives."

Lance Quinn, Pastor of Grace Advance,
Grace Community Church, Sun Valley, California

—m—

"I commend Dr. John Street for assembling such a 'championship' team of writers to produce this superb volume for men (Proverbs 27:17). The authors major on the certainty of powerful, biblical truth rather than manipulative, psychological technique. The book's content proves to be both preventative and corrective, as well as personal and practical. A 'must read' label should be stamped on every cover."

Dr. Richard Mayhue, Executive VP and
Dean of The Master's Seminary

—m—

"John Street and his team have made a significant contribution to men who want to help one another grow in Christ. Reading this book is like going out for a steak dinner with your best buddies. Forget the frills and doilies—this is a meal for real men who intend to get to a more authentic place in their relationship with the Lord, together. Feasting on the Word with your friends—there are few things better than that. Bring a hearty appetite...steak sauce optional."

Steve Viars, Senior Pastor, Faith Church,
Lafayette, Indiana

—m—

"I have great memories of teaching biblical counseling at The Master's College and supervising a few of these men with their writing projects. I thought at the time, *These topics are so well done that they ought to be published to help others with their various struggles in the faith.* In God's providence (and thank you, John) it has happened, and I'm delighted to recommend this book with its wide scope of practical topics to churchmen everywhere."

Dr. Stuart W. Scott, Associate Professor of Biblical Counseling,
The Southern Baptist Theological Seminary

MEN
COUNSELING
MEN

JOHN D. STREET

HARVEST HOUSE PUBLISHERS
EUGENE, OREGON

Cover by Dugan Design Group, Bloomington, Minnesota

Cover photo by © Clarissa Leahy / Cultura Creative / Alamy

Back cover author photo by Lukas VanDyke

This book contains stories in which the contributors have changed people's names and the details of their situations in order to protect their privacy. There are also fictitious accounts used for illustration purposes only.

MEN COUNSELING MEN
Copyright © 2013 by John D. Street Jr.
Published by Harvest House Publishers
Eugene, Oregon 97402
www.harvesthousepublishers.com

Library of Congress Cataloging-in-Publication Data
    Men counseling men/John D. Street, Jr., general editor.
        p.cm.
    Includes bibliographical references.
    ISBN 978-0-7369-4926-2 (pbk.)
    ISBN 978-0-7369-4927-9 (eBook)
    1. Church work with men. 2. Men—Pastoral counseling of. 3. Pastoral counseling. I. Street, John D., 1952-
    BV4440.M46 2013
    259.0811—dc23

        2012028982

Printed in the United States of America

    13 14 15 16 17 18 19 20 21 / LB-KBD / 10 9 8 7 6 5 4 3 2 1

To the thousands of biblical counseling students,
both undergraduate and graduate,
who have studied at The Master's College and Seminary,
and to their counselees—may this book be a blessing!
To Jesus Christ belongs all the glory and honor,
both now and forever.
Amen!

Acknowledgments

I wish to personally thank each of the men who have so faithfully contributed to this labor of love. Twenty-two men, in hopes that the body of Christ will be enriched and blessed, have put hundreds of hours into the writing of this volume. It is our desire to see this book equip men who are earnest in using the Bible to effectively counsel other men who are struggling with serious issues of the soul.

My appreciation goes to Nathan Busenitz, who helped me to "kick-start" this book, and to my son, Jay Street, who assisted in the editing process. Also to all the faculty and staff in the Biblical Counseling office of The Master's College—both present and in the past. Your investment in the lives of men and women around the world has helped to bring about biblical change in many lives to the glory of God. In addition, it has been a joy to work with Steve Miller at Harvest House Publishers. He has been both gracious and extremely helpful throughout the writing process.

Special thanks goes to my precious wife, Janie Lynn Street, who has spent countless hours editing and formatting this work into a presentable form. Without her, this book would not have made it. Thank you, Sweetie!

Contents

Foreword

The important book you now hold in your hands is written with the strategic intent of being simple and straightforward. The various contributors to this volume have sought to bring basic biblical truths to bear upon the current challenges that professing Christian males face in our world. The book's wide array of authors, coming as they do from various walks of life, humbly desire to communicate solid, scriptural answers for their assigned subject and they do so with genuine care and Christlike compassion. This is what I so appreciate about this book. It is nothing more (but certainly nothing less) than an attempt to practically teach powerful, divine truth within the context of the Christian man's everyday life struggles.

Although some of the issues discussed in this book will be seen by doubters as much too complex to be handled with the Bible alone, each and every writer unequivocally affirms the absolute sufficiency of God's Word. While it is readily acknowledged that the specific issues addressed in these chapters have the potential to bring much hurt and heartache to men's lives (as sinful choices always do), those men who choose to apply the biblical principles that are thus proposed from these pages will find both great hope and profound joy in their obedience to Scripture's infinitely wise cures.

This unified approach in ministering to people is something that has, in general, uniquely marked the biblical counseling movement over the last 40 years. When I became president of The Master's College in 1985, I sought to bring all the students in every academic discipline under this same unswerving commitment to the doctrine of the total sufficiency of God's Word. Now, almost 30 years later, and to use this but one example, the biblical counseling degree programs we offer are now the largest of their kind in the United States.

Over this span of time, we have seen thousands of our students trained to teach and practice biblical counseling all around the world. God sovereignly honors His sufficient Word.

My sincere thanks go to Dr. John Street, the editor of *Men Counseling Men,* who also capably oversees the undergraduate and graduate programs in biblical counseling at The Master's College. It is my earnest prayer that God would continue to honor the efforts of so many as they labor in the ministry of seeing more and more people transformed by God's Word and for His glory.

John MacArthur

Pastor-Teacher
Grace Community Church
Sun Valley, California

President
The Master's College & Seminary

Preface

John D. Street

I became interested in biblical counseling because I wanted to help people, but it ended up helping me first. That is what caught me totally off guard."

Several men have confessed this to me after being exposed to biblical counseling. And that was precisely my experience when I was first introduced to it. Biblical counseling fundamentally changed me, because it helped me address serious issues in my own heart. The way I viewed God and the circumstances of life permanently changed for me. In fact, knowing every contributor to this book, I can attest to the fact that each one could make a similar claim. They are writing not only as active and experienced counselors, but also as men who have been personally transformed by the very biblical truths they explain throughout this book. After reading it, you may have a similar confession.

All counseling is about change. Every psychotherapeutic theory seeks some type of change in the counselee's life. But there is a major problem that is fundamental to the field of psychotherapy. It may surprise you to learn there are over 300 distinctive theories of psychotherapy in the world today. Depending on the type of therapy you receive, the end product or goal in counseling will always be different from system to system.

Now, if you knew that there were over 300 distinctive approaches to anesthesia, would you go into surgery? Most people would not, because the fact there are so many approaches—and therefore, so many possible outcomes, some of which could be very uncertain—could mean they might die or be maimed for life.

Yet when it comes to counseling, we will often surrender our most vulnerable and hurting people to some unknown psychotherapist without a clear knowledge of his goals. In stark contrast, every Christian understands that exposure to God's Word in counseling should have one uniform result—Christlikeness! This is always the goal of genuine biblical counseling.

Every contributor to this book understands and agrees with this one Christ-focused goal for counseling. The apostle Paul had the same goal in his personal ministry of God's Word, which he presents in Colossians 1:28: "Him we proclaim, warning everyone and teaching everyone with all wisdom, *that we may present everyone mature in Christ.*" He had this focused purpose throughout his entire ministry, whether he was preaching or counseling.

Notice as well how Paul repeated the word "everyone" three times in this brief verse. He was emphasizing the individual ministry of the Word in his proclamation of the truth with the goal of Christlikeness. This is biblical counseling and this is the central focus of the principles for personal ministry that are found in *Men Counseling Men*.

Men Teaching Other Men

Christian men with the right theological training and experience in counseling should be modeling and training other men how to counsel from the Bible. The twenty-plus gifted men who have contributed to this book have the theological training and counseling experience to be models and teachers of counseling. I wish you could meet them personally, for their most notable traits are their humble attitudes, their passionate love for the Lord and His Word, and their gracious love for the people they counsel. Their sacrifice of countless hours of extensive research and writing for this book is purely for the glory of God and the benefit of other men. There will be no personal monetary reimbursement for their efforts. All financial proceeds from the sale of this book will go toward scholarships for men who desire to receive accredited graduate training in biblical counseling in the Master of Arts in Biblical Counseling (MABC) program at The Master's College in Santa Clarita, California. These contributors are truly faithful men who have sacrificed considerably in order to provide this tool for those who desire to equip themselves for counseling biblically, and I am grateful for each of them.

When the apostle Paul wrote to the young man Timothy about the training that should go on in the church, he admonished him, saying, "What you have heard from me in the presence of many witnesses entrust to faithful men who will be able to teach others also"[1] (2 Timothy 2:2). Dedicated men, with this admonition in view, have written this book to help men like you counsel men more effectively using God's Word. In short, real biblical counseling is a ministry of faithful Bible exposition that is done with a balance of grace and truth (John 1:14,17).

Distinctives of Biblical Counseling

What are the critical assumptions that lie behind each chapter and make the counsel in this book distinctively Christian? No one counsels from a neutral, unbiased point of view. Any counselor who is honest will admit that he operates with certain assumptions that make his counseling work. This is true for biblical counseling as well. Here are five important assumptions that find their source in biblical theology and form the basis for the instruction in this book on how to help men effectively counsel other men:

1. God and His Word Are the Focus of All Counseling

Human psychology makes *man* the center of all counseling. Every problem is about *man's* feelings, *man's* experience, *man's* actions, and *man's* reactions. As a result, success in counseling is evaluated by how a man feels, or whether his experiences are more pleasant, or whether he is acting or reacting productively with his problems. Biblical counseling is concerned with all of these as well, because godly counselors deeply care about the condition of their counselee. But, by way of contrast, biblical counselors view these human experiences as symptoms, not the ultimate source of the problem at hand. The central focus of real biblical counseling is not man and his problems; rather, the central focus is God's glory and how man is handling his problems from *God's* perspective. God is the central figure in biblical counseling, not man (2 Corinthians 5:9).

This book does not view the Bible as merely one source among other equally authoritative sources of counsel. It views the Bible as *the final authority*, and holds that the Bible is sufficient to deal with all the nonorganic problems that a man may encounter (2 Peter 1:3). In other words, this is a Christian counseling book that holds a high—or better, a *supreme*—view of the insight, wisdom, and authority of God's Word in counseling. For a more complete discussion about the Bible's sufficiency, see chapter 1, "Understanding Biblical Counseling."

2. The Local Church Is the Primary Context for Counseling

God gave the church as a gift of grace to people who have the greatest problems of the soul. There is no establishment of counseling clinics in the New Testament—just the church. By design, God intended for the church to be the place where the greatest struggles and difficulties of life find their answers (Romans 15:14; Galatians 6:1). Theology is life. Pastors should counsel and train men and women in the church with theology so that they too can address serious soul problems (Ephesians 4:11-16).

Counseling done under the authority of godly elders in a local church has credibility as well. There can be immediate personal and doctrinal accountability for the counsel that is given. When a church that is serious about good doctrine actively takes this type of direct oversight, then people who are receiving counsel have caring supervision (1 Thessalonians 5:14). The local church is a perfect setting for counseling because the counselors are often working with people they know and can benefit from the insights of the pastoral staff in better shepherding the counselee. There are many wonderful advantages when a cure of the soul is accomplished under the discipleship of a loving church.

Counseling is also a ministry to the needy. When the church is involved in counseling, there is no need for charging a fee. Counseling is a ministry of the Word to people who have struggles that extend to several areas of their life, and oftentimes one of these struggles is financial difficulties. Charging a fee for counseling can be oppressive to someone who already has a host of challenges. Again, the church is the perfect context in which people can receive help without having to worry about the burden of another monetary obligation (3 John 7; cf. Genesis 14:21-24).

3. The Gospel of Jesus Christ Is Critical to Every Counseling Problem

The most critical soul problem for every man is his standing before God. Every counseling problem goes back to how much that man loves God and how much he loves others (Matthew 22:37-40). Counseling can easily become evangelism if that man has never been regenerated by the saving grace of the Lord Jesus Christ. There are many who profess to be Christians, but it is not uncommon to find professed Christians who are not genuine believers. This is such an important issue that we've included a section in this book on communicating the gospel of Jesus Christ in counseling (see "The Gospel for Men" in Appendix One).

In addition, this book is also dedicated to the theological premise that grace drives the process of change in the believer commonly known as *sanctification*. God's grace is a central motivator when it comes to change and growing in Christ. His grace is a like a trainer that teaches the believer to increasingly deny the sinful passions that afflict his life (Titus 2:11-14)—a lifelong process that will continue until he reaches his glorified state (Romans 8:23-25). Grace daily reminds the Christian man of his righteous standing before God in Jesus Christ and how he now lives without condemnation (Romans 8:1). A personal knowledge of this undeserved grace is what sparks a fire in the heart of a believer and prompts him toward more holy living. This is why it's so crucial to communicate God's grace to those who are being counseled.

4. Only the Sovereign Work of the Holy Spirit Changes People

Human counselors cannot change anyone. They can only provide guidance that may or may not be followed by counselees. But counselees, on the other hand, may change their outward behavior for a time because of some perceived threat or to achieve some possible reward, yet if this change is not from the heart, they will eventually return to their old way of life (Proverbs 26:11). Biblical counselors understand that real heart change comes from the sovereign work of the Holy Spirit in the heart of a man as he hears the Word of God and mixes his hearing with faith (John 3:6-8; 16:8-11). Ultimately, there are no techniques or counseling strategies that change people. Counselors are responsible for being faithful to communicate God's Word, which alone is able to discern "the thoughts and intentions of the heart" (Hebrews 4:12). Only then will the Holy Spirit work, according to His perfect timetable, in the heart of the counselee (Ephesians 6:17).

5. Scripture Teaches a Complementarian View of Marriage and Family

This is a very important principle for a Christian counselor who must address family issues. Scripture recognizes the distinctive roles of a man and woman as being designed by God. An egalitarian believes that a husband and wife have equal authority in marriage. But a complementarian believes the husband should assume loving leadership of his wife and home (1 Corinthians 11:3; Ephesians 5:22-25; 1 Timothy 2:13-15; 3:4-5). Contemporary egalitarian perspectives that are unnaturally forced upon the Bible erode the biblical uniqueness of the sexes and destroy the divine design of spousal roles. Just as there exists an equality among the persons of the Godhead—God the Father, God the Son, and God the Holy Spirit—there also exists a functional subordination within the Trinity (John 14:10; 16:7). In a similar manner, there is a functional subordination in marriage. The apostle Paul said that the relationship a husband has to God and then to his wife is comparable to Christ's relationship to His Father: "I want you to understand that the head of every man is Christ, the head of a wife is her husband, and the head of Christ is God" (1 Corinthians 11:3). Here, the concept of being a "head" refers to immediate authority.

In Scripture, a husband's authority is always described within the context of preferring his wife before himself and loving her with a greater love than the human tendency for a man to love himself (Ephesians 5:28-29). And the Christian wife is always to be the complement to her husband by submitting to his leadership, respecting him, and helping him. Harmony in the home is predicated upon following this biblical structure. Christian counselors understand that a vibrant and vigorous Christian home is one in which the man assumes the role of leadership in both the home and the church.

Building on a Biblical Foundation

The counseling principles within this book are powerful because they are built upon biblical precedent. It is my hope that as you read and study this volume you will find it to be a great tool in your ministry bag. Whether you read this book in a private context, for a class, or with other men in a study group, our hope is that your insight into God's Word and into His people will grow. To Jesus Christ belongs the glory, both now and forever. Amen!

Part 1

A Man and the Word

1

Understanding Biblical Counseling

Joshua Clutterham

What is biblical counseling?

Whole books have been written to answer this question alone, and it's a good question to ask, for the answer will help shape the way in which we fulfill this crucial ministry task. This chapter will aim at a basic introduction to biblical counseling by surveying its approach to communication and the counseling meeting, its place within the church and society, and its foundations.

But before we answer that question, it is important to pause and note this very crucial point: Biblical counseling is unshakably anchored to the authority and sufficiency of the Bible. That is, biblical counseling is defined by the Bible—not the author who is currently selling the most books or giving the most presentations—and it is exemplified by the God-man, Jesus Christ. "Understanding Biblical Counseling" or "What Is Biblical Counseling?" chapters may rise and fall over the years, but the Word of God stands forever (Isaiah 40:8).

That which claims to be biblical counseling but fails to be *biblical*—that is, consistent with the Bible rightly interpreted—is a poor witness. Likewise, that which claims to be instruction in biblical counseling but bears no resemblance to Jesus Christ—doesn't speak the way He speaks, or sound the way He sounds, or share His message, or operate with His worldview—will be exposed as counterfeit. Let this chapter, then, and those that follow be examined for biblical integrity. They have been written with the hopes of withstanding the test and challenging us toward knowing the Lord more and His Word more profoundly. The biblical call to love our neighbor as ourselves as an expression of love to God finds its application in "speaking the truth to others"—what we call counseling.

A Biblical Approach to Communication

Biblical counseling could be defined simply as "a biblical approach to communication"— or, as another has described it, "intentionally helpful conversations."[1] But how does your communication relate to counseling?

Everyone counsels. That means you—yes, you—are already a counselor, whether you have accepted the title or not. Every time you share an opinion that communicates values or a system of belief, you counsel. Think back to the last time you gave advice, instructed someone, or related a past experience to help another person in a similar predicament. In every case, you were counseling. And the question is not *whether* you counseled, but whether your counsel could be considered *good*.

For the biblical counselor, the evaluation of "good" is marked by two loaded elements: Does your counsel *speak the truth*? And is it *motivated and consistent with love*? (Ephesians 4:15). Good counsel must have both. Neither polls nor personal opinion determine truth and love; God defines truth and love in the pages of the Bible. Take a moment to appreciate the gravity of the following thought: Every word ever spoken by every person who ever lived will be judged by God using these two standards (Matthew 12:36-37; Ephesians 4:25,29). Thus, because every word counsels and because all persons may be labeled as counselors, it is vital to see biblical counseling as an approach to communication.

Speaking a single ordinary word requires a complex system of brain-to-body processes—controlling approximately one hundred different muscles.[2] "Yes," "No," "Maybe"—what a workout! Yet there is something even more extraordinary about speaking than that. You might observe this extraordinary experience on a daily basis with your spouse or a friend at the office. Their approach to life and conversations are so subtly unique. That is where the extraordinary enters in. Biblical counseling is at its root supernatural, involving the actual Spirit of God sending out His counsel through biblical counselors who teach and apply the Word of God to the needs of another person.

As godly communication, biblical counseling is the right message at the right time presented in the right way. Think of the effect a single word can have. In a busy parking lot, a mother cries out "Stop!"—saving her child from a fatal collision. A father slowly speaks his son's name with that certain gravity of correction, and the boy takes notice. These words counsel, and the Bible speaks of their value: "A word *fitly spoken* is like apples of gold in a setting of silver" (Proverbs 25:11). The New Testament, likewise, commonly promotes this type of communication: "Let no corrupting talk come out of your mouths, but only such as is good for building up, *as fits the occasion*, that it may give grace to those who hear" (Ephesians 4:29).

Now, words that build up and give grace are not always soft. It is love that controls the approach. If my mother had softly said, "Stop" in that parking lot, I probably would not be writing this chapter now. Love thundered that message to my young ears. So too the Bible has many words for godly communication: warn, admonish, counsel, speak truth, remind, encourage, exhort, among many others. At times, godly communication proceeds through actions without a word: shedding tears at the side of someone grieving, or jumping for joy with someone who is rejoicing (Romans 12:15). In all cases, the substance of the message is *truth* as defined by the Bible, and the goal and manner is *love*.

Every word sent out from Jesus' mouth never failed to have both of these elements. Imagine that—never a careless word, nothing said in haste or that He wished He could take back. No other human being can claim to have done the same. We sin so often and easily in our speech and verify the Scripture passage that says, "No human being can tame the tongue. It is a restless evil, full of deadly poison" (James 3:8). Temptations in this area arise so quickly. A neighbor in the community accuses you falsely, and in response you quickly formulate every ounce of criticism you ever had about him in slanderous character assassination. Or a friend in a high-pressure situation betrays your trust, and you immediately tear him down, sever the relationship, and consider him your enemy. Frequently such responses are blurted out in an instant, and are accompanied by negative (sinful) emotions or attitudes.

Jesus was both falsely accused and betrayed, and was tempted as we are, but responded in a radically different way than you and I are prone to: "He committed no sin, neither was deceit found in his mouth. When he was reviled, he did not revile in return; when he suffered, he did not threaten, but continued entrusting himself to him who judges justly" (1 Peter 2:22-23). Understand the contrast: We sin instinctually—from our very nature—but He *never* sinned, never ceased to speak the truth in love. How? The truth—as God defines it—was not only what Jesus spoke, but was also who He was: "I am the way, *and the truth*, and the life" (John 14:6). Biblical love was not just something Jesus did in a series of isolated events; it was His essence and mission:

> Beloved, let us love one another, for love is from God, and whoever loves has been born of God and knows God. Anyone who does not love does not know God, because God is love. In this the love of God was made manifest among us, that God sent his only Son into the world, so that we might live through him (1 John 4:7-9).

The center of the Christian message and the essential core of all biblical counseling is that Jesus, who existed eternally as God, came down from heaven and became a man, lived a life of unceasing and perfect love for God and neighbor, died in the place of sinners (and never sinned Himself) to bear the penalty of righteous wrath for their sins, rose to life to conquer death and give life to those who believe, presently intercedes for His followers, and anticipates a future return when He makes all things new and establishes a never-ending kingdom. (The Bible calls this message "the gospel.") It is the life of Jesus Christ living in Christians that transforms them into people who also speak the truth in love, equipping them to bring words of hope and life to others in the most complicated and dire situations.

Counseling As We Think of It

Far more weighty matters devastate people than mere words or short statements are capable of resolving: uncontrolled grief over losing a loved one, suicidal depression, marriage crises, the worry and panic over a big decision, employment turmoil, the damage of sexual immorality, and severe financial burdens, to name a few. Biblical counseling is not a well-wishing effort, but an arduous self-sacrifice to extend God's Word and join another's burden in order to see that person be transformed from the inside out, begin to worship God, and move in a godly direction with his life toward a greater resemblance to Jesus.[3] In the context of these severe problems, the simple definition of biblical counseling must yield to the thorough.

On the complex end of the spectrum, biblical counseling is *the whole counsel of God delivered in a systematic, understandable, relevant, and loving manner.* The whole counsel of God—every last piece, fully known without contradiction, fully distinguished from another and ready to fit an infinite number of scenarios—absolute truth and unending love condensed into words, sentences, pauses, questions, and answers. But be careful not to create an artificial difference between *real* counseling and biblical counseling. For example: Describe the counseling scenarios of every resident of a psychiatric ward; "the whole counsel of God" can make the matter plain with a wisdom that can transform everyone involved. He has made His wisdom known to us in the pages of the Bible (Psalm 19:7), and in the person of Jesus Christ (1 Corinthians 1:30). To all matters of life the Bible speaks, and with an authority surpassing any theorist and practitioner of a modern psychology. Biblical counselors, equipped with a thorough knowledge of the Bible and skilled in presenting it in an understandable, relevant, and loving way, aim to interject that wisdom from above—the counsel of God—into these counseling opportunities. And the Spirit of God, working through the Word of God and using these ministers of the Word, transforms lives.[4] Every contributor to this book has seen it happen—it is biblical, and it is *real.*

Biblical Counseling in the Church and Society

Over the course of the last century, secular psychological thought has slowly infiltrated the American Protestant church and replaced the biblical foundations for preaching, counseling, and ministry. The biblical counseling movement within the church is an attempt to expose this calamity and return the church to the Bible as the authoritative guide for how Christians ought to think and counsel one another. The term *psychology* represents the "study of the soul." However, because the soul is immaterial and cannot be examined directly, the field of modern psychology seeks to study the "mental and behavioral characteristics of an individual or group."[5] Psychologists seek to understand why people do what they do (psychology), and how change can be achieved when beneficial (psychotherapy). Biblical counseling then, itself, qualifies as a psychology.[6] Its foundations and methods may not agree with the mainstream positions in the field—though consensus is not really a characteristic of modern psychology[7]—but it nonetheless presents a perspective on all essential elements of the term so that it qualifies as a contender among the psychologies. And the hero among them is biblical counseling—as we, the contributing authors of this volume, contend.

All psychologies operate from worldviews, and all the sciences—even the most objective—are carried out by scientists who could not deny that they themselves have a system of values, a belief system, a way of looking at the world, and that those elements have at least some small influence on how they approach their work. David Powlison writes, "Christianity is a psychology in that it involves a true knowledge of people and true knowledge of God."[8] Biblical counseling, as a psychology, shares this trait—building its philosophy and method of counseling from its worldview.

Edward Welch proposes four striking tenets of the Christian worldview with radical implications for counseling: "(1) The Christian worldview is unique in that it begins with God; (2) the Christian worldview speaks with depth to the observations of modern psychology; (3) the Christian worldview speaks to critical psychological phenomena rarely addressed in secular theories; and (4) the world makes no sense apart from a Christian worldview."[9] All people live and speak from individual worldviews. This worldview is formed from what a person thinks (impacted by his culture, parents, traditions, beliefs, etc.) and what this person loves (what rules his heart). When the combination of these two is lived out, the Bible calls it worship. (The object of worship is identified by the focus of each element.)

The following call to worship, by Francis of Assisi, has been a beloved hymn of the church for centuries:

> All creatures of our God and King,
> Lift up your voice and with us sing
> Alleluia! [Praise the Lord!]
> Alleluia! [Praise the Lord!]

The audience here is comprehensive—"*all* creatures." Its message is directive and clear: "Praise the Lord!" The Christian worldview begins, exists, and ends with God. The apostle Paul wrote it this way: "From him and through him and to him are all things. To him be glory forever" (Romans 11:36). God created mankind first and foremost as *worshippers*, persons who would see God as the ultimate worthy object of their worship. His very design and purpose is a function of worship—believing God's Word concerning all matters, and loving God above all else (Exodus 20).

The Bible calls the immaterial part of mankind the "heart," and describes how God's original design was for everything it produces—every thought, intention, affection, action, spoken word, etc.—to serve as an act of worship that glorifies the God of the Bible. Consequently, mankind experiences trouble in this life when he acts contrary to this design and fails to worship God—in a word, sin. Think of an automobile designed to be fueled with regular gasoline. If you fill the gas tank with diesel fuel, it won't take very long for all the functions of that automobile to shut down. But when that same automobile is filled with the right fuel and maintained properly, it can run for hundreds of thousands of miles. Mankind was designed to function as a worshipper of God for eternity, and the intent was for all aspects of his life to be acts of worship to the living God.[10]

A Foundational Theology for Biblical Counseling

A belief system or worldview that revolves around God would accurately be described as a *theology*, since the "study of God" dominates its perspective on everything. "Speaking the truth in love," our theme phrase for the early part of this chapter, is said to produce the following result: "We are to grow up in every way into him who is the head, into Christ" (Ephesians 4:15). This latter phrase contains the most basic elements of a theology of biblical counseling: who people are in relation to God, and what God expects of them. (To be clear, a growing understanding of all the Bible's teachings is vital for building a thorough theological basis for counseling wisdom and skill, and should be pursued.) This phrase says something about people in process. There is a present condition and a destination, but a transformation is needed for people to get from one to the other. Verses 17-24 of the same passage frame this process with three instructions: put off your old self (verse 22), be renewed in the spirit of your mind (verse 23), and put on the new self, which is holy and righteous like God (verse 24).

Put off. How did man get to a place where he now needs fundamental change? In the beginning, God created man in His own image (Genesis 1:26-27), and placed him in this world as a representation of what He is like. Despite being surrounded by what can only be described as a "very good" environment (Genesis 1:31; 2:7-15), and having unhindered fellowship with God (Genesis 2:16-25), man rebelled against God by breaking the one prohibition given him (Genesis 2:17; 3:6) and received the consequence of his trespass (Genesis 2:17; Romans 6:23): he began to exist in the status of whole-person corruption and decay (Romans 3:10-18) in a world cursed with corruption and decay (Genesis 3:14-19; Romans 8:20-23), and to have a broken relationship between he and God (Genesis 3:23-24; Romans 3:23). This whole-person decay—rooted in his very heart (Genesis 4:3,5; Romans 1:21)—put him at enmity with God.

Because Adam represented all of mankind, this consequence was subsequently passed down to every generation. Thus every human born thereafter has been adversely impacted by the first man's trespass (Romans 5:12). Yet God made a way for His enemies to turn from their sin, to be delivered from their decay, to be reconciled as friends and children of God (Romans 5:6-11), to await a final removal of cursed corruption and decay (1 John 3:2), and once again reflect God's glorious likeness (Romans 5:2; 8:23-25)—though at present we battle to live wisely by God's Spirit (Romans 8:13-14),[11] a life of progressively refined worship (Romans 12:1).

The need for change then exists, first and foremost, because people fail to worship God. Instead, they worship some aspect of the creation (Romans 1:25)—usually themselves—through some cleverly concealed strategy. Now, when people worship something or someone other than God, their actions *always* reflect what they are treasuring. The Bible labels these actions "sin" and identifies them as affronts to God: "Now the works of the flesh are evident: sexual immorality, impurity, sensuality, idolatry, sorcery, enmity, strife, jealousy, fits of anger, rivalries, dissensions, divisions, envy, drunkenness, orgies, and things like these. I warn you, as I warned you before, that those who do such things will not inherit the kingdom of God" (Galatians 5:19-21). A theology of biblical counseling clearly identifies these actions as sin, but is even more interested in exposing the system of worship at their root by the light of God's Word (Hebrews 4:12-13), and by outshining the treasured object of that system with the light of life, Jesus Christ (John 3:19-21).

Put on. As the destination, the standard for change is Jesus (Ephesians

4:20). Why? Jesus, the God-man, perfectly pleased God in every respect (Matthew 3:17; 17:5). He displayed, as a human being, what loving God perfectly and loving one's neighbor perfectly looks like. And it is God's desire that people be conformed to resemble Jesus, so that they too might give God the glory due His name.

Be renewed. Finally, the process of transformation takes a person from what he is presently and grows him up—along with the rest of the church—to correspond to Jesus Christ in resembling His character. Clearly this transformation involves a ceasing of the works of the flesh and a putting on of a new, Christlike pattern of behavior. This shift involves a radical work of change. As wrong worship is the root of all sin, and right worship is at the core of righteous living, a transfer of worship must take place. The person must transfer his worship from the undeserving object or person who is currently receiving it, and focus it upon Jesus Christ, who infinitely deserves it. And this transfer is a work of God: one must *be* renewed by God—that is, do an about-face away from sin, and walk toward Jesus Christ (e.g., 1 Thessalonians 1:9).

For this transformation and transfer to take place, a person must see the glory of God as greater than that to which he has been ascribing importance and admiration in his heart. And the most powerful message of the glory of God is represented in the Christian gospel, which concerns both (1) the grand theological picture of God delivering people from His wrath, redeeming His creation from the curse of sin through the death of Jesus on the cross, and preparing for an eternity of restored worshippers rehearsing His glory; and (2) a focused picture of the glory of God in the person of Jesus in every account given to us in the Gospel narratives. For example, have you ever considered the glory of God in the person of Jesus turning water to wine? Have you ever known anyone in your entire life with the power to intrinsically transform as He did with a word? Yet seeing Jesus with this accuracy takes the lens of repentance and faith.

The Christian life begins when this message of the glory of God, by the work of the Holy Spirit, powerfully generates a new life of faith within a person (Romans 1:16-17). The Spirit, using this message and its implications, continues to inspire faith throughout the Christian's life. The Bible describes the one who is not a Christian as dead and unable to respond to spiritual impulse

(Ephesians 2:1-3). The Christian, however, has been made alive to respond to spiritual stimuli (Ephesians 2:4-10). The Holy Spirit convicts the Christian of sin through the use of the Word of God, and energizes the Christian's faith so that he once again comprehends from the heart the glory of God in the face of Jesus. The biblical counselor, then, seeks to display the glory of God through the person of Jesus to inspire a counselee's transfer of worship from that which is undeserving to Him who is the joy of man's desiring, and then the biblical counselor seeks to practically guide the counselee in extensions of that worship through word and deed.

The Bible calls this process of change *sanctification* and presents it as happening progressively (2 Corinthians 3:18; Philippians 2:12-13). The biblical counselor is called to be faithful to continue coming alongside the counselee to promote repentance, consistently teaching and displaying the glory of God in the person of Jesus, and waiting upon the Holy Spirit of God to bring about right worship in the heart. When repentance and faith occur, right worship resumes, and new successes in following after Jesus in loving God and loving others emerge—in other words, "we grow up...into Christ" (Ephesians 4:15).

Biblical Counseling's Foundational Doctrine

The Bible, as used by God in a person's life, is the foundation for biblical counseling. How can we be so confident to build an approach to counseling from the Bible? Given the weighty task of addressing some of the most difficult issues in human experience, it has a lot of expectations to live up to. The Bible's claims about itself, however, show its sufficiency to meet those challenges. Although all doctrines of the Bible are vital to an understanding of biblical counseling, one specific doctrine has emerged as preeminent: the sufficiency of Scripture. This doctrine is a historical teaching of the church, especially highlighted during the time of the Protestant Reformation[12]—a subset of the Reformation pillar *sola scriptura* (Scripture alone). And the biblical counseling movement has demonstrated the need for that same teaching to be reemphasized and clarified for the church today.

Sufficient is that which is "enough to meet the needs of a situation or a proposed end."[13] It is important to understand the purpose or goal of the Bible in order to evaluate its sufficiency for counseling. The doctrine of the sufficiency of Scripture teaches that God has designed a comprehensive resource for man—His inspired, inerrant, infallible, and authoritative Word—to cooperate with the Holy Spirit's work of salvation and to wisely guide through *all matters of life* either by direct command or precept. Thus Scripture prepares a person for salvation through making one wise in the knowledge of God (Psalm 19:7), and also instructs the Christian's gradual growth in pure worship by training in holy character (2 Timothy 3:14-17). The Holy Spirit brings a biblical man to believe the truth of His sufficient Word and enables him to obey it by faith.

Affirmation for the Doctrine of Sufficiency

The church has historically looked to three primary passages of Scripture to affirm the doctrine of sufficiency; however, every text of Scripture assumes that it be understood in the context of sufficiency without explicitly mentioning the doctrine. Those texts are Psalm 19:7-11, 2 Timothy 3:14-17, and 2 Peter 1:3-4 (see also verses 16-21). These texts stress the Bible as the sufficient guide for knowing God, worshipping God, and obeying Him by faith.

Sufficiency in Psalm 19

Psalm 19:7-11 introduces seven terms and descriptions for describing Scripture, each corresponding to an avenue of effect:

> The law of the LORD is perfect,
>   reviving the soul;
> the testimony of the LORD is sure,
>   making wise the simple;
> the precepts of the LORD are right,
>   rejoicing the heart;
> the commandment of the LORD is pure,
>   enlightening the eyes;
> the fear of the LORD is clean,
>   enduring forever;
> the rules of the LORD are true,
>   and righteous altogether.
> More to be desired are they than gold,
>   even much fine gold;

> sweeter also than honey
>   and drippings of the honeycomb.
>
> Moreover, by them is your servant warned;
>   in keeping them there is great reward.

This psalm of David speaks to the value of God's revelation to man. Verses 1-6 speak of God's revelation of Himself to all mankind, of which the surrounding creation is a major element. However, Scripture—here referred to as "law," "testimony," "precepts," "commandment," "fear," and "rules"—is contrasted as the unique source of revelation needed to change the heart of man and make him wise. Every counseling issue you ever encounter could relate to the need for at least one of these effects to occur in the life of the person you are seeking to help. Scripture was designed with those needs in mind.

Sufficiency in 2 Timothy 3

In 2 Timothy 3:14-17, the apostle Paul alluded to Psalm 19.[14] He wrote,

> As for you, continue in what you have learned and have firmly believed, knowing from whom you learned it and how from childhood you have been acquainted with the *sacred writings, which are able to make you wise for salvation* through faith in Christ Jesus. All Scripture is breathed out by God and profitable for teaching, for reproof, for correction, and for training in righteousness, that the man of God may be complete, equipped for every good work.

Several key phrases might highlight the strong support this text proposes for the doctrine of sufficiency. First, the text suggests an extreme dependence on the Word of God by the recipient of Paul's letter—Timothy. Second, "wise for salvation" speaks to the total transformation of a person beginning with initial sanctification, continuing with progressive sanctification, and culminating in final sanctification: a change of the comprehensive nature of a person.[15] It gives a direct link between this passage and all that David wrote about the Scripture in Psalm 19. Third, "for teaching, for reproof, for correction, and for training in righteousness" places the Scripture as the comprehensive guide for human personality and behavior change. And fourth, it describes the person who has come to Scripture for a sufficient guide as being *complete* and *equipped for every good work*, which is the hope of every biblical counselor.

Sufficiency in 2 Peter 1

A third claim in the Bible regarding its sufficiency appears in 2 Peter 1:3-4. It reads,

> His divine power has granted to us all things that pertain to life and godliness, through the knowledge of him who called us to his own glory and excellence, by which he has granted to us his precious and very great promises, so that through them you may become partakers of the divine nature, having escaped from the corruption that is in the world because of sinful desire.

This text states explicitly that the knowledge of God given to man suffices for everything that pertains to matters of life and godliness. No issue of counseling falls outside those categories. Moreover, this passage focuses on God's prophetic revelation written down in the pages of Scripture, not just revelation knowledge in general. This observation is confirmed later in the passage when Peter speaks about an extraordinary experience in which God's power revealed Jesus in transcendent glory to himself and two other disciples with him on a mountain in northern Israel (Matthew 17:1-9). There, Jesus was transfigured: His face shone like the sun; His clothes became white; and He spoke with Moses and Elijah about His coming death and resurrection. And Peter and his friends fell to their faces with great terror before Jesus' glory. He related this experience as follows:

> We did not follow cleverly devised myths when we made known to you the power and coming of our Lord Jesus Christ, but we were eyewitnesses of his majesty. For when he received honor and glory from God the Father, and the voice was borne to him by the Majestic Glory, "This is my beloved Son, with whom I am well pleased," we ourselves heard this very voice borne from heaven, for we were with him on the holy mountain (2 Peter 1:16-18).

Despite the awesome nature of that experience, and the fact it happened right before his eyes, Peter went on to make this striking statement about Scripture:

> And we have something more sure, the prophetic word, to which you will do well to pay attention as to a lamp shining in a dark

place, until the day dawns and the morning star rises in your hearts, knowing this first of all, that no prophecy of Scripture comes from someone's own interpretation. For no prophecy was ever produced by the will of man, but men spoke from God as they were carried along by the Holy Spirit (2 Peter 1:19-21).

Peter was more confirmed to know that Scripture was God's very Word, and that it was intended to lead mankind through the darkest experiences of life, than he was comfortable believing his own eyes. Are you kidding us, Peter? We place so much of our confidence in what we see with our natural eyes! Like doubting Thomas, we are reluctant or refuse to believe something until we see it and place our hands on the matter (John 20:25). Over the years I have seen many physically blind men place full confidence in walking by the "light" of a cane or the hand of a trusted friend. Perhaps the fact this amazes me points to my own blindness—that I have trouble believing that depending on the surety and love of another could surpass the trust I have in myself and my own perception. (Open the eyes of my heart, Lord, and the hearts of all of us who counsel biblically!)

Certainty About the Doctrine of Sufficiency

God, who is the ultimate Lover of mankind (John 3:16), provides us with plenty of certainty regarding the sufficiency of His Word:

- the knowledge of God necessary for a life of worship (Psalm 19:8),

- since it is foremost a testimony of God's glory (Psalm 19:8),

- to make the matters of the heart evident (Proverbs 20:5; Hebrews 4:12-13),

- to make man truly wise (Psalm 19:7),

- to guide him through life in a rewarding way and warn him about life's dangers (Psalm 19:11),

- to provide all knowledge needed for repentance and training in righteousness (2 Timothy 3:16),

- so that he is capable of pleasing God by faith in word and deed (2 Timothy 3:17).

The Counselor and the Doctrine of Sufficiency

An immediate implication of this doctrine of sufficiency is that the biblical counselor must thoroughly know the Word of God, and counsel with it as his exclusive authority, sufficient source, and guide. The doctrine assures that the answers for all matters of life lived before God are contained in Scripture, yet those answers must still be plucked from its pages and implanted into the mind of the counselor so that his words truly represent God.

The counselor's approach to counseling would then involve a careful investigation of Scripture for assistance in interpreting the problem at hand. Only the Word of God allows the counselor to see God's diagnosis of the counseling problem. The Bible may not use the same terminology as modern psychology, but it does speak with greater authority.

The counselor would also do a survey of Scripture for assistance in formulating the solution. Only God's Word speaks absolute truth concerning the solutions to all counseling problems and provides comprehensive direction (Psalm 119:105,130).

Last, the biblical counselor will need to know Scripture well so he can discern how to communicate the counsel and its necessary implications (confession, repentance, reconciliation, etc.) in a manner that resembles how Jesus Christ would give counsel (with gentleness, humility, helping the weak, encouraging the fainthearted, admonishing the unruly, patient with all, among many other qualities—Matthew 11:28-30; Galatians 6:1-2; 1 Thessalonians 5:14). To accomplish all this, the counselor's mastery of the Word must be strong, not superficial.

A New Beginning

Much more could be said, and will be said in the subsequent chapters of this book. This chapter was only an attempt at an introduction. Did biblical counseling make a good impression? Inasmuch as the discipline and practice of biblical counseling seek to model the character of Jesus Christ and the qualities and values of the Bible, its nobility should have ravished you. But if that didn't happen, consider this chapter to have been a muddled veil, and please try to meet biblical counseling on better terms with the help of the chapters to follow and other introductions. (Some additional resources have been suggested in the "Recommended Resources" list at the end of each chapter.) Do not consider this the end, but rather a new beginning—

- a beginning of refreshment for you who are weary biblical counselors, to reengage in the hard labors of your ministry;

- a beginning of a blessed lifetime of biblical counseling study and ministry for you who are newcomers;

- a beginning of reexamining your foundation for you who have known a different approach to counseling; or

- a beginning of a new relationship with Jesus Christ for you who never heard of His glory before you came to this chapter.

However you may have come, biblical counseling is pleased to have met you.

Recommended Resources

Biblical Counseling as an Approach to Communication and Counseling

Beevers, E. Bradley. "Watch Your Language!" *The Journal of Biblical Counseling*, 12, no. 3 (Spring 1994): 24-30.

Powlison, David. *Speaking Truth in Love*. Greensboro, NC: New Growth Press, 2005.

Biblical Counseling in the Church and Society

MacArthur, John, and the Master's College Faculty. *Counseling: How to Counsel Biblically*. Nashville, TN: Thomas Nelson, 2005.

Piper, John. *Desiring God*. Sisters, OR: Multnomah, 2003.

Powlison, David. "A Biblical Counseling View." In Eric L. Johnson. *Psychology & Christianity: Five Views*. Downers Grove, IL: IVP Academic, 2010.

———. *Seeing with New Eyes*. Phillipsburg, NJ: P&R Publishing, 2003.

Welch, Edward T. "A Discussion Among Clergy: Pastoral Counseling Talks with Secular Psychology," *The Journal of Biblical Counseling*, 13, no. 2 (Winter 1995): 23-34.

Biblical Counseling's Foundations

Adams, Jay. *A Theology of Christian Counseling*. Grand Rapids, MI: Zondervan, 1979.

Lambert, Heath. *The Biblical Counseling Movement After Adams*. Wheaton, IL: Crossway, 2012.

Powlison, David. *The Biblical Counseling Movement*. Greensboro, NC: New Growth Press, 2010.

———. "Counseling is the Church." *The Journal of Biblical Counseling*, 20, no. 2 (Winter 2002): 2-7.

Tripp, Paul David. *Instruments in the Redeemer's Hands*. Phillipsburg, NJ: P&R Publishing, 2002.

Biblical Counseling Today

The Biblical Counseling Coalition (BCC)—website: http://biblicalcounselingcoalition.org

The Christian Counselor's Education Foundation (CCEF)—website: http://ccef.org

The National Association of Nouthetic Counselors (NANC)—website: http://nanc.org

2
Counseling Men
with the Bible

John D. Street

There are many men who profess to give biblical counsel, but not everyone who makes this claim is truly biblical. Some insist they are Christian counselors because they use the Bible in their counseling, but cults and false religions use the Bible and they are not biblical. Just because a man uses the Bible in his counseling does not mean he gives biblical counsel.

So what makes counsel biblical? The short answer to this question has two parts. First, your counsel will be biblical when, after careful study, you arrive at the same meaning of the biblical text that was intended by the original author for the original audience of Scripture. Second, your counsel will be biblical when you correctly understand the situation of your contemporary audience—your counselee. To sum up, counseling that is faithful to the Bible effectively communicates the original meaning of the biblical text in a way that is relevant to the situation and heart of the person you are counseling.[1]

Jason was a young Christian man who struggled persistently with lustful voyeurism on the Internet. He asked his pastor if there was a mature Christian man in the church who would counsel him on ways he could gain victory over this lust that seemed to have such a hold on him. Steve, a well-respected married man in the congregation, loved helping younger men and had a reputation of being a counselor who genuinely loved those whom he counseled. Steve agreed to counsel Jason. Early on Saturday mornings they began meeting at the church office—a private setting—for some personal counsel.

Half of the first session was spent in prayer seeking God's help to defeat this powerful enemy of lust that had so consumed Jason. During the rest of the counseling session Steve questioned Jason concerning the frequency and means he would use to indulge his pornographic cravings. This was a much larger problem in Jason's life than was first reported. However, aside from this sinful struggle, Jason had a good Christian testimony among other people inside and outside the church. So Steve was fairly confident that he was working with a true believer after reviewing the gospel with him. In addition, Jason evidenced a real desire to change. There were times during the counseling session Steve could see Jason's sincerity in his tear-filled eyes. However, change was going to be much more difficult than Jason had imagined.

Steve understood that Jason needed some immediate biblical help and hope for change that would make a lasting difference. With exuberance in his voice he asked Jason to turn in his Bible to 2 Timothy 2:22 and read it out loud: "Flee youthful passions and pursue righteousness, faith, love, and peace, along with those who call on the Lord from a pure heart." Then Steve continued, "Let me explain how important this verse is to your situation." With the help of the training he had received in the biblical languages at a Christian university, Steve proceeded to explain to Jason the meanings of the key words in this verse.

"I want you to focus on the word 'flee' in this verse," Steve said with a compassionate confidence. "My study Bible notes tell me that this word, in the original Greek text, is an imperative—a command. It means 'to escape, avoid, or shun.' Is that what you have been doing with this Internet pornography?"

Jason hung his head despondently, "No, I believe I've pursued it instead of running from it."

Steve then said, "Now notice how the apostle Paul refers to 'passions.' They are dangerous and destructive sins that come from deep within. But this is not just any type of passion; it is 'youthful passion.' This is a type of sexual lust that young people are especially susceptible to. Do you see that?"

After a moment of reflection, Jason responded, "Yes, this is something that is far more powerful than I ever imagined. I can really relate to what Paul is saying here. This sexual passion has been in control of my life for too long now. I really want to get rid of this."

"There is great news in this verse for you, Jason!" Steve announced with excitement. "Our apostle does not just tell us what to flee; he also directs us where to go. You are to 'pursue righteousness, faith, love, and peace.' These are very specific things we are going to examine in future sessions together. I want you to purchase a good Bible dictionary so you can study each of these words before our next meeting. There is so much here, it will take us some time to flesh it all out." Steve ended this first session with an expectant prayer of hope, and both men left with great anticipation about their upcoming counseling sessions together.

The next session, however, did not go as well. Jason had not only done his homework on 2 Timothy 2:22, but being the diligent student that he was, he had studied the entire chapter and consulted some good commentaries on Paul's purpose in writing the book of 2 Timothy. After opening in prayer, Steve asked Jason why he looked so confused and anxious. "Well," Jason said somewhat apologetically, "I did everything you asked me to do, and I do not see how this verse has anything to do with my problem. It seems to me that sexual lust is not the problem that Paul addresses in this chapter. After careful study, it appears that the apostle is admonishing the young pastor, Timothy, about his tendency to involve himself in passionate theological debates with disagreeable people who are teaching false doctrine in his congregation. In fact, the verses immediately after verse 22 clarify that Paul warns Timothy not to be quarrelsome but be patient with argumentative people and not allow his passion for the truth to cause him to overreact when he is challenged."

An uncomfortable silence settled in the room as Steve reread 2 Timothy 2:22-26 to himself. Jason was right. Verse 22 did not have anything to do with sexual lust and temptation. In fact, it *was* about Paul admonishing a young pastor's undiscerning exuberance to involve himself in passionate debate with false teachers. Steve realized that even though his motivation was good as a counselor, he had inappropriately used this Bible verse as a proof text without considering its context. He felt embarrassed and ashamed because he knew he should have guided Jason through well-studied Scripture instead of handing out Bible verses without careful consideration. It bothered him that his careless mishandling of God's Word might have deceived another less discerning and sincere counselee. Steve realized then that if he was going to be a good biblical counselor, he needed to better understand and practice good principles of biblical interpretation.

Men who struggle with deep problems of the soul need men who are competent in understanding the Bible correctly for counseling. Steve knew the Bible had answers for Jason's burning lust, but he had used the Word inappropriately and wasted an opportunity to really help him. A man who counsels with the Bible must be well informed on good principles of biblical interpretation in order to be an effective biblical counselor. The remainder of this chapter is intended to help men show their true love for Christ by being better students of His Word.

Knowing the Bible Well

Starting with a Good Bible Translation

To be a good counselor, a man must start with a reliable translation of the Bible. It is important to remember that the original Scripture texts were written in ancient Hebrew, Aramaic, and Greek.[2] For most people throughout history, this means that the original manuscripts of the Bible were not written in their native language. In order for people to read and understand God's Word, translations had to be made from these original languages into a multitude of other languages.[3] Because of this reality, a conscientious counselor will always want to ask, "What translation of the Bible in my language is best to use for counseling?"

If you desire to be true to the original meaning of Scripture, then it is vital that you choose a translation that most closely communicates the original meaning intended by the biblical author. God is the author of Scripture, but He elected to use intermediate human authors, divinely guided by the Holy Spirit (2 Peter 1:20-21), to give us the sixty-six inerrant, inspired, canonical books of the Bible that we have today. These books constitute the holy Word of God.

Selecting a good Bible translation in order to properly minister the Word of truth in counseling will require great care. There are a multitude of different types of Bibles available, and deciding on the best translation for any competent counselor will require a little thought and research. Here are four guidelines for your consideration:

First, choose a Bible that is a *translation* and not a *paraphrase*. A popular paraphrase Bible is a Trojan horse in counseling. That is, it will promise immediate relevance, and may even appear to give your counselee quick understandable guidance, but often it will not offer the most reliable representation of what God actually intended to say in the original text. Paraphrase texts are full of interpretations of what the text actually says. Remember, your counsel will only be as authoritative as it accurately represents what God truly has said. Paraphrase Bibles are subjective commentaries on the Bible; they are not careful translations of the actual words of God. They can be used as a supplement to a faithful translation in limited ways, but should never be seen by you or your counselee as stating what God is really telling you to do. In a similar manner, gender-neutral renderings of the Bible are not faithful to the words of God. Instead, they seek to change the original meaning of the text to fit the expectations and demands of an egalitarian culture. Good counselors stay away from any translation that rewrites the Word of God in an attempt to appease cultural mores.

Bibles that are so-called "dynamic" translations are more reliable than paraphrase versions, but still maintain a high degree of interpretation in their published versions. A good Bible to use in counseling translates words, not meanings, where the Bible translator has chosen reliability over readability.[4] Even though every good translation has a certain element of interpretation in it, it is vital that the translator limits interpretative opinions, no matter how well-informed they might be. It is imperative for the translated text to remain true to the actual Hebrew, Aramaic, and Greek words God has given. To attempt to make a translation of the Bible immediately understandable ignores the obvious fact of its "otherness." What I mean by otherness is that the Bible is an ancient document written in a different culture with a different language to a different people with different customs. When a translator, in the name of readability, removes these distinctive features in the translation process, then the original meaning of the text is often lost or made more vague and replaced with the translator's opinions and biases. The job of getting to the actual meaning of the text should be left up to the reader of the translation and not be presumptively assumed by the translator.

Second, a translation completed by a team of scholars rather than by one translator is always to be preferred. There are some good translations that have been made available by single translators,[5] but they will always have weaknesses because every translator has certain limitations. A team of good language and Bible scholars, with a high view of Scripture that is committed to the inerrancy, inspiration, and supremacy of God's revelation, is more likely to produce a reliable translation of the Bible that is suitable for counseling.[6]

Third, a reliable Bible is one that has been translated from recognized Hebrew and Greek critical texts. Latin texts are not reliable, since they are a translation themselves. Even translations that come from the Septuagint (the first Greek translation of the Hebrew Old Testament) are using a secondary source and not the primary Hebrew source.[7] The Old Testament should be translated from the standard Hebrew Masoretic text; the New Testament should be translated from a Greek "critical" text.[8] These critical texts are compiled on the basis of the best scholarship in analyzing the earliest and most reliable manuscripts of the New Testament available today.

Fourth, use a translation that will encourage the study of the meaning of the words and the ancient cultures of the Bible. Often, modern translations attempt to "dumb down" the Bible to our society and culture. Significant meanings and applications are lost when the translator removes all the distinctive features of the ancient languages and cultures. When a translator changes the actual words of Scripture, then the cultural bias of the translator frequently overrides and fundamentally changes the original meaning. The more a Bible student is in touch with the "otherness" of the Bible, the more memorable and life-changing its truth.

For example, in dealing with Jason's sexual sins, suppose counselor Steve had chosen to cite Matthew 5:28 from the paraphrase version called *The Message*. This paraphrase renders this verse as saying, "Don't think you've preserved your virtue simply by staying out of bed. Your *heart* can be corrupted by lust even quicker than your *body*. Those leering looks you think nobody notices— they also corrupt" (Matthew 5:28 MSG). Someone like Jason could benefit from the idea that lust is dangerous, but the original text is much more explicit and helpful for the real change that must occur with Jason. A better translation (English Standard Version) translates Jesus' words, "I say to you that everyone who looks at a woman with lustful intent has already committed adultery with her in his heart."

This translation makes it clear that our Lord is actually saying that the heart of a lustful person and the heart of an adulterer are exactly the same. It is not just the behavior of "leering looks" that needs to change, but the inner condition of Jason's heart. First-century pharisaical teaching advocated that as long as a person did not sin externally, like committing adultery, they were guilt-free. In contrast, Jesus taught that the internal condition of a man's heart is more important to God. Jason—because of his lustful looking—was just as much an adulterer as a man who had been physically unfaithful to his wife. The more accurate rendering of Matthew 5:28 puts Jason's sin in a very vivid light. *The Message* emphasized the outer behavior; a good translation of the Bible will more clearly communicate Jesus was addressing the inner heart.

In a paraphrase, the effect of adding man's ideas and words to the original text significantly alters the original thought or intent of the text. "Staying out of bed" or the words "your heart can be corrupted by lust even quicker than your body" are not the actual words of Jesus. By contrast, the more precise terminology of committing "adultery with her in his heart" is. The actual words of Jesus will bring a man to see his heart more clearly, leading him to repentance. The biblical counselor who desires to communicate God's actual thoughts to a counselee must use a faithful translation of the Bible that is true to the original words of God.

Exegeting the Context

To exegete a text is to thoroughly study it so one can properly explain its meaning. A significant part of that study involves exegeting the context, which means coming to understand a Scripture passage the way the original author intended it to be understood. A counselor will be unable to help a victim of suffering with the genuine hope and promises of God if he does not understand the correct meaning of God's promises. It is also impossible for a counselor to correct the sin of a counselee if he does not properly understand the admonitions of Scripture. The meaning of God's promises and admonitions becomes clearer with good contextual exegesis. Good counseling begins with good doctrine, and good doctrine begins with good exegesis.[9]

Overcoming Interpretative Bias

Everyone who reads the Bible brings a certain interpretative bias to the words they read. A counselor who is a good interpreter of Scripture must

understand his own personal bias before he proceeds to represent God's Word
in his counsel. Sometimes bias can be good, especially when it involves a high
view of the Word of God. For example, when the interpreter reads the Bible
as the *inspired* Word of God, the interpreter's assumption or bias is reliable.
This means its source is understood as coming from God ("breathed out by
God," 2 Timothy 3:16-17).

Likewise, when the Word is judged as *inerrant*, the interpreter's assumption
is reliable. *Inerrancy* means that the revelation of its truth is absolutely perfect,
since the Author of Scripture is an absolutely perfect God (Psalm 12:6; Proverbs 30:5). And when the Word of God is seen as *sufficient* and *superior*, the
interpreter's assumption is reliable. These definitive adjectives mean that when
Scripture speaks to matters of the soul and its problems, there is nothing that
is left out or that supersedes it (Psalm 33:10-11; 2 Peter 1:3,19-21). Secular
psychological theories are unnecessary and destructive to effective counseling if
the Word of God is truly *sufficient* and *superior*. (For more on the sufficiency of
the Word of God in counseling, read chapter 1, "Understanding Biblical Counseling.") These functional assumptions have to do with how the counselor views
the entire Bible. They are good and helpful. But interpretive bias can also be
harmful if it misrepresents, deludes, or distorts God's Word.

Why did Steve misapply 2 Timothy 2:22 to Jason's situation? Because both
his previous experience of hearing the verse taught and his personal reading in
various Christian books had biased him to this incorrect understanding. He
believed the verse was referring to sexual lust, but in reality it was referring to a
youthful passion to argue with false teachers. Steve had failed to study the verse
for what it meant within its context, and he had allowed his interpretative bias to
rule his use of the verse while counseling Jason. This demonstrates how a counselor's *preunderstanding* of a text has the potential to mislead a counselee into a
false application of a text.

Often this kind of preunderstanding can be greatly influenced by a counselor's theological agenda. A counselor may have an honorable agenda yet may
end up using the wrong biblical texts in order to further his agenda. Steve
wanted to address Jason's sinful lust and voyeurism on the Internet. That's an
honorable agenda. But he used the wrong passage to do so. It appeared to him
that the words in 2 Timothy 2:22 fit the counsel he wanted to give to Jason.
His theological agenda drove his use of that verse when he should have taken

care to find verses that were appropriate to Jason's problem. This highlights the importance of properly understanding a given text within its biblical context.

What's more, a counselor's immediate culture will always have an unconscious impact upon interpretative conclusions. This culture can involve his church, Bible study, Sunday school, Christian music, hymns, sermons, reading, friends, coworkers, art, and more. Culture is constantly creeping into a counselor's interpretation of the Bible, frequently predetermining a false understanding of selected verses. At this point the interpreter is not reading the Bible for what it says; he is reading it through the prism of his culture.

At times the culture may be instructive to a proper interpretation of the text. For example, if a counselor resides in suburban America, the suburban culture of materialism may serve as illustrative support for texts that warn of the spiritual dangers of material abundance (Proverbs 30:7-9; Luke 18:18-23). On the other hand, it can just as easily hurt if the counselor assumes that such texts are only warning the millionaires and billionaires of this world. On the flip side, if the culture of counseling were set in the context of the slums of Haiti, then the spiritual dangers of poverty would be better understood (Ephesians 4:28).

A counselor's culture will stonewall proper biblical interpretation when the counselor arrogantly assumes that his cultural perspective is the most correct way to read the Bible. Theologian Kevin Vanhoozer has called this an interpretative issue of pride. Such an assumption, he comments, "encourages us to think that we have got the correct meaning before we have made the appropriate effort to recover it. Pride does not listen. It knows."[10] When a counselor believes his cultural perspective is preeminent, then he refuses to seriously study Scripture for what it says.

Understanding Historical-Cultural Context

The effective antidote to a counselor's invasive cultural bias is an informed understanding of the biblical culture in which the biblical text was written. The better the counselor comprehends the ancient culture and history of the scriptural text, the more accurate will be his interpretation and application. In short, to be a proper interpreter, you must carefully study the historical-cultural background of the text.

Getting a sharp focus on the historical-cultural background of any biblical text involves three focal points.

Focus on the Human Author

God inspired all of Scripture, but used specially selected human authors to reveal His specific will without overruling their distinctive writing style, personality, and unique use of vocabulary. Each of these factors is highly influenced by the culture of the writer. The better you know the personal history of the original author, the better you will understand his words.

Explore the background and ministry of the human author as you study the passages you will use in counseling. Good Bible dictionaries, encyclopedias, and commentaries are helpful study aids that will supply much of an author's personal history in a condensed format.[11] Even more reliable will be the study of the author's background using the Bible as your main source. For example, if you are counseling a Christian who is overwhelmed with guilt and sorrow due to some past failure or sinful deed, you'll find it helpful to take him to a passage like Romans 8:1 and read the freeing words of the apostle Paul: "There is therefore now no condemnation for those who are in Christ Jesus."

What makes Romans 8:1 so profound is the background of the man who wrote this verse. In his misplaced zeal for God, Paul had severely persecuted Christians in the early church (Acts 9:21). Prior to his conversion to Christ he had made it his mission to imprison those who followed Christ, possibly even participating in putting many of them to death. This explains why he said of himself in 1 Timothy 1:15, "The saying is trustworthy and deserving of full acceptance, that Christ Jesus came into the world to save sinners, of whom I am the foremost." In light of that, read Romans 8:1 again—slowly.

A good interpreter will earnestly seek to discover the personal history of the author, the actual date of writing, the type of ministry he had, his relationship to the people to whom he wrote, and the purpose of his writing. When an interpreter digs into the personal history of a biblical author, the actual words of the text come alive and help ensure the proper use of texts for counseling purposes.

Focus on the Human Audience

Biblical counselors should also consider that the Bible was God's Word to someone else before it was God's Word to them. Since God chose to reveal His Word to that original audience first, it is imperative that the original audience and their situation be taken seriously. Who are the people to whom the author writes? What circumstances are they facing?

Thinking back to our case study—if Steve had studied the life of Timothy, to whom Paul wrote the epistle of 2 Timothy, he would have known that Timothy was not struggling with sexual lust. In his youthful exuberance, Timothy did struggle with another form of lust. He could be passionately quarrelsome and argumentative as a young pastor, especially when he believed he was on the side of truth (cf. 2 Timothy 2:23-26). Counsel offered from the Bible is more likely to be accurate and authoritative when the counselor takes the original audience seriously.

Another example of why consideration for the author and human audience is important can be seen when it comes to offering counsel from selected portions of Old Testament wisdom literature (e.g., Proverbs, Ecclesiastes and Job).[12] The Old Testament wisdom books are good source material for a counselor so long as they are properly interpreted and applied. Solomon wrote the majority of the book of Proverbs, and a few other men of God contributed some portions.[13] Solomon's primary audience is his sons (Proverb 4:1), and frequently he focused on one son at a time (e.g., Proverbs 1:10; 2:1; 3:1). The wisdom of Proverbs can easily be seen as familial instruction of a loving father to his son.

As you study the historical-cultural background during the time of Solomon, you quickly realize the necessity of parents providing their children with wisdom for life because of the difficulties and temptations they faced growing up in a culture of abundance. Sending young men out into a culture filled with the temptations of sex, greed, and violence without godly wisdom is like sending them into the Australian bush without instruction on poisonous snakes, spiders, and plants. Death is unavoidable for the uninformed. With many looming dangers facing the young and naïve, it is not surprising Solomon said to his sons, "Whoever listens to me will dwell secure and will be at ease, without dread of disaster" (Proverbs 1:33).

A careful study of ancient wisdom literature of the time (ca. 1000 to 930 BC) reveals that the father/son motif was also used in wisdom writings to refer to any teacher/student relationship. This wisdom was not restricted to a father-and-son relationship alone. It was intended for use with anyone who desired to be wise in living. When you understand the intended audience of Proverbs, you begin to see that its wisdom extended beyond the narrow confines of a father's instruction to his son. Anyone attempting to face the temptations and dangerous pitfalls of life—and survive—would be wise to follow its insights.

With this broader audience in mind, Steve could use Proverbs to help Jason understand that when he refuses to follow its wisdom, tough days lie ahead. In Proverbs, there are several sobering texts that warn young men of sexual temptation and its destructiveness (5:3-23; 6:23-35; 7:4-27). It is interesting to note that Solomon's warnings can go beyond reference to an actual woman and can include an imaginary seductive woman who is the make-believe product of a man's lurid fantasies (6:18; the Hebrew concept of heart involves the thinking, purposing, and planning of the mind and desires[14]). In addition, Solomon makes clear that the real temptation is not external, but is rooted in the heart of a man (4:23; 6:18,25; 7:25). This speaks directly to Jason's lustful voyeurism on the Internet. Wisdom teaches us that no matter how attractive the woman, she cannot tempt a pure heart (cf. Genesis 39:6-10). Conversely, if Jason refuses to follow godly wisdom, difficult times will follow his life (13:15,21).

Focus on the Biblical History and Culture

A biblical counselor who is serious about interpreting Scripture accurately will also have a keen eye for distinctive clues on the history and culture of ancient times, and the circumstances in which the writing took place. This would include social customs, political arrangements, geographical highlights, religious rites and rituals, economic conditions, and historical references. When these are properly identified, they will help to paint a more comprehensive backdrop for understanding the verses within the setting in which they were originally communicated. When the original history and culture are clarified, the individual words and phrases of the text take on a new and more vibrant meaning. This then makes application more precise and profound.

Let's assume that after careful study of the history and culture of 2 Timothy, our counselor Steve had a better grasp of its setting and purpose as he counseled Jason. Then he would be able to share with Jason the fact that the author, Paul, had serious concerns about Timothy weakening under the heavy pressure of pastoral ministry—a pressure brought on by difficult people

(1:6-8,13-14). He wanted Timothy to endure, not cave in to pressure, and remain faithful to his calling. This instruction is magnified by Paul's personal example—at the time he wrote this, he was in a Roman prison (1:16; 2:9). Historically, it is safe to assume that Paul had been rearrested under the violent persecution brought on by the Roman emperor Nero (ca. AD 66-67). Paul's difficulties were further heightened by the fact he had been forsaken by many of his closest friends, who feared coming under that same severe persecution (cf. 1:15; 4:9-16). Yet in spite of all of this, Paul remained faithful to his calling and his Lord. This made him a tremendous example for Timothy to follow for his life and ministry.

In like manner, even though 2 Timothy 2:22 has nothing to do directly with the topic of sexual lust, there is an overarching admonition in this epistle that could be used in the course of counseling Jason. Steve could use the historical background and admonition of 2 Timothy with all of its imperatives, and the example of its author, to help to strengthen Jason's resolve to remain faithful to his Lord and not give in to the temptation to sin. Understanding the historical and cultural background of any book of the Bible helps the imperatives appear less arbitrary.

Examining the Literary Context

Interpreting the literary context of a passage involves answering two critical questions: First, what is the genre of the passage? And second, what is the surrounding and immediate context of the passage?

The term *genre* is a Middle French word used to denote "kind" or "sort." In answering the question, "What kind of writing did the author utilize?" the meaning of a text becomes clearer. For example, one would not read a church newsletter the same way he would a love letter, for the two texts have different purposes and styles. So it is with Scripture: some is narrative, a telling of events; some is poetic; some is prophetic; some is historical, etc. If you need help with determining the genre of literature that you are studying, go to a good Bible commentary, Bible encyclopedia, or hermeneutics textbook. The credibility of a counselor's biblical guidance is greatly enhanced through this kind of study.[15]

The second question regarding the literary context of a passage considers both the verses immediately surrounding the passage at hand, as well as the broader subject matter of the book in which the passage is found. For this reason a good counselor should be dedicated to reading the entire book carefully and repeatedly. Bible teacher John MacArthur encourages Bible students by saying,

> That is the method I use to prepare my messages. I read through the passage I'm studying over and over again until it fills my mind. I suggest that as you read, you jot down the major themes of each chapter on a three-by-five card. Every day as you read the book, look at the card and read through your list. You will soon know by heart the main points of each chapter.[16]

Exceptions can be made for books like Psalms and Proverbs, which are compilations of a variety of subject matters into whole chapters or groups of verses. In all other books of the Bible, extended argumentation can be found. For example, in many of the early chapters of his epistles, Paul described the Christian's standing in Christ (for example, Romans 1–11 and Ephesians 1–3). When this is the case, the sentences are often written in the indicative—that is, as statements of truth. They emphasize the believer's standing because of the saving grace of Jesus Christ. Then in the remaining chapters of these epistles, and directly because of the Savior's grace, Paul gives the imperatives— that is, commands for godly living that grow out of the truth statements (as in Romans 12–16 and Ephesians 4–6).

Why is this important in understanding the overall flow of thought in a biblical book? Because the author intends the indicatives to properly motivate the imperatives. Obeying these commands from the heart is possible only because of the ongoing enabling grace of Jesus Christ in sanctification (Titus 2:11-12). A counselor should help the counselee understand that obedience is properly motivated when the accomplished work of Christ is remembered and appreciated.[17] This would be an example of the importance of understanding the macroscopic—or bigger picture—view of the literary context of any biblical passage.

Priority should be given to the *immediate* context in determining the meaning of a passage. This is the microscopic view of literary context—in this case, the verses immediately before and after the text at hand are examined. What do the paragraphs, sentences, and words mean in the surrounding context and in the text itself?

This is what Jason realized his counselor had failed to do, and this was an embarrassment to Steve. But what hurt Steve most was the fact that he had failed his Savior by misrepresenting His Word. If he would have just studied the literary context of the passage along with the surrounding verses, he would have discovered that his preunderstanding of 2 Timothy 2:22 was built upon a false presumption. He believed himself to be a good biblical counselor, but found that due to his carelessness he was no better than a cult leader who mishandles the Bible for personal gain. As a result, Steve resolved to be much more careful in his study of the passages he used for counseling, even if it took many hours for him to gain the understanding he needed.

There is one more important aspect of counseling that must not be overlooked before it can be properly called biblical.

Knowing the Counselee Well

The best counsel comes from a man who takes the time to get to know his counselee well. For you to do effective biblical counseling , it is not enough to know your Bible well. Knowing your counselee is extremely important, for that will enable you to apply the truths of the Bible in a meaningful and appropriate manner.

This may very well be the most difficult part of counseling. There is a sense in which the Bible is a stationary document.[18] It will not resist the counselor's scrutiny! A counselee, on the other hand, is a moving target. Whereas the Bible is rooted in the unchanging, immutable character of God (Numbers 23:19; Malachi 3:6; James 1:17), your counselee is constantly changing, hiding, and calculating. It is not unusual for a counselee to be the "artful dodger" when it comes to changing and growing into Christlikeness.

It is important for a counselor to actively pursue a knowledgeable relationship with the person he counsels. He must get involved in his friend's life and gather appropriate data.[19] Otherwise he will simply dispense the Bible instead of ministering it. This is what makes for good discipleship. Counseling is a type of discipleship that is problem-focused. It stands to reason that merely teaching truth from the Bible correctly is insufficient if the counselor misunderstands the counselee and his problem.

Jason came to counseling thinking that his main problem was Internet pornography; Steve began his counsel accepting Jason's assumption. But the wasteful hours Jason spent feeding his lust on the Internet was not the core problem. His Internet surfing for pornography was a symptom of a much deeper problem. Understanding this problem would help Steve to determine which biblical passages he could use to help Jason.

Scripture illustrates the tendency of God's people to simplistically interpret external evidences without taking the time to investigate deeper for the truth. For example, the priest Eli believed Hannah to be drunk, when in actuality she was praying silently, with her lips moving (1 Samuel 1:13). He failed to question her and simply jumped to a wrong conclusion. The rich young ruler incorrectly assumed he was ready for Christ's kingdom, but Jesus demonstrated he was not ready by asking him to give away his riches and follow Him (Mark 10:17-23). The young ruler was unable to comply because he loved his wealth more than he loved Christ. In each of the above cases, superficial observations led to false conclusions. Effective counselors understand that symptoms are merely clues to more serious core problems.

Therefore, wise biblical counselors get at the issues of the heart that activate the symptoms. They understand that the main occupation of the heart is worship, and that troubling external symptoms are an indicator that something is seriously wrong in a person's heart. A wise counselor will be able to draw this out of the heart (Proverbs 20:5), even though the counselee may not understand or be willing to acknowledge the real source of the problem (Proverbs 12:15; 16:2; 21:2). What motivations are ruling in the heart of the counselee? The only way these may be discovered is by the wise use of God's Word by a counselor (Hebrews 4:12)—by one who is willing to build a trusting relationship with the counselee so that the counselee understands that the counselor has his long-term welfare in mind.

Once there is a correct understanding of both the symptoms and the source of the counselee's problem, then the counselor can select the appropriate biblical texts for implementing God's solution to the problem. This is the compatibility challenge. Just as a Honda carburetor is not compatible with a Ford engine, it is foolish to apply inappropriate passages to a counselee's problems. What biblical passages are appropriate and compatible in getting at the heart of the counselee's problem? It is when a counselor is both case-wise and Bible-wise that a good matching of Scripture to the heart problem is likely to be found. In some more difficult cases, a counselor may need to consult with another wise Christian counselor or some biblical counseling resources in the search for compatible passages. There are many excellent resources listed at the end of this book that may be of help when doing such research.

Merging Knowledge of the Bible and the Counselee

During the fourth counseling session with Jason, Steve came to realize the heart issues that were at stake in Jason's problem. Jason shared that his struggle went way back to early puberty. This was when he began to actively seek out provocative stimulation by any means possible. Steve inquired about Jason's home life as a boy, and discovered he was raised as an only child by unbelieving parents who constantly fought each other. By the time he was 18 years old, his parents divorced. Steve probed, "When you were young, what did you do while your parents fought?" "Oh," Jason revealed, "I would run to my room, lock the door, and hide under my bed."

"What did you do under the bed?" asked Steve.

"I would read comic books while I listened to my parents argue and fight," said Jason. "Sometimes, when they became violent, I wanted to escape the harsh realities of my real world and withdraw into my comic world."

"I've seen those comic books," Steve said. "They exaggerate the physical attributes of women."

"That's right," Jason agreed. "That is when masturbation began to take such dominant control of my life."

This was beginning to make more sense to Steve. From the time Jason was a child, he had learned to deal with the unpleasant circumstances of life by escaping into an unreal world of make-believe. It was a fake world that promised him love and favors. But he discovered that the promise was a lie, because it actually made him intensely selfish, alienating him from real people and imprisoning him with a horrible bondage. Now that Jason was a Christian, he knew this is not what life was supposed to be. He knew that his self-indulgent lifestyle was a huge offense to the gospel and the Lord he loved.

It was now obvious to Steve what needed to happen in Jason's life. He proceeded to help Jason understand the righteous judgment of God in response to sin, and that Jesus Christ had saved him from this judgment through His atoning death. Before Steve was finished, Jason was in tears. He carefully explained Ephesians 2:1-10 verse by verse, helping Jason to refocus his understanding that as a sinful rebel against God he is undeserving, a man under an awful judgment. "But God, being rich in mercy…made us alive together with Christ—by grace you have been saved" (2:4-5). Steve then explained the glories of Jason's position in Christ. All the grace-filled truths of Ephesians 2 were like a cool breeze through Jason's soul.

Then Steve called Jason's attention to Paul's admonition to Titus: "The grace of God has appeared, bringing salvation for all people, training us to renounce ungodliness and worldly passions, and to live self-controlled, upright, and godly lives in the present age." Jason understood that it was the grace of the Lord Jesus Christ that was now compelling him to make significant changes away from a life with a *self-deserving* attitude to a life with an *undeserving* attitude so that he would bring glory to Christ. This meant not only being *saved* by grace, but *living* by grace.

But Steve was not finished. The worship of Jason's heart was completely wrong. He idolized pleasure and personal comfort to the point that he was willing to sinfully indulge his sexual fantasies to escape his unpleasant circumstances. At the very core of his sexual lust was a heart of greed. His heart had become stubborn and demanding. It sought images that appealed to his sexual desires and would bring him temporary delight. But these images also brought a selfish captivity and consumed him with an ugly covetousness.

Steve had Jason turn to Ephesians 5:3 and asked him read it out loud: "Sexual immorality and all impurity or covetousness must not even be named among you, as is proper among saints." Steve went on to explain to Jason that the term "sexual immorality" is one Greek word (*porneia*) and refers to any illicit sexual activity. It was a broad term that would include Jason's Internet voyeurism. The phrase "must not even be named among you" is stated as a command. The main reason Jason had allowed his problem to continue for so long was that he had never recognized how his heart idol of comfort was feeding his covetousness. It was time for Jason to repent of this god he wrongly worshipped in his greedy heart. Steve then pointed out the proper example Moses set in rejecting the indulgences of Egypt and all of their accompanying pleasures, taking the harder road by following righteousness (Hebrews 11:24-25). Jason had to make this same choice and make it stick.

Finally, Steve showed Jason Ephesians 5:4, which presents a life of greed being replaced by a life of thanksgiving. He proceeded to describe a life filled with a rich gratitude because of the saving grace of the gospel. This was the only type of life that would bring Jason lasting change. In their final counseling sessions together, Steve helped Jason to gain a thoroughly biblical understanding of thanksgiving on account of who he was in Christ, and presented Jason with practical barriers he could erect to make it hard for him to return to his lustful activities.

Providing Effective Biblical Counseling

Because Steve had taken the time to study God's Word more diligently and get to know Jason's heart motivations, real and effective biblical counseling took place. The thorough and accurate handling of the Bible in counseling reaps spiritual benefits in the lives of both counselor and counselee. The counselor grows in faithfulness to communicating God's truth correctly and effectively, while the counselee discovers God's solutions to his problems in a very clear exposition of Scripture.

In short summary, as a biblical counselor, it's important to…

- use a good translation of the Bible that focuses on accuracy over readability.

- identify the authorial intent of the passage, which will help to overcome errant preunderstandings and theological biases that might cloud the true meaning.

- carefully study the historic-cultural (including original author and audience) and literary contexts of a passage. This will help you to overcome interpretative bias.

- carefully study your counselee and his symptomatic behaviors so that you can correctly determine the underlying purposes and desires of the heart that are causing the symptoms. Upon determining these wrong purposes and desires of the heart, you can then call your counselee to repentance.

Recommended Resources

Adams, Jay E. *Fifty Difficult Passages Explained.* Stanley, NC: Timeless Texts, 2008.

Duvall, J. Scott, and J. Daniel Hayes. *Grasping God's Word: A Hands-on Approach to Reading, Interpreting, and Applying the Bible.* Grand Rapids, MI: Zondervan, 2005.

Kaiser, Walter C. Jr., Peter H. Davids, F.F. Bruce, and Manfred Brauch. *Hard Sayings of the Bible.* Downers Grove, IL: InterVarsity Press, 1996.

Ryken, Leland, and C. John Collins. *The Word of God in English.* Wheaton, IL: Crossway, 2002.

Zuck, Roy B. *Basic Bible Interpretation.* Colorado Springs, CO: David C. Cook, 1991.

3

Hope for Men in Despair

Nathan Busenitz

Hardship follows some people through life more closely than others. Horatio Spafford was one of those people. A wealthy Chicago attorney, committed Christian, and friend of the famous evangelist D.L. Moody, his story has been told many times. Like a nineteenth-century Job, his sufferings only increased the perseverance of his faith, setting him apart as an example of the hope-filled life that is available to God's children no matter what their circumstances. In the midst of great personal tragedy, his proper perspective prevailed.

Spafford's trials began with the great Chicago fire of October 1871, which nearly ruined him when his real estate investments literally went up in smoke. Two years later, the businessman decided to take his family on vacation to Europe. The trip was scheduled for November 1873. Unexpectedly detained by last-minute business, Spafford was forced to delay his passage to Europe. So he sent his wife, Anna, and four daughters on ahead, planning to follow them a few days later. Never did he imagine that his family's ship, the SS *Ville du Havre*, would never reach its intended destination. Striking another vessel while at sea, it sank to the ocean floor in less than fifteen minutes. All four of Spafford's daughters—Annie, Maggie, Bessie, and Tanetta—were killed. Incredibly, his wife survived, sending her husband the tragic telegram: "Saved alone."

Spafford immediately left Chicago to join his wife in Wales. En route, he came to the approximate place where his daughters had died. The grieving father would later recount that, at that very moment, he felt peace like a river despite the billowing sorrows of the surrounding sea. Only his hope in God allowed him to respond to his grief not in despair, but by penning the words to the famous hymn "It Is Well with My Soul." In the moment of his greatest sorrow, he found comfort and consolation in the fact that his soul was safe in the hands of God.

Spafford experienced peace in the midst of the storm not because his circumstances were easy, but because his heart was anchored in the bedrock of biblical hope.

Our Hopeless World

Spafford's hope-filled example provides a startling contrast to the fear and despair that characterizes so many people in contemporary American society. According to the National Institute of Mental Health, some 40 million American adults claim to suffer from anxiety disorders.[1] The American Foundation for Suicide Prevention adds that approximately 19 million have been diagnosed with clinical depression, and that every day more than a hundred Americans take their own lives in suicide (making it the tenth-leading cause of death in the United States).[2]

Countless others endure daily feelings of apprehension and despondency. Airline passengers worry about the safety of their flights; mourners grieve despondently at the loss of loved ones; patients agonize over the deadly dangers of their medical conditions; businesspeople fret because of the economy; and collegians cower at the uncertainty of whether they will achieve their career goals. It's no wonder that stress, worry, depression, and guilt run rampant in our culture. The clock is ticking, life is short, and people are looking for a safe, unfailing place in which to put their trust.

Of course, the postmodern consensus is that no such place exists. We are told that hope is relative, like everything else. To many, even the word *hope* carries no sense of certainty. Comments such as, "I hope I win the lottery" or "I hope it doesn't rain tomorrow" flood everyday conversations, evidencing both the whimsical and unfounded desires of many. In modern society, hope is a dream or a chance, a penny tossed carelessly into a fountain. It guarantees nothing and instills no confidence. It is a fairytale, a rabbit's foot, or a shooting star—it is a *wish*, and nothing more.

Sadly, feelings of hopelessness and despair are not solely the property of secular culture. Writing in *Christianity Today*, Duke University professor of psychiatry Dan G. Blazer explains that studies of religious groups, [including] evangelical Christians, reveal no evidence that the frequency of depression varies across religious groups or between those who attend religious services and those who do not. So in a typical congregation of 200 adults, 50 attendees will experience depression at some point, and at least 30 are currently taking antidepressants.[3]

Amidst sickness, suffering, and doubt, many self-proclaimed Christians are following those in the unbelieving world down a hopeless path. But they need not do so.

The Biblical Definition of Hope

The unbelieving world views hope as a fantasy. But the Bible declares that there really is such a thing as true hope—a hope that is absolutely sure. That hope is found in God and the unfailing promises of His Word. Though many could be cited, here are a few passages of Scripture that make the point:

- "Why are you cast down, O my soul? And why are you in turmoil within me? Hope in God, for I shall again praise him, my salvation" (Psalm 42:5).

- "I wait for the LORD, my soul waits, and in his word I hope; my soul waits for the Lord more than watchmen for the morning, more than watchmen for the morning. O Israel, hope in the LORD! For with the LORD there is steadfast love, and with him is plentiful redemption" (Psalm 130:5-7).

- "Blessed is he whose help is the God of Jacob, whose hope is in the LORD his God, who made heaven and earth, the sea, and all that is in them; who keeps faith forever" (Psalm 146:5-6).

- "As for the rich in this present age, charge them not to be haughty, nor to set their hope on the uncertainty of riches, but on God, who richly provides us with everything to enjoy" (1 Timothy 6:17).

- "...in the hope of eternal life, which God, who never lies, promised before the ages began and at the proper time manifested in his word through the preaching with which I have been entrusted by the command of God our Savior" (Titus 1:2-3).

- "Let us hold fast the confession of our hope without wavering, for he who promised is faithful" (Hebrews 10:23).

As these verses aptly demonstrate, true hope is found by looking to the Lord, resting in His powerful provision, and clinging to the promises of His Word. *To hope in God is to fix your eyes on Him and His promises rather than on your own personal circumstances no matter how difficult they may be.* If God is the source of your hope, it will never fail because He never fails. Those who hope in Him will never be disappointed (Romans 5:5).

According to Hebrews 11:1, the life of faith is defined by "the assurance of things hoped for." Like the notable saints depicted in Hebrews 11, believers today are called to confidently embrace the promises of God's Word and act upon them. The hope of resurrection, the hope of heaven, and the hope of being like Christ are not examples of wishful thinking—they are divine guarantees. They are realities, not whimsical desires; they are absolutes, not possibilities; they are true, and they have bearing on our lives.

Unlocking Your Spiritual Hope Chest

The life of hope begins at the moment of salvation, when a sinner repentantly turns away from sin and wholeheartedly embraces the Lord Jesus Christ in saving faith. As Paul told the Philippian jailer, "Believe in the Lord Jesus, and you will be saved" (Acts 16:31). He later explained to the Christians in Rome, "If you confess with your mouth that Jesus is Lord and believe in your heart that God raised Him from the dead, you will be saved" (Romans 10:9). The Bible describes the reality of salvation as a new birth (John 3:3; 1 Peter 1:23), in which those who were formerly sons of disobedience are adopted into the family of God (Romans 8:14-16; Ephesians 2:1-10).

In describing our new identity as children of God, the Bible speaks of a heavenly inheritance that every Christian can anticipate. Romans 8:17 declares that we are "heirs of God," meaning that we will receive an endowment from God that is far greater than anything we could ever imagine (see also Ephesians 3:6; Titus 3:7; 1 Peter 1:3-4,7). The believer's inheritance—a God-guaranteed hope chest filled with divine promises—is detailed throughout the New Testament. Here is a sampling of the promises that our heavenly inheritance includes:

- The promise of Christ's return (Philippians 3:20; 1 Thessalonians 4:13-18; Titus 2:11-14).

- The promise of being with the Lord forever (2 Corinthians 5:8; 1 Thessalonians 4:17).

- The promise of bodily resurrection (Acts 23:6; 1 Corinthians 15:20-23; Philippians 3:10-11,21).

- The promise of being made perfectly righteous (Galatians 5:5; 2 Timothy 4:8; Hebrews 11:7).

- The promise of everlasting life (John 3:16; 1 Corinthians 9:25; James 1:12; 1 John 2:17).

- The promise of heavenly reward (2 Corinthians 5:10; Ephesians 6:8; Colossians 3:24; Revelation 22:12).

- The promise of eternal rest (Hebrews 4:1-11; Revelation 14:13).

- The promise of a new heaven and earth (2 Peter 3:13; Revelation 21:1-2).

Those are only some of the absolute guarantees that we, as believers, can eagerly anticipate in the life to come! Of course, being God's child means that He has given you promises for this life as well. The Bible associates these promises, too, with the concept of hope. So they are also part of our spiritual hope chest. Here are a few examples:

- The promise that we can trust God in every situation (Psalm 9:10, 56:3; Nahum 1:7).

- The promise of God's sovereign protection (Psalm 25:20-21; 2 Corinthians 1:10-11).

- The promise of God's providential care (Jeremiah 14:22; Matthew 6:31-34; 1 Timothy 5:5).

- The promise that we can find true satisfaction in God (Psalm 62:5; 1 Timothy 6:17).

- The promise that we have been given every spiritual blessing in Christ (Romans 5:1-2; Ephesians 1:3).

- The promise that God uses trials to build spiritual character and bring joy in our lives (Romans 5:3-5; James 1:2-3).

- The promise that we cannot lose our salvation (2 Corinthians 1:22; 5:5; Ephesians 1:13-14).

- The promise that nothing can separate us from the love of God in Christ (Romans 8:31-39), and that He will never leave us nor forsake us (Hebrews 13:5-6).

As heirs of God, believers receive infinite benefits for both this life and the next. Hope is not limited only to what comes after death. Rather, our hope chest is brimming with promises for the present as well as the future.

When we consider the marvelous promises that comprise our spiritual hope chest, it changes the way we think about this life. It was Paul's hope-filled perspective that enabled him to respond to hardship with confidence and joy. In 2 Corinthians 4:16-18, he explained,

> We do not lose heart. Though our outer self is wasting away, our inner self is being renewed day by day. For this light momentary affliction is preparing for us an eternal weight of glory beyond all comparison, as we look not to the things that are seen but to the things that are unseen. For the things that are seen are transient, but the things that are unseen are eternal.

Paul invited others to share that same perspective. As he told the Ephesians, "…having the eyes of your hearts enlightened, that you may know what is the hope to which he has called you, what are the riches of his glorious inheritance in the saints, and what is the immeasurable greatness of his power toward us who believe" (Ephesians 1:18-19). When believers center their attention on "the hope to which he has called you" and "the riches of his glorious inheritance," their lives are radically changed—not because their circumstances change, but because their perspective is reoriented and renewed.

In the midst of difficult circumstances—when Christians experience times of deep discouragement and are even tempted to despair—they need to remember to keep their eyes on the source of their hope, the Lord Himself (Hebrews 12:1-2). They must talk truth to themselves, rather than listening to the doubts of their hearts. By renewing their minds with the promises of God's

Word, prayerfully depending on Him, and putting on the hope of salvation like a helmet (1 Thessalonians 5:8), believers can find *joy*, *peace*, and *spiritual victory* in the midst of any suffering or adversity. These three benefits come to the believer who puts his hope in God, the only truly effective remedy for the doubt and dismay that are often linked with difficult trials and temptations. Let's consider them briefly:

Hope Produces Joy in the Midst of Difficult Trials

Life often brings circumstances we don't understand, hardships that seem unbearable, and times that are really tough. It might be a death in the family, a lack of financial security, a personal health problem, or simply the pressures of a hectic schedule. Yet, no matter the situation or the supposed cause, Christians can trust in the fact that God is in control (1 Chronicles 29:11-12). He is our help and our refuge (Psalms 50:15; 59:16). And He will allow us to experience only that which is possible for us to endure (1 Corinthians 10:13) and that which will result in our spiritual good (Romans 8:28).

Even in the midst of severe trials and tribulations, hope enables us to find joy. Here are three reasons why:

Trials Force Us to Depend on God

In Romans 5:3, Paul explained that we "exult in our tribulations, knowing that tribulation brings about perseverance" (NASB). James echoed that same truth in James 1:2-3 when he wrote, "Count it all joy, my brothers, when you meet trials of various kinds, for you know that the testing of your faith produces steadfastness." In both of those passages, the point is clear: hardship produces perseverance.

What is *perseverance*? It is the ability to endure by waiting on the Lord; it is the power to weather any storm because permanent shelter has been taken in God. As David joyfully explained in Psalm 5:11, "Let all who take refuge in you rejoice; let them ever sing for joy, and spread your protection over them, that those who love your name may exult in you." Perseverance is possible, not because of our own inner fortitude, but through the strength and grace that God supplies (2 Corinthians 12:9; Philippians 4:13).

Trials generally involve the loss of something we hold precious—whether it's our health, our home, our loved ones, or our job. By taking away what we hold dear on this earth, trials compel us to look to God; they force us to depend on Him. And rightly so. Only on the solid rock of His strength can we survive the storm—all other ground is sinking sand. Trials, then, teach us perseverance because they force us to wait on the Lord and rely on His power and faithful provision (see Lamentations 3:20-25). In this way, they bring us into a closer communion with our loving heavenly Father. That deepened relationship brings profound joy, even in the midst of suffering.

Trials Are for Our Spiritual Good

Not only do trials produce perseverance, they also result in holiness in our lives. Romans 5:4 refers to this as "proven character" (NASB) and James 1:4 as spiritual maturity. While life's hardships are never enjoyable, God always uses them for our benefit. The author of Hebrews explained it this way: "All discipline [which comes in the form of trials] for the moment seems not to be joyful, but sorrowful; yet to those who have been trained by it, afterwards it yields the peaceful fruit of righteousness" (Hebrews 12:11 NASB). Thus we can rejoice, even in the worst of times, because we know that God is in the process of refining us. We may not understand everything that is involved. We may not have all our questions answered. But we can rest confidently in the reality that God loves us (1 John 4:11,19) and wants us to be holy (1 Peter 1:15-16). Andrew Murray summarized it this way:

> First, He brought me here, it is by His will I am in this strait [narrow] place: in that fact I will rest. Next, He will keep me here in His love, and give me grace to behave as His child. Then, He will make the trial a blessing, teaching me the lessons He intends me to learn, and working in me the grace He means to bestow. Last, in His good time He can bring me out again—how and when He knows. Let me say I am here, (1) By God's appointment, (2) In His keeping, (3) Under His training, (4) For His time.[4]

Knowing that God uses trials to produce sanctifying results in our lives enables us to have joy in spite of the sorrow.

Trials Cause Us to Long for Heaven

Trials not only point us to a faithful God, they also remind us that this world is not our home. Only in heaven will we enjoy a perfect existence that is free from the stain of sin and suffering. In describing the new earth, the apostle John noted that one day Christ "will wipe away every tear from their eyes, and death shall be no more, neither shall there be mourning, nor crying, nor pain anymore, for the former things have passed away" (Revelation 21:4). In the life to come, there will be no more sorrow, sadness, sickness, or suffering. What a wonderful reality that is for us to eagerly anticipate! It was the hope of the reversal of the curse for which the apostle Paul groaned in Romans 8:23-24. It was this hope that motivated the heroes of Hebrews 11 to endure suffering and affliction in this life because "they desire[d] a better country, that is, a heavenly one" (verse 16).

The reality for Christians is that what we suffer in this life is only temporary. One day we will no longer experience trials of any kind. The effects of sin and the curse will be gone. The temporary afflictions of this world are producing for us an eternal weight of glory (2 Corinthians 4:17). Thus, we can rejoice, with the apostles, that we are counted worthy to suffer for His name's sake (Acts 5:41). Moreover, when death comes knocking, we do not grieve as those who have no hope (1 Thessalonians 4:13). Such a perspective is possible because we look forward to a place where sorrow and suffering are gone.

Hope Brings Peace in the Midst of Daily Trouble

Trials refer to specific times of significant hardship or adversity. But what about the everyday troubles and concerns that we face? How does hope safeguard our hearts against the constant cares of everyday life? The Lord Jesus addressed that very issue in Matthew 6:31-34. In that passage He instructed His followers with these words:

> Therefore do not be anxious, saying, "What shall we eat?" or "What shall we drink?" or "What shall we wear?" For the Gentiles seek after all these things, and your heavenly Father knows that you need them all. But seek first the kingdom of God and his righteousness, and all these things will be added to you.

> Therefore do not be anxious about tomorrow, for tomorrow will
> be anxious for itself. Sufficient for the day is its own trouble.

Rather than growing anxious (like unbelievers do), the children of God need to trust the providential care of their heavenly Father.

The apostle Paul exemplified that kind of settled confidence in the Lord throughout his life and ministry. From an earthly standpoint, Paul had plenty of reasons to worry. Jewish antagonists wanted to kill him. Gentile opponents thought he was a fool and a menace to society. He had experienced great physical hardship for the sake of the gospel (2 Corinthians 11:23-27). Even within the churches he had planted, false teachers posed a constant threat. In situations in which most of us would have complained, become worried, or grown discouraged, Paul reacted differently. He was under house arrest in Rome when he penned Philippians 4:6-7. Yet in spite of his troubling circumstances, he wrote, "Do not be anxious about anything, but in everything by prayer and supplication with thanksgiving let your requests be made known to God. And the peace of God, which surpasses all comprehension, will guard your hearts and your minds in Christ Jesus." In just those two verses, Paul articulated four means by which hope overcomes worry.

Hope Meets Fear with Faith

Because he put his hope in the Lord Jesus, trusting Him for the outcome, Paul could *not be anxious about anything* even when his circumstances were far from easy (see Philippians 1:19-20). No matter how bad the situation became, he remained calm and settled. Just a few verses later, the apostle would add:

> I have learned in whatever situation I am in to be content. I know
> how to be brought low, and I know how to abound. In any and
> every circumstance, I have learned the secret of facing plenty and
> hunger, abundance and need. I can do all things through him who
> strengthens me (Philippians 4:11-13).

How could Paul be content and at peace in any circumstance? He found his strength in Christ—keeping his focus on the Savior rather than the situation.

Because Paul's hope was in the Lord, he chose to cling by faith to God's promises rather than worry about anything. As Christians, we too can hope in God rather than our circumstances (see 1 Peter 5:7). The God whom we serve is far greater than any fear we might have.

Hope Counteracts Worry with Worship

Paul continued by telling the Philippians that they should respond to "everything" in life "with thanksgiving." Instead of worrying about the details of what may or may not happen, believers are to praise God for His faithfulness. In Philippians 4:8, Paul implored believers to think about things that are true, honorable, and just. When we worry, our minds concentrate on things that are harmful and often imaginary. Instead, we ought to be meditating on those things that we know are right and true—such as God's power, goodness, and trustworthiness. God's promises, rather than the potential troubles of the future, ought to govern our thoughts and actions.

Hope Responds to Problems with Prayer

Paul commanded his readers that, rather than worrying about their problems, they were to take their burdens to the Lord "by prayer and supplication." In 1 Thessalonians 5:17, he echoed this with the instruction to "pray without ceasing." Ironically, believers often find consistent prayer hard to practice; but they find it easy to worry continually. A hope-filled response turns worries into prayer requests and reminds us to depend on the Lord for strength and wisdom (James 1:5).

Hope Replaces Pressure with Peace

In Philippians 4:7, Paul assured his readers that when they rest in God, His peace will comfort them. Instead of being consumed by anxiety, we can experience comfort and rest when we choose to rely on God. Worry never brings happiness—instead, it brings agitation, stress, and tension. God, on the other hand, promises peace "which surpasses all understanding" to those who hope in Him. That kind of peace can never be disrupted by changing circumstances, because it is anchored in the One who never changes.

For unbelievers, happiness is based on circumstances. If things are going well, happiness comes easy. When things go badly, peace and joy are nowhere to be found. In contrast, *the happiness of hope is based on certainty.* God has made promises, and those promises will not change or fail no matter what troubles we face in this life. While the world's happiness is flippant and fleeting, the peace of God is eternal. The joy we find in Him transcends the daily sorrows and setbacks of this life.

Hope Motivates Victory over Deadly Temptations

We've seen that a hope-filled perspective produces joy in the midst of difficult trials and brings peace in spite of daily troubles. But how does hope strengthen believers so that they can stand victoriously against deadly temptations?

The battle against sin and temptation is a constant reality (Ephesians 6:10-18). As those who have been saved from sin, we are called to put off our old way of thinking by renewing our minds with the truth (Ephesians 4:22-24; Philippians 4:8). We are to deny sinful deeds and replace them with the fruit of the Spirit (Galatians 5:19-24). Through the power of the Spirit (Romans 8:13), we are able to put to death wicked attitudes and actions (Colossians 3:5). Though we will never be sinless until we reach heaven (1 John 1:8-10), we are commanded to diligently seek godliness (2 Timothy 2:22), knowing that the Lord "loves him who pursues righteousness" (Proverbs 15:9). Practically speaking, holiness manifests itself in our lives through heartfelt obedience to God's commands. Even the term *holiness*, referring to separation, points to this idea—we are to separate ourselves from the sinful activities of this world so that we are more fully devoted to God.

The pursuit of holiness is a continual struggle (see Romans 7:15-24). Yet God is faithful, not only to forgive His children when they fail (Psalm 32:1-5), but also to sanctify and purify the lives of those whom He has saved. The wonderful reality, then, is that although the process of our sanctification takes discipline and hard work (1 Timothy 4:7), God gives us the power to fight and promises us the ultimate victory (see Philippians 2:12-13; 1 Thessalonians 5:23-24).

Not only is God our source of strength in the midst of temptation, He also gives us great motivation to obey—motivation that is intrinsically tied to our hope. Here are three reasons hope should motivate your daily obedience:

You Will Give an Account to Christ

Knowing that we will one day appear before the Lord to give an account for our lives is a powerful motivation for continued faithfulness. As Paul explained in 2 Corinthians 5:9-10, "Whether we are at home or away, we make it our aim to please him. For we must all appear before the judgment seat of Christ, so that each one may receive what is due [or be rewarded] for what he has done in the body, whether good or evil." Paul made it his ultimate goal in life to please and glorify the Lord, knowing that one day he would stand before Christ to be rewarded for his steadfast service (see 2 Timothy 4:8).

Believers, of course, are saved by grace alone through faith in Christ (Ephesians 2:8-10). Our salvation is possible through God's free gift of grace, which is bestowed on all who genuinely repent and believe (Romans 10:9-10). It is not the result of our good works. At the same time, however, the Bible teaches that believers "will all stand before the judgment seat of God" (Romans 14:10), where they will be given heavenly rewards for their faithfulness in this life. Just as an exceptional employee receives a bonus or an outstanding soldier a decorative medal, Christ's loyal servants will be rewarded for their heartfelt obedience.

It is helpful to remember that God is not impressed with the mere outward appearance of righteousness. He does not reward actions or words that come from a hard, selfish heart. The Lord knows the thoughts of men (Jeremiah 17:9-10). He is well aware of our motives (Proverbs 16:2). So unless our works stem from a genuine desire to please Him, there is no reward. After all, the Pharisees did good works. But because they did them with wrong motives, they did not receive our Lord's approval (Matthew 6:1-6).

Hope-motivated holiness, then, stems from a genuine desire to love the Lord and keep His commands (Mark 12:30; John 14:15), knowing that we will one day see Him face to face. Even if no one notices our acts of obedience, God sees and knows—the motivation is not human recognition, but rather to be pleasing to Him (Colossians 1:10). Having been saved by grace through faith alone, we subsequently work hard to be found faithful as His servants (Matthew 25:21).

God's Promises Are True

Second, hope motivates holiness because hope believes the promises of God over the promises of sin. In reality, temptation—which is where sin always begins (James 1:13-15)—is nothing more than a promise (albeit a false promise), claiming that true happiness is actually found in disobedience. Satan used this very tactic in the Garden of Eden when he promised Eve that by disobeying God, she and Adam would be like God Himself (Genesis 3:5). That promise was a deadly falsehood.

On the flip side, God also makes us promises. He promises that He knows what is best for us. He promises that He loves us as His children. He promises that sin has terrible consequences, but that obedience brings blessing. As one writer put it, "Faith [and hope] and holiness are inextricably linked. Obeying the commands of God usually involves believing the promises of God."[5]

So when temptation comes, the Christian has a choice. Faced with two sets of promises, the believer must decide which promises to believe. Both offer happiness and fulfillment. Both claim to have your best interests in mind. And yet, as we know from Scripture and experience, the promises of sin are always false; they always disappoint and lead to negative consequences. The promises of God, however, are always true; they never disappoint, but rather, always result in blessing and joy.

When we choose to believe God's promises consistently, a life of holiness is the inevitable result. The boastful pride of life (1 John 2:16 NASB) can be combated by embracing God's promise that those who are "poor in spirit" and "meek" will be "blessed" (Matthew 5:3-5). The humble receive grace (Proverbs 3:34 NASB) and will be exalted in due time (James 4:10; 1 Peter 5:6). On the other hand, those who are proud will be brought low (Job 40:12; Psalm 18:27) and destroyed (Proverbs 15:25; Isaiah 2:17).

The desires of the flesh and of the eyes (1 John 2:16)—including sexual sins, self-indulgence, laziness, covetousness, and greed—can also be combated with the promises of Scripture. Time and time again, God guarantees that these sins will lead to ruin and heartache (Proverbs 5:20-23; 11:6; 13:4; 20:1; 27:20). He further promises that lasting satisfaction and true fulfillment can only be found in Him (Ecclesiastes 2:25; 12:13-14). When we try to satisfy our hearts with sinful substitutes, we replace the spring of living water—which continually satisfies—with broken cisterns that are all dried up (Jeremiah 2:13).

Sin takes place, then, when we doubt the promises of God and, instead, choose to believe the false promises of temptation. As Christians, we must use "the sword of the Spirit, which is the word of God" (Ephesians 6:17) and coun-teract the lies of sin with the truth of Scripture. In so doing, we will choose the path of life rather than the way of death (Psalm 119:9-11).

Divine Encouragement Is Promised

As we fight against sin, our gracious heavenly Father encourages our hearts in several important ways. First, He promises His children that their future is secure. With that in mind, after discussing his own struggle against tempta-tion, Paul joyfully announced, "There is therefore now no condemnation for those who are in Christ Jesus" (Romans 8:1). We can be encouraged to keep fighting because we know that once we are part of God's family we will never be disowned. When we do fail, He is faithful to forgive (1 John 1:9). There is nothing, not even our own sin, that can separate us from His love (Romans 8:38-39).

Second, God cheers our hearts by reminding us that our struggle here is only temporary. One day our battles with sin will be no more; our past fail-ures will be history; our wrong choices will be forgotten. The resurrection body God creates for us will have no sinful remnant, nor will our heavenly home have any external solicitations to sin. We will be perfect forever. The hope of that future reality ought to motivate our holiness in the present (1 John 3:2-3).

Finally, God comforts us by promising that the process of spiritual growth that He began when He called us to Himself will ultimately finish. While this does not excuse laziness on our part, it does mean that we can depend on Him as we strive to be holy. What Paul told the Philippians is true for all Chris-tians—namely, that "he who began a good work in you will bring it to com-pletion at the day of Jesus Christ" (Philippians 1:6; see also 2 Thessalonians 2:13; 1 Peter 1:2). By relying on His Spirit, His strength, and His Word, we can be confident that we will find victory as we diligently pursue Him each day.

In all of this, our love for Christ is the fuel that powers our holy living and obedience. Hope is an intrinsic part of this equation. When we look to our heavenly reward, we are looking ultimately to pleasing and glorifying Christ. When we choose to believe the promises of God rather than the promises of sin, we are choosing to trust in Christ and His Word—recognizing that Jesus alone can truly satisfy us. And when we look to His promises to encourage us along the way, we are relying not on ourselves but rather on His perfect power.

The author of Hebrews powerfully summarized the perspective that should characterize our lives: "Let us also lay aside every weight, and sin which clings so closely, and let us run with endurance the race that is set before us, looking to Jesus, the founder and perfecter of our faith, who for the joy that was set before him endured the cross, despising the shame, and is seated at the right hand of the throne of God" (Hebrews 12:1-2).

Where Is Your Hope Built?

The overwhelming testimony of Scripture is that lasting hope is found in God alone—whether in the midst of difficult trials, daily troubles, or deadly temptations. While people are often enticed to look elsewhere, their search is a vain endeavor. Medication may make them feel better, alcohol may dull their senses, entertainment may help them escape, other enterprises may distract them—yet all of those are only temporary fixes. They are like bandages on cancer. They can never actually solve the problem; they can only cover it up for a time.

Only a heart that has been changed by Jesus Christ and that looks to God for its strength can enjoy true hope. The promises of God can be trusted because God cannot lie; they can be enjoyed because they were given for our spiritual good; and they can be embraced forever because they are eternal.

Are you discouraged? Are you disheartened and downcast? Is your life not what you desire? Is the guilt of your sin too much for you to bear? Do your problems feel insurmountable or your struggles too painful to endure? Do you not know that there is hope—*real* hope—in God? Jesus said, in Matthew 11:28, "Come to me, all who labor and are heavy laden, and I will give you rest." The question is, Will you come? Or will you look for your hope in the things of this earth, things that can never satisfy and will ultimately only disappoint? In this same vein, John Gill wrote:

> God is faithful to all His promises, nor can He fail, or deceive; He is all wise and foreknowing of everything that comes to pass; He never changes His mind, nor forgets His word; and He is able to perform, and is the God of truth, and cannot lie; nor has He ever failed in any one of His promises, nor will He suffer [allow] His

faithfulness to fail; and this is a strong argument to hold fast a profession of faith.[6]

Our search for help, then, must begin with the One who will never fail, for only He offers true hope.

Recommended Resources

Adams, Jay E. *A Theology of Christian Counseling*. Grand Rapids, MI: Zondervan, 1979.

———. *The Christian Counselor's Manual*. Grand Rapids, MI: Zondervan, 1973.

Bridges, Jerry. *Trusting God: Even When Life Hurts*. Colorado Springs, CO: NavPress, 2008.

Busenitz, Nathan. *Living a Life of Hope*. Uhrichsville, OH: Barbour Publishing, 2003.

Lane, Timothy S., and Paul David Tripp. *How People Change*. Greensboro, NC: New Growth Press, 2008.

4

Man and the Meaning of Life

Andrew D. Rogers

The first time I truly thought seriously about the meaning of my life was at my father-in-law's retirement party. Many people stood up at the podium and told a variety of anecdotes about him. They spoke about his character, his mannerisms, and his attitude toward life and work. Some had some funny stories to tell, while others had more serious things to share. While I sat listening to what was being said, I was struck by questions about my own life. Had it amounted to anything? Was I on track to living a meaningful life? At the end of it all, would my life have amounted to anything of significance?

What about you? Have you ever asked yourself, *Is there any purpose to my life? Is there any real meaning to it? Is there value in what I do?* It seems that everyone faces these questions at one time or another. We want to know that the life we live is meaningful. We want to know whether our life will count in some way.

If your day-to-day life has not yet triggered these thoughts, or you haven't pondered them for a while, usually all it takes to bring them to the surface is a sudden tragedy. Going to a funeral tends to bring these questions to our attention. Funerals are like splashes of cold water on a sleepy face. They wake us up and make us think about reality—about life and death. King Solomon, in the Old Testament book of Ecclesiastes, wrote that it is better to attend funerals than go to parties (7:2). That's because we are more lucid about our lives during funerals. He is not saying that parties are bad, but unlike parties, funerals cause us to think seriously about life. We don't normally ponder the meaning of life at parties. Funerals strike us with the frailty of life and cause us to reflect on how we are spending our time.

The meaning of life has been the subject of much philosophical, scientific, and theological speculation throughout history. There have been a large number of solutions offered from many different cultural and ideological backgrounds. Here are just a few:

- The meaning of life is acquiring the greatest knowledge.

- Life's true meaning is becoming self-sufficient.

- Live your life the way you want as long as everyone else is okay with it.

- Live in a way that brings about the greatest happiness to the greatest number of people.

- Live life as if everything is worthless.

- Determine your own meaning.

Solomon, one of the great kings of Israel, had much to say about living a meaningful life. He was the son of King David, and God had granted him more wisdom than any other person (1 Kings 3:12). During his life he accumulated great wealth (1 Chronicles 29:25) and taught and arranged many proverbs (Ecclesiastes 12:9). He started out well, but then he made many serious mistakes. Later in his life he became concerned about those who would live on after him, that they would make the same mistakes he had made. By direction of the Holy Spirit of God, Solomon wrote Ecclesiastes to warn others not to go down the same dead-end streets he had.

Reading Ecclesiastes is like listening to an older man share not what he had done right, but what he had done wrong. We learn from this great book what will not satisfy, what will not make life worth living, and what is utterly useless and "a striving after wind" (Ecclesiastes 1:14). Along the way, Solomon helps us see what will bring about a meaningful life. M. James Sawyer describes the book of Ecclesiastes like this: "The book is a record of a search for the key to life. It is an endeavor to give meaning to life...If you want the key you must go to the locksmith who made the lock."[1]

Our Struggle to Find Meaning in This Life

Solomon observed two truths about life: It is meaningless, and it is monotonous. He said, "Vanity of vanities...vanity of vanities! All is vanity" (Ecclesiastes 1:2). From a mere human perspective, life is vain, useless, and meaningless.

To demonstrate this, Solomon pointed to the monotony of life. He mentioned six facts about life to prove his point. One, people come and go—they are not permanent. "A generation goes, and a generation comes" (Ecclesiastes 1:4). Two, look at the sun. It rises and it sets only to rise and set again and again and again (verse 5). Three, the wind blows one way, and then another. Like a dog chasing its tail, the wind goes around and around and around (verse 6). Four, look at the rivers and the sea. The streams run to the sea, but the sea doesn't overflow (verse 7). By appearance, none of these activities accomplish anything.

Think about your typical day. You get up, eat, go to work to make money so that you can eat and have a place to sleep, go home, eat, and go to sleep. The next day? You get up, eat, go to work, go home, eat, and go to sleep. The next day? You get the picture. Life is monotonous and seemingly meaningless.

The fifth fact about life that Solomon identified is that our appetites and desires are never satisfied (verse 8). Remember Thanksgiving? You ate so much that you might have said, "Oh, that was so good. I'm stuffed. I won't ever have to eat again." The very next day or maybe even later during the same day, you went into the kitchen to make yourself one of those incredibly delicious leftover turkey sandwiches. Or perhaps you have seen a car that made you say, "Wow—I will never have to see another car. That was the car of all cars." But in short time, we won't be so satisfied that we don't have to see another car.

The sixth and final fact that illustrates the monotony of life is history. History simply repeats itself. There is "nothing new under the sun" (verse 9). Things only appear new because we forget the past (verses 10-11). Solomon shows how nature, man, and history all portray the monotony of life. And this monotony demonstrates the meaninglessness of life and begs the question, "What does man gain by all the toil...?" (verse 3).

Solomon said that human wisdom is impotent when it comes to discovering the meaning of life. No matter how much we try to figure it out, we can't.

More often than not, we just make things worse. It seems that the best we can do is deliver solutions that create new problems. Drug commercials tell us how a drug might solve a certain problem, but then they spend just as much time telling us about the possible *new* problems that will be created by the drug. We created remote controls to make life easier, but then how much time and effort do we waste looking for it when it is lost or misplaced? We can't turn on the television and watch it until we find the remote, right?

So is there any meaning to this life? Is it possible to live a meaningful life? Can our lives genuinely amount to anything? If so, how? What can we do to live a life of meaning?

Our Search for Meaning in the Wrong Places

We saw earlier that there are many theories about the meaning of life. Solomon tested these theories almost 3000 years ago. In Ecclesiastes, he tells us of an experiment he conducted to see if meaning can actually be found in this life. He identified five areas in which people attempt to find meaning—all of which are still pursued today.

Pleasures

The first area is pleasure. We seek to find meaning in what makes us happy—in what is enjoyable to us. Solomon says in his heart, "I will test you with pleasure; enjoy yourself" (Ecclesiastes 2:1). He says, "I searched with my heart how to cheer my body with wine…and how to lay hold on folly, till I might see what was good for the children of man to do under heaven during the few days of their life" (verse 3). We might hear similar sentiments like this from men who say, "Eat, drink, and be merry; for tomorrow you die."

Solomon concludes that pleasure-seeking in its various forms is meaningless because it ultimately accomplishes nothing (verse 2). Sensual gratification, while pleasing for the moment, yields no lasting benefit (verses 3,8,11). What do brief bouts of laughter and pleasure actually accomplish? Just look at late night TV shows and sitcoms. They are perhaps the epitome of what Solomon is speaking about. The canned laughter is piped in to make you think that what is said is actually funny.

What can I do to feel good all the time? What can I do to pleasure myself? No matter what I do—how pleasurable it is, it is fleeting and short-lived, and simply brings no lasting satisfaction. The human heart will always want more. These things will not satisfy your thirst for a meaningful and satisfying life. However, you can find pleasure in the mundaneness of life by seeking your pleasure in a right relationship with God (verse 25).

Projects

The second place we look for meaning are our projects. These are the things that we build or achieve in our lives. Solomon built big houses, fruitful vineyards, and extravagant gardens and parks. In ancient times, such gardens and parks, which were constructed by the wealthy, often contained refreshing streams, cool shade, and all manner of fruit trees. Sometimes they also contained wild animals. Basically, Solomon built his own animal theme park. In Palestine, where winter rainfall has to be stored to compensate for the long drought of summer, ponds of water or rock-cut reservoirs were of such importance that their structure was a worthy boast for a king.

This wasn't something that any of us could just build with some materials from our local do-it-yourself store. Even for Solomon, this was a magnificent achievement (Ecclesiastes 2:4). None of the projects on *Extreme Makeover: Home Edition* and other home improvement shows can compare to what Solomon created.

As was the case with selfish pleasures, Solomon found that the satisfaction derived from home improvement projects is only temporary (verses 4-6,11). I remember being so happy with myself after building a shed from the ground up to match the side of the house. We sold the house only a few months later. Solomon expressed my sentiments well: "I hated all my toil in which I toil under the sun, seeing that I must leave it to the man who will come after me" (verse 18).

Possessions

Our possessions are another area in which we seek to find meaning. We have heard men say, "Whoever dies with the most toys, wins." Jesus, however, said, "What does it profit a man to gain the whole world and forfeit his soul?"

(Mark 8:36). Possessions, like pleasure and projects, will not provide meaning for us. In fact, Solomon concluded that wealth and possessions actually bring more problems than they are worth. He had more than any other person before him and after him (Ecclesiastes 2:7-8). He got whatever he wanted (verse 10). He deprived himself of nothing. And yet he found this too to be meaningless (verse 11).

Solomon discovers that wealth actually brings anxiety rather than fulfillment (Ecclesiastes 5:10-11). People who possess a lot of money and material possessions are rarely pleased or satisfied with what they have. The more we have, the more people there are who will take what we have. From family to friends, to accountants and attorneys, there will be plenty of people to take our wealth. And the more money we make, the more time we will spend thinking about what to do with it. Ultimately, all we can really do with our possessions is look at them (verse 11).

Money can easily consume us. We have to work hard to keep it. Possessions can be easily lost and keep us up at night (verse 14). We hear stories of people who started out in life with little to nothing, and they say those were some of the most enjoyable and freeing years of their lives. Just because we have wealth doesn't guarantee we will actually enjoy it. You can have everything you ever want, but if God doesn't give you the power to enjoy what you have, then you won't (Ecclesiastes 6:1-2).

It isn't how much we have that brings about meaning. Instead, it is how much we enjoy what we have. Only God can give that kind of enjoyment. The story is told of a rich industrialist who was disturbed to find a fisherman sitting idly by his boat. The industrialist asked, "Why aren't you out there fishing?"

"Because I've caught enough fish for today," was the reply.

"Why don't you catch more fish than you need?" asked the rich man.

"What would I do with them?"

"You could earn more money and buy a better boat so you could go deeper and catch more fish. You could purchase nylon nets, catch even more fish, and make more money. Soon you'd have a fleet of boats and be rich like me."

"Then what would I do?" asked the fisherman.

"You could sit down and enjoy life."

"What do you think I'm doing now?" said the fisherman.

Education

The fourth area in which people seek meaning is education. We often put our hope in learning, discovery, and ingenuity. We believe that gains in knowledge and technology will enhance our lives. The first set of commercials for the microwave oven promised a better family life. Because we would spend less time cooking the family meal, we would have more time to spend with our families. How's that working out for you in your home?

Solomon found that human knowledge has its advantages, but ultimately it also is vanity. Why? He said that the same fate awaits both the fool and the wise person—they will die (Ecclesiastes 2:15). And there is no guarantee that the wise person would ever even make a name for himself. As a fool will die and not be remembered, so too the wise person (verse 16).

Employment

Many of us attempt to find meaning in our work. What we do for a living is often seen as what brings about true meaning. We want to know that what we do is significant. The reason unemployment is so debilitating to us is because we want to do something meaningful. Yet Solomon pointed out that not even our work and labor will satisfy us. Eventually someone else will benefit from your work, and who knows how that person will treat or care for what you did (verses 18-19)? Sometimes the fruit of your labors is left for someone else to enjoy and benefit from, even though he did nothing to work for it.

We see this sometimes in the world of sports. We have seen football coaches get fired from their job because they failed to reach the Super Bowl. They reached the playoffs almost every year of their tenure, but just couldn't seem to win "the big one." So the team hires a new coach, and the very next year, the team goes to the Super Bowl. Now, did that coach really achieve that on his own? No—he benefitted from the long, arduous, and persistent labors of the preceding coach. He built on the foundation that his predecessor worked so hard to put together. Frustrating, right?

The task of looking for meaning in this world is wearisome. Eventually Solomon came to the end of his rope. He was utterly grieved and frustrated to the point of despair (verse 20). The search for meaning is so burdensome that a person will not find rest or sleep (verse 23). Is it any wonder that there are so many advertisements for drugs to help us sleep and calm our minds?

We are looking for meaning in all the wrong places. Even the people who appear the most successful in life have expressed disappointment, bitterness, and even committed suicide after going down these dead-end streets in their search for meaning. They spend years pursuing what the world has to offer, and they end up experiencing innate dissatisfaction.

Is there any answer? Is there any hope? Solomon said there is. Put a relationship with God into the picture, and everything changes. "There is nothing better for a person than that he should eat and drink and find enjoyment in his toil. This, I saw, is from the hand of God, *for apart from him who can eat or who can have enjoyment?* For to the one who pleases him God has given wisdom and knowledge and joy" (verses 24-26). After conducting his experiment in search of meaning, Solomon concluded that apart from God, there is no meaning.

Our Search for Meaning in the Right Place

You would think that unlimited pleasure, projects, possessions, education, and employment would bring about unlimited satisfaction and a life filled with happiness and meaning. However, no matter how enjoyable these are, without God, they are fleeting and short-lived, and do not bring satisfaction to our thirst for meaning.

> Every pursuit to which the typical [man] might attach significance and value is ultimately meaningless apart from God's blessing. It does not matter whether the pursuit is a thirst for wisdom and knowledge or a search for pleasure or a drive to work and advance or an exclusive focus on oneself or a desire for wealth; without God it only amounts to "a chasing after the wind." The Lord wants people to be happy, but happiness (like everything in life) must be understood in relation to God's will.[2]

Place Your Trust in the Sovereignty of God

The first place to search for meaning is in the sovereignty of God. God has created life to be meaningful only in Him. That is how He has created us (Ecclesiastes 3:11-14). This doesn't mean that pleasure, possessions, projects, education, and employment are wrong, or that you can't find any joy or satisfaction in them. The point that Solomon is making is that these areas of life *by themselves* will not bring any meaning to our lives. It is in God and being rightly related to Him that we find meaning.

God is your holy Creator (Genesis 1). He is righteous and kind (Psalm 145:17). We, on the other hand, are not. We are sinners before God and deserving of death—complete separation from God for all eternity (Romans 3:23; 6:23). As sinners, we are enemies of God and we are helpless and hopeless to save ourselves. We are in desperate need of someone to save us. Herein lies the mercy and justice of God. In His mercy He provides His one and only Son, Jesus Christ, to die as our substitute on the cross for our sins (John 3:16; Romans 6:23). At the cross, the sinful life we live was credited to Him as if He lived it and the perfect life He lived is credited to us as if we lived it (2 Corinthians 5:21). And those of us who put our faith in the finished work of Christ on the cross take part in what is sometimes referred to as the "great exchange"—His life for ours.

Christ has made it possible for you to be reconciled to God by faith. You must put your trust in the finished work of Christ for the forgiveness of your sins. It is only through Christ that you can be rightly related to God (John 14:6). Meaning to life starts here.

Solomon said that "[God] has made everything beautiful in its time" (Ecclesiastes 3:11). We find meaning when we place our trust in the wisdom and sovereignty of God, when we trust His design and His provision of Jesus Christ for our sins. Only when we find our joy in Him can we have a right perspective on wealth and possessions and have the power to enjoy them (Ecclesiastes 5:19).

Prioritize God in Worship

The second place to find meaning is in worshipping God. The apostle Paul, in the book of Romans, exhorts us to present our lives to God—to sacrificially and submissively place ourselves under His authority (Romans 12:1). This means seeking His will and His desire in everything we say, think, and do. One way we do this is through our approach to the corporate worship of God. Solomon warned us to be careful when we approach public worship services. We should go with the intent to listen (Ecclesiastes 5:1). We don't go to church to tell God what to do, but to listen to what He says. We are to keep in mind the infinite difference between Him, our Creator, and us, His creation (Ecclesiastes 5:2). We should approach God with unending respect and awe.

We are to thank God daily for the life he has given us. Whether we have little or much, we are to enjoy what God has given us and to choose to worship Him in the mundaneness of life. After all, enjoyment does not come from possessions or from riches. Meaning in life comes from knowing the living God and taking everything from His hand with thanksgiving, whether pain or pleasure. Seeing your lot in life through a vital worship of God will provide you with inexpressible joy.

"Better is a handful of quietness than two hands full of toil and a striving after wind" (Ecclesiastes 4:6). Instead of being thankful for what we have, we often complain about what we don't have. As we worship God, He gives us the power to enjoy what we have. "For he will not much remember the days of his life because God keeps him occupied with joy in his heart" (Ecclesiastes 5:20). In other words, Solomon is saying that time flies when you're having fun.

That doesn't mean that life is absent of pain and suffering. Rather, it means that our joy is not tied to our circumstances but to the Lord, who never changes. "Though the fig tree should not blossom, nor fruit be on the vines, the produce of the olive fail and the fields yield no food, the flock be cut off from the fold and there be no herd in the stalls, yet I will rejoice in the Lord; I will take joy in the God of my salvation" (Habakkuk 3:17-18).

Pursue the Wisdom and Counsel of God

The third place in which we can find meaning is the wisdom and counsel of God. Human wisdom has some value. It will help us to fix our car and maintain our house. However, it's limited. It cannot make sense of life. It cannot explain what happens or what will happen. From a mere human perspective, life just seems to happen by chance. The race is not always won by the fastest. Battles are not always won by the strongest (Ecclesiastes 9:11).

Every year at my junior high school, we hosted a week of various competitions between teams of students. Each of us would arrange our own teams. One year, my team competed in the finals. The last event was a game of tug-of-war.

The other team was bigger and stronger. They outweighed us by a couple hundred pounds. Needless to say, we didn't have a chance of winning. Therefore, we decided to concede. We weren't going to concede without having some fun, though. Our plan was to begin strong and see what we could do, but as soon as the other team began to pull us, we were going to let go of the rope and let them win by falling to the ground.

Well, as anticipated, the other team began to pull us, and we let go of the rope. With a great thud, the other team fell to the ground. We conceded with fun. What happened next took everyone by surprise. When the other team fell, they didn't hold on to the rope long enough to pull the flag at the middle of the rope over the line. The crowd began yelling for us to pick up the rope and pull. We did, and we won. That was an unexpected turn of events.

When life doesn't go as expected, human wisdom sits and scratches its head, trying to figure out what just happened. Yet the Bible affirms that even the most seemingly random event is in God's hands. "The lot is cast into the lap, but its every decision is from the LORD" (Proverbs 16:33).

While human wisdom cannot make sense of the world, God's wisdom can. It can explain what happens and what will happen. Christ's death on the cross is a perfect example. For many, putting our faith and trust in a man who died on a cross seems foolish (1 Corinthians 1:18). God, however, was pleased not to save us through human wisdom, but through divine wisdom (verse 21). What seems foolish to man is wise to God.

As finite human beings, we simply don't know how God will work things out. That is why we need to trust God's wisdom—to do as He says, believe what He promises, and leave the outcome to Him. "Blessed is the man who walks not in the counsel of the wicked...but his delight is in the law of the LORD, and on his law he meditates day and night...In all that he does, he prospers" (Psalm 1:1-3).

In particular, Solomon taught us to be wise in three areas: our behavior, our decisions, and our speech. When it comes to behavior, just as a dead fly in a bottle of perfume will give off a bad stench, one mistake can deface our character and reputation (Ecclesiastes 10:1). Therefore, don't be careless about your behavior, and use self-control (Ecclesiastes 10:4).

Second, when it comes to decisions, we should take care to know the inherent risks and prepare accordingly. If you are digging a hole, then beware of the risk of falling in (verse 8). Also, plan ahead for what you need before you proceed with your plan. If you are planning to cut wood, then sharpen the edge of your ax (verse 10).

The third area that calls for wisdom is our speech. Wise words have good effects (verse 12). Unfortunately, many of us pay less attention to our words than we should. Foolish words cause misery and anguish, and eventually they consume us. Scripture tells us there is coming a day when we will give account for every careless word we speak (Matthew 12:36). Therefore, we should strive to speak thoughtfully and carefully.

All of this takes effort, which means we cannot afford to be lazy about life. "Through sloth the roof sinks in, and through indolence the house leaks" (Ecclesiastes 10:18). The flat roofs in ancient Israel were covered with clay and lime. Without proper maintenance, a roof would eventually crack and allow rainwater to seep into a house. Constant effort and attention were needed to make sure that didn't happen. Likewise, we must be diligent about wise living and put forth the necessary and persistent effort to learn from God how to wisely and skillfully live our lives.

Practice Being a Good Friend and Companion

God provides comfort and strength through friends and companions, who are gifts from God. Solomon identified four benefits of having a companion (Ecclesiastes 4:9-12): One, a companion can help increase the rewards of our labors. Having two or more to share the burden of any business endeavor will multiply the return. Two, a companion will help in times of trouble. Three, a companion will help bring comfort in times of agony and distress. And four, having one or more people in your life makes failure less likely.

We often seek out friends and companions on the basis of how they'll benefit us. "How will being friends with that person benefit me?" But rather than seek to network with others for our own benefit, we should plan to provide these benefits of companionship and friendship to others. Be a good friend and companion to your wife and family, to your friends, and to the church, seeking the good of others (Matthew 22:37-40; Philippians 2:3-4). Let the people around you benefit from being your companion and friend. With love, speak the truth to them (Ephesians 4:15), encourage and build them up (Ephesians 4:29), and seek to stir them to love and good deeds (Hebrews 10:24).

Solomon also mentions enjoying our wives and seeing them as precious gifts from God (Ecclesiastes 9:9). Rejoice in your wife and be satisfied with her (Proverbs 5:18-19). You are responsible to satisfy yourself with her, and likewise give yourself to her that she might be satisfied. Delight in her and, as Proverbs 5:19 says, "be intoxicated" with her. Having a wife is a good gift from God (Proverbs 18:22). The most practical way we thank God for our wives is by remaining faithful to them. "So guard yourselves in your spirit, and let none of you be faithless to the wife of your youth" (Malachi 2:15).

Purpose to Give 110 Percent to Life

You may have had a physical education teacher or coach say to you, "Now go out there and give it 110 percent." Strictly speaking, that doesn't quite make sense because we all know it's impossible to give more than 100 percent. We know that the exhortation to give 110 percent is simply another way of saying we should go all-out and do our very best. Well, that's what Solomon commanded us to do. He listed four ways we are to approach life with a 110-percent effort.

First, we are to be generous. The context here is that we cannot control the outcome of anything we do. That uncertainty can sometimes promote stinginess. Solomon, on the other hand, said that instead of holding back...give. "Cast your bread upon the waters...Give a portion to seven, or even to eight" (Ecclesiastes 11:1-2). Give, and give broadly.

Second, we are to be courageous. Being generous is risky. Minimizing the risk is the best we can do; we can't ever eliminate it. Again, you cannot control the outcome, and that is what normally keeps us from being liberal with our possessions. "If I let Larry borrow my car, he won't replace the gas, and he'll leave all his trash in it." "If I let the Smiths use our home, they might break something." "If I give the Randolphs money, we won't be able to..."

We can seek to minimize the risks by being prudent, but even then, we are to give and invest in people's lives generously, holding our possessions loosely, not letting the fear of the unknown keep us from the great opportunity to be a blessing. "Do not withhold good from those to whom it is due, when it is in your power to do it" (Proverbs 3:27).

Third, we are to be proactive. Many of us have a long list of would'ves, should'ves, and could'ves. We *would* have done this…we *should* have done that…we *could* have done it…but we didn't. We are often paralyzed by the fear of failure. Because of that, we wait for just the right conditions before we act. The man who waits for the wind and the clouds to be just right before planting will never plant (Ecclesiastes 11:4-5). If we sit around waiting for the perfect conditions before we act, we won't. We can't completely control whether we might succeed or fail, so we may as well go for it. If I had waited for "just the right conditions," I probably would have never gotten married.

And fourth, we are to work hard. Be industrious (Ecclesiastes 11:6). "Whatever your hand finds to do, do it with your might" (Ecclesiastes 9:10). Give to this life. Often we are told how to *get* the most *from* this life. Instead, consider *giving* as much as you can *to* this life.

Be generous, be courageous, be proactive, and be industrious.

Our Steps to Building a Meaningful Life

The meaning of life is found in our relationship to God. It is He who puts meaning into all we say, think, and do. Solomon sums up the meaning of life with these two resolutions: make God the center of our attention, and make God the object of our obedience.

Make God the Center of Our Attention

Let's worship and serve God while we can. The days are coming when our bodies and faculties will make it more and more difficult to serve Him (Ecclesiastes 12:1). As I grow older, I hear myself saying the things I thought only old men say: "My bones ache all the time." "I'm so stiff, I can barely move." One day, when coaching baseball, I spent a whole afternoon working with the catchers. I was bending down and shooting straight up for a good two hours. The next day? Oh, the agony! I was miserable. I was suffering the consequences of getting older.

We won't always be able to do what we do now. What we can do now is temporary, and not something to take for granted. Solomon said to worship and serve the Lord while we can.

Make God the Object of Our Obedience

The second resolution from Solomon is to make God the object of our obedience. This world teaches us to obey our passions and desires. "Do what feels good." "Do what's right for you." There is no meaning in that; Solomon proved it. After carrying out his pursuits, he concluded, "The end of the matter; all has been heard. Fear God and keep his commandments, for this is the whole duty of man. For God will bring every deed into judgment, with every secret thing, whether good or evil" (Ecclesiastes 12:13-14). How many trees have been sacrificed to provide the paper secular philosophers have needed in order to ponder and pontificate the meaning of life? All that has been needed to figure out the meaning of life took only one tree—the tree that became the cross on which Jesus died.

Finding the meaning of life begins with your attitude and approach to the cross. Do you fear God, acknowledging Him as the sole creator of the universe, almighty, perfect, and holy? Does that fear produce a humble response, whereby you willfully and joyfully place yourself under the authority of Jesus? Do you know that all that we say, think, and do will someday be judged by Him?

The meaning of life is not living for us, but for God and others (Luke 9:23). This is the key that unlocks the meaning of life. We start by being reconciled to God through Jesus Christ. Have you humbled yourself before God, acknowledging your sinfulness and need for a Savior? By faith, do you believe Jesus Christ is God and that He purchased your pardon and forgiveness on the cross? Do you believe He rose again? Do you believe that this is His gracious gift to you? Confess your sins to God, turn from them, and ask God to forgive you. Be reconciled to God. To find out more about the gospel, see "The Gospel for Men" in Appendix One on page 387.

Second, you must increase your knowledge of the character and promises of God. You do this by taking the time to read the Bible on a regular basis and paying close attention to what God reveals about Himself. The Psalms and the Gospels are great places to start.

Third, make God your first priority with regard to your time and decisions. How does God want you to spend your time? Are you seeking His counsel concerning how you live? Do you consult the Bible when you make decisions? Do you seek out biblical counselors who can help you carry out Scripture's commands? Taking the time to read Galatians, Ephesians, and Colossians is a good start. Pay close attention and try to identify all the resources you have in Christ—resources made available to you by God's grace. And observe how you are expected to live your life as a result of those gracious resources.

Fourth, practice being a good friend, husband, and father. Start by asking your friends and family to provide honest input about your effectiveness in being a good friend to them. Identify ways you have been selfish in your relationships, looking to your friends only for what they can give to and do for you. May we turn from those selfish ways, ask their forgiveness, and determine specific ways we can be a good friend and companion.

Fifth, make the most of the life God has given you. Use what God has given you and invest it in the lives of people. Don't hold back. Don't make excuses. Consider what prestige, prominence, and possessions God has given you, and instead of thinking about how those things benefit you, think about how you could use them to benefit others. For example, let's say I have been given access to a certain airport lounge because of my travel status with a given airline. I should consider how I might be able to use that status to benefit a fellow traveler by inviting him to be my guest in that lounge.

The Whole Duty of Man

Life without God is monotonous and meaningless. Though we may attempt to build a meaningful life through pleasure, projects, possessions, education, and employment, all of these will fail. The power to enjoy and live a meaningful life comes from God alone. We must place our trust in His sovereignty, prioritize Him in worship, pursue His wise counsel, practice being a good friend, and purpose to give 110 percent. As Solomon observed, "The end of the matter; all has been heard. Fear God and keep his commandments, for this is the whole duty of man" (Ecclesiastes 12:13-14). As you commit to living this out, remember these encouraging words from the apostle Paul: "I am sure of this, that he who began a good work in you will bring it to completion at the day of Jesus Christ" (Philippians 1:6).

Recommended Resources

Bridges, Jerry. *You Can Trust God*. Colorado Springs, CO: NavPress, 1989.

Mayhue, Richard. *Seeking God: How to Develop an Intimate, Spiritual Relationship*. Scotland, UK: Christian Focus, 2000.

Nelson, Tommy. *A Life Well Lived: A Study of the Book of Ecclesiastes*. Nashville, TN: Broadman & Holman Publishers, 2005.

Piper, John. *Don't Waste Your Life (Group Study Edition)*. Wheaton, IL: Crossway, 2003.

Tripp, Paul David. *A Quest for More: Living for Something Bigger Than You*. Greensboro, NC: New Growth Press, 2008.

5

Developing Discernment as a Counselor of Men

Chris Kropf

Imagine you're not feeling well. So you go to your doctor. He asks you about your symptoms, runs some tests, and diagnoses you. If the diagnosis is strep throat, he may prescribe antibiotics and rest. However, if you're diagnosed with kidney disease, he may prescribe blood pressure medication, annual checkups, and a change in diet. Why the difference in prescriptions? There's a difference because a diagnosis will vary depending on the path one must follow in the hopes of arriving at a cure.

The same is true spiritually. How you diagnose a problem leads inevitably down a path toward solving that problem. Imagine your five-year-old son bonks an innocent kid on the head and takes his toy. What caused the problem? If your answer is that your son's love tank was running on empty, the solution you're likely to propose might be to connect with your child better and help build his self-esteem. But if your answer is that your son was born into sin and bonked the other kid on the head because he's naturally selfish, a more appropriate solution would be to discipline your son and make it clear that it is wrong to selfishly take another child's toys. The first diagnosis prompts you to do whatever you can to fill your son's love cup. The second diagnosis sends up a red flag, reminding you of the sinner that your child is, and leading you to intervene by showing your son his need for a Savior. Christ is the solution to his problem; He is his only hope. And you need Christ to enable you to parent your son wisely.

As you can see, the diagnoses lead in two different directions. The first drives your counsel away from Christ, the second drives you and your son toward Him.

Every religion, worldview, and counseling system seeks to answer the following question: Why do people do what they do? You will learn throughout this book that we do what we do because of what is in our heart. Jesus taught that it is "out of the abundance of the heart the mouth speaks" (Matthew 12:34). His appraisal of our souls—His psychology, if you will—revealed the truth that "out of the heart come evil thoughts, murder, adultery, sexual immorality, theft, false witness, slander" (Matthew 15:19). That is why Proverbs 4:23 warns us, "Keep your heart with all vigilance, for from it flow the springs of life."

If you're going to develop discernment in counseling and discipling men, you not only need to be able to answer the question, Why do men do what they do?, you also need to be able to answer the question, Why do men have the problems they have?

It doesn't take much investigating to see that there are numerous approaches to finding the answers. For example, the world-famous psychologist Carl Jung proposed an archetype male hidden in the unconscious part of man—much like a real but intangible image of a man that is revealed through dreams, fantasies, and images from the aboriginal self. For Jung, this unconscious entity was a great guide and friend to the conscious self and something to explore for insight and self-knowledge. He labeled the inner "feminine side" of man the anima. By getting in touch with his feminine side, a man can explore new worlds of thinking, feeling, and self-expression. For Jung and his followers, men have problems because they fail to explore their unconscious and allow it to guide their conscious self.

The American poet Robert Bly has diagnosed modern men as half-adults trapped between childhood and maturity. The decline of the father's role in the home and absence of rites of passage create a vacuum in which boys grow up without gender-specific instruction. Bly finds great significance in mythology for teaching men what it means to be a man and has dedicated an entire book to the lessons men can learn from *Iron John*, a Brothers Grimm fairy tale.

In response to the perceived feminization of men there is an entire men's movement with organizations dedicated to helping men find themselves, define their gender role, and improve their legal rights. In his book *Wild at Heart*, John Eldredge addresses this feminization of men, proposing his own answer as to what ails men. In his opinion, every man has been dealt a wound as a child, most often from his father, and is in need of finding authentic masculinity in order to heal and get his heart back.[1]

To these diagnoses and solutions you can add a chorus of other ideologies that are not gender specific. Some say we are merely the products of our environment. Others say our family and culture determine who we are. Still others say the explanations are purely biological. Some attribute our problems to irrational and destructive thought patterns. Still others say we just need to be resocialized, tweak our self-talk, and perhaps use meds to take the edge off.

But the question about why men do what they do is answered in God's story. By walking through the history of God's redemption of His people, we discover in the Bible the much-sought-after answers. God's story, in a nutshell, looks like this: God created all things; through Adam the world fell into sin; God is redeeming the world through Christ; and history will culminate in future perfection in the new heavens and the new earth.

According to the Bible, men have the problems they have because of evil. The curious thing about evil is that it is two-dimensional. Evil threatens us from without (what others do to us) and wells up from within (the wickedness we conceive in our own hearts). It comes at us *and* it's something we participate in. When God created Adam and Eve, they lived in perfect harmony with Him in the garden. However, Genesis 3 records the deception of the serpent (the evil from without) and the fall of Adam and Eve and all of mankind into sin (the evil from within). We all suffer from a Genesis 3 hangover!

Sinners and Sufferers

In other words, we suffer and we sin. You can rightly call people suffering sinners and sinning sufferers. When I counsel men, I always ask myself, *Am I dealing primarily with a sinner or a sufferer?* Of course, the answer is both to some extent. That is why I use the word *primarily*. If I'm helping a husband who has committed adultery against his wife, I tend to treat him as a *sinner*. Now in saying that, I'm sure his wife has not been perfect. He does suffer from being married to a sinner, like all married people do. However, the Bible is clear that adultery breaks the covenant a husband has made with his wife. To portray this husband as a well-intentioned person who was driven by his own emotional needs to seek love outside of marriage for whatever reason is pure foolishness. It leaves the adulterer's self-pity and self-righteousness intact and fails to acknowledge the exceeding sinfulness of his sin. Christ had to pay the death penalty on the cross for his adultery.[2]

On the other hand, suppose I'm counseling a man whose wife has committed adultery against him. He has been betrayed. I'm overjoyed to see him confess how his own sin has damaged the marriage and I'm willing to work with him on that. However, I'll treat this man as a *sufferer*. My primary role is to teach him how to repent of his sin, love his wife through this difficulty, and if possible, reconcile his relationship with his wife.

If you're going to grow in discernment as a counselor of men, you have to be able to help *sufferers* and *sinners*. In the remainder of this chapter, my goal is to give you a start on how to discern which of these two diagnoses best describes your counselee, and then how to counsel him accordingly.

Regardless of whether you counsel a sufferer or a sinner, there are some goals that should remain the same. You should work at building a friendship with that person, give him hope with the promises we have in Christ, gather information about his problem, and use God's Word to wisely speak truth in love to him. However, some of those goals will look a little different depending on whom you're dealing with.

Common Goals

Build Friendship

The book you are reading has the word *counseling* in it. Often when people think of a counselor, they imagine a person making an appointment and meeting with an expert of some sort. They might even imagine a patient lying on a couch. That mental picture of counseling applies to formal counseling, however. Few counselors do formal counseling, but all counselors model behavior, thinking, and values to those who seek help. They influence others and give advice. This modeling and advice-giving is what I like to call informal counseling.

Whether you are helping a man in a more formal counseling setting or informally, your first goal should be to build a friendship with him. You shouldn't hold him at arm's length or fail to get emotionally involved. You should be passionate about helping your friend! If you do not make this person your friend, then how will you treat him—in a disinterested or condescending way? Will you have a cool rather than a warm interaction with him such that he perceives that you view him as a problem, and not a person? If you deliberately work to keep a "professional distance" between you and him, do you expect that he will then *trust* you as his counselor/advisor?

Think of it this way: Whenever someone comes to you for advice, he is asking himself a number of questions. Things like, "Do I trust you?" "Can you help me?" "Am I going to be completely honest, or will I cover up details of my situation I'd rather not share?" If you want to really help someone, you have to build a friendship such that the other person trusts you and knows you are an ally who cares for him and has his best interests at heart.[3]

If you ever counsel in a more formal ministry context, chances are you'll find it necessary to counsel men you may have never met. You can't help someone if you don't know him. With your first meeting your friendship is just beginning, so you have to take time to learn a little bit about his life story, his family, and what he is passionate about. Try your best to connect with him. Share a little bit of your life. Though you have to be wise about what you share, transparency in friendship and in a counselor is always appreciated.

If you find yourself helping someone you are already friends with, ask yourself this: *I know a lot* about *Joe but do I really know him?* Men tend to settle for some pretty shallow relationships. The women have us beat on this one. Whenever there is a gathering at someone's house, the women end up in the living room talking about eternal realities, and we men stand around the chips and salsa talking about the Super Bowl. We know each other's names, who is married to who, and who has which children, but we have no idea about what each man is burdened by or struggles with.

If you are currently helping someone you're already friends with, allow me to ask you some questions: Do you really know him? What are his burdens? What are his temptations? What does he live for? What does he tend to crave, want, desire? Does he struggle with the love of comfort? Is he passive? Is he a Type-A person who comes off as domineering? Has he alienated the people around him because of his control issues? No matter what his situation, be it primarily *sinner* or *sufferer,* you can and should get to know him better.

Give Hope

Another common goal is giving your counselee hope. The implementation of this goal, however, will be somewhat determined by his role in his predicament.

Hope for the Sufferer

If you are helping a sufferer, the first words out of your mouth should be words of hope. You must know this about hope: biblical hope is not an "I hope so" kind of hope. Hope in the Bible is offered as a "sure hope" based on the unchanging character of God and His faithful promises. This kind of hope brings great encouragement and a substantial confidence that can be found nowhere else in this world.

God offers us plenty of hope in Scripture. I recommend starting with biblical truths that fit your friend's situation or have already encouraged you in your own life. For example, one promise that is especially precious to me is the assurance of God's presence in the middle of our suffering. He tells us not to fear; He is with us. "I will never leave you nor forsake you" (Hebrews 13:5). God has not forsaken your friend or left him to his own devices. He will be there for him and extend grace and mercy that will help him get through the suffering.

The Bible is full of promises for sufferers. One of my favorites is Psalm 34:18: "The LORD is near to the brokenhearted and saves the crushed in spirit." Our God is "the Father of mercies and God of all comfort, who comforts us in all our affliction, so that we may be able to comfort those who are in any affliction, with the comfort with which we ourselves are comforted by God" (2 Corinthians 1:3-4). "As a father shows compassion to his children, so the LORD shows compassion to those who fear him. For he knows our frame; he remembers that we are dust" (Psalm 103:13-14).

What comfort do you find in Scripture? What passages give you hope? How have you been comforted by God in your previous afflictions? You can start by sharing that which has given you comfort, and that, in turn, will comfort your friend.

Hope for the Sinner

If your friend is ensnared in sin, the hope you give is different. The hope you offer sinners is the assurance that God is willing to forgive him and help him overcome the sin he is trapped in. Jesus is a great Savior who saves men who have sinned greatly. The hope offered is mercy and grace. Men tend to justify their sin, make excuses for it, shift the blame to others, or do whatever they can to cover it up. Those who are willing to come out into the light and call their sin what God calls it—and repent and believe in Christ alone—receive mercy and forgiveness.

I've often noticed with curiosity that there are more women than men asking for counseling at our church. Why is that? Could it be that women have more problems than men? Actually, I'm convinced that the men in our church have just as many, if not more, problems than the women. The trouble is that too many of us aren't comfortable with asking for help. We are determined to look like we have it all together. It is our pride that keeps us from admitting we need help with thorny issues, bearing burdens, and resisting temptations. If your friend has gotten as far as sharing his sin with you and asking for help, that is significant, and he has put himself in a good place. God opposes the proud and gives grace to those who humble themselves by confessing their sin and asking for help (James 4:6; 1 Peter 5:5-7).

A key verse that has given me hope in the middle of my temptations is 1 Corinthians 10:13: "No temptation has overtaken you that is not common to man. God is faithful, and he will not let you be tempted beyond your ability, but with the temptation he will also provide the way of escape, that you may be able to endure it." God promises to be faithful and not allow me to experience temptations that are more than I can handle. And He promises a way out. This gives me great hope because it is a promise that no temptation presents a hopeless situation where I am bound to sin. There is always a way out, and it begins with the gospel of Jesus Christ. I urge you to read Appendix One, "The Gospel for Men," for a clear explanation of how solutions to difficult situations are found in the gospel (see page 387).

I also like Philippians 1:6: "I am sure of this, that he who began a good work in you will bring it to completion at the day of Jesus Christ." There are no unfinished projects in God's garage. He is working to make me more like

Jesus. That is why He says that those whom He has called to salvation are "destined to be conformed to the image of his Son" (Romans 8:28-29).

Gather Information

From the Sufferer

If your friend has recently lost a loved one, you can probably skip asking questions and, at first, just focus on being available. However, if you're trying to help someone resolve a problem, it's necessary for you to gather information that will enable you to offer wise and appropriate advice. Proverbs 18:13 says, "If one gives an answer before he hears, it is his folly and shame." To diagnose a problem before you have all the facts is foolishness. Remember my earlier example of the husband who was betrayed by his wife's adultery? Before you can offer counsel, you need to find out what happened. How did he find out? Who did his wife cheat with? Is his wife begging for his forgiveness, or does she want to run off with the other guy? Will he forgive her? Because every situation is different, it's not possible to provide a list of one-size-fits-all questions. You'll need to vary your questions according to the circumstances. However, there is one question that I think is always helpful to ask.

I've learned to ask sufferers to share with me their biggest fear in the middle of their situation. Their answers will give you plenty of insight into what they are going through. You can respond with promises from God's Word that address their fear, and encourage them to trust those promises while you work together toward solutions.

From the Sinner

If your friend is entangled in sin, try to identify what is going on behind his sinful behavior. What does he want? What does he crave? What does he desire? One pastor phrased the questions this way: "What do you want that you're not getting?" And, "What are you getting that you do not want?"

You'll also want to determine when he tends to be tempted the most. Is it at a certain time of day, or in certain kinds of situations? Try to gather as many facts as you can. If there is conflict with another person involved, remember that "the one who states his case first seems right" (Proverbs 18:17). If you truly want to be a peacemaker in the middle of a conflict, you'll need to hear the other person's side of the story as well.

Speak Truth in Love

Good counseling can be summarized simply as wisely speaking the truth with love.[4] It is good to lend a sympathetic ear and provide a shoulder to cry on, but eventually you need to speak helpful truth into your friend's life—and as hard as that might be, it is a very loving thing to do. If you've turned to the Bible to give him hope and comfort, you have probably already done this. However, wisely speaking the truth in love goes beyond just offering encouragement and giving hope. There are times when correcting wrong thinking or giving practical advice comes into play. Here are a few things to consider.

Embracing God's Purposes

When someone goes through deep suffering, we never want to see him lose his identity in his suffering. For example, the man who loses his wife through divorce may begin to identify himself as a loser, a divorcee, a failure. In the midst of all that's happening, we need to remind him his real identity is defined by his relationship to God: he is loved, adopted into God's family, forgiven, cleansed, a friend of God, a recipient of mercy and grace, etc. As you stress your friend's identity in these terms, he will come to embrace the purposes of God for him in the middle of his suffering.

Now, God has so many different purposes for our suffering that I cannot list all of them here. However, allow me to offer a few key purposes that apply to most—if not all—situations:[5]

- *God uses suffering to make us more mature Christians.* "Count it all joy, my brothers, when you meet trials of various kinds, for you know that the testing of your faith produces steadfastness. And let steadfastness have its full effect, that you may be perfect and complete, lacking in nothing" (James 1:2-4).

- *God uses suffering to wean us from our favorite sins.* "Before I was afflicted I went astray, but now I keep your word…It is good for me that I was afflicted, that I might learn your statutes" (Psalm 119:67,71).

- *Gods uses suffering to humble us and force us to look to Him for help.* "My grace is sufficient for you, for my power is made perfect in weakness" (2 Corinthians 12:9).

We also never want to see men turn bitter in their suffering. This is a big temptation—it is easy for someone to become angry with God and let bitterness about broken relationships, diminished health, and lost loved ones fester. The severity of a person's suffering may tempt him to believe that God isn't good. That is why passages like Romans 8:28 are so precious: "We know that for those who love God all things work together for good." God is good.

The temptation toward bitterness in suffering is one reason God gave us the Prophets and the Psalms. Consider how many of the prophets argue with God and how many of the psalms are laments. I once heard a Jewish man say, "You Christians read your Bibles to know God. We Jews read to argue with God." He has a point: The prophets and the psalmists are frank about their frustration with God, and we can learn from their candor and the answers they learned from their questioning. The book of Psalms is always a source of comfort for people who are suffering.

Our tendency to become bitter when life gets difficult is a key reason God commands Christians to be forgiving of others. We have been forgiven of every sin we've ever committed. And those who have received grace are commanded to be gracious with others. When Peter asked about forgiveness, Jesus told a story about a servant who owed a king more debt than he could ever repay. The king graciously forgave him and cancelled his debt. However, after the servant's massive debt was forgiven, the same servant went out and threw a fellow servant into prison for failing to repay him a small debt. When the king found out what had happened, he was furious and threw the first servant into prison. Jesus ended the story this way: "So also my heavenly Father will do to every one of you, if you do not forgive your brother from your heart" (Matthew 18:35). Those who have received grace are not allowed to be graceless. Those who have received mercy are not allowed to be merciless.

Bringing About Restoration

If your friend is trapped in sin, you need to speak the truth in love in an effort to restore him. Though the specific passages you use will vary based on the situation, the tone of how you do this is captured in a number of passages. For example, Jesus said,

> What do you think? If a man has a hundred sheep, and one of them has gone astray, does he not leave the ninety-nine on the mountains and go in search of the one that went astray? And if he finds it, truly, I say to you, he rejoices over it more than over the ninety-nine that never went astray. So it is not the will of my Father who is in heaven that one of these little ones should perish (Matthew 18:12-14).

And in Galatians 6:1, the apostle Paul said, "Brothers, if anyone is caught in any transgression, you who are spiritual should restore him in a spirit of gentleness. Keep watch on yourself, lest you too be tempted." In other words, you are on a rescue operation to save your friend from himself and from God's judgment.

So often we think of addressing sin as being confrontational. The word *confrontation* conjures up images of heated discussion, raised voices, and condescending rebukes. I'm convinced this view also provides us an excuse to avoid talking about a person's sin. How many times have you heard someone say, "I'm not very good at confrontation"? How many times have you said that yourself? The passages I cited above say nothing about confrontation. Jesus paints a picture of a lost sheep that was being rescued. Paul deliberately used the word "restore" in Galatians 6:1.

Imagine what would happen if someone said to you, "I know Joe is going to destroy himself, but I'm just not good at restoration." I don't know about you, but I would disagree!

We are all able to help bring about restoration. We're not necessarily talking about confrontation here—we're talking about helping someone who has lost his way and encouraging him to be reconciled to God before he dishonors the name of Christ, hurts more people, and destroys himself. You may not like having a difficult conversation. You may find yourself shying away from potential conflict. And in the end, your brother may resist your help and end up not being restored. Not every story has a happy ending. But my question to you is this: Are you willing to make an attempt to gently restore your brother in the Lord? Will you go out and make an effort to help him?

Addressing Motives and Intentions

As you do this, remember to point your friend to Scripture passages that apply to his specific sin. And make sure your instruction doesn't deal solely with his outward behavior. You want to work with your friend on the level of what he is wanting, desiring, craving. What does God say about what he's wanting? What fundamental change is needed in his life? You don't want to just address the behavior, but the heart behind the behavior.

Imagine for a moment you're helping a guy who struggles with outbursts of anger. Christians and non-Christians alike can see that the anger is destructive and will ruin all his relationships. However, you need to get past the outward behavior and ask him what is so important that he's blowing his top over it in the first place. What is it he longs for? Respect? Success? Control? Power? Comfort? He can't be devoted to Christ and continue to pursue these things with so much passion that he responds with outbursts of anger when he doesn't get his way. He cannot allow such inconsistency in his life. Christ has called him out of the world and saved him so that he will make God's name look great, not live for his own purposes. That is what Paul meant when he said that Jesus "died for all, that those who live might no longer live for themselves but for him who for their sake died and was raised" (2 Corinthians 5:15).

God's Word addresses our behavior—do not cheat on your wife, do not lie to God and others, show kindness and love to others, etc. But the Bible also exposes the motives behind our behavior. That is why Hebrews 4:12 calls it "living and active...and able to judge the thoughts and intentions of the heart" (NASB). In John 12:42 we learn that "many even of the authorities believed in him [Christ], but for fear of the Pharisees they did not confess it, so that they would not be put out of the synagogue." This was during the week before Jesus was crucified. John adds the reason why: "For they loved the glory that comes from man more than the glory that comes from God" (verse 43). The Bible has an uncanny way of exposing our motives.

Bringing About Change

However, the Bible does more than just expose motives and intentions. It also insightfully points the way home. Consider for a moment how timely God's Word is for handling problems in the family. A good example of this appears in Titus 2:4, where Paul instructs Titus to teach the older women to "encourage young women to love their husbands, to love their children, to be sensible, pure, workers at home, kind, being subject to their own husbands, so that the word of God will not be dishonored" (NASB). There are two different Greek words translated "love" in the New Testament—*agape* love is self-sacrificial love, and *phileo* is a love that is kindly affectionate or fond of someone. The word Paul uses for what young wives and mothers need to learn is *phileo*. How many mothers have you met who would throw themselves in front of a bus to save their children (*agape* love) but you get that feeling they are annoyed by them (a lack of *phileo* love)? Young mothers often need to work at enjoying and being fond of their children. Do you see how God's Word gets right to the heart of what really needs to change?

Chances are, if you're reading this chapter, you're not a mother. However, you may be a husband. What does the Bible say to husbands? In Ephesians 5:22-33, God gives instructions to both husbands and wives. He instructs the wives to be submissive to their own husbands, yet this command is made to wives only once. Husbands, on the other hand, are commanded to love their wives with an *agape* love *four times*. Now that is insightful! Why is it that we husbands tend to ignore family life and engross ourselves in our careers? Because we love ourselves. Why is it that we seldom lift a finger to clean the house or take out the trash? Because we love ourselves. What is the number one way we husbands hurt our marriages? By having little room in our hearts for anyone but ourselves. The point of God's instruction in Ephesians 5:22-33 is clear: We husbands have to turn from a love of self to a love for our wives in self-sacrificial ways—ways that may mean sacrificing our most cherished goals and ambitions.

Keys to Progress

God's Word provides more than adequate guidance for developing the discernment that is needed for Christian men who counsel other Christian men. This discernment takes in consideration the need to distinguish sinner from sufferer, offer loving friendship and biblical hope, get all the information, and speak the truth in love. In these ways we can help men who are struggling.

Counseling others requires more than just dispensing a doctrinal truth from the Bible and expecting the counselee to understand and apply it. Working with someone through their problems with the Scripture is a bit of a process—a process that's been described in this chapter. You can use these guidelines as a grid through which to view your progress in helping someone. This grid should not be used as a formula for every situation—it can be adapted to varying circumstances and needs. Ultimately your goal is to be able to answer these questions:

- Are you building a friendship with this brother in Christ?

- Have you given him hope?

- Do you know the full story, or do you need to ask him or another person for more information?

- What passages of Scripture will you use to speak truth to him in a way that is helpful?

If you love your brother in Christ, you will be able to help him—whether sinner or sufferer.

Recommended Resources

MacArthur, John, ed. *Counseling: How to Counsel Biblically*. Nashville, TN: Thomas Nelson, 2005.

Powlison, David. *Seeing with New Eyes*. Phillipsburg, NJ: P&R Publishing, 2003.

———. *Speaking Truth in Love*. Greensboro, NC: New Growth Press, 2005.

Tada, Joni Eareckson, and Steven Estes. *When God Weeps*. Grand Rapids, MI: Zondervan, 1997.

Part 2

A Man and His Emotions

6

Men and Depression

Robert B. Somerville

What do you do when the counselor wakes up depressed and that counselor is you? That was my situation after prolonged back pain culminated in two months of total debilitation, which in turn was preceded by two years of overwork and emotionally draining counseling. I thought I was just having a difficult recovery from surgery until my wife said, "I think you're depressed." It was then I realized that I had become the poster boy for clinical depression. I, the always-cheerful, whistling pastor and now college professor, was going through a major depressive episode. Suddenly, all that I had taught for 40 years about the sufficiency of Christ and His Word would be put to the test.

In the 1970s I had written a seminar on depression based on the life of Elijah. Could the principles I taught at that time see me through this dark and seemingly endless tunnel? Would I ever have hope and be able to give it to others again?

Praise God! After going through the crucible of depression myself, my message has not changed. I teach the same truths—now with more sympathy and thankfulness.

Defining Depression

What are the symptoms of depression? While there can be different degrees of depression from mild to severe, there are some common characteristics that identify it. They are a depressed mood, a markedly diminished pleasure in activities, significant weight gain or loss, insomnia, psychomotor agitation, loss of energy, feelings of worthlessness or excessive guilt, diminished ability to think, indecisiveness, and recurrent thoughts of death or suicide.[1] I experienced all of these.

King David described the agony of this desperate state when he said, "My bones wasted away through my groaning all day long" (Psalm 32:3). The mental pain is excruciating and there seems to be no way of escape. One can't even escape it in sleep. When combined with physical pain and exhaustion, depression is an incomprehensible horror. One truly wishes to die.

A Common Problem

Depression is a common problem. For the person who struggles with it, there's comfort in knowing that one is not alone in this malady. Yet there are many who go through it and never share their struggles with anyone. One man confessed to me that he would soak an old sweatshirt with his tears on his way home from work each day. Although this went on for a considerable length of time, he never told his family. Other people, by contrast, are willing to share their experiences freely.

Depression afflicts even God's most faithful servants. A pastor of a large church called and told me of his experience with severe depression and said he had to take five months off from work to recover. There are many godly men in the past who have endured severe bouts of depression, including Martin Luther, the great reformer; William Cowper, the prolific hymn writer (who attempted suicide on at least five occasions); and Charles Spurgeon, the prince of preachers.

And today in the twenty-first century, depression is still a major problem. A *Newsweek* cover story dated February 25, 2007, predicted that six million American men would be diagnosed with depression that year. Yet millions more suffer silently, unaware that their problem has a name or unwilling to seek treatment. In her article "Men and Depression," Julie Scelfo writes,

> Although depression is emotionally crippling and has numerous medical implications—some of them deadly—many men fail to recognize the symptoms. Instead of talking about their feelings, men may mask them with alcohol, drug abuse, gambling, anger or by becoming workaholics. *And even when they do realize they*

have a problem, men often view asking for help as an admission of weakness, a betrayal of their male identities.

The result is a hidden epidemic of despair that is destroying marriages, disrupting careers, filling jail cells, clogging emergency rooms and costing society billions of dollars in lost productivity and medical bills. It is also creating a cohort of children who carry the burden of their fathers' pain for the rest of their lives (emphasis added).[2]

So we see that depression is a snare that has been trapping men throughout history and up to our present age. It attacks Christians and non-Christians alike, the weak and the strong. Is there any escape? God promises, "No temptation has overtaken you that is not common to man. God is faithful, and he will not let you be tempted beyond your ability, but with the temptation he will also provide the way of escape, that you may be able to endure it" (1 Corinthians 10:13).

A Case Study in the Life of Elijah

Let's look at the prophet Elijah and see what we can learn from God's Word about how to counsel the depressed. Read through 1 Kings 17–19, and then let's walk through it together here.

Identify Contributing Factors

When we are depressed or counseling someone in that state, we want to know where these negative feelings come from. What has happened to change a confident, capable man into a helpless child? In Elijah's case, what caused this fearless prophet—who defeated 450 Baal worshipers—to become a groveling refugee begging God to take his life? What were the contributing factors that led to Elijah's breakdown and depression?

Conflict and Confrontation

Because Elijah was faithful to God's Word, he lived a life of confrontation. King Ahab ruled over Israel at this time, and he was the most wicked king up till now (1 Kings 16:33). He provoked God to anger, so God called His prophet Elijah to stand against him. Elijah had to confront Ahab face-to-face when he predicted the drought God would bring upon Israel. He then went into hiding for three-and-a-half years while Queen Jezebel killed every true prophet she could find. Then Elijah had to come out of hiding and confront the king again. The king, of course, reversed the charges and blamed *Elijah* as the troubler of Israel—not himself (1 Kings 18:17-18).

Elijah even had to confront the widow who would be his lifeline when his brook hideout dried up. He had to call on her to trust the words of a stranger who promised that her oil and flour would not run out if she gave him her last meal. Then he had to face her wrath and grief when her son died and she blamed him for it.

The confrontations climaxed on Mount Carmel when Elijah invited the whole nation to watch him in a battle with 450 prophets of Baal and 400 prophets of Asherah. The prayer contest was 850 to 1, to see which god would answer by fire and prove himself to be true. The false prophets were in a frenzy, calling on their god from morning until past noon, leaping about the altar, and cutting themselves with swords until their blood gushed out on them. How this must have brought sorrow and anger to Elijah, seeing God's people mixing worship of the one true God with Baal worship! He was calling upon the Israelites to decide who they would follow. Imagine the tension!

Physical Exertion Plus Emotional Tension

Then came Elijah's turn to call upon God to set afire the altar upon which he would place his sacrifice. But first he had to rebuild the altar, which had been comprised of twelve heavy stones. Then he dug a deep trench around it, slayed the animal, and placed it upon the altar. Next he urged the people to pour water onto the altar and into the trench—three times. He went through all this work out of the compassion of his heart, for this was a last-ditch effort to see God's nation rescued from self-destruction. You can imagine the emotional tension Elijah felt as he waited to see if God would answer his outrageous request with fire. He knew that if God didn't answer, his life was over.

Sure enough, fire came down and consumed the offering, the wood and the stones, and even the water in the trench. Elijah must have been filled with joy and relief. What elation he must have felt as revival broke out and the people declared, "The LORD, he is God" (1 Kings 18:39).

But his job was not done. Now he had to oversee the capture and execution of the 450 prophets of Baal. He could not let any of them escape. And it was also time for him to pray for rain to bless the nation as the people returned to worshipping the one true God. He told King Ahab to enjoy a meal while he climbed the mountain to persevere in prayer to God so that rain would be restored to Israel.

What an incredible victory for Elijah! But as we're about to see, even in our times of greatest usefulness, victory, and success, we may be just a step away from falling into the darkest of depression.

Another Death Threat

Elijah may have beaten Ahab and all the false prophets, but he hadn't beaten Jezebel. Now all her fury was directed at him. And while the people may have turned back to God, they weren't ready to stand with God's prophet when it would cost them. So Elijah turned tail and ran for his life. Instead of asking God to strengthen him for the next battle, instead of remembering the power of God, he trusted his own two legs to get him out of trouble.

Self-Reliance, Self-Focus, and a Failure to Trust the Power of God

Men often fall at their strongest point. Moses, the meekest of all men, lost his temper with the people of Israel and struck the rock. Abraham, the man of faith, hid behind his wife and called her his sister. John, the man who eventually became known as the apostle of love, wanted to call down thunder and judgment on those who were casting out demons in the name of Christ. Peter, the bold spokesman for the apostles, quaked at the voice of a maid who, the night before Jesus' crucifixion, accused him of being one of Jesus' followers.

Whenever we fail God, it's because we're relying on our own strength instead of humbly admitting our weakness and asking God for the grace to see us through the challenge we're facing.

Isolation, Fatigue, Hopelessness

Elijah was not only running *for* his life, now he was running *from* his life as well. He was tired of being the lone voice for truth. He was tired of the death threats. He was tired of the faithless people. He just wanted to be alone. He traveled about 80-120 miles to Beersheba in Judah, but evidently he felt that wasn't far enough. He left his servant there and went a day's journey into the wilderness by himself, sat down under a juniper tree, and "asked that he might die, saying, 'It is enough; now, O LORD, take away my life, for I am no better than my fathers'" (1 Kings 19:4).

Here Elijah is—physically and emotionally spent, all by himself in the wilderness, forgetting his recent victory, crying out in utter despair. He now thinks of himself as useless, as a failure. He prays according to his feelings instead of praying according to God's promises or power as he had before. He begs God to take his life.

When you are depressed, you filter all positive information through a negative grid and nothing is encouraging, happy, or good. And even if it is good, you just figure it doesn't apply to you anymore. You doubt your salvation. You center your thoughts and actions on yourself. It is all "Woe is me."

When I faced my bout with severe depression, I don't know how many times I prayed and wished for God just to take me home. I didn't believe I would ever experience normal emotions again. I felt like I had lost my mind. As Proverbs 18:14 says, "A man's spirit will endure sickness, but a crushed spirit who can bear?"

So what led to Elijah's broken spirit? What was the pattern of Elijah's life up to this point? When the Lord said something to him, did he obey? Had Elijah been directly in the center of God's will? The answer is absolutely and unequivocally "Yes!" It was Elijah's obedience that had led him into conflict and confrontation. And that, in turn, led him to a place of physical and emotional exhaustion. It was then, in his frailty, that he succumbed to self-reliance and despair.

Our Vulnerability

As men, our natural inclination is to want to be strong and in control. That's our manly calling, but in our pride we fail to admit our human frailty and lack of control over circumstances or the health and virility of our bodies.

Though as Christians we have spiritual life, physically, God has made us of clay—we are vulnerable to weakness, sin, disease, and yes, depression. There are many physical factors that can lead us into depression. These include exhaustion from years of overwork, serious injury, chronic pain, or insomnia. Improper diet or eating disorders can be a great contributing factor, as well as diseases such as hypoglycemia or thyroid issues.

Depression can also be triggered by overwhelming grief from a failed marriage, a rebellious child, severe financial problems, or the death of a loved one. Depression can also originate from personal failures and disappointments— hope that has been dashed over and over again. It can result from failing to handle the normal responsibilities of life in a biblical way. It can come as a consequence of sins such as worry, anxiety, or fear.

Like Elijah, you may encounter depression in the line of duty as you serve your family and the church. You may find yourself hit by wave after wave of opposition until you collapse in exhaustion. But just as God brought angels to minster to Elijah, and He brought an angel to minister to Jesus as He prayed in the Garden of Gethsemane, He also wants to care for you and restore you to do His will in His power.

God the Counselor

How did God handle His servant's depression? Can you imagine God saying, "Okay, Elijah, if that's what you really want"—then zap!—He takes Elijah home! God could have done that, but He didn't. What did He do instead?

Rest and Physical Nourishment—Tokens of His Grace

God gave His servant physical rest. We read that Elijah lay down and slept. God didn't rebuke him for his depression and for asking to die. In fact, God made sure that Elijah was one of the two men in the Old Testament who never died! God is longsuffering and remembers that we are but dust (Psalm 103:14). He let Elijah sleep, for sleep refreshes the mind and the body. In this sense, sleep is definitely a gift.

God also gave Elijah physical nourishment. An angel woke him up and told him to eat. God provided a freshly baked cake and a jar of water. This all happened a second time as well. The sleep, the angel, and the food and water were all proofs of God's love for Elijah. We are told that Elijah "went in the strength of that food forty days and forty nights to Horeb" (1 Kings 19:8).

Here we see that God, the Great Counselor, addressed Elijah's physical needs first. This affirms the definite connection between the mind and the body. John Piper points this out when he says, "What we should be clear about… is that the condition of our bodies makes a difference in the capacity of our minds to think clearly and of our souls to see the beauty of hope-giving truth."[3]

In my case, I needed to take time off from teaching to recover. Part of my recovery plan was the physical therapy, nutritious meals, and supplements that would help restore my health. The biblical counselor must work alongside medical doctors to see if there are any underlying physical causes for the depression. But what if that physician recommends psychotropic drugs?

Are psychotropic medicines always necessary to bring healing? We must consider that these drugs deal with the outer symptoms of depression, not the underlying cause. Dr. Ed Welch, in his book *Blame It on the Brain*, counsels us to use them carefully and sparingly:

> If the person is not taking medication but is considering it, I typically suggest that he or she postpone that decision for a period of time. During that time, I consider possible causes, and together we ask God to teach us about both ourselves and him so that we can grow in faith in the midst of hardship. If the depression persists, I might let the person know that medication is an option to deal with some of the physical symptoms.[4]

In my situation, after a lengthy period of time and with the advice of biblical counselors and physicians, I realized that a short-term antidepressant would help my body regain its emotional and physical balance quicker. It very gradually took effect and, combined with everything I was doing spiritually, the depression began to lift and my thoughts and feelings finally returned to normal. I was able to get back to teaching and off the medication in six months. The medication was not my first or only course of action; it was a gift of God's grace and used after only much careful consideration.

The biblical counselor must also help his friend to make a plan for the ongoing care of his body to avoid a relapse into depression. As I look back on my situation, I now realize that I had probably sinned against my body by overtaxing it beyond its limits. The consequence was that everything ended up being taken from me—my job, my ministry, and even my ability to think clearly or feel normal. By God's grace, those things were removed only temporarily. But to prevent a recurrence, I needed to set some guidelines for the future. I also came to realize that God was more interested in my heart before Him than all my service for Him. If I could never serve Him again, I could still praise Him by faith, whether or not my normal feelings or employment ever returned. I resolved to remember my vulnerability and weakness, and to not trust in my own strength.

Awareness of His Power

God did not try to cure Elijah's depression with a pep talk to boost his self-image. He just showed Himself to Elijah, and that was enough. God called His servant to come out of the cave and stand on the mountain—the same mountain where God had revealed Himself to Moses and where He had given the Law. Then God passed by with a wind so strong that it "tore the mountain" and shattered the rocks, but the Lord was not in the wind, nor the earthquake, nor the fire. He came and spoke to Elijah in a gentle whisper. Elijah faced the thundering elements with awe, but he covered his face in the presence of that quiet voice (1 Kings 19:11-13). He covered his face even as the angels do (Isaiah 6:2), for no one can see God and live (Exodus 33:20).

We too must know God. We must know the God who gave the Law with trumpet blast and earthquake and smoke, the God who is a consuming fire, the God whom we can never please in our own strength because even our best efforts are tainted (Isaiah 64:6), the God who doesn't wait for us to come to Him. Rather, He comes to us. He clothed Adam and Eve. He provided the ram in the thicket so Abraham didn't have to slay his son. He revealed Himself to Moses as the God who is compassionate and gracious; slow to anger and abounding in steadfast love (Psalm 103:8). He gave His only Son to be the perfect sacrifice that would take away our sin (Romans 5:8-9). Do you know and love Him? Do you fear Him? Do you trust Him?

Often depression can occur when we feel like a failure, and that is likely to happen anytime we are trusting in ourselves. Rather, we must trust in Jesus, who was the only perfect man. He has taken our sin and given us His righteousness. He will give us the peace *of* God, which comes from peace *with* God.

I came to know this peace with God when I was thirteen years old, right after my father died suddenly of a heart attack. My mother took my sister and me into her arms with perfect peace, saying, "We know where Daddy is, and we know we'll see him again." But I didn't know the assurance that I would see him again. I decided then and there that I needed to make a change—instead of trusting myself to be good enough to get into heaven on my own, I needed to trust in Christ as my Lord and Savior. To know peace with God, we have to humble ourselves, admit we are sinners in need of a Savior, and fall on God's mercy and grace. When we do, God receives us with open arms, forgives us, and makes us His blood-bought children with all of His resources available to us. His love motivates and empowers us to trust Him through the dark times.

God's Voice and Awareness of His Presence

Back to Elijah's encounter with God—the Lord was not in the wind, earthquake, or fire, but He revealed Himself in "a sound of a gentle blowing" (1 Kings 19:12 NASB). Faith comes by hearing and hearing by the Word of God; miracles and signs only prepare the way. God asked Elijah what he was doing—why had he neglected his duties, deserted his people, and hidden from an impotent queen when such a God of power was on his side? From behind his cloak, Elijah poured out his fear and frustration before the Lord. It was not for lack of zeal that he had run away, but because he had lost all hope of success. Scared and alone, he felt it was useless to try any longer. God conde-scended to answer Elijah's every complaint with his next commission.

When you're in the midst of depression, you don't feel God's presence. You are in the ditch and you can't see out. You think the light at the end of the tunnel is a train coming at you. And you long for the voice of God to tell you what He wants of you. It comes, dear sufferer, in the still small voice of *His Word*, just as clearly as it did for Elijah.

I went to the Word of God for my comfort and direction. The Psalms and other Scriptures can become an oasis in the desert that soothes and calms the soul. I spent a lot of time in the Psalms, where David, who experienced depression often, poured out his soul to God. David confessed there were times when he could not see his God, and he laid bare his doubts, anxieties, and anguish of soul. And God was always faithful to pull him out of the miry pit and set his feet upon a rock—prompting David to lift up a song of praise to his God (Psalm 40).

Men, God's Word is sufficient. It speaks to us of hope because of the Father's favor and our Savior's unquenchable love for us—truths we need to have drummed into us over and over again. Scripture assures us that "His divine power has granted to us all things that pertain to life and godliness, through the knowledge of him who called us to his own glory and excellence." This is through the agency of "his precious and very great promises" found in His Word (2 Peter 1:3-4).

When I was battling depression, I knew it was important to spend time in God's Word and fill my mind with the truth, for I needed this as an antidote to my negative thinking and the lies of Satan. But I needed my counselor to hold me to it. He had me examine the Scriptures daily and journal what reasons I learned there to respond in obedience and praise. Could God even use my weakness? Yes, His power is perfected in our weakness (2 Corinthians 12:9).

Don't think you are being hypocritical if you read the Bible when you don't feel like it. You might wonder why you should read if your brain will not engage. Why bother if, an hour later, you're going to forget what you just read? You must read out of faith and obedience. God's Word will restore your soul. It will revive you and strengthen you and enlarge your heart (Psalm 119:25-32). Keep listening to that still, small voice—the voice of God in His Word!

A Proper Perspective

When Elijah poured out his frustrations to God, he complained, "The people of Israel have forsaken your covenant, thrown down your altars, and killed your prophets with the sword, and I, even I only, am left" (1 Kings 19:10). But was he truly the only one left? God gave His servant a proper perspective of the facts. He said there were 7000 in Israel who hadn't bowed the knee to Baal. Elijah had chosen to forget about faithful Obadiah and the 100 prophets he had kept hidden in caves. He had chosen to forget about his own faithful servant, whom he left before his journey into the wilderness. And there were more on his side than he even knew about. God gave him hope by reminding him of His remnant.

Like Elijah, we too choose to forget our blessings. And so God gives us hope by giving us counselors who help us think on what is true, honorable, right, pure, and lovely (Philippians 4:8).

In my depression, I too needed the proper perspective—I needed to be encouraged over and over again with the truths of the gospel. Though I am more sinful and flawed than I realize, I am also more welcomed, loved, and forgiven than I dare to hope because I have placed my faith in Jesus' substitutionary death for me on the cross. He isn't through with me yet!

A Task to Accomplish

After God had gotten Elijah's attention, He gave His servant an assignment. He had more for Elijah to do. God wanted him to go in the strength of that sleep and food for 40 days and forty nights to the mountain of God to prepare him for a new commission—to anoint a king of Aram for the purpose of destroying Baal worship in Israel, Jehu as king of Israel to wipe out Ahab's wicked family, and Elisha as Elijah's successor. Elijah's work would not be in vain; others would carry it on. God commanded him to get moving, and Elijah, out of love and trust for God, got up and did what God commanded him to do, with the strength that God had provided.

What God Wants You to Do

Every Christian is a servant of the Lord, and we're called to do His work until He takes us home. So when depression comes, what can we do to keep moving forward and making ourselves available for His use?

Commune with Him Through His Word and Prayer

As I battled through my time of depression, I was challenged to memorize portions of Scripture and pray them back to God. One such passage was 1 Peter 5:5-11, which lists truths I needed to focus on—that the God of power promises to *restore, confirm, strengthen* and *establish* us as we humble ourselves under His mighty hand. This portion of Scripture was a great encouragement to me, and I prayed to that end. God doesn't call us to do anything that His Son was not willing to do. Jesus, the very Son of God, humbled Himself, taking the form of a bondservant, and became obedient unto death to redeem us!

Now, we can't clothe ourselves in humility and bear our anxieties on our own—only Jesus could do that for us. But one way we *can* humble ourselves is to pray and seek God's strength in everything, casting our anxieties on Him. Why? Because God cares for us! (1 Peter 5:7). We don't have to suffer in silence. We can cry out to our Father. David did: "Out of the depths I cry to you, O LORD!" (Psalm 130:1). He hears, and He will answer.

My wife, Mary, and I dug into biblical accounts of people who experienced times of deep despair—people such as Elijah, David, and Job—and what they went through. I was encouraged by each of the accounts of these men who knew God and yet struggled mightily with doubt and despair. God met them where they were, and brought them out to a place of usefulness.

Mary posted scriptural promises all around our apartment. Everywhere I looked, a verse of hope confronted my negative thinking. We quoted Psalm 23 and read *Valley of Vision*, a marvelous collection of Puritan poems and prayers, each night before bed to be reminded of our Good Shepherd and the riches of His matchless grace. One such prayer in part reads like this:

> O Lord God, teach me to know that grace precedes, accompanies and follows my salvation. That it sustains the redeemed soul. That not one link of its chain can ever break. From Calvary's cross wave upon wave of grace reaches me, deals with my sin, washes me clean, renews my heart, strengthens my will, draws out my affection, kindles a flame in my soul, rules throughout my inner man, consecrates my every thought, word, work, teaches me Thy immeasurable love.[5]

Seek Counsel

Every man needs the encouragement and accountability found in the body of Christ. I entrusted myself to a biblical counselor from our church (and another from my work) for man-to-man help. They prayed with me and empathized with me in the pit, but with a hand up. They assured me of my secure position as a child of God—that nothing could take me out of His hand even though I felt lost. They always took me to the Word of God, where real hope is found. They assured me that God had a plan for me in this suffering, and that He would be faithful to bring me through. They helped me sort out "false guilt" (guilty feelings) from what would be real guilt—sins that grieve the heart of God. They encouraged me to confess those sins and to know that they were forgiven despite what my feelings were telling me (1 John 1:9).

Seek Forgiveness for Known Sin

Whereas the secular world approaches depression by seeking to minimize people's guilt, we as believers can face our sins because the price for them has been paid and God's great love and forgiveness motivate us to deal with them. We can pray with the psalmist, "Search me, O God, and know my heart! Try me and know my thoughts!" (Psalm 139:23). Much of the time we live our lives with faults that we're incapable of seeing. It's the covert sins of the heart like pride, self-justification, self-righteousness that we are often blind to. Only when the searchlight of the Spirit exposes the sin and melts our hearts in brokenness do we change. Sin and resulting guilt often go hand-in-hand with depression. With confession and repentance there is forgiveness and sweet release! Scripture tells us that if we confess and forsake our sin, we will obtain mercy (Proverbs 28:13).

When depression has ensued because we have responded sinfully in anger and bitterness to hard situations in life, a counselor can help us sort out a plan of action to get energy directed toward repentance and biblical problem solving. As we learn to thank God for our trials and overcome evil with good, burdens are released and depression is lifted.

I knew that my suicidal thoughts were sinful and needed to be confessed to God and to my family—for my own protection. But I still battled with guilt. How could I be a Christian if I had such wicked desires? I wrestled with whether to participate in the Lord's Supper during church services. I should refrain if I was harboring unconfessed sin, but if I was willing to forsake that sin I had to partake if I wanted to remember that my sins were washed away by the blood of the Lamb, not by self-chastisement. I had to believe what I could not feel and take communion in faith during this dark night of the soul. I needed to realize that it is not immunity to temptation that makes me right with God, but the death of Christ and His righteousness that has been put to my account. I need not wallow around in guilt; I could bask in the forgiveness that I have in the shed blood of Christ.

In examining my heart, I also found that the desire for control and comfort was an idol that needed to be thrown down and replaced with a new way of thinking—that suffering is part of the Christian life, and that we are called to it in the fellowship of Christ's suffering and a platform for the gospel (Romans 8:17; Colossians 1:24-29). The destruction of idols is a great cure for depression!

Seek to Know Christ Better in the Fellowship of His Suffering

To know Christ is worth more than anything else in life. In the course of my depression it seemed that I had lost everything, but I had to keep reminding myself, *I haven't lost Christ.* Rather, I was experiencing what the apostle Paul called the "fellowship of His sufferings" (Philippians 3:10 NASB). Knowing Christ in a deeper way is better than having a healthy body and mind. My prayer was to be able to say with Paul:

> Whatever things were gain to me, those things I have counted as loss for the sake of Christ. More than that, I count all things to be loss in view of the surpassing value of knowing Christ Jesus my Lord, for whom I have suffered the loss of all things, and count them but rubbish so that I may gain Christ, and may be found in Him, not having a righteousness of my own derived from the Law, but that which is through faith in Christ, the righteousness which comes from God on the basis of faith, that I may know Him and the power of His resurrection and the fellowship of His sufferings, being conformed to His death; in order that I may attain to the resurrection from the dead (Philippians 3:7-11 NASB).

Seek Help Through the Church

At first I didn't want to be with people because they would ask questions about how I felt. I didn't think that they wanted to hear that I felt like dirt. But I decided to tell them the truth: "I don't feel well at all, but I know God is good and He will sustain me. My future is secure in Him."

When we are struggling, we need to be honest and be willing to accept help from the body of Christ. I had always been the giver and minister to others. Now it was time to receive. I was deeply humbled by the outpouring of notes of encouragement and calls from my colleagues, students, fellow church members, and pastors. Men came to sit with me and just be there, seeing that I didn't want to talk. Meals were brought, family members came to lend support from across the country, and our daughter came all the way from South Africa. God made provisions for me through His loving family, and I was to receive it all with thanksgiving.

When you find yourself wanting to withdraw from others, you need to utilize the provision that God has made for this very purpose—the body of believers, the church (Hebrews 10:24-25). My wife encouraged me to go against my desires and drove me to church because I wasn't able to drive. The church is where we find sustenance for the hunger in our souls through the preaching of God's Word and encouragement to persevere as brothers and sisters in Christ share the comfort they also have received from the Lord (2 Corinthians 1:4). We must allow those who have been through this valley to tell us their stories, and let them help shine light on our path.

Seek to Live a Structured Life

My counselors encouraged me to keep doing those things which I could do. People who are not in a severe state of depression should continue carrying out their normal duties. Pulling back from meaningful work can end up adding to the depression. Living a structured and productive life is a very important part of keeping our health up.

I had a schedule of things that I did every day. I was not called to do demanding things, but to be faithful in the things that I could do (Matthew 25:21). Besides the reading, journaling, and doing some minor work-related tasks, I had to do physical therapy that was required to help my back. I was asked to write some notes of encouragement to others each day by email—this would help me to look beyond my own needs. I could reach out to others who could be suffering as well and be in need of God's help.

As we are faithful to reach out to others, God ministers to us and gives us the joy of knowing the smile of His approval. When we think that we are unable to do what is necessary, we can ask God for His strength (Philippians 4:13).

Reading to my wife was another thing I could do, for that had been my pattern all through our years of marriage. During the long days I read book after book on the gospel, soaking us in the truth about what Jesus Christ has already done on our behalf. I was blessed to have a wife who directed her energies to helping me get through this in every way—being there to feel my sorrows, to listen, and to encourage me with the truths about who I am in Christ. Needless to say, this time drew us closer together as a couple.

Trusting in God

Since recovering from my period of depression, God has assured me that He has more for me to do. I was able to return to teaching and preaching again, all praise to God. He has given me the desire to share my experience with others so that they too can be encouraged to trust Him in times of testing and persevere—all by God's grace and for His glory.

If you are in the midst of depression, my heart goes out to you. I have seen the horrors up close. It truly is a battle for your life. The good news is that God is redeeming our brokenness! He knows all about your suffering. Our Savior is a man of sorrows and acquainted with grief. He understands! And one thing you can rest assured in is that this loving God has allowed these trials to come into your life with a purpose for your good (Romans 8:28-29). He is the blessed controller of all things, and He wants to make you more like His Son.

Know, dear brother, that your trials are momentary in view of eternity and are working an eternal weight of glory (Romans 8:18). "Weeping may tarry for the night, but joy comes with the morning" (Psalm 30:5). Until then, fight the good fight of faith, and rest in His love.

Recommended Resources

Bridges, Jerry. *Trusting God: Even When Life Hurts.* Colorado Springs, CO: NavPress, 2008.

Fitzpatrick, Elyse M. *Because He Loves Me: How Christ Transforms Our Daily Life.* Wheaton, IL: Crossway, 2008.

———. *Comforts from the Cross: Celebrating the Gospel One Day at a Time.* Wheaton, IL: Crossway, 2009.

Harris, Greg. *The Cup and the Glory.* The Woodlands, TX: Kress Christian Publications, 2006.

Mahaney, C.J. *The Cross Centered Life: Keeping the Gospel the Main Thing.* Colorado Springs, CO: Multnomah Books, 2006.

Miller, Paul E. *A Praying Life: Connecting with God in a Distracting World.* Colorado Springs, CO: NavPress, 2009.

Piper, John. *When the Darkness Will Not Lift: Doing What We Can While We Wait for God—and Joy.* Wheaton, IL: Crossway, 2006.

Tada, Joni Eareckson, and Steven Estes. *When God Weeps.* Grand Rapids, MI: Zondervan, 1997.

Welch, Edward T. *Depression: A Stubborn Darkness.* Winston-Salem, NC: Punch Press, 2004.

7

When a Man Gets Angry

Wayne Erick Johnston

Michael came home after a long day at work. His kids—ages four and eight—greeted him at the door, and the hardworking man gave each of them a big hug. His wife welcomed him with kind but tempered words. It had been three months since his last outburst of anger, but tonight he would reset the clock. *I'm tired*, he thought as he plopped down on the couch and turned on the football game. *I worked hard today. Tonight is for me.*

When Michael's favorite quarterback threw an interception that was returned for a touchdown, he yelled an obscenity and slammed his fist on the table. During a key point in the game, his eight-year-old asked for help with his homework. "Can't you see I'm watching football?" Michael responded harshly. The boy burst into tears and ran upstairs to his room. Michael cursed and hollered to his wife in the next room, "It's your fault that he's so weak." Following the boy upstairs, she coolly replied, "When I come back down I'm switching channels to my reality show."

Michael's anger raged. "You know what? It's all yours!" he exclaimed as he stormed to the garage, slamming his fist hard against the wall on his way out. After midnight, he finally went back into the house again. He entered his bedroom to find his wife lying at the far edge of the bed, refusing to talk.

Five years prior, Michael had become a Christian. Like most guys at church, he loved God and really loved his family. He read his Bible. He had friends. Michael had changed, repenting of many of the sins that had ruled his life before he believed in the gospel—but not his anger. In his own home, that sin continued to damage his relationships with his wife and children.

Michael had two kinds of anger. Most days, his anger was held inside. That anger was like embers in a fireplace—not very noticeable to people, but they were present within him, and they were burning. At other times, his anger raged like a whole room on fire. This anger was dangerous to others, and it did serious damage. According to the Bible, both kinds of anger are sinful. His anger was sin against God and sin against his family. "Wrath is cruel, anger is overwhelming" (Proverbs 27:4). "A man of wrath stirs up strife, and one given to anger causes much transgression" (Proverbs 29:22).

Anger is a big problem for many men, yet God has a solution to man's anger. As we begin to examine this solution, let's look first at a four-part process for biblical change—change from the sin of anger to the practice of holiness:

Recognize Sinful Anger > Change the Desires > Trust God's Promises > Replace Anger with Love + A Forgiving Heart

So far, Michael was stuck on part one: He did not yet recognize his anger as sinful. Once this happens, men are able to overcome their sinful anger by God's grace and through His sufficient Word. To see what it takes to defeat anger, read on. God's Word offers hope for change.

Recognize Sinful Anger

A friend once asked, "Is anger really *my* fault?" The simple answer is yes. Our culture, however, excuses sin. We are often taught that all people are good, and that if we do sin, it is because we are victims of being sinned against, or a bad childhood, or a chemical imbalance. In this belief system, you are not responsible or guilty for your sinful anger.

The Bible, however, does not agree. "The anger of man does not produce the righteousness of God" (James 1:20). God is holy and right; man's anger goes against what is right. Jerry Bridges said it well: "In facing up to our anger, we need to realize that no one else *causes* us to be angry. Someone else's words or actions may become the occasion of our anger, but the cause lies deep within us—usually our pride, or selfishness, or desire to control."[1] We are responsible before God for our anger. The first step toward overcoming our sinful anger is admitting that it exists.

The Bible describes anger in a manner that helps us recognize it in our own lives. Colossians 3:8 gives us five manifestations of anger: "Now you must put them all away: anger, wrath, malice, slander, and obscene talk from your mouth." Each of these five words tells us something about anger. "Anger" translates a general word that encompasses the four words that follow. The word rendered "wrath" means rage, heat, and a fury as unpredictable as the wind. "Malice" comes from the Greek word translated "evil" and conveys cursing or speaking evil lies about a person. "Slander" refers to insults or speaking in opposition to another. "Obscene talk" is filthy, improper street language. Which of these five terms best describes your sins of anger?

There is good news for us as Christian men. With the help of the indwelling Holy Spirit, we can "put to death the deeds of the body" (including sins like anger) according to Romans 8:13, and instead, do what is right (Romans 6:19). In a nutshell, that's the key to defeating anger: recognize it, and then kill it. The Spirit helps us do this. In the rest of this chapter, you will read more truths from the Bible about putting your anger to death.

Wrong Desires Cause Anger

When we want something for ourselves and don't get it, we are tempted to become angry. These wrong desires are described in James 4:1-2: "What causes quarrels and what causes fights among you? Is it not this, that your passions are at war within you? You desire and do not have, so you murder. You covet and cannot obtain, so you fight and quarrel."

Do you see a progression? A person wants something for his own benefit. He doesn't get it. So then he feels evil passion, he fights, and he rages with anger. Think about the last time you got angry. What did you want that you were not getting?

Anger Multiplies Sin

The sin of anger causes other sins. We can see this in Genesis 4:3-10, an account of the very first counseling case. The writer of Genesis reports that "Cain was very angry, and his face fell" (verse 5). Apparently, God had asked Cain and his brother, Abel, for offerings of sacrificial animals. Abel was a keeper of sheep and brought the sacrifice God requested. Cain, however, worked a garden and brought a sacrifice from there. The Lord rightly had regard for Abel's offering, but not for Cain's. What wrong desire caused Cain's anger? Cain *wanted* something, but it was not to obey God. Whatever his wrong desire was, he was not getting what he wanted. In response, he became "very angry." And so it is with us. Often we desire something other than obeying God, and then we get angry when we do not get it.

How did God reply to Cain's wrong desire and subsequent anger? The Lord first asked two questions: "Why are you angry, and why has your face fallen?" (verse 6). We can be sure that God knew the answers to both questions. Perhaps He asked so that Cain would think about the answers for himself. If so, Cain probably realized that his wrong desire was the reason for his anger, and his face showed his unhappiness.

Then our Almighty Creator God, the first biblical counselor, gave Cain the solution to the problem of anger due to wrong desires: "If you do well, will you not be accepted?" (verse 7). In other words, if Cain would choose a different desire—to obey God rather than to want what he wanted—God would accept him. The Hebrew text literally says, "Will there not be a lifting up of your face?" Not only would right desires result in restoration to God, they would also result in a different mood. Cain would be content rather than angry.

Finally, God warned Cain about the consequences of continuing in anger: "If you do not do well, sin is crouching at the door. Its desire is for you, but you must rule over it" (verse 7). Sadly, Cain did not follow God's counsel.

Cain's anger then produced more sin—a terrible sin. He did not do well. He did not rule over sin. Instead, he "rose up against his brother Abel and killed him" (verse 8), and then lied to God about it—yet another sin. The first murder on earth occurred as a result of anger. Your anger may not result in murder, but it is sin, and it will likely result in *more* sin.

Sin harms others by stirring up strife and inflicting cruelty upon others. My own sinful anger once produced another more serious sin. When I was 25, there was a conflict in my family. Unkind words had been spoken by me and to me. I desired to be heard and obeyed. The choice was mine: continue with anger caused by wrong desires, or choose the right desire of honoring God (which would result in loving and forgiving people). Sin was crouching at my door. I needed to kill it. Instead, I continued in anger. I was holding a big ceramic bowl of salad. In one horrible moment, I lost control, yelled at my family members, and threw the bowl across the yard, where it broke against some rocks. It was a moment which I immediately knew I could not take back. My actions had a negative impact on those relationships for years afterward.

The first step in the process of replacing anger with doing right is recognizing our own sinful anger. This includes acknowledging the wrong desires behind our anger as well as the further sin that has been caused by it. What do we do when we realize that our anger and our desires connected to it are sin against God? We confess to God that we have sinned, and we choose to turn away from that sin and to not continue in it (Psalm 32:1-6; Revelation 3:19). By God's grace, we do not need to follow the pattern of sins being multiplied by our anger. Rather than indulge in anger (as I had years ago), we as Christians have the freedom to defeat our sinful desires through the power of the Holy Spirit.

Change the Desires

The second step in the process of biblical change from the sin of anger to holiness is to change your desires.

Recognize Sinful Anger > Change the Desires

Wrong Desires: Idols

Earlier we saw that it is wrong desires that cause anger. To further understand what this means, it will be helpful to consider James 4 in greater detail. Here we learn that Christians are to replace *idols* with the desire to obey God (James 4:6-10). An idol is anything that we want more than obedience to God. In the example of Michael—the angry husband and father—his desire was to please himself first. That was his idol, and it played out in his desire for a night that revolved around what *he* wanted. This idol was threatened by his team's lack of performance and his son's interruption. If Michael had wanted to obey God more rather than seek his own satisfaction, he would not have sinned by becoming angry. Instead, he would have dealt with each matter in a way that honored God, showed love and kindness to his family, and upheld his biblical roles as a husband and a father.

Typically, anger is an unrighteous reaction to someone or something. Robert Jones explains, "Our anger is a *response against* something. It does not arise in a vacuum or appear spontaneously…our active hearts are always responding to the people and events in daily life" (emphasis in original).[2] It may seem difficult to replace idols with the desire to obey God, but God gives us hope. We Christians *do* change because we are born of God (1 John 5:3-5). Not only that, but the death Christ died "he died to sin…So you also must consider yourselves dead to sin and alive to God in Christ Jesus" (Romans 6:10-11). Sin no longer holds ultimate power over the Christian!

Over the years, I have asked Christian men the following question: "What do you want that results in you becoming angry?" That hasn't been a hard question for them to answer. They know what makes them angry. One man said, "I want my wife to follow our budget. She's always spending our savings money. Because of my anger, I spend less and less time around her." Another said, "My wife is always arguing…about nothing. It's probably wrong when I explode, but at least she stops then." Another man said, "I just want my kids to do what I say. When they screw up, I get so mad and it comes out when I discipline them." Another man used colorful language to describe his boss, then said, "He makes my life miserable. I hate going to work."

Each man described an idol—something he wanted more than he wanted obedience to God. The first man desired his wife to be responsible with the finances so much that he sinned by becoming angry. The second wanted peace more than obedience to God. In such situations, a man's desire must be to obey God, not to make his own life easier. With that mind-set, he would choose patience over anger. If he has the right desires, he can freely express love to his bride, even if she sins. The man with disobedient children must view their sins as primarily against God, not him. Then he will teach and train them—not in anger, but in love (Proverbs 4:1-6). The man with the difficult boss must change his desire by choosing to work for God, not for man (Colossians 3:23-24). If he did, he would be content to honor God with his good work. In that case, because of love for God, he would not even think of damaging his testimony of the gospel to his employer by sinning in anger.

So it is with each of us. If our core desire is to obey God rather than fulfill our wants, we will be able to choose kindness, forgiveness, and love instead of responding in sinful anger when we don't get our way.

Right Desires: Love Jesus Christ and Love People

Jesus said, "If you love me, you will keep my commandments" (John 14:15). Love for Jesus is the right desire. It results in change from sinful anger to keeping His commands.

I love Jesus Christ. He was faithful to obey God the Father to the point of death on a cross (Philippians 2:7-8). He refused to sin when faced with temptations far beyond any that I will ever face (Matthew 4:1-11). He also loved me, though I was dead in sin (Romans 5:8). Jesus Christ now lives in me (John 17:23); He is my life (Philippians 1:21). Times of reading the Bible result in great joy because that's how I come to understand more about Christ. I worship Him as my Lord. I take courage in Him and strive to emulate Him (Philippians 2:5-11).

This love for Jesus strengthens me when I am tempted to become angry. It results in a change of desires. I now want to keep His commandments, rather than fulfill some selfish desire. Because God provides, in His Word, all I need to grow in righteousness (1 Peter 2:1-3), right desires to know Him and love Him will change me from an angry, sinful man to a loving, obedient man.

A second right desire, love for people, also produces right actions. Jesus said, "A new commandment I give you, that you love one another: just as I have loved you, you are also to love one another. By this all people will know that you are my disciples, if you have love for one another" (John 13:34-35). Having a Christlike love for people helps us to replace anger with the actions of love: "Love is patient and kind...it is not arrogant or rude. It does not insist on its own way; it is not irritable or resentful...Love bears all things...endures all things" (1 Corinthians 13:4-7).

When you and I are committed to loving people the way Jesus Christ loved us, then the times when we are sinned against, treated unfairly, or disrespected will no longer be about us not getting what we want. Instead, our love for people will transform these situations into opportunities to be like our Lord Jesus Christ—who, when He was sinned against and treated unfairly, did not retaliate in anger (1 Peter 2:21-24).

If you now recognize the wrong desires behind your sinful anger, take time now to repent (Psalm 51), and turn instead to the desires of loving God and loving people. Ask God for help with following through on this decision.

Read James 4:1-2 and use the following assignment to help you identify your desires and grow stronger in Christ:

- What desires tempted you to get angry this week?
- What other circumstances created the temptation to become angry?
- What did you do when you were tempted?
- When you wanted to love Jesus Christ by obeying His commands, what did you think and do?
- When you wanted to love people (John 13:34-35, 1 Corinthians 13:4-7), what did you think and do?
- Summarize your progress in changing your desires over the past week and over the past month.
- Confess sin. Repent. Pray for help. Fight the battle with temptation. Plan what to do next.
- Give thanks to God for His grace, which is causing your growth.

Trust God's Promises

The next part of the process of changing from the sin of anger to obedience is trusting the promises God has given in the Bible:

Recognize Sinful Anger > Change the Desires > Trust God's Promises

We have some amazing promises from God. They are true and they will never fail, so we should choose to believe them. They give us hope, and we can live by them.

Hope Begins with the Gospel

Every man who believes in the gospel and has turned *from* living for self and sin *to* honoring Jesus Christ as Lord is a Christian (Romans 3:23-26; 6:4-14).

In Romans 6:6-11, speaking of Christians, the apostle Paul said that we *were formerly* enslaved to sin, but that we have *now* died (to sin) with Christ.

If we believe this is true, how will we view ourselves? Here's Paul's answer: "So you also must consider yourselves dead to sin and alive to God in Christ Jesus." Every time we are tempted to be angry, we should think what is true: "I am no longer sin's slave. I *died* to sin. I *can* change." As Christians, we are no longer hopeless slaves to the sin of anger. We can trust this promise from God.

A Gospel Story

Before we became Christians, we were all slaves of sin: "We ourselves were once foolish, disobedient, led astray, slaves to various passions and pleasures, passing our days in malice and envy, hated by others and hating one another" (Titus 3:3). I was no different. One of my biggest sin struggles was anger.

Though my anger was not often visible, it was there. I thought my father and others were unfair, so I was angry and told myself that they were wrong. The Titus 3:3 characteristics of sin described me in my anger. I was foolish. I was led astray in thinking that people owed me their approval. I was a slave of my own passions and pleasures and I wanted life to revolve around me. I passed my days hating others because they didn't do what I wanted.

My father was also a slave to the sin of anger. His anger was sometimes more visible than mine, for a similar reason: He also desired that people would deal with him in the ways that he wanted them to. When he didn't get what he wanted from people, he held it in for a long time. But when it came out, he stared people down and drank and yelled. He did this when people failed. He did this when he failed. He did this when life got hard. He displayed the Titus 3:3 traits of sin as well. He was foolish in that he knew *about* God, but he would not *honor* Him as God. He was led astray because he thought that he could control people and circumstances with anger. He passed his days hating others because they didn't help his problems go away.

For guys like us, who had never believed in the gospel, wrong desires were overpowering. We wanted what we wanted, and did not care that we were sinning against God with our anger. Romans 8:7-8 says it this way: "The mind that is set on the flesh is hostile to God, for it does not submit to God's law, indeed, it cannot. Those who are in the flesh cannot please God." My father and I refused to turn from sin. We were slaves to it. We *could not* please God because we were choosing to set our minds on the flesh—on our own selfish and sinful desires.

By God's grace, when I was seventeen, I believed the gospel and turned from my idols of sin and self to Jesus Christ as Lord. It was extremely humbling to die to myself and to begin a new life of serving him as my Master. A year later, my father did the same. Titus 3:5-7 describes this transformation: "He saved us, not because of works done by us in righteousness, but according to his own mercy…through Jesus Christ our Savior, so that being justified by his grace we might become heirs according to the hope of eternal life." We were saved by mercy and given new life through Jesus Christ. Life was no longer about us, but Christ. Pride was gone; joy had come. We changed from focusing on what we wanted from people, and instead desired to honor Christ by loving people His way, including each other. God deserves all the glory for changing our lives, making them new and different.[3]

If you have never repented from your sin, believed in the truth of the gospel, and turned from living for yourself to honoring Jesus Christ as your Lord, I invite you to do so now. The cross of Jesus Christ is the way for new life with God, with new desires that result in freedom from sin's rule over you. It is a life lived in God's forgiveness and love. For more about this, you can read Appendix One, "The Gospel for Men," on page 387.

Hope in Jesus Christ

Jesus Christ broke the cycle of sin. Everyone who has ever lived has sinned at some point when tempted—except Jesus. First Peter 2:23 tells us how He dealt with temptation: "He…continued entrusting himself to him who judges justly." Jesus was confident that God, His Father in heaven, was in control of His circumstances. He also knew that His Father would strengthen Him to resist the temptation to sin, and He did. Earlier in the same verse we read, "When [Jesus] was reviled, he did not revile in return; when he suffered, he did not threaten." Jesus resisted the temptation to act in anger by entrusting Himself to the Father. This should serve both as hope for us and as an example to follow. Verses 21-22 tell us, "Christ also suffered for you, leaving an example, so that you might follow his steps. He committed no sin."

We also follow Jesus' example in this way: "If when you do good and suffer for it you endure, this is a gracious thing in the sight of God" (verse 20). This is a helpful principle to understand. We all know what it is like to do the right thing and suffer for it. You tell the truth when others are lying, and they get mad at you. Or you refuse to watch pornography with the other guys at work, and they mock your manhood. We are tempted to respond in anger at such injustice. But in Christ, we have an example of how to avoid the temptation to become angry. First, we know that God is aware of what's happening, and we are to pray for His help to resist the temptation to sin. Then, we are to do what Jesus did: We are to refuse to retaliate or threaten those who wrong us. Then when it all ends, we will not have sinned.

This is our time, Christian brothers, to be courageous. In John 16:33, Jesus told His followers to have hope in Him: "In the world you will have tribulation. But take heart; I have overcome the world." There will be hard times in this world, and Stuart Scott encourages us to expect this and stand strong:

> It is important that you not entertain the thinking, "This is impossible!" or "I'll never be able to change!"...With God's grace, God's Word, and your sincere efforts, you will be able to change... remember that being tempted is not a sin, but following through with sinful anger is. Do not grow weary in "well-doing"...[4]

Jesus Christ overcame the world. He was tempted, yet never sinned. Because He is in us (Galatians 2:20) and we are in Him (John 15:4), we *can* defeat sin, including anger. Trust His promises!

Hope from God's Word

Through His promises in the Bible, God provides hope for Christian men who seek to defeat sin. Jesus Himself spoke of the sufficiency of His Word to enable us to overcome sin when He prayed to God for us future believers: "Sanctify them in the truth; your word is truth" (John 17:17). We can change by replacing sin with doing right (being sanctified) through God's Word. (For practical resources that make use of God's Word to bring about real and lasting change, see the recommended resources list at the end of this chapter.)

James 1:2-4 reveals a promise from God that we can trust. He will use difficult times in our lives, along with His work in us, to produce greater strength to overcome sin: "Count it all joy, my brothers, when you meet trials of various kinds, for you know that the testing of your faith produces steadfastness. And let steadfastness have its full effect, that you may be perfect and complete, lacking in nothing."

When we find ourselves under the weight of adversity, we can take courage because Jesus Christ has overcome the world (John 16:33). We also know that God has promised to provide strength to help us resist temptation (1 Corinthians 10:13). The result is that we are able to endure in the face of difficult circumstances.

I have a buddy who was a bodybuilder when he was in his twenties. Recently, while I was training with him, he pushed me to the point where I could not lift the weights one more time. I know this because he was standing above me and grabbed the bar so it didn't fall on my head! At the gym, we expend physical energy until eventually our muscles can't lift that weight even one more time. That's how the human body works. But it's different for Christians with regard to the human soul. Because God is strengthening us, when we remain under the weight of hard times, the result will be a greater endurance to continue on. However long the suffering lasts, we can last longer because God is at work in us. That is the message of James 1:2-4.

Trusting this promise from God can transform our lives. Although we fight difficult battles against sin, we have hope in the weapons God has given us. This interaction with the Almighty Creator is so invigorating that we can actually have joy while we are in the midst of hardship.

As a biblical counselor, I have seen God's faithful work in men who learned to trust His promises of hope as they faced difficult times. I encourage you, as a man who is in Christ, to trust God's promises in your battle to kill sinful anger. Doing so results in a fresh, strong interaction with the Almighty God—and victory over sin.

Complicating Factors

God will never allow us to be tempted beyond what we are able to handle (1 Corinthians 10:13). Yet when we experience someone's anger against us, this will increase the temptation for us to become angry. As Proverbs 15:1 says, "A harsh word stirs up anger" (Proverbs 15:1). So how can we tap into the promise in 1 Corinthians 10:13 when we find ourselves in a situation that riles up our anger?

Matt grew up in a home where he did not hear soft answers but rather harsh words from his father, which often stirred up his anger. Tyler's mother ruled the home with her temper, so his anger was kindled frequently. Brian's boss makes a practice of motivating him through threats and tirades, so he is tempted to be angry himself. In all three cases, not only are these men being sinned against by the anger of others, they are also being exposed to unbiblical patterns for leadership, which can end up influencing them to think, speak, and deal with their roles of authority in the same way. Such influence can be detrimental, which is why the Bible warns, "Make no friendship with a man given to anger, nor go with a wrathful man, lest you learn his ways and entangle yourself in a snare" (Proverbs 22:24-25).

So what are Matt, Tyler, and Brian to do? And what are we to do when we find ourselves in similar situations? As Christians who trust God's promises, we can remember that we will never be tempted to sin to such a degree that we cannot resist the temptation. God is faithful; He will not let us be tempted beyond our ability to handle it (1 Corinthians 10:13). What's more, God's grace is sufficient for us to resist temptation (2 Corinthians 12:9-10). So no matter what the situation, it *is* possible for us to resist and endure.

Replace Anger with Love + A Forgiving Heart

So far we have considered what the Bible says about sinful anger and how to defeat it; we must change our desires and trust God's promises. Now we turn our attention to the final part in the process of overcoming sinful anger: replacing anger with love and forgiveness.

> Recognize Sinful Anger > Change the Desires > Trust God's Promises > Replace Anger with Love + A Forgiving Heart

By God's grace, we can and must defeat of our anger and replace it with love toward God and others. As believers we have the desires to love Jesus Christ, keep His commandments, and to love people. And we can look to Scripture for truths and promises that can help us defeat sinful anger. For example, in Ephesians 4 the apostle Paul explains the biblical dynamic of growth in righteousness. Our responsibility as Christians is to do two things: "Put off your old self, which belongs to your former manner of life and is corrupt through deceitful desires, and...put on the new self, created after the likeness of God in true righteousness and holiness" (verses 22-24). We are to lay aside doing wrong and replace it with doing right. Later in this landmark passage on Christian change, the specific sin of anger is listed, along with the corresponding righteousness with which to replace it. This is very practical! "Let all bitterness and wrath and anger and clamor and slander be put away from you, along with all malice. Be kind to one another, tenderhearted, forgiving one another, just as God in Christ forgave you" (verses 31-32).

This specific teaching is for us. When we are tempted to get angry, we must choose instead to be kind, tenderhearted, and to forgive as God in Christ forgave us. Put another way, "As the Lord has forgiven you, so you also must forgive. And beyond all these put on love" (Colossians 3:13-14).

We know what love is because we know how Jesus Christ gave His life for the forgiveness of our sins (Galatians 1:4). We trust in His blood as the means of our redemption (Romans 3:24-26). That is the core of the gospel (Ephesians 2:1-10). So when Colossians 3:13 tells us to put on love, we know we can. "We love because he first loved us" (1 John 4:19). Because we have received this pure love from God, we can and must choose to love—even when we are tempted to be angry.

We must also replace anger with a forgiving heart. When we came to Christ in repentance and faith, God forgave us by choosing not to remember our sins against us (Jeremiah 31:33-34). So when someone wrongs us and we are tempted to be angry, we should instead love that person and seek to reconcile the wrong through repentance and forgiveness. If I love my angry boss in the same way that Christ loved me, then my greatest desire will be to reconcile our relationship, and not seek revenge or return evil for evil. When my goal is love and reconciliation, the temptation to retaliate in anger is easily set aside. Instead, I will actively seek ways to show kindness. I want to do this because I am mindful of the much greater forgiveness I have received from God.

If we choose love and forgiveness, we can overcome anger. Jerry Bridges explains the options: "...we must believe that God is absolutely sovereign in all the affairs of our lives (both the 'good' and the 'bad')...We must realize that any given situation that tempts us to anger can drive us either to sinful anger or to Christ and His sanctifying power."[5]

How will we do it? How will we become skilled at replacing anger with love and forgiveness? We must develop new habits of thinking and doing. For example, when another person's words or actions tempt you to become angry, a new pattern of thinking might be, *How can I love this person?* and *What sins must I be ready to forgive?* Or you can ask yourself, *How can I show kindness to this person who has sliced me with his words?*

When you apply God's Word and develop new patterns of thinking and actions, you'll see real change take place in your life. And you'll see change in the people around you as well. They will respond to your new kind and loving ways, which is a far cry from the anger you formerly dished out. While some past relationships damaged by anger might not change, others will, and God will use your obedience to glorify Himself and to build love in your relationships with others.

Doing All in Love

The four-part process to defeating sinful anger is to recognize it, change your desires, trust God's promises, and replace anger with love and a willingness to forgive. When you no longer respond to people in anger, you will bring honor to God. So "be watchful, stand firm in the faith, act like men, be strong. Let all that you do be done in love" (1 Corinthians 16:13-14).

As you commit yourself to real and lasting change, may God strengthen you through His Word and His grace to live for His glory.

For More In-depth Help

Scripture and Daily Journal for Anger

Memorize These Scriptures

Genesis 4:6	Proverbs 19:11	James 1:19-20
Proverbs 14:29	Proverbs 29:22	James 4:1-2
Proverbs 15:1	John 13:34-35	
Proverbs 16:18	Ephesians 4:31-32	

Complete This Journal Daily

What happened just before I was tempted to get angry?

What I thought—

What I wanted—

What emotions I was feeling—

When tempted to choose anger, this is what I did and said—

Why I did that—

What Bible verse best describes my response—

What were the right things to want and do (include Scripture)—

Prayer

Give thanks to God for helping you to replace anger with righteousness, and confess your sin and repent of it.

A Christian's Daily Guide to Dealing with Sin

When I Have Sinned

Confess sin: Psalm 32:3-5; 1 John 1:9

Regret sin: 2 Corinthians 7:9-10

Repent of sin: Psalm 51:16-17; Proverbs 28:13; Revelation 3:19

Turn from sin and toward righteousness as a slave: Romans 6:11-12,19

Confess sin to those you've sinned against and make restitution: Matthew 5:23-24

When I Have Been Sinned Against

Do not take into account sins suffered: 1 Corinthians 13:5

Forgive because you have been forgiven so much: Isaiah 53:3-5; Matthew 18:21-35; Ephesians 4:32

Think what is true: Philippians 4:8

Hope from God's Word

Memorize the Scriptures of Hope from This Chapter

Genesis 4:6-7	2 Corinthians 12:9-10	Hebrews 12:1-3
Psalm 119:9-11	Galatians 2:20	James 1:2-4
John 13:34-35	Philippians 1:21	1 Peter 2:1-3
John 16:33	Philippians 2:5-11	1 John 3:16
John 17:23	Philippians 2:7-8	1 John 5:3-5
Romans 6:6-11	Titus 3:3-7	
1 Corinthians 10:13	Hebrews 4:12-16	

Daily Meditate on Two of the Verses Above and Consider with God

Because these promises are true, what must I think about God, my circumstances, and my desires?

Recommended Resources

Bridges, Jerry. *Respectable Sins.* Colorado Springs, CO: NavPress, 2007.

Jones, Robert D. *Uprooting Anger.* Phillipsburg, NJ: P&R Publishing, 2005.

Scott, Stuart. *Anger, Anxiety, and Fear.* Bemidji, MN: Focus Publishing, 2009.

Strauch, Alexander. *If You Bite and Devour One Another.* Littleton, CO: Lewis and Roth, 2011.

8
Handling Emotional Extremes

Mark C. Chin, MD

I remember the first and only time I have ever witnessed my father weep. We were sitting alone together, having a conversation in his kitchen. He had just emigrated from Canada to the United States for the purpose of living closer to his two sons. By all appearances, this should have been a joyous reunion. It would be years, however, before I would make the connection between the stir of overwhelming emotions my father expressed that day and those associated with his traumatic flight from post-World War II Communist China to Canada as a 13-year-old boy. Regardless of the circumstances, such an open display of grief and sorrow was hardly the norm for an Asian male of my father's generation. At that moment I was baffled, clueless, and anxious. All I could do was watch and pray. The God-given irony was that after nearly a decade of "handling" other people's emotional extremes as a family physician—extremes that were often associated with diagnoses such as bipolar disorder, depression, or schizophrenia—here I was, face-to-face with my father's outpouring of emotions…feeling confused, powerless, and overwhelmed.

As Americans, we live in a feelings-driven culture, one that celebrates the open expression of intense emotions. Yet the task of handling emotional extremes—whether extreme sorrow, anger, or fear—is often a difficult, confusing, and frightening one, especially when it directly involves us or those we dearly love. Unchecked, emotional extremes have the power to dominate the entirety of our lives and the lives of those around us, often bringing with them unwanted loss of control, vulnerability, shame, and tenacious patterns of self-destruction.

Every year, Americans spend tens of billions of dollars on medication and therapy, not to mention the amount spent on alcohol and street drugs, in an attempt to alter or control their feelings.[1] The prevailing psychiatric and psychological models—ones that have proposed subconscious conflicts, environmental influences, neurochemical imbalances, or organic disease as the alleged root causes of persistent emotional extremes—have yet to be proven definitively or provide a definitive cure.[2] The unwanted feelings that seem to wreak havoc in our lives continue to torment us, bearing the ugly testimony that we, as human beings, are broken, self-destructive sinners. It is a testimony that shouts for a word of hope from God, our sovereign Creator. It is a testimony that screams for a Savior. Praise God, He has mercifully given us both. In them, He has given us a definitive diagnosis and a certain cure that redeems and renews the whole man, including his emotions, for the glory of His grace in Christ.

What God's Word Has to Say About Our Emotions

God's Word is no stranger to emotions or emotional extremes; neither is our Great High Priest. He is the One who has fearfully and wonderfully made each one of us, including our emotional framework. He has been tempted and challenged in every way that we have, yet triumphed over all sin. He is intimately aware of our emotional struggles. Of them His Word has much to say, providing us with the truth in Him that sets a heart free to serve Him with joy and gladness, even in the face of intense suffering.

The Bible likens the nature of our emotions, such as that of anger, to a fire, as in the case of a man named Elihu, who *burned* with anger (Job 32:5) or the enemies of David, whose anger was *kindled* against him (Psalm 124:3). Feelings may start as small as a spark, but unchecked or fed, be they feelings of anger, sadness, fear, anxiety, or grandeur, they can quickly become a contagious fire that consumes the entirety of a life, body, and spirit. By the time they become a problem for ourselves or others, often we have a forest fire on our hands, one that has been burning at various degrees and places in our lives for years, forging deeply ingrained patterns of emotionally controlled behavior that frequently obscure the source and triggers of the initial spark.

Yet God's Word also clearly states, as in Proverbs 15:13, Ecclesiastes 7:9 (NASB), or Matthew 5:28 and 15:19, that the primary source of both our thoughts and feelings, be they happy or sad, is our heart, the "mission control" center of our lives. Our circumstances, the actions of others, physical illness, or the biochemistry of our brain may fan the fire or provide the fuel, but the initial spark originates in the inclination, desires, and content of our heart, the source of what that great preacher Jonathan Edwards refers to as our "affections."[3]

So often in our struggles with emotional extremes, we forget that we and our emotions were created for a purpose. God created man to bear His image—to be like Him, to serve Him, and to be with Him. To us He gave the capacity to love Him and to love our fellow man for His glory. To this end God gave us emotions as the expression of the fundamental desires and inclination of our hearts—wonderfully complex "smoke detectors" that communicate the nature and magnitude of the fires burning in our hearts. As such, our emotions play a significant role in the way in which we relate and respond to God and to one another.

In and of themselves, emotions are not sinful, even when they are intense, as in the case of someone grieving over the death of a loved one. Clearly Jesus was a man of intense emotions, a man of sorrow who was well acquainted with grief. The difference, however, between Jesus and us is that our fallen hearts, as the prophet Jeremiah noted, are deceitful above all things, wicked, and desperately corrupted by sin (Jeremiah 17:9). The fundamental desires and inclination of our depraved hearts, unlike Jesus, are usually intent on loving *self* rather than God, *self*-serving rather than God-serving.

The emotional patterns of our lives are all too often an expression of this truth. Ugly emotions are the fruit of ugly hearts. When our emotions, be they mild or extreme, are the expression of ungodly desires that run contrary to the will and Word of God, they are participants in our sin and in the sinful patterns of behavior that inevitably follow. What, then, does our emotional behavior—our patterns of joy and sadness, peace and anger—reveal about our hearts' true desires and inclination? A quick inventory with pen and paper of the triggers that provoke a given emotion in our life—the words, actions, events, or people that provoke joy or anger, fear or peace—reveals much about the desires and priorities of our heart.

The biblical truth as to the source and nature of our feelings is illustrated by the testimony of a dear saint whom I had the privilege of ministering to while he was dying of cancer. In his last days, as his cancer increasingly distorted his brain function, he episodically struggled with fear, anxiety, and panic attacks that shook his entire physical frame in response to recurrent frightening visual hallucinations. At this point, the best that medication could do was to take the edge off his physical agitation or provide sedation.

During these episodes, a family member would hold his hand, call him by name, and speak God's truth to him. The family member would gently and quietly inform him that his hallucinations were not true and that he had nothing to fear because Christ was with him. She would then read to him Scripture that would directly address his feelings of fear and reassure him of his certain hope in God's protection. The testimony of this saint's heart prior to these episodes and throughout his battle with cancer was one of a heart overflowing with the love of Christ, inclined toward the will and Word of God, desirous of His glory even in his own present suffering. His emotional response to his family's ministry to him during these times of cognitive confusion, fear, and anxiety reflected such a heart. He received a calm amidst the storm that can only come from above, one that allowed his entire person, including both his physical and emotional frame, to rest peacefully in the truth of God's Word in Christ.

Peter, the Disciple of Great Emotion

The apostle Paul tells us, "No temptation has overtaken you that is not common to man. God is faithful, and he will not let you be tempted beyond your ability, but with the temptation he will also provide the way of escape, that you may be able to endure it" (1 Corinthians 10:13). This is no empty promise. Scripture and the history of the church testify to God's faithfulness in fulfilling this promise in the lives of His precious saints. Moses, Samson, David, Elijah, Jeremiah, Paul, Martin Luther, and William Cowper, to name just a few, all struggled with emotional extremes just like you and I. They were all frail, emotional, less-than-perfect men who struggled and stumbled, at times miserably, under the burden of their emotions and in the face of great adversity and temptation.

Yet the love and grace of God through faith was the difference in their lives, enabling them to seize His way of escape and endure. In the end they triumphed as mighty men of faith, enjoying a sweet fellowship with God that redeemed their emotional extremes for His glory.

Perhaps one of the most detailed and instructive accounts of such a path of redemptive grace is the life of the apostle Peter. A quick glance at any of the Gospels reveals a brash, unrefined, passionate—on at least one occasion, violent—young manual laborer. He was a sinner who struggled with the intense ups and downs of poor impulse and emotional control as a characteristic pattern of his life, a sure recipe for disaster in any era. Peter would always remain a man of great emotions, even as God had made him so for His glory. But by the love of Christ, he would glorify God as a man of redeemed emotions, a godly leader whose heart overflowed with the love, hope, and joy of Christ.

A Gospel Love: Given and Received

The difference-maker in the life of Peter was Jesus Christ and nothing less than the enduring presence of His gospel love, given and received. This gospel love is a far cry from the warm, fuzzy, fleeting feeling that all too often characterizes the deceitful and disappointing love of our times. It was and is a divine *agape* love that intentionally chose a rough, hotheaded, sinful young fisherman to be not just any disciple, but to be a beloved disciple, an intimate companion, and a leader of disciples.

It was a love that transformed Peter's life, including his emotions, into a song of divine grace in praise of His Savior and Lord. It was a love that Jesus first gave to Peter in the form of a divine command and promise: "Follow me, and I will make you fishers of men" (Matthew 4:19). Many preachers have interpreted this verse as some sort of optional invitation. But a careful study of the original Greek command permits no such interpretation. "Come now! Come immediately!" This was no self-improvement sales pitch or friendly invitation to a better life. It was a divine confrontation with the living Word of God, a gospel love that authoritatively demanded an immediate all-or-none response: Obey or disobey the Word of God! Submit to His Lordship or rebel! My friend, the love of Christ demands no less of you and me.

Few of us think of love in terms of command and obedience. Yet in John 15:10, Jesus directly links the keeping of His commands with abiding in His love. Our legalistic hearts often distort this message, somehow believing that we must earn His love through our obedience. Our libertine hearts attempt to remove obedience and submission from His love. The gospel love of Jesus that redeems our sinful lives will have neither. His love comes before, not after obedience, not as a reward but as a prerequisite for it. "God shows his love for us in that while we were still sinners, Christ died for us" (Romans 5:8).

Gospel obedience is a willing embrace of God's divine love by faith in Christ alone. It sets apart a life entirely for the holiness of Christ, refusing to obey the strong self-serving desires of our past life, the source of our sinful emotions (1 Peter 2:1). It is a Spirit-led gift of grace, an expression of faith, which humbly submits the entirety of a life to His Word and His Lordship. It is a lifelong commitment to live for Christ and not for self that Christ Himself demands of us.

Gospel obedience is the Spirit-paved path to true emotional freedom and self-control that begins and ends in the love of Christ. This truth was not lost on Peter (1 Peter 1:14-15,22-23). He immediately embraced Christ's love by obeying His command. He submitted the entirety of his life—including his emotions—to the will of God, the Word of God, and the Lordship of Jesus Christ. He abruptly broke with his past, leaving everything to follow Jesus as Lord and Master. Peter, of course, would continue to struggle with both sin and poor impulse control throughout his discipleship. However, the pattern of his life would be one of progressive and enduring humble submission to the Word of God. The love of Christ demands no less of us.

Certainly this is no easy task. Each of us has areas in our lives where we struggle to obey Christ. Each of us has things in our lives that we are reluctant to surrender control of—even to Christ. More often than not, these are the parts of our lives that are ruled by intense emotions. Frequently they are tied to raw wounds, deep hurt, and real pain, past or present. Sure, we all want the love of Christ. But are we willing to relinquish control over our pain or hurt? Are we willing to expose raw wounds? Are we willing to be humbled and hurt in the process? Are we willing to surrender our emotions to His command?

We see these gods at play all too often in the lives of men who have been hurt even while serving in church ministry or in their families. Deacons, elders, seminary grads, and pastors—no one is exempt. When called upon to reconcile, forgive, and pursue unity in the simple and direct way Christ commands, delay is all too often the rule rather than the exception. Excuses abound. "It's just too hard right now." "It doesn't feel right." "Why me?" "Why does everything have to be so difficult?" "Why doesn't *he* change?" "You don't understand." "Our case is different." "I don't want to make a mistake by moving too fast." "I'm just not ready yet." The challenge here is that the command of Jesus' love, "Come now!" affords us no such luxuries.

Christ Himself demonstrated that the obedience of gospel love is often difficult, painful, and humiliating, always requiring a death to self and a submission of our feelings to the will and Word of God. Being nailed to a cross was hardly something that felt good or easy, but it was a pure expression of the love of God in Christ for you and me. When it came to dying for your sins and mine, Jesus did not hesitate. He did not delay. He did not allow His feelings to dictate the terms of His actions or behavior as so remarkably demonstrated in the Garden of Gethsemane (Luke 22:42), but rather, He submitted His feelings to the will and Word of God. Our refusal to do likewise in the name of dying to our sins or those of others, whatever the pain or hurt, is essentially the coronation of those sins, along with all the feelings that accompany them, as lords of our lives. Who or what will rule your life and mine?

All too often, when it comes to something we feel strongly about, we delay, waiting for Jesus to work on our terms and not His. We treat Jesus like a buddy or a pet. Jesus is neither. He is Savior and Lord. To delay is to refuse Him. To refuse Him is to disobey. Few of us are willing to admit that a refusal to obey God's Word, whatever the excuse, is a willful choice of self over Christ and a flat-out rejection of His love. Essentially, we are telling Jesus that we do not trust Him to handle the most painful and sensitive parts of our lives. We are saying that we can do a better job of managing our problems and our emotions than He can.

Herein lies one of the root causes of the destructive emotional extremes in our lives, an area of our heart given over to a prideful self-love and self-confidence that requires everyone, including Christ, to conform to the demands of the things we feel strongly about. Delay in obedience in these areas only fans the flames, allowing our emotional extremes to go unchecked, building behavioral patterns that are controlled by the emotions of self-love and self-confidence rather than the Word of God. Redemptive change in our lives and our emotions cannot happen until that self-love is replaced with the love of Christ, until we embrace His gospel love through the obedience of faith, until God's Word—not our feelings—rules our lives. A quick, prayerful inventory with pen and paper of the areas we struggle to obey Christ in, and the emotions that accompany these struggles—whether it be anger, jealousy, envy, anxiety, fear, sorrow, or despair—will usually point toward the true gods of our life, the puppet-masters of our emotional extremes, the roots of our self-love and self-confidence.

The gospel command, "Come now! Follow Me" is, in essence, a command of repentance—a command to walk away from those false gods and to let Christ rule our lives instead. It is one of the greatest expressions of divine love in the history of the world. Gospel obedience is the way we receive this offer of divine love. This is our first step toward Christ's victory over our emotional extremes. Are you ready to obey His command?

Gospel Truth: Given and Received

If the love of Christ that conquered Peter's emotional extremes began with a command, it continued in the form of a most personal gospel truth. Peter's problems, emotional or other, did not suddenly end with his initial obedience. In fact, as he submitted his life to Christ, Peter's emotional challenges only increased, exposing his emotional vulnerabilities and his shortcomings even more. His life was clearly more painful and his failures more obvious after Christ than before.

These are often the very things we all fear in following Christ. Yet this was no accident or abandonment by Jesus. Rather, it was further evidence of Christ's sovereign love at work in Peter's life, beginning the process of rebuilding Peter into a true child of God. The purpose of Christ's sovereign love was clearly not to create a more successful and happier life for Peter. Rather, it was to mold Peter into the image of Christ for the glory of God (Romans 8:28-29). To do so, Peter's life needed to be rebuilt upon the truth of God's Word (Matthew 7:24). This was one of the primary ways in which Jesus poured His divine love into Peter. It involved not just instruction in the truth, but also the painful process of exposing and removing the untruth that Peter's life had previously been built upon.

Letting Go of Destructive Thinking

Like all of us, Peter brought a substantial amount of emotional baggage and messed-up thinking into his relationship with Christ, much of which was built around the world according to Peter rather than Christ. Peter's life needed to be emptied of the love and truth of Peter so that it could be filled with the love and truth of Christ. This is clearly demonstrated in Jesus' famous rebuke of Peter's fierce objection to the cross in Matthew 16:23: "He turned and said to Peter, 'Get behind me, Satan! You are a hindrance to me. For you are not setting your mind on the things of God, but on the things of man.'"

So many of the destructive patterns of sinful emotions trace their roots to recurrent patterns of untruthful and unbiblical thinking. These are sinful and destructive patterns of thinking that all of us, to varying degrees at various times, have succumbed to. Jesus points out that they are the fruit of hearts and minds set upon—or as Jonathan Edwards would say, inclined toward—the things of man rather than the things of God. In Peter's case, as seen in Matthew 16:23, Jesus identified the content of such thinking as a sinful opposition to the cross.

As happened with Peter, many of the difficult emotions we struggle with are directly connected to a deep-seated refusal to allow ourselves or the ones we love to suffer for the glory of God, according to His will and His Word. Jesus identifies the source of such thinking: Satan, the father of lies (John 8:44). Later in his life, Peter would warn the believers in the early church to be on the alert, prepared to stand firm in the faith and to resist the devil, who prowls like a roaring lion seeking someone to devour (1 Peter 5:8-9). Peter knew from firsthand experience that the devil devours lives by sowing lies that oppose and distort the truth of the cross.

Furthermore, Peter had the spiritual scars to show that the devil is a master at preying upon our weaknesses, both physical and spiritual, at those times when we are least on our guard—times of success as well as times of suffering. During times of suffering, the devil brings the lies of "Why me?" During times of success, he brings the lies of "Because of me." Many of the sinful and destructive emotional extremes in our lives are built upon these two lies that distort the truth of the cross.

The truth that Peter's life needed to be built upon was the reality of our sinful total depravity and, therefore, our desperate need to participate in the cross of Christ through fellowship with Him—whatever the cost. The lie that needed to be destroyed was the notion of a gospel, a Savior, and a saint without a cross. This lie from the devil needs to be destroyed in all our lives. This is why Jesus, immediately after rebuking Peter, addressed the disciples with the following truth: "If anyone would come after me, let him deny himself and take up his cross and follow me" (Matthew 16:24).

Are we ready to die with Christ?

Receiving the Truth of the Cross

A very sweet Christian patient of mine suffered the tragic and heartbreaking loss of her children to illness. For some time after the loss of her last living child, her encounters with me were filled with inconsolable grief and rage, uncharacteristic for her but most understandable in light of her loss. There was nothing I could do or say to ease her pain or dampen her rage. She would just repeat to me over and over again while crying in anger, "No one should have to bury their children."

Months later, she appeared in my office with a smile on her face. She said to me, "Dr. Chin, I know what my problem was. My pastor told me I was angry with God. You know what? He was right. I'm no longer angry with God."

Too often we do not want to believe that the truth of the cross applies to us or to someone we love. We would prefer to believe the devil's lie that somehow there's a way around the cross. We would rather hold onto our pain, our hurt, our fear, and our anger, trying to manage them ourselves. In doing so, we reject the only true comfort and hope that can heal such pain and sorrow, the comfort and hope of the cross that comes from a God who is intimately acquainted with the sorrow, grief, and pain that accompanies the loss of an only child. How much of our emotional extremes are tied to things which we are unable to let go of, things in our lives that we are unwilling to surrender to the cross of Christ?

Though Peter continued to struggle with unbiblical thinking, Jesus never gave up on him. To Peter's credit, he always received Jesus' rebukes well, a testimony to the magnitude of his love and reverence for his Lord and Savior. Though Peter's life was painfully broken by following Jesus, his life was also rebuilt by the love of Christ and the truth of the cross. To the end, he never lost sight of the necessity of the cross. To those believers who had begun to suffer persecution and were about to suffer even more, Peter gave this exhortation (reminiscent of Jesus' rebuke to him in Matthew 16:23): "Since therefore Christ suffered in the flesh, arm yourselves with the same way of thinking, for whoever has suffered in the flesh has ceased from sin, so as to live the rest of the time in the flesh no longer for human passions but for the will of God" (1 Peter 4:1-2).

This gospel truth made Peter a powerful leader in the face of persecution and an incredible comforter of those who suffered for Christ. Truth given and truth received transformed a proud, impulsive know-it-all into a humble, restrained servant of the cross, one who was willing and able to endure whatever pain and suffering this world could bring for the name of Christ and the will of God. How willing are you and I to receive the rebuke and discipline of Christ's Word? How willing are we to reject the devil's lies for the truth of Scripture? How willing are we to submit to the oversight of godly men and serve the body of Christ, embracing the cross as we do so? How willing are we to receive the truth of the cross? It is the truth of the cross that redeems the heart of our emotions.

Grace: Prepared and Given

Truth without grace is a harsh master—every counselor, pastor, and friend needs to remember this. The beauty and glory of Jesus' ministry to Peter was the way in which He, the perfect incarnation of both these divine attributes (John 1:14), lovingly poured them into Peter's life without ceasing. For those of us who have the privilege of ministering to friends or family struggling with emotional extremes, we would do well to pay close attention to the ways in which Jesus ministered to Peter. He didn't just preach a sermon or throw Bible verses at Peter. He shared His life with Peter, giving of His fullness, grace upon grace (verse 16). He literally fed Peter. He healed Peter's mother-in-law. He cared for all Peter's needs and He washed his feet.

Jesus didn't simply offer to pray for Peter. He taught Peter how to pray and invited Peter to participate in some of his most intimate times of fellowship with the Father and the Spirit as He withdrew from the world to be alone with the Father and the Spirit in prayer. Inasmuch as prayer is an expression of humble dependence on the grace of God for all things, the life of prayer that Jesus shared with Peter modeled and shared the only life possible for a servant of God, a life of grace by faith.

As we minister to those who are struggling with emotional extremes, we who claim to be the children of God's grace need to follow Christ's example. There is a time to lovingly call for obedience to Christ. There is a time to lovingly impart truth. There is a time to care for physical and family needs. There is also a time to share God's grace by sharing the fellowship we have with God in Christ, through corporate worship, through time in the Word, through songs of praise, and especially through prayer with those who are too ensnared by the bondage of sin to do any of these things on their own. This is what Jesus did for Peter. He carried Peter in grace even as He does us. He shared His life with Peter, and then sacrificed it for Peter's sins.

The problem, however, was that for much of Jesus' earthly ministry, Peter felt he didn't need grace. That Peter loved Christ deeply is without question. There was nothing that Peter was not willing to do for Jesus, but he was determined to prove it in his own way. Peter possessed a mentality common to many Christian men, one that plays a significant role in patterns of emotional extremes. Peter was determined to prove his own self-worth. He possessed an abundance of what the Bible refers to as confidence in the flesh. As such, he had little time for grace. This, in many ways, accounts for Peter's poor impulse control as well as his moments of personal despair and "low self-esteem."

With the best of intentions, Peter was determined to succeed at doing what was right. Always confident in his ability to make things right, he persistently attempted to set things straight as he saw fit, whether it be rebuking Jesus for promising the cross, refusing to let Jesus wash his feet, or cutting off someone's ear to defend Jesus. So often Peter was determined to be a man's man. Grace was for wimps who couldn't succeed on their own. Inevitably, Peter, like all of us who have travelled this path, crashed and burned miserably, experiencing the discouragement and despair of repeatedly and pathetically failing to meet his own personal expectations, especially that of proving his self-worth in the eyes of his Master. Such was the case when Peter denied Jesus—not once, but three times—within twenty-four hours of confidently declaring that he would defend Jesus to the point of laying down his own life for Him.

Yet Christ, no matter how miserable or pathetic Peter's failure, never stopped loving His disciple. That's because Christ's love for Peter was never based on Peter's performance. It was based on the love of the Father and the grace of the cross. This was a truth Peter desperately needed to receive. One of the most surprising gifts of love that Jesus would ever give to Peter was the sovereign opportunity to sink painfully and fail miserably under his own efforts. By allowing Peter to shoot himself in the foot, Jesus allowed Peter to see the reality of his own pathetic inadequacy, his lack of faith in Christ, and his desperate need for grace.

As humbling and painful as this path was, it was the necessary preparation for the grace of the cross. Peter was learning, under Jesus' loving oversight, the invaluable lesson of the cross, that the best we have to offer is simply not sufficient to follow Christ and to please God. The harder we try, the worse we make things. We need a Savior. We need a substitute. We need atonement and forgiveness for trusting ourselves rather than Christ. We need grace— a grace that can only come from the cross—to deliver us from our miserable offenses and failures. Without grace, no man can stand together with Christ. By the time Jesus looked at Peter after he had denied Jesus three times, Peter knew without a doubt that no man is good enough to serve Christ; no man is capable of saving himself.

Of those who struggle with persistent patterns of emotional extremes, many whom I have had the privilege of serving have endured lives of heartbreaking pain and suffering. For some, much of the pain and suffering was the consequence of personal sin. For others, it was initially the result of other people's sin. For many, it was a combination of both.

Many of these people find themselves wracked by guilt, unable to forgive themselves for what they have done or believe themselves responsible for. Others start out unwilling to forgive those who have hurt them and then eventually end up being unable to forgive at all. The longer they try, like Peter, to fix or control things on their own, the worse things get. As well, their emotional extremes become more intense and recurrent. Behavior patterns of withdrawal, lashing out, and alienation become normative. Feelings of anger, guilt, rage, anxiety, fear, grief, and sorrow, like forest fires, consume them, ultimately breaking them down both physically and spiritually.

At the end of the day, what is needed is not more self-esteem, better medication, or things to make us feel better about ourselves. What is so desperately needed is a heart that is ready to receive the forgiveness and grace that only Christ can give. Whatever painful path of failure and suffering gets us to that point of brokenness and poverty of spirit is indeed a divine gift of both love and grace. Are you ready to receive His grace?

Grace Received

After His crucifixion and resurrection, Jesus came to Peter where He had first found him, fishing on the Sea of Galilee. This time, however, Jesus found a different man from the brash, self-confident, fisherman eager to follow the Messiah and King. This time He found a man with no confidence in the flesh, very aware of his desperate need of a Savior. This time He found a broken man who was truly poor in spirit, ready to receive the forgiveness and grace of the cross, ready to inherit the kingdom of heaven. In Jesus Christ, the risen Savior and Lord, Peter finally found what he so desperately needed—everything his discipleship, including his emotional ups and downs, his miserable failures, and the sorrow of sin had been preparing him for. Though the words between them on that beach were few, what passed between them was monumental. "Do you love me?...Feed my sheep." Grace prepared, grace given, and grace received.

Peter's first epistle would suggest to us that the apostle ended his life with a markedly transformed heart, a sober-minded, self-controlled, vigilant heart overflowing with love, hope, and joy inexpressible—all in the face of horrific personal suffering and abuse. The love, truth, and grace of Christ, given and received, produced incredible fruit in Peter's life. God would use Peter to accomplish great things for His glory, including the founding of His church at Pentecost. The lessons of the cross he received by way of his own personal brokenness would become foundational for the early church, encouraging and inspiring suffering saints to set their hope fully on the grace of Christ in the face of brutal persecution while not giving in to the passions of their former lives. As a result, the world would never be the same.

In the end, Peter, the disciple who once shunned the cross, would literally embrace it. His life stands, from beginning to end, as an inspired testimony to the hope of the cross and the unceasing love of Jesus Christ, his Lord and

Savior. It is a tribute to the One who does more than just "handle" the emotional extremes of His saints. He redeems them for His glory, by the unceasing love, truth, and grace of His cross that transforms broken sinners into songs of divine praise.

Are you ready to receive what He has already given?

Recommended Resources

Fitzpatrick, Elyse, and Laura Hendrickson, MD. *Will Medicine Stop the Pain? Finding God's Healing for Depression, Anxiety, and Other Troubling Emotions.* Chicago: Moody Publishers, 2006.

MacArthur, John. *Twelve Ordinary Men: How the Master Shaped His Disciples and What He Wants to Do with You.* Nashville: Thomas Nelson, 2002.

———. *Anxious for Nothing: God's Cure for the Cares of Your Soul.* Colorado Springs, CO: David C. Cook, 2006.

Mack, Wayne. *Anger & Stress Management God's Way.* Greenville, SC: Calvary Press, 2004.

Welch, Edward T. *Addictions, a Banquet in the Grave: Finding Hope in the Power of the Gospel.* Phillipsburg, NJ: P&R Publishing, 2001.

Living with Severe Physical Affliction

Jeff Lair

It was a challenging, increasingly painful season of my life. At age twelve, I began to experience arthritic-type pain in my hips. Over the course of time, the pain in my hip joints increased while my mobility significantly decreased. Through orthopedic doctor visits, I was diagnosed with a rare degenerative genetic condition.

The first to be affected were my hip joints due to an irregularly formed ball-and-hip socket. Friction occurred when I walked and ran, resulting in an inflamed joint. Over the duration of ten trying years, from age twelve to age twenty-two, I visited numerous orthopedic doctors for answers to my worsening condition, with no success. But finally, a breakthrough occurred: An orthopedic doctor at Johns Hopkins Hospital confidently looked me in the eye and said, "Jeff, you are a candidate for hip replacements." Words cannot describe what this news meant to me.

In 1990, both of my hips were replaced. Due to a bicycle accident, a partial hip replacement occurred in 1994. In 2000 and 2001, both hips were replaced again due to wear and tear of the joints and femur bones. In 2008, I underwent four surgeries to replace bone-on-bone ankle arthritis. All in all, by the grace of God, I have had *nine* surgeries on my hips and ankles between 1990 and 2008. Currently, my day-to-day activity is fairly free of pain, but I still experience the arthritic deterioration of other joints in my body.

It goes without saying that physical affliction[1] can pose one of the most challenging trials for a Christian. In my experience, severe affliction impacts not only the body, but also one's emotional and spiritual well-being. The duration of physical suffering may last a week, months, years, and even end in death. Where do you turn for real encouragement when you face the reality that your pain, suffering, lack of mobility, and dependence on others has become the norm? When it comes to your physical hardship, how are you to think and live in a way that glorifies God—that is, how can you live in a *God-honoring* way that is *consistent with the character and gospel-centered will of Jesus Christ?*

If you have turned to this chapter for answers to these questions, I am thrilled you are here! My goal is to offer you practical, Bible-based counsel and encouragement that will help you recognize how to glorify God and love others *through* your physical affliction, not merely *in spite* of it. This is what God graciously allowed me to learn over time throughout the duration of my severe physical affliction.

The focus of every believer in Christ Jesus, regardless of the condition of their bodies, must be on *right thinking, right living,* and *right loving* of God and others according to God's Word. This focal point is intensified and sharpened when God allows acute physical pain and disability. The human tendency is to recoil from the affliction. However, the man who desires to "do all to the glory of God" (1 Corinthians 10:31) will persist in this trilogy of right thinking, living, and loving. However, a tension exists between what is right thinking and what is wrong thinking about physical affliction, and where there is wrong thinking, there is a need for change.

Wrong Thinking About God

For what possible reasons would Christians have wrong thoughts about God in relationship to their physical affliction? First, we may not know enough about God's unchanging character, let alone rely on it. Second, we may lack an understanding about who God is. Third, we may have a low view rather than a high view of God. Fourth, we may have a low view of others.

Whatever the case might be, in order for us to live with a physical affliction in a way that glorifies God, wrong thinking—including a low view of God and a low value of others—*must* be addressed. Once wrong thinking is addressed, it is possible for us to identify and apply right thinking and right responses, and bring honor to the Lord in the midst of physical affliction.

There are many potential wrong thoughts we can have about God in relation to physical affliction, and why such affliction happens to you or me. We'll consider three of them here:

1. God Does Not Really Care

The belief behind this wrong thought is that if God cared, He would not send suffering. We conclude those who are loved or loved more do not suffer or should not suffer as much. In addition, it is easy to think that God is "out to get us" or that our suffering is a result of some specific sin in our life. However, even if physical suffering *is* the result of some sin, it does not change (malign) God's love for you.

2. God Has Not Allowed This for My Good

It's easy to come to this conclusion when physical affliction limits our mobility, reduces our physical strength, does not allow us to do the things we like to do, causes us to be dependent on others, and causes unnecessary disruptions in our life. How can any good come from diabetes, cancer, multiple sclerosis, or chronic pain? Yet, such a self-focused perspective ignores the tremendous value of how our *responses* to physical suffering can be a blessing and encouragement to others. As they see that the source of our strength is God and that He uses suffering for our good, others might be encouraged to turn to Him, too.

3. God's Will Always Involves Physical Healing

This view is frequently based on references in both the Old and New Testaments that show God, Jesus, and the disciples healing the sick (e.g., Genesis 20:17; Psalm 103:3; Matthew 4:23; 10:1). If healing happened in the Bible, then why doesn't it happen today, and why doesn't it happen to me? Sadly, this view misses the point that there are many instances in Scripture when people were not healed. For example, the apostle Paul, who begged three times for God to remove his thorn in the flesh, was *not* healed (2 Corinthians 12:7-10). Ultimately, God is more interested in growing us in righteousness for His glory than He is in healing us.

If you have wrong thoughts about physical affliction, you will also have a low view of God. While you may not think that is the case, anytime you fail to fully believe all that God has said concerning Himself and His promises, you have a low view of Him. This necessarily affects how you think about your affliction. Why is this? Because it is impossible to understand the purpose of physical affliction apart from the One who controls all things. An unbeliever or someone who has a low view of God will not—in fact, *cannot*—trust in God's sovereign control. The fact of God's sovereignty means that all things that come to pass are permitted by Him, and He is in complete control of what happens. "Who has spoken and it came to pass, unless the Lord has commanded it?" (Lamentations 3:37). A worldly perspective assumes that God is weak and unable to stop or eliminate physical affliction, or that God is unloving, uncaring, or simply unwilling to help.

What happens when we have a low view of God, or when we do not trust that God is good, loving, and in control of all things? The result is that we end up questioning why God, *who is always good*, allows chronic pain or a terminal illness into our lives. The Bible says, "You [God] are good and do good" (Psalm 119:68). We do not know, or perhaps we forget, that God is trustworthy and reliable. "Those who know your name put their trust in you, for you, O LORD, have not forsaken those who seek you" (Psalm 9:10). We miss the blessing of walking in obedience to God and all that He has for us. "I am sure of this, that he who began a good work in you will bring it to completion at the day of Jesus Christ" (Philippians 1:6).

Ultimately, a low view of God results in an unbiblical perspective about God's character and purposes and destroys any confidence we might have to trust in His perfect plan. This, in turn, leads to despair and hopelessness.

Right Thinking About God

To understand and know the character of God is essential for right thinking about Him. This cannot be overemphasized! J.I. Packer writes, "It [knowing God] is the most practical project anyone can engage in. Knowing about God is crucially important for living our lives."[2] Packer continues, "Disregard the study of God, and you sentence yourself to stumble and blunder through this life blindfolded, as it were, with no sense of direction and no understanding of what surrounds you."[3]

Because physical affliction can challenge your faith and reveal your heart more than any other experience, knowing and trusting in God are critical to your faith. Do you respond to suffering by honoring the Lord, or do you complain, become bitter, and have a pity party? If the answer is the latter, then you have likely lost sight of God's sovereignty, or His complete control over all things, and other vitally important attributes such as His love, goodness, faithfulness, and wisdom. By contrast, when you have a right knowledge of God regarding His character, His attributes, and His promises, you'll be mindful of the many evidences that you can indeed trust Him. If you do not truly know and trust God's character, you cannot have the hope, peace, and joy that flow from knowing and applying His will for your life despite your circumstances.

We are to "count it all joy...when you meet trials of various kinds" (James 1:2). It is not simply *going* through trials that matters, but *how* you go through them that determines whether you bring glory to God. God is not only concerned about the end goal, but also the *process*. Do you believe God is at work in and through you, even during the most difficult and trying times? He is. Knowing God and trusting in Him as the lover of your soul—as well as the controller of all things, including the trials and suffering you face—is a major key to a satisfying and joyful life in the midst of physical suffering.

As you see your physical affliction through the lens of God's Word and His unchanging character, "you see Christ in your problem," Dr. Jay Adams writes.[4] He says the following will occur:

> This viewpoint will determine your fundamental stance toward trouble, which, in turn, will affect your attitudes and all of your actions. When hard times come and persist, and you feel as though you were chained to a problem, unable to move, you will know that your chains are the bonds of Christ. Every believer who ever achieved anything for Him suffered—and took this viewpoint toward trouble (see Genesis 50:20; Hebrews 11:24-26,35). If you want to serve Christ well in trouble, you too must have the same viewpoint; there is no other way to do so.[5]

Knowing God's characteristics is essential for our growth as Christians. Let's look at two of His attributes—His sovereignty and His love—and see how they help us to grow in godliness and glorify Him as we joyfully respond to physical affliction.

God's Sovereignty

God is sovereign over all things—that is, He is in complete control. What a promise to rely on and trust in, especially when suffering physical affliction! If God were not sovereign, He would not be God, nor could He be trusted even through the most difficult trials. Jeremiah the prophet wrote, "Who has spoken and it came to pass, unless the Lord has commanded it? Is it not from the mouth of the Most High that good and bad come?" (Lamentations 3:37-38). To know that God is sovereign is to look at both sides of a coin. On the one side of the coin, you must know God. On the other side of the coin, you must know that God knows you. Contemplating both truths—the knowledge of who He is and that He knows who you are—allows you to confidently rest in His care. You will be able to say with Job (the same Job who suffered severe physical affliction, and in one day lost ten children and his complete economic livelihood of thousands of sheep and hundreds of camels and oxen), "Shall we receive good from God, and shall we not receive evil?" (Job 2:10).

The first side of the coin, knowing God, means that we believe He is in control and at work in our lives for our good and His glory. "We know that for those who love God all things work together for good, for those who are called according to his purpose" (Romans 8:28). God works *all things* for our good. This is an encouraging truth to rest in and rely on through the seasons when we cannot see God at work. Sometimes we may not know why something happens in our life. We cannot always know God's ways because His ways are not like ours (Isaiah 55:8-9). Nevertheless, we must still walk by faith and trust Him (Hebrews 11:6).

God is in control of every event and circumstance that takes place in our lives. "I make known the end from the beginning, from ancient times, what is still to come. I say: My purpose will stand, and I will do all that I please" (Isaiah 46:10 NIV). Because God is in control of every event in our lives, we must "give thanks in all circumstances; for this is the will of God in Christ Jesus for you" (1 Thessalonians 5:18).

You may be asking, "Am I to give thanks for my cancer, diabetes, or pain that keeps me up at night, along with a laundry list of all the unpleasant circumstances that result from my physical affliction?" The answer is yes. The Lord commands us to be thankful in *all* things. We are never promised that the Christian life will be one of ease and comfort. Trials and difficulties will come to God's people, and God promises to be with us at all times and to strengthen us (Psalms 18, 46, 91, 121).

From the grand scheme of God's great design of His creation to daily circumstances in life, God is in control for the good of His children. It is essential for us to not only know these truths, but to believe them with all of our heart.

> Behold, the eye of the LORD is on those who fear him, on those who hope [trust] in his steadfast love, that he may deliver their soul from death and keep them alive in famine. Our soul waits for the LORD; he is our help and our shield. For our heart is glad in him, because we *trust* in his holy name. Let your steadfast love, O LORD, be upon us, even as we hope [trust] in you (Psalm 33:18-22).

Jerry Bridges writes, "If we are to trust God, we must learn to see that He is continuously at work in every aspect and every moment of our lives."[6] Knowing God is in control is vital for right thinking about God in our relationship with Him so that we might stand firm in the faith and glorify His name through physical affliction.

So, *knowing God*—or understanding that He is in control—is one side of the coin. The flip side of the coin is to understand that *God knows you*. He is intimately acquainted with each Christian as His own child. This intimate relationship can be likened to that of a shepherd who knows his sheep (Psalm 100:3). God knows everything about His children—what we do, what we think, where we go, and what we say (Psalm 139:1-4). He knows that we are physically frail (Psalm 103:14). He knows our prayers before we say them (Matthew 6:8). He knows our hearts (Jeremiah 17:9-10). J.I. Packer succinctly summarizes this great reality that God knows His children, saying, "What matters supremely...is not, in the last analysis, the fact that I know God, but the larger fact that underlies it—the fact that He knows me. I am graven on the palms of His hands. I am never out of His mind."[7]

Knowing that God knows us is a great comfort, encouragement, and strength. We can receive comfort from knowing that He daily bears our burdens and disappointments, and lovingly exhorts us to cast our cares upon Him (Psalm 68:19; 1 Peter 5:6-7). As Paul said, God "did not spare his own Son but gave him up for us all." That being the case, "how will he not also with him graciously give us all things?" (Romans 8:32).

We can be strengthened to keep pressing on, knowing that His grace is sufficient to sustain us even in our weaknesses. As God said to Paul, "My grace is sufficient for you, for my power is made perfect in weakness." How did Paul respond? "Therefore I will boast all the more gladly of my weaknesses, so that the power of Christ may rest upon me" (2 Corinthians 12:9).

Knowing that God is in complete control of your life is foundational to right thinking when going through physical affliction. He is trustworthy, and He can be relied on without reservation.

God's Love

The Bible also tells us that "God is love" (1 John 4:8,16). This is another attribute of God we must know and rely on. It is inherent to who God is and must be remembered when living through physical suffering. "In this is love, not that we have loved God but that he loved us and sent his Son to be the propitiation for our sins" (1 John 4:10). The God of creation and Ruler of the universe loves us. And His love is not dependent on *what you do* or *do not do*. This is clear from 1 John 4:10—we did not love God; He loved us first (see verse 19). Because His love is not dependent in any way upon us, it is an ever-abiding truth that God's love is sure for all eternity and can be trusted.

Let us now turn our attention to four important characteristics of the love of God—specifically, that His love is active, everlasting, consistent, and that nothing can separate us from it.

His Love Is Active

One key aspect of God's love is that it is active, not passive. God gave His one and only Son to die on the cross for our sins. In ancient times, crucifixion was a death reserved only for the worst of criminals. The suffering we face is nothing compared to the tremendous suffering Jesus endured. Jerry Bridges writes, "If we want proof of God's love for us, then we must look first at the cross where God offered up His Son as a sacrifice for our sins. Calvary is the one objective, absolute, irrefutable proof of God's love for us."[8]

His Love Is Everlasting

God's love is not only active; it is everlasting. The psalmist knew this when he wrote twenty-six times in succession, "His steadfast love endures forever"

(Psalm 136). No matter what we face in physical affliction, we can rest in the fact that God is eternal and so is His love. A.W. Pink wrote, "How tranquilizing for the heart: since God's love toward me had no beginning, it can have no ending! Since it is true that 'from everlasting to everlasting' He is God, and since God is 'love,' then it is equally true that 'from everlasting to everlasting' He loves His people."[9]

His Love Is Consistent

God's active love for us would be enough through His Son's death on the cross (Romans 5:8), but consider this: *Every day* He shows His love for us. The prophet Jeremiah called this to mind, and so should we: "This I call to mind, and therefore I have hope: The steadfast love of the LORD never ceases; his mercies never come to an end; they are new every morning; great is your faithfulness" (Lamentations 3:21-23). It is through *His great love* that hope is a daily reality amid suffering physically. This hope rests with confident expectation that God is true to the promises of His Word and is faithful.

Nothing Can Separate Us from His Love

Through the most difficult, painful, and discouraging times we will ever face in physical affliction, this is a promise from God's Word that *we must believe*. Nothing, absolutely *nothing*, can separate us from the love of God! "I am sure that neither death nor life, nor angels nor rulers, nor things present nor things to come, nor powers, nor height nor depth, nor anything else in all creation, will be able to separate us from the love of God in Christ Jesus our Lord" (Romans 8:38-39). The apostle Paul experientially knew that nothing could separate him from God's love. We, too, can rest in this promise as we know God's great love.

The active, eternal, consistent, and inseparable love of God are promises to take to heart, rely on, and remember. God's awesome love was actively demonstrated through Christ's death on the cross (Romans 5:8). He thought rightly, submitting His life to His heavenly Father in the midst of His suffering, and so must we (1 Peter 2:23).

Renewing your mind on the promises of God's Word (Romans 12:2) is essential for right thinking about God and the physical affliction you live with. Through consistently renewing your mind on the Scriptures, you gain right thinking about God and right thinking for why God has allowed physical suffering into your life.

Next, it is important to know how God commands us *to live* with physical affliction for His glory.

Right Living: Love God and Love Others

Given that the chief end of man is to glorify God and enjoy Him forever (John 17:3,21-23; 1 Corinthians 10:31), we can rightly conclude that a major purpose for physical affliction in our lives is for God's glory (John 9:3). There are many ways we can glorify God. Let us look specifically at glorifying God by *loving Him* and *loving others*.

Jesus Christ is our example to know and model in the midst of our own physical suffering. It was the *love* of His Father that motivated Christ in His thinking and His responses (John 14:31), including His perseverance in the midst of great physical suffering and in His bearing the wrath of His Father for the sins of the world. It was this same love that compelled Him to humble Himself by becoming obedient to the point of death—even death on a cross (Philippians 2:3-8). It is why Christ—even though He asked that another way might be possible to love and glorify the Father—was able to head toward His death with a heart of love, saying, "My Father, if it be possible, let this cup pass from me; nevertheless, not as I will, but as you will" (Matthew 26:39).

Jesus not only continually loved God the Father with all His being amidst His suffering, He also humbly loved His disciples to the point of suffering and dying for them. "This is my commandment, that you love one another as I have loved you. Greater love has no one than this, that *someone lay down his life for his friends*" (John 15:12-13). Every Christian can proclaim with Paul that "the Son of God...loved me and *gave himself* for me" (Galatians 2:20; see also Ephesians 5:25).

By now you may recognize that Jesus' sacrificial love of God and people was simply the outworking of the two biblical commandments that Jesus authoritatively stated were the greatest:

> He said to them, "You shall love the Lord your God with all your
> heart and with all your soul and with all your mind. This is the great

and first commandment. And a second is like it: You shall love your neighbor as yourself. On these two commandments depend all the Law and the Prophets" (Matthew 22:37-40).

Jesus truly came to fulfill the Law and the Prophets (Matthew 5:17), including the two greatest commandments, in the fullest sense. This means He was there to bring about both the salvation of sinners and the eventual fulfillment of the prophecies concerning God's judgment upon mankind (Matthew 22:37-40; see also Amos 8:1-10; Luke 23:41-46). Where Adam failed, Jesus prevailed (Romans 5:12-21).

Despite expectations to the contrary, God's people were forewarned that the true Messiah's appearance would be marred beyond human resemblance (Isaiah 52:14); that He would be wounded for their transgressions and crushed for their iniquities; that He would bear chastisement that would bring peace; that healing would come by means of suffering (His "stripes") (Isaiah 53:5). This Messiah, God's supreme suffering Servant, was to make many to be accounted righteous, and He has done so by way of the cross (Isaiah 53:11; Romans 5:19).

Subsequently, as believers in Jesus Christ, we are to "walk in the same way in which he walked" (1 John 2:6). That means we ought to continually reflect the character of Christ in all that we say and do out of our love for Him and the spread of His gospel (Matthew 28:18-20; John 14:15). Jesus made it clear that a "great" disciple is one who humbly strives to be the greatest servant of all (Mark 10:42-45).

I am therefore convinced that it is essential for those of us who live with physical affliction to know and constantly live out the two greatest commandments. Why? Because your love for God is a direct reflection of how well you know Him and think about Him. That is why it is important to have a right view of God and think rightly about God. As you understand God's immeasurable love for you and as you grow in that love, you demonstrate the love relationship you have with God by your love for Him and your obedience to His Word.

Loving God

Loving God means to love Him selflessly with your entire being. There is no reservation in expressing your love to God. It is to be done with *all* of your affections, thoughts, and pursuits focused on glorifying God. Jesus said, "If you love me, you will keep my commandments" (John 14:15). It is through your *love* for God that you live to obey His Word. Practically speaking, you will endeavor to have a thankful heart for His goodness and grace to sustain you, rather than have a complaining spirit (2 Corinthians 12:9-10; Philippians 2:14-15). You can rejoice in the midst of your trial as God uses it to grow your faith and mature you in Christ (James 1:2-3).

Loving Others

In addition, loving your neighbor is a direct result of loving God. It is because of God's love for you that you have the ability to love others. And it is because of your love and gratitude toward God that you desire to love others. As you live with a physical affliction, you have the great privilege of showing God's love through serving others. When the apostle Peter wrote his first epistle, he was writing to believers who were encountering severe persecution for being Christians. His letter was intended to encourage them and to instruct them as to how they should respond to the relentless oppression. He admonished his fellow believers to love one another—even in the midst of great suffering: "Finally, all of you, have unity of mind, sympathy, brotherly love, a tender heart, and a humble mind. Do not repay evil for evil or reviling for reviling, but on the contrary, bless, for to this you were called, that you may obtain a blessing" (1 Peter 3:8-9).

Let God Work Through Your Afflictions

No matter how physically impaired you may be, there are opportunities to serve others. For example, you could write notes of encouragement to missionaries, your pastor, or to others who need to be encouraged. You can pray regularly for others—this is a significant way in which to further the work of the gospel (Colossians 4:2). Furthermore, when you recognize it, a tremendous testimony of God's grace has been woven through your life that you could share with others to encourage them. The apostle Paul, who was familiar with much suffering, wrote, "Blessed be the God and Father of our Lord Jesus Christ, the Father of mercies and God of all comfort, who comforts us in all our affliction, so that we may be able to comfort those who are in any affliction, with the comfort with which we ourselves are comforted by God" (2 Corinthians 1:3-4).

Think about all God has graciously taught you through your physical affliction. You can share these lessons with others. What's more, God may have used your affliction to open doors for you to share the good news of the gospel with many different people. He may have brought into your life doctors, nurses, medical staff, caregivers, or strangers who ask, "What happened to you?" This, of course, allows you to share what God has done in your life, and lets you proclaim Jesus to a lost and dying people. The apostle Paul saw God at work in his circumstances, even while in prison, and affirmed that "what has happened to me has really served to advance the gospel" (Philippians 1:12). In our affliction, we need to be mindful that God wants to work through us, and have the same response as Paul.

Believer in Christ, you have a sure way to live with a physical affliction *to the glory of God* in accord with His Word! It comes through recognizing when your thoughts are incorrect and by renewing your mind according to the character of God and what is true based on His written Word (Romans 12:1-2; Philippians 4:8-9). Through renewing your mind on right thinking, you can live a life that glorifies God through serving others and not your own selfish desires (Philippians 2:1-4). God's grace is abundantly sufficient to enable you to do this! Yes, God's grace is abundantly sufficient to enable you to show the love of Christ through the proclamation of the gospel—even *through* your physical affliction—to those who are without hope and in need of the Savior, Jesus Christ.

Recommended Resources

Adams, Jay E. *The Biblical View of Self-Esteem, Self-Love, and Self-Image.* Eugene, OR: Harvest House, 1986.

———. *Christ and Your Problems.* Phillipsburg, NJ: P&R Publishing, 1971.

Bridges, Jerry. *The Joy of Fearing God.* Colorado Springs, CO: Waterbrook Press, 2000.

———. *The Practice of Godliness.* Colorado Springs, CO: NavPress, 1996.

———. *Trusting God.* Colorado Springs, CO: NavPress, 1988.

Harris, Greg. *The Cup and the Glory*. The Woodlands, TX: Kress Christian Publications, 2006.

Lloyd-Jones, D. Martyn. *Spiritual Depression: Its Causes and Cure*. Grand Rapids, MI: William B. Eerdmans, 1965.

Mack, Wayne A., and Deborah Howard. *It's Not Fair! Finding Hope When Times Are Tough*. Phillipsburg, NJ: P&R Publishing, 2008.

Piper, John, and Justin Taylor. *Suffering and the Sovereignty of God*. Wheaton, IL: Crossway, 2006.

Tozer, A.W. *The Knowledge of the Holy*. New York, NY: HarperCollins Publishers, 1978.

Welch, Edward T. *When People Are Big and God Is Small*. Greensboro, NC: New Growth Press, 1997.

10

Contentment for Men

Dwight D. Ham

We live in a culture that puts a high value on being happy and having the kind of success that is expected to be the perfect picture of contentment. The assumption of many people is that those who have attained worldly success and are achieving their goals in life are fulfilled and therefore happy, which presupposes they are also content. In fact, the idea of experiencing happiness is so embedded in our culture that we have Happy Meals, happy hour, and we are cautioned, "Don't worry, be happy!" The Walt Disney Company's vision statement at one time was "to make people happy," and while you are in their parks, you are told you are in "the happiest place on earth."

This happiness imperative carries over into our lives both in business and in the home. Men are expected to be the perfect employee, the most prosperous business owner, the most successful investor, the top student, the finest athlete, the greatest dad, the providing husband, the spiritual leader, the best handyman, the creative problem solver who fixes anything and everything, and the list goes on. And a man's arrival at one or more of these lofty goals is supposed to epitomize happiness and success—and therefore, contentment.

But are such achievements and the attainment of lofty goals the pathway to contentment? If this were true, it would then be possible to measure contentment by looking merely at the outward achievements of man.

I can honestly say that at times I have been sucked into this abyss of thinking that somehow I would be happier and therefore more content if I had some outward achievement or position of influence that would "make life more fulfilling." Yet that's merely a human perspective, and it would mean that happiness and contentment are based on our circumstances. But no matter how fulfilling something looks based on its outward appearance, ultimately, our circumstances can never bring real contentment, no matter how ideal they might seem.

That is why we should be encouraged by the words of the apostle Paul, who stated that he *learned* to be content no matter what his circumstances: "Not that I am speaking of being in need, for I have learned in whatever situation I am to be content" (Philippians 4:11). In other words, he could know contentment even in the worst situations—his contentment wasn't based on what was happening around him.

The Bible makes it clear being content is something that must be *learned* while living in obedience to Jesus Christ each day in the midst of our circumstances whether we are happy or sad, whether or not we have attained "success" in life.

In Search of Being Content

The search for contentment is not new. Man has been in pursuit of this elusive quality since the beginning of time. In fact, the first two people on earth were not content to live in the garden God had prepared for them, where it certainly could be said that "they had it all." They had ample food, no weeds to pull, no diseases to fight, and no severe weather patterns or natural disasters like earthquakes. They were in perfect health, and didn't have to worry about security because that was already provided for in an intimate relationship with the all-powerful God of the universe

"Wow," you say, "I want that!" Well, that is what it was like for Adam and Eve. But they were not content. Instead, they had a desire to be like God, to be independent of God, to know as much as God did about good and evil—all of which resulted in their being deceived by Satan. Through their disobedience, sin was introduced into the world (Genesis 2:17; 3:1-6).

Adam and Eve thought they would find contentment in their independence from God. Instead, they found they were discontent. And they became fearful as well, for they recognized that they were naked and without protection (Genesis 3:7).

Very little has changed since then. Man today continues to search for contentment, and he still cannot find it, even in our fast-paced, technologically advanced world. Like Adam and Eve, people today are looking everywhere for that fleeting treasure—except to God. This age of consumerism, with its mass marketing of materialistic values and possessions, deceptively convinces man that contentment is found through having things such as popularity, success, position and power, status, the ability to go places and see the world, wealth, beautiful homes, expensive automobiles, independence, freedom, unbridled sexual encounters, relationships, self-awareness, and self-esteem. Creature comforts are sought instead of the Creator Himself, who made all things for man to enjoy.

What's more, contentment cannot be measured—not in the same way you determine the value of your investment portfolio or your personal net worth. Rather, it is left to the individual to determine the degree of contentment, joy, and peace he is experiencing in his life. Yet there is nothing in life that brings true satisfaction except for Jesus Christ. All other means of fulfilling the desires and lusts of the heart bring man to the point of self-pride and a false sense of accomplishment, and do not bring true contentment. Contentment is not found in the endless pursuit of happy experiences or anything that we do that is perceived to have some measure of success. Even getting a hold of "enough religion" to feel good about oneself does not bring contentment.

With the ever-increasing standard of living that is enjoyed in America and Western Europe—a standard far exceeding that known by any generation that has lived before—today's societies are producing more citizens than ever who are unhappy and overwhelmed by feelings of depression.[1] More than anything else, people are striving to be satisfied—satisfied with their lives, surroundings, relationships, income, status, reputation, skill level, physical appearance, or meaning and purpose for living. And yet they are failing. They are having trouble realizing satisfaction, even when they attain all their dreams and expectations.

The person who ventures to find satisfaction and contentment through what the world offers and not through a living relationship with God through Jesus Christ will not understand what true contentment is. To many this may appear to be an extraordinary claim, but when we understand that God created man in His own image and for the purpose of glorifying Himself (Isaiah 43:7), then we'll realize that only God can give us the contentment we so greatly desire.

The Biblical Meaning of *Contentment*

The Hebrew word translated "contentment" in the Old Testament means "fullness, abundance, and sufficiency."[2] This word often refers to God when the Lord calls himself *El Shaddai*—that is, the God who possesses everything and who is able to bring forth everything out of His fullness, "the Almighty One." In the New Testament, the Greek term translated "contentment" brings two thoughts together—"self" and "being sufficient." The term speaks of having sufficiency for ourselves or with ourselves. We can only be content when we have enough, and we have enough when we no longer desire anything more. Contentment, therefore, involves self-sufficiency or having enough, whether with much or with little. It doesn't have anything to do with having a large quantity of things, but with the fulfillment of desire.[3] Pure contentment has to do with God bringing forth all that we need to be satisfied with in life.

Furthermore, biblical contentment is an attitude that involves the whole person. The *intellect*, the *emotions*, and the *will* are all working together to bring about contentment. For example, the *intellectual* element turns to Scripture and searches out the promises of God and His beneficial care and sovereignty over all areas of life, understanding that God is in control in the worst of situations as well as in the best (Ecclesiastes 7:14). The *emotional* element involves an overwhelming sense of joy and graciousness in living, coupled with a heart that is calm and peaceful, independent of circumstances. The element of the *will* involves a conscious and intentional change of direction in life, turning from living for selfish purposes and "me-theism" (the worship of self, where all of life centers upon our own selfish interests, desires, and wants) to loving and trusting God in each circumstance of life.

Some people think that being content is the same as passivity—that is, not pursuing goals. Others think it's the same as asceticism—denying oneself the creature comforts of the modern world. Still others say it is achieved through mental gymnastics, whereby one determines to be content against all odds. These wrong assumptions completely miss the biblical truth about contentment, because they leave God out of the picture. Biblical contentment is being thoroughly satisfied with all that God has graciously provided.

What's more, it matters what we are content *with*. To be content with pride, rudeness, anger, an undisciplined life, poor relationships, broken promises, and irresponsibility is not God's idea of contentment. On the contrary, the

Christian must never be content to live in the flesh. Peter admonished early Christians, "As he who called you is holy, you also be holy in all your conduct, since it is written, 'You shall be holy, for I am holy'" (1 Peter 1:15-16). The apostle Paul said it this way,

> Those who live according to the flesh set their minds on the things of the flesh, but those who live according to the Spirit set their minds on the things of the Spirit. *For to set the mind on the flesh is death, but to set the mind on the Spirit is life and peace* (Romans 8:5-6).

Those Christians who turn away from the flesh will find peace—contentment—by living according to the Spirit of God. We are called *holy,* and a byproduct of holy living is contentment.

Perhaps you think that this attitude is beyond your ability to attain, so there's no hope for you. Yet even the godliest of men, the apostles and writers of Scripture, had much to learn. Paul may have learned to be content through the circumstances he encountered, yet he did not think of himself as being perfect or having achieved his goals (Philippians 3:12-14). He still had his struggles (see Romans 7:15-25). Just because a person lives contentedly in Jesus Christ does not mean his life is free of struggles, temptations, and difficulties, and that he does not need further maturing in his relationship with the Lord (James 1:2-4; 2 Corinthians 12:9-10). Even though Paul had learned contentment, he still pursued growing more and more like Jesus Christ. The fact he had learned contentment didn't mean he had arrived.

The Enemy of Contentment

Why is contentment so elusive? Why is it so hard to acquire this godly quality? The answer to this question can be found in the writings of Israel's third king, Solomon. He wrote the book of Ecclesiastes in part to reveal the heart of man, which strives to acquire the things of this world and yet is never satisfied. In the first two chapters, Solomon chronicled all of the ways in which he pursued what his heart desired. As we read this journal or memoir, we are blessed that he included mention of the futility of chasing after things, which he calls "vanity and a striving after wind" (Ecclesiastes 1:14). Here is how he described the human experience:

- "the eye is not satisfied with seeing" (1:8)
- "nor the ear filled with hearing" (1:8)
- "his eyes are never satisfied with riches" (4:8)
- "his appetite is not satisfied" (6:7)

It's obvious, both from Solomon's testimony and what we see around us today, that the things of this world—worldly pursuits—cannot satisfy the human heart. But men chase after these things regardless of that truth!

The more complete answer to this problem is found in the prohibition stated in the tenth commandment, in Exodus 20:17: "You shall not *covet* your neighbor's house; you shall not *covet* your neighbor's wife, or his male servant, or his female servant, or his ox, or his donkey, or anything that is your neighbor's." Here, covetousness refers primarily to an inordinate desire or to a desire for anything that is forbidden. It is a desire for that which belongs to another, lusting after that which is not yours, especially in the realm of material things. Covetousness frequently involves dishonest gain (Exodus 18:21), *the desire to have more than one possesses* (Luke 12:15), an intense love or lust for gain (Romans 1:29), greed (Luke 12:15 NASB), or an inordinate love of money (1 Timothy 6:10).[4] Coveting involves a man's inner being, including the thoughts, desires, imaginations, and lusts.[5]

What we're up against here is a covetous heart. We all know how the human heart works—the minute we are told we can't have something, that is the very thing we want and have to have! "The tenth commandment, rather than making us less covetous, actually stimulates 'every kind of covetous desire' (Romans 7:8). To say '*don't*' makes us aware of desire; it does not quench it. It takes the work of God's Spirit to redirect our passions and give us contentment in those things that God intends for us to have."[6]

This is exactly why Paul wrote to the Philippians that he had *learned* the joy of contentment in every situation. Paul's learning the mystery of being content was born out of having an understanding of his sin nature—his own inclination toward coveting. When he wrote to the church in Rome, Paul explained that just because the heart covets when it hears, the command *not to* does not mean the Law is sin to us. In fact, he affirms,

What shall we say then? Is the Law sin? May it never be! On the contrary, I would not have come to know sin except through the Law; for I would not have known about coveting if the Law had not said, "YOU SHALL NOT COVET." But sin, taking an opportunity through the commandment, produced in me coveting of every kind (Romans 7:7-8 NASB).

Paul was saying that if it were not for the Law giving him enlightenment, he would not have realized his internal struggle with sin. This is true of every believer. But because we have the Law, we are aware that we have hearts that crave for things they must not crave.

So what can we learn about fighting covetousness, a great enemy of contentment?

Let's be clear on this point: Desire alone is not wrong, nor is the ability to enjoy the good things of life sinful. Rather, covetousness is desire run amuck. The tenth commandment makes it obvious that it is wrong to desire those things that are not your own, such as another's home, your neighbor's wife, their gardeners and housekeepers, their car or deluxe camper, or anything that belongs to them (Exodus 20:17). However, it is completely acceptable to desire and take pleasure in your own house, wife, and possessions, since these are gifts from God. "Enjoy life with the woman whom you love all the days of your fleeting life which He has given to you under the sun; for this is your reward in life and in your toil in which you have labored under the sun" (Ecclesiastes 9:9 NASB). God has given the man who fears Him enjoyment with his wife for all his days as a reward for his toil. God also gives wealth for the righteous to enjoy.

Furthermore, as for every man to whom God has given riches and wealth, He has also empowered him to eat from them and to receive his reward and rejoice in his labor; this is the gift of God. For he will not often consider the years of his life, because God keeps him occupied with the gladness of his heart (Ecclesiastes 5:19-20 NASB).

Keep in mind that the enjoyment of God's good gifts is not for selfish purposes. Instead, we can enjoy them knowing that they are the fruits of living in obedience to the Lord and keeping Him first place in our hearts' desires.

When a good desire is left unchecked, it can easily be tainted by our coveting heart. Desire progresses to a need, an "I deserve it" attitude, and ends in "I must have it or else!" The lustful passion of a covetous heart is in a constant state of want and is never satisfied. Instead of receiving enjoyment from the Lord for the things it has, the covetous heart rushes to fulfill its own desires and evil passions with its own schemes and plans.

This, in turn, breeds even more discontentment because these passions can never be fully satisfied by things and possessions. This becomes fertile ground that Satan uses to tempt us—to ignite the inclinations of the heart so that we end up seeking satisfaction apart from God. That is why we must keep our desires in check. Otherwise, our hearts will deliberately mislead us and rationalize our wants and lustful desires. As the prophet Jeremiah observed, "The heart is deceitful above all things, and desperately sick; who can understand it?" (Jeremiah 17:9).

The Steps to Contentment

How was the apostle Paul able to deal with his sinful, covetous heart in such a way that he could declare that he was content in *every* situation?

The man who desires true godly contentment will do two things: First, he will repent of the sin of covetousness. As Paul described the struggle that believers have with indwelling sin, he cried out in desperation, "Wretched man that I am! Who will deliver me from this body of death?" (Romans 7:24-25). His answer is swift and sure: "Thanks be to God through Jesus Christ our Lord!"

Paul wrote Romans 1–6 to reveal the utter sinfulness of man and the complete redemption that is found for him in Christ. "While we were still weak, at the right time Christ died for the ungodly...God shows his love for us in that while we were still sinners, Christ died for us" (Romans 5:6,8). The sinful, coveting heart rightly deserves the wrath of God. But God has shown mercy, and "God's kindness is meant to lead you to repentance" (Romans 2:4). To repent means to turn; to repent in the biblical sense means to turn away from sin and to God in faith. In other words, a repentant sinner renounces sin (both in thought and action), leaves that way of life behind, and turns in faith to Christ to live for Him, and not for selfish desires. This is the first step toward contentment.

The second step to attaining true contentment is to develop a heart of gratitude for the great grace of God. His grace does more than just save us from punishment for our sin. It also enables us to live a life of godly contentment. "The grace of God has appeared, bringing salvation for all people, training us to renounce ungodliness and worldly passions, and to live self-controlled, upright, and godly lives in the present age" (Titus 2:11-12). This is where the real learning begins—or the training, if you will.

Training in Contentment

It takes serious training and focus to win the prize in an athletic competition. Whether running in a marathon, or competing in a swim meet or a gymnastics competition, the athlete will undergo many hours of endless and difficult training. He must train the muscles in his body to meet the demands of the event with regard to muscular strength and physical endurance. This training requires discipline and self-control—the athlete must engage in a consistent pattern of behavior that will favorably prepare him for the competition (2 Timothy 2:5). Bad habits have to be replaced with good habits, and lack of focus has to be replaced with concentration and single-mindedness. Training also requires learning the rules of the competition. If an athlete doesn't follow the defined rules, he can be disqualified from competing.

Training to compete in a sport, however, is not the same as just going out and "playing" the sport. A person who only plays a sport doesn't need to engage in a regimen of daily workouts, long hours of repetition in practice, and the specialized instruction that refines one's ability to perform exceptionally well. Those who merely play a sport may be curiosity seekers, weekend warriors, or individuals who simply want to stay fit—they're not serious athletes. What's more, the fullness of what a sport offers cannot be judged by the performance of those who merely play in it. Only the serious athlete who excels in a sport is able to demonstrate what is capable of being achieved in any given sport.

The Training

When Paul spoke of learning contentment and maturing in Christ, he was speaking of the serious athlete who is preparing to participate in competition. Many believers only attempt to "casually" learn contentment, and once

CONTENTMENT FOR MEN
Diagram #1

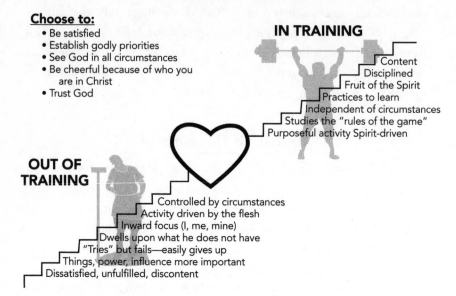

Choose to:
- Be satisfied
- Establish godly priorities
- See God in all circumstances
- Be cheerful because of who you are in Christ
- Trust God

IN TRAINING

Content
Disciplined
Fruit of the Spirit
Practices to learn
Independent of circumstances
Studies the "rules of the game"
Purposeful activity Spirit-driven

OUT OF TRAINING

Controlled by circumstances
Activity driven by the flesh
Inward focus (I, me, mine)
Dwells upon what he does not have
"Tries" but fails—easily gives up
Things, power, influence more important
Dissatisfied, unfulfilled, discontent

they realize this is going to require consistent practice, fervent discipline, constant hope, and a complete reliance upon God and understanding of biblical truth—as well as the possibility of failure—they shrug off taking part in the competition and decide instead to sit in the stands. They become spectators rather than participants because they already "tried it" and found it to be hard, or were met with failure. They were not willing to sustain the effort required to experientially and purposefully learn biblical contentment. "Trying something out" and then giving up becomes the enemy of learning, and contentment becomes elusive to these people. Always trying and forever attempting to learn, but never fully training in the manner that prepares them for the competition, they are unwilling to "go the distance" in learning biblical contentment.

As is true with any endeavor in the Christian life, change from sinful habits (the covetous pursuit of things) to godly habits (an attitude of contentment) requires a dual process. It requires the joint effort of the believer *and* the Spirit of God. This is confirmed by Paul in Philippians 2:12-13: "Work out your own salvation with fear and trembling, for it is God who works in you, both to will and to work for his good pleasure." It is clear: We work, and He works in us! Paul made the same point in Ephesians 2:10: "We are his workmanship [He works], created in Christ Jesus for good works [we work], which God prepared beforehand [He works], that we should walk in them [we work]." We have God's help as we make those choices in Diagram #1 to be satisfied, to establish godly priorities, to see God in all circumstances, to be cheerful, and to trust God.

Furthermore, the athlete who trains consistently and builds the necessary strength and endurance to perform the sport well is more free in the competition to perform at optimum potential than the athlete who did not show up for practice, kept a poor diet, allowed his muscles to weaken, and did not sufficiently learn the rules of the competition. So it is with learning contentment. The Christian who studies God's Word (2 Timothy 2:15), prays (Psalm 34:6), confesses sin (1 John 1:9), follows the example of those who are mature in their Christian experience (Philippians 4:9), thinks on those things that are good and perfect (Philippians 4:8), practices being holy by taking hold of his thought life (2 Corinthians 10:5), keeps check on his desires (Hebrews 13:5; 11:24-25), and sets godly priorities that are consistently practiced (Joshua 24:20-24) will learn to be content and is more free to be used of God by the power of the Holy Spirit residing within him. A heart that is full of godliness (Hebrews 10:19-25) will be motivated to do the work of learning how to be content because it pictures the life and example of Jesus Christ.

The Results

The process of being more like Christ, which results in contentment, involves growing in holiness by (1) putting off attitudes, thoughts, and actions that demonstrate a heart full of discontentment and covetousness, and (2) putting on Spirit-filled attributes such as love, joy, peace, patience, kindness, goodness, faithfulness, gentleness, and self-control (Galatians 5:22-23) that will build contentment. This unique scriptural process of *putting off* and *putting on* by the renewing of the mind (Ephesians 4:22-24) is an integral part of growing in Christ. In this process you learn to live not in the pattern of this world, but in God's transforming power. Your efforts in putting off the old self that is full of discontentment (grumbling, quarreling, anger, dissention, greed, covetousness, pride, selfishness, fault-finding, negativism, impatience,

regret, disappointment) and putting on the new self that is content with attitudes that are Christlike (Philippians 2:5) are energized by the transforming
power of the Holy Spirit in your inner being (Ephesians 3:16). This is what it
means to do all things through Christ's strength. The believer who overcomes
a covetous heart (Romans 7:7-8,24-25), finds contentment in his inner being,
where the Holy Spirit resides, as he throws off attitudes and behaviors that lead
to discontentment.

What was the circumstance and outcome of Paul's contentment? According
to 2 Corinthians 4:7-9, "We have this treasure in jars of clay to show that this
all-surpassing power is from God and not from us. We are hard pressed on every
side, but not crushed; perplexed, but not in despair; persecuted, but not abandoned; struck down, but not destroyed" (NIV). More specifically, it looks like this:

- hard pressed on every side—the pressure of Paul's situation
   – but not crushed—his contentment in that situation

- perplexed—the mental anguish of the trial
   – but not in despair—his Christ-centered hope in that trial

- persecuted—the trial of his faith
   – but not abandoned—knowing that Jesus promised to be
     with him always

- struck down—physically beaten
   – but not destroyed—not defeated spiritually because of
     God's strength working in him.[7]

When Paul referred to himself and his ministry partners as being "jars of
clay," he affirmed that the Master delights in using simple jars of clay, not beautiful urns or expensive china that are empty and fragile. We should be content
to be humbly used of God in every state, every circumstance, to carry out His
work by His all-surpassing power.

> Not that I am speaking of being in need, for I have learned in what-
> ever situation I am to be content. I know how to be brought low,
> and I know how to abound. In any and every circumstance, I have
> learned the secret of facing plenty and hunger, abundance and
> need. I can do all things through Him who strengthens me (Philip-
> pians 4:11-13).

Christians will encounter a variety of conditions while in this world. Some situations will produce great need, and others will provide plenty. In the midst of these conditions, Christians who know what it is to be in want or to have plenty will also know how to carry themselves in this varying state of affairs. And in this mixture of circumstances, God will show His people how to avoid the sins common to those who are in need or in prosperity, and enable them to be content in whatever circumstance they may find themselves.[8]

Joy and Learning Contentment

It's not surprising that the overriding theme of Paul's letter to the Philippians is joy. In the letter he called Christians to "rejoice in the Lord always" (4:4). Paul used such phrases as "make my joy complete" (2:2 NASB), "welcome him in the Lord with great joy" (2:29 NIV), "so you too should be glad and rejoice with me" (2:18 NIV), "I always pray with joy" (1:4 NIV), "I rejoiced greatly in the Lord" (4:10 NIV), and "Because of this I rejoice. Yes, and I will continue to rejoice" (1:18 NIV). Paul is known to be the theologian of joy because the word "joy" appears 326 times in the New Testament, and of those, 131 are found in the ten letters that are usually attributed to Paul.

Paul taught that joy was not just an emotion or a feeling, but a state of mind characterized by peace and an attitude that is focused outwardly beyond self-interest and the general circumstances of life. Joy in the Christian life is possible in spite of the ups and downs, the moments of elation or depression we experience from day to day. The Christian can experience joy regardless, because joy sees beyond the circumstances to the One who is sovereign and above all circumstances, Jesus Christ. Having God's joy is irrespective of events. It is a confident way of looking at life that is established by faith in Jesus Christ, who is in complete control of everything that happens, causing "all things to work together for good to those who love God, to those who are called according to His purpose" (Romans 8:28 NASB).

It is certainly fitting that the apostle Paul, who knew and expressed joy in his life, would proclaim to the Philippians that he had learned the secret of being content. Paul wrote to the church in Philippi while in chains (Philippians 1:7,13,17) in a Roman prison when he boldly professed, "I have learned to be content in whatever circumstances I am" (Philippians 4:11 NASB). The word translated "learned," as used in the original Greek text of this verse, means to learn something experientially that is beyond just intellectual knowledge. It refers to something that is actually being practiced in your life by appropriating that which is true. Paul *learned* contentment by consciously and deliberately *choosing* to be joyful through every conceivable and possible human circumstance and event.

Therefore, even though we can know contentment *independently* of circumstances, it must be proven and learned *in the midst* of circumstances. Those who are in Christ understand intellectually that they are to be content, but the experiential *learning* takes place in the midst of circumstances by making an effort to practice biblical contentment—which, in turn, brings fullness of joy.

CONTENTMENT FOR MEN
Diagram #2

Contentment

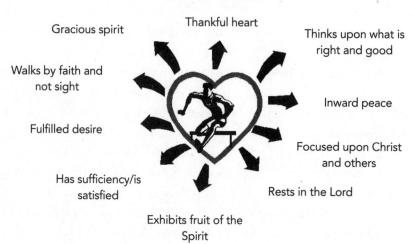

Gracious spirit

Thankful heart

Thinks upon what is right and good

Walks by faith and not sight

Inward peace

Fulfilled desire

Focused upon Christ and others

Has sufficiency/is satisfied

Rests in the Lord

Exhibits fruit of the Spirit

On this foundational basis, Paul can say that he has *learned* to be content in all circumstances. As he spiritually grew and matured in his faith in Christ— as he worked to discipline himself as an athlete who prepares for the competition—he *structured* his life to make those things a priority that were focused on Christ and others. Those who follow Jesus Christ can take encouragement from Paul's example. Part of learning to be content is learning obedience to God by looking to the sufficiency of Jesus Christ in all matters. Contentment by the world's standards is void of satisfaction, providing no ultimate and good eternal outcome. For us who are Christ followers, spiritual maturity is a result of the work of the Holy Spirit as we continue to walk by faith in putting off sin and putting on righteousness. And when we are content, we are showing evidence of a changed life, which brings honor and glory to the name of Jesus Christ and to God the Father in heaven.

CONTENTMENT FOR MEN
Diagram #3

The Wise Heart

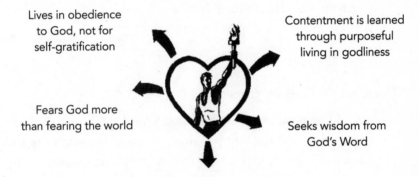

Lives in obedience to God, not for self-gratification

Contentment is learned through purposeful living in godliness

Fears God more than fearing the world

Seeks wisdom from God's Word

Circumstances are used by God instead of circumstances dictating personal satisfaction

A satisfying benefit of contentment is the discovery of godly wisdom, which we find described in James 3:17: "The wisdom from above is first pure, then peaceable, gentle, open to reason, full of mercy and good fruits, impartial and sincere" (James 3:17). The contented heart is a teachable heart, a heart that is satisfied by godly wisdom. Because this heart is no longer running after the empty pleasures of this world, and instead it seeks godly contentment, it will be, as James said, peaceable. It will be a wise a heart that lives in obedience to God, not for self-gratification; a heart that fears God more than it fears the world; a heart that does not allow circumstances to dictate its joy; a heart that seeks wisdom from God's Word; and a heart that knows that contentment is learned through purposeful, godly living.

The promise for a wise man who is content in the Lord and has a heart of peace is that he will bring a harvest of righteousness (James 3:18). That is, he will continually bear righteous fruit in his life. Just imagine what that harvest of righteousness will produce in your life—peace and contentment in your business dealings, your family, your relationship to your possessions, and the goals you set for your life. And as you exhibit this peace and contentment, you'll make it possible for others to see where true contentment can be found.

> To be content as a result of some external thing is like warming a man's clothes by the fire. But to be content through an inward disposition of the soul is like the warmth that a man's clothes have from the natural heat of his body.[9]
>
> —Jeremiah Burroughs

Questions for Personal Growth

1. Read Philippians 4:11-12. Write out what it means to be content in every circumstance. Can you think of any circumstances in which you would not be happy but could still find contentment?

2. Why do you think contentment involves the whole person—the intellect, the emotions, and the will? Why is contentment not just a feeling?

3. Why is contentment something to be mastered in the Christian life—and not just given as a gift by virtue of your life in Christ?

4. Read Proverbs 3:5. What does it mean to lean on your own understanding? Why are you told to trust the Lord with all your heart and not with something else? In what areas of your life do you need to trust the Lord more from your heart and less with your own understanding? How will this help you to be more content in your circumstances?

5. Do you think it is possible to have joy in your Christian life and *not* be content? Why or why not?

6. What does it mean to you to be a citizen of heaven (Philippians 3:19-21)? How does this relate to learning contentment? What are some ways you can remind yourself of your citizenship in heaven?

Recommended Resources

Burroughs, Jeremiah. *The Rare Jewel of Christian Contentment*. Carlisle, PA: The Banner of Truth Trust, 1998.

Fitzpatrick, Elyse. *Idols of the Heart: Learning to Long for God Alone*. Phillipsburg, NJ: P&R Publishing, 2001.

Lloyd-Jones, D. Martyn. *The Path to True Happiness*. Grand Rapids, MI: Baker Books, 1999.

Lundgaard, Kris. *The Enemy Within*. Phillipsburg, NJ: P&R Publishing, 1998.

Watson, Thomas. *The Art of Divine Contentment*. Morgan, PA: Soli Deo Gloria Publications, 1997. Reprinted from the 1835 edition published in London by the Religious Tract Society.

Part 3

A Man and His Relationships

How to Develop Biblical Relationships

S. Andrew Jin

It is no mystery that many people today struggle with interpersonal problems. Take a moment to consider all the people you come into contact with on a daily basis, and you will quickly recognize how common and pervasive these problems are. Just this week, you might have heard the complaints of a friend who recently fought with his wife because they both have different expectations of their relationship. Or perhaps you heard a coworker ridiculing your boss because of a personality flaw or a disagreement over how something should be done. Unfortunately, it is almost an everyday experience to encounter and hear about conflicts, insults, and misunderstandings.

Sadly, Christians are not immune to interpersonal problems. Many believers who profess to know God and His Word lack a biblical understanding of how to build good relationships with one another, and this is clearly evidenced by the many divided churches and broken Christian homes all around us. More and more, the health and condition of relationships between professing believers is becoming like the health and condition of relationships between unbelievers. And many times, the relationships between believers are in a worse state than those between their unbelieving counterparts.

The Plan

Thankfully, Christians do not have to approach interpersonal problems in the same way as those who do not know Christ. We have the inerrant, completely sufficient Word of God (cf. 2 Peter 1:3), which helps us to develop and maintain an accurate view of God, ourselves, and others, laying the groundwork for cultivating biblical relationships. More specifically, a study of the "one another" commands in Scripture can help us understand not only what biblical relationships are, but also how to nurture and cultivate them.

According to Stuart Scott, a personal relationship can be defined as "an interconnection with the persons to whom we have commitment or responsibility."[1] Applying this to Christians, we can define a personal relationship as *an interconnection or association one Christian has with another Christian*. In this chapter, we will see how *biblical* relationships can be cultivated by exercising the "one another" commands found in Scripture.

An Introduction

The Bible teaches that people were created to worship. The problem, however, is that those who have not experienced new life in Christ have a natural disposition to worship people and things—including self (Romans 1:25).

We who have regenerate hearts, however, know we are to worship God. How is this properly done? Jesus answered this question with two simple yet profound commands. These two commands reveal God's desire that believers have a right relationship with Him and with one another. These two commands also sum up for us the entirety of God's commandments, the fullness of His Law. We find them stated in Matthew 22:36-40:

> "Teacher, which is the great commandment in the Law?" And he said to him, "You shall love the Lord your God with all your heart and with all your soul and with all your mind. This is the great and first commandment. And a second is like it: You shall love your neighbor as yourself. On these two commandments depend all the Law and the Prophets."

Because the focus of this chapter is personal relationships, we want to concern ourselves with how to "love your neighbor as yourself." And it is the "one another" passages in the Bible that help us to understand, in practical terms, how God wants us to love our neighbor.

At the same time, it's important for us to realize that our relationship with God and our relationships with one another are intricately linked. As we love other believers by obeying the "one another" commands, we are in fact loving God (1 John 3:11,23; 4:7,11-12). In other words, as we practice the "one another" commands, we demonstrate our love of God through our love of others.

The rest of this chapter surveys a sampling of the "one another" commands in Scripture, which, properly understood and diligently applied, will equip you to build truly God-honoring relationships with other believers. For your reference, a complete list of the "one another" commands is presented in Appendix Four on pages 419-422.

The Commands

Prefer One Another

"Love one another with brotherly affection. Outdo one another in showing honor" (Romans 12:10).

Explanation

Paul issues the command to outdo or prefer one another shortly after he urges his readers to "present your bodies a living sacrifice, holy and acceptable to God, which is your spiritual worship" (Romans 12:1). The ideas are clearly connected. Your proper treatment of other believers in love is linked to having a proper love for and worship of God.

The specific command in the verse is to "outdo," which carries the sense of giving preference. "Honor" is merely the manner in which preference is to be given. Douglas Moo, in his commentary on the book of Romans, helps explain the application of the command. He writes, "Paul is then calling on Christians to outdo each other in bestowing honor on one another; for example, to recognize and praise one another's accomplishments and to defer to one another."[2] Preferring one another involves deferring or yielding to the other person. In obedience to this command, you must consider whether you are willing to yield your desires for the sake of your brother or sister whom you seek to love.

When people choose to prefer others, it is typically motivated by what they can receive in return or how it makes them feel. For example, an employee might go out of his way to praise his boss in the hopes of setting himself up for a promotion. A young man might compliment a gal or buy her gifts in the hopes of influencing her decision about pursuing a dating relationship. Unlike the way those in the world seek to prefer one another for selfish gain, a believer's giving of preference to others is not to be based on external factors such as physical attractiveness, social status, or economic standing. It is not to be dependent upon a person's education level, type of personality, or family background. Our giving of preference is to be based solely on the fact that the other person is a brother or sister in Christ. The fact that you have been made one in Christ should be motivation enough to seek another person's interests above your own (Philippians 2:3-4).

Giving honor to others means treating them with special respect. The word "honor" in Romans 12:10 communicates the idea of treating something as valuable. According to Scripture, the foundational reasons you are called to value your brother or sister are that God has created you both in His image (Genesis 1:27), and He has purchased you both by the blood of Jesus Christ (Acts 20:28; 1 Peter 1:18-19). Preferring one another is not about flattering others or pretending that they are better or wiser than you. It is about genuinely giving others special, serious consideration.

Application

- How are you *purposefully* seeking to prefer others over yourself?
- Specifically, whom can you prefer over yourself this week? Make a list of five believers you can prefer with honor. How can you make the other person "weigh heavy" in your life this week? List three specific ways you can do this for each person.

Speak Truthfully to One Another

"Therefore, having put away falsehood, let each one of you speak the truth with his neighbor, for we are members one of another" (Ephesians 4:25).

Explanation

The command to speak truthfully to one another is embedded in a context in Ephesians where Paul is explaining the practical outworking of the gospel. This "one another" command appears in a passage that addresses unity in the body of Christ (Ephesians 4:3). Paul strongly emphasizes that we are to be one in Christ, and this requires that you put aside your former manner of life and put on your "new self" (Ephesians 4:22-24). And one way to be consistent with your new identity in Christ is to work toward the unity of the body by speaking truthfully to one another.

Of course, this means that you must make every effort not to lie. The present tense of the command indicates ongoing action, and can be translated "speak truth continually." Believers are to have a habit of speaking the truth with one another. They are not to be associated with lying, but must be characterized by truth. Truth is a vital and foundational aspect of a trusting relationship. Without truthfulness, a biblical relationship cannot occur. How can you successfully build a loving relationship on falsehoods and lies? Repeated lies destroy the trust in a relationship.

Not only are you to speak the truth, but you are called to do so "in love" (Ephesians 4:15). Truth not spoken in love can be quite harmful. For example, you might say to a woman, "That is a beautiful black dress you are wearing today. You are always the best dressed and ever so stylish!" This may be a true and sincere statement, but it would be an incredibly inappropriate comment if it were spoken at a funeral to a woman who has just lost her husband. Even when a statement is true, it must be spoken at the appropriate time and with love for the hearer in mind. Otherwise, it will not benefit the listener. Truth must be spoken in love.

Application

- With Ephesians 4:25 in mind, confess and repent of a recent conversation in which you did not speak truth. Contact the person who heard you so that you can confess your sin and seek that person's forgiveness.

- Read Ephesians 4:15. Recall a recent conversation in which you failed to speak the truth in love. How could you have handled matters differently?

- When are you most prone to speak falsehood? What circumstances influence your decision not to speak truth?

Be Kind to One Another

"Be kind to one another, tenderhearted, forgiving one another, as God in Christ forgave you" (Ephesians 4:32).

Explanation

As is the case with speaking the truth to one another, the command to be kind to one another is given in the context of maintaining unity in the Spirit (Ephesians 4:3). This too comes as a result of laying aside the old self and putting on the new self (verses 22-24). The last three chapters of Ephesians offer numerous applications for the "putting off and putting on" process through a string of negative ("don't do") and positive ("do") commands. Sinful habits must be replaced with godly habits. The chart below helps delineate the "put off" and "put on" teaching of Ephesians 4:22-32.

Ephesians 4:31 and 32 are inextricably linked. In order to "put on" being

Ephesians 4	Put Off	Put On
verses 22-24	Old self, which belongs to your former manner of life and is corrupt through deceitful desires	Renewed in the spirit of your mind, and to put on the new self, created after the likeness of God in true righteousness and holiness
verse 25	Put away falsehood	Speak the truth
verse 28	No longer steal	Labor, doing honest work with his own hands
verse 29	Let no corrupting talk come out of your mouths	Only such as is good for building up, as fits the occasion, that it may give grace to those who hear
verses 31-32	Let all bitterness and wrath and anger and clamor and slander be put away from you, along with all malice	Be kind to one another, tenderhearted, forgiving one another, as God in Christ forgave you

kind to one another, you must necessarily "put off" bitterness, wrath, anger, clamor, slander, and all malice. If the sins listed in verse 31 are present in your life, it will be impossible for you to show the acts of kindness that verse 32 requires. Thus, it is essential that you first confess and repent of the things you are to "put off." This is the first step toward obeying the command to be kind to one another.

The kindness you show others is to be consistent and continuous. Believers are to show a "sweet and generous disposition"[3] toward one another. According to verse 32, this kindness is particularly exercised in forgiving one another. Interestingly, Paul used the same word in Romans 2:4 to describe God's attitude toward believers prior to salvation: "Do you presume on the riches of his kindness and forbearance and patience, not knowing that God's kindness is meant to lead you to repentance?" What an amazing statement! It is not the wrath and anger of God that leads sinners to repentance, but the kindness of God. God's tender-heartedness and forgiveness are what draws sinners to Jesus Christ. In the same way, believers are not called to be angry with one another. Instead, they are called to show others the same kindness that they received at salvation.

This principle holds true even in basic areas of life, such as our conversations. Proverbs 15:1 states, "A soft answer turns away wrath, but a harsh word stirs up anger." Imagine if someone came to you fuming with anger and using harsh words. How would you respond? Understandably, it would be difficult to respond with kindness. On the other hand, if that person came to you with gentleness and sweetness of speech, you would find it easier to be receptive. Likewise, by showing kindness to others, you can make it easier for them to respond with kindness to you. Your kindness might even help to diffuse a potentially volatile situation.

Believers should be known for their tender hearts and forgiving attitudes. And we need to recognize that God's Word does not limit our showing this kindness only to those who are easy to love. We are to show kindness even to those who are unlovable. It helps to remember that God loved us when we were unlovable—we are to show that same kind of love as well.

Application

- Consider a recent incident with a fellow believer in which you found yourself tested in the area of kindness. What did you need to put off? What did you need to put on?

- Can you think of times when God made His love evident to you even when you were unlovely? What do you think prompted God to show such love? What do you need to "put on" so you can show this same kind of love?

Forgive One Another

"Be kind to one another, tenderhearted, forgiving one another, as God in Christ forgave you" (Ephesians 4:32).

Explanation

"I'm really sorry about that." "Please accept my apologies." While these statements might be said with complete sincerity, they are inadequate substitutes for "Please forgive me."

Some Christians might not discern the difference between merely apologizing and asking for forgiveness. Here's the distinction: When two people have experienced conflict, for one to say, "I'm sorry" only communicates that person's remorse over what he has done. It focuses solely on the offender's own feelings. By contrast, saying, "Forgive me" confesses that a wrong has been committed against another person and there is a desire to pursue reconciliation. In this case, the other person's hurt is in focus. The difference may seem subtle, but it is significant.

A lack of forgiveness may occur because of one's outright refusal to grant it or simply because of one's lack of understanding about biblical forgiveness. In today's feeling-oriented society, people have confused granting forgiveness with overlooking sin, excusing sin, or accepting apologies. However, Scripture is very clear when it speaks on the topic of forgiveness.

First, it is important to understand that forgiveness is a matter of obedience. In Luke 17:1-4, when Jesus gave instruction about being willing to forgive repeatedly, the disciples responded by saying, "Increase our faith!" (verse 5).

They thought their problem was a lack of faith for being able to forgive, but Jesus corrects their thinking, describing how even a little faith the size of a mustard seed could move a mulberry tree! When it came to forgiveness, their problem was simply a refusal to obey. Jesus pointedly illustrated this truth by referring to a servant's obedience simply because of who his master was (verses 7-10). Likewise, Christians should forgive one another simply because of who their Master is—the Lord Jesus Christ. A failure to forgive is not due to a lack of faith; it's due to a refusal to obey God.

Another important aspect of forgiving one another is that forgiveness is a transaction. Forgiveness should be sought in repentance, and then forgiveness should be granted (verse 3). Many conflicts between Christians remain unresolved because this transaction does not occur. Instead, people resort to saying, "I'm so sorry. Please accept my apologies." And the typical unbiblical response is "That's okay," or "Apology accepted." These statements do not accomplish anything substantial, for they don't necessarily include forgiveness in the picture. However, when people seek and grant forgiveness as instructed by the Bible, a wonderful transaction occurs. Jay Adams points out that granting forgiveness is about making a threefold promise:

1. I will not bring the matter up to you.

2. I will not bring the matter up to another.

3. I will not bring the matter up to myself.[4]

To "forgive and forget" is not only unbiblical, it is also virtually impossible. When Christians forgive one another, they are not promising that they will never remember what happened. Rather, the one who forgives is promising that he will not continue to hold the offense against the other, either outwardly in his speech or actions or internally in his thoughts.

It is not easy for someone to ask for forgiveness. It is harder still for someone to grant it. But the reason any believer should be willing and able to forgive is because of the forgiveness he has received from God (Matthew 18:21-35). When it came to your salvation, God was willing to forgive your insurmountable debt owed to Him. The forgiveness you are asked to show others is meager by comparison. Any failure on your part to forgive others exposes a lack of understanding or appreciation of God's forgiveness. Understanding properly the command to forgive one another is a vital part of helping resolve problems in relationships.[5]

Application

- List the names of people from whom you need to seek forgiveness. Write out in detail exactly what you will say as you confess the wrongdoing and seek forgiveness from that person (see Luke 15:18-19). Also, confess and repent of your sins to God.

- Are there people who have asked for your forgiveness to whom you have not granted forgiveness? If so, what steps do you need to take to forgive them in a biblical manner?

Bear with One Another

"...bearing with one another and, if one has a complaint against another, forgiving each other; as the Lord has forgiven you, so you also must forgive" (Colossians 3:13).

Explanation

This command to bear with one another must be read in context with the preceding verse: "Put on then, as God's chosen ones, holy and beloved, compassionate hearts, kindness, humility, meekness, and patience." God's call to bear with one another involves "a willingness to bear with those whose faults or unpleasant traits are an irritant to them...'bear with' suggests the thought of putting up with things we dislike in others."[6] This is certainly not an easy task. Instead of complaining when others are difficult to love, believers are called to endure and be patient with them. First Corinthians 13:7 reminds us that bearing all things (including people) is part of what it means to show love.[7]

It is hard enough to be consistently pleasant to those we generally get along well with. What a seemingly impossible task to bear with those who are difficult to like! However, God's Word says to do just that—bear with (that is, love) those who are unlovable.

Why do we get annoyed by others? You might be surprised to hear that the root of this annoyance may not be the other person's behavior or personality.

Rather, the root of the problem may actually be in the heart of the one who is annoyed. Getting easily annoyed with others is a manifestation of pride rearing its ugly head. When we get annoyed, we are basically saying that we are less annoying than the other person. We are saying we are better than the other person. We fail to realize that it is impossible to see others correctly when there are logs in our eyes (Matthew 7:1-5).

Before you allow yourself to become annoyed with others, take some time to examine your own heart. As believers, we are redeemed sinners, which means we will continue to sin because we are not yet perfect. It is helpful to remember how often others need to bear with us. This will help us to repent of any pride in our own hearts and to bear with others.

Application

- In what ways have you recently displayed impatience toward a fellow believer?

- Under what circumstances or situations do you find it most difficult to "bear with one another"? List three of them, and specify ways that you can show love in each situation.

- Read Matthew 7:1-5, and examine your own life. How are you making it difficult for people to deal with you? How are you causing unnecessary "patient forbearance" on another believer's life?

- Read the chapter entitled "A Husband's Resolve—Humility and Service" in Stuart Scott's *The Exemplary Husband* for excellent biblical teaching on pride and humility in a man's life.

Stir up/Stimulate One Another

"Let us consider how to stir up one another to love and good works" (Hebrews 10:24).

Explanation

According to one Christian author, "The reality of Christian love should be demonstrated in the personal relationships and mutual concerns of the Christian community."[8] Christians are called to stir up one another to love and good works. It is important to read Hebrews 10:24 together with the verse that follows. Together, the two verses read, "Let us consider how to stir up one another to love and good works, not neglecting to meet together, as is the habit of some, but encouraging one another, and all the more as you see the Day drawing near."

Christians are called to gather together because church is where they can find mutual encouragement. There is great importance in the regular gathering of the saints. The author of Hebrews even stresses the urgency of meeting together—because the day of the Lord is drawing near. When the church gathers and its members show practical concern for one another, this distinguishes them as a community from those outside. Believers should exhibit a concern for one another that nonbelievers do not have.

Acts 15:39 is the only other passage in Scripture that uses the Greek term that is translated "stir up." It states, "There arose a sharp disagreement, so that they separated from each other." You may be asking, "What does this passage have to do with stirring up one another to love and good deeds?" The word translated "stir up" or "stimulate" in Hebrews 10:24 is translated "sharp disagreement" in Acts 15:39. The connection may seem strange, but it is significant for a proper understanding of Hebrews 10:24. The word can be translated "stimulate, sharp disagreement, irritation." It is used negatively in Acts and positively in Hebrews. Just as there was a negative provocation between Paul and Barnabas in Acts, there should be a positive provocation among believers according to Hebrews. Believers are called to "provoke" other believers to love and good deeds.

To stir up a fellow believer is a conscious and intense action. "Good works" are tangible expressions of care and love that are expected of all believers (see Ephesians 2:10). Christians need to be catalysts for one another so that all can demonstrate love and good deeds to others.

Application

- In what ways do you "positively provoke" or "stir up" others to love and good works? Are you a catalyst for others?
- List five people whom you can stimulate to love and good works this week. Note specifically how you will do this.

Be Hospitable to One Another

"Show hospitality to one another without grumbling" (1 Peter 4:9).

Explanation

To "show hospitality to one another" is an interesting command. Paul lists this as a specific requirement for elders (1 Timothy 3:2; Titus 1:8), and for any widow who would receive financial support from the church (1 Timothy 5:10). Peter, more generally, indicates that it is a requirement for all believers.

The term that is translated "hospitality" in 1 Peter 4:9 is often misunderstood. It literally means "love of strangers." Believers are called to be lovers of strangers! This is certainly a foreign concept in contemporary Western culture. These days, people (even Christians) are generally told to be wary of strangers and to stay away from them. The thought of lending a room to a complete stranger free of rent is a totally foreign concept today.

In Peter's day, however, hospitality was viewed differently. Showing love to strangers was extremely important in the early church, as it facilitated the spread of the gospel. Many travelers—such as letter carriers, pastors, and teachers—relied upon the hospitality of believers. Hotels in those days were not like hotels today. "It was undesirable to lodge in public inns, which were often the scene of drunkenness and impurity; the Christian's faith had cut him off from the pagan practices that generally prevailed there."[9] Furthermore, believers often needed to find refuge in Christian homes whenever they were fleeing from persecution.

First-century believers also practiced hospitality by holding church services in their homes. Romans 16:5 and 1 Corinthians 16:19 testify to the fact that some graciously opened their homes for worship meetings. A key reason for this is that in many places during the earliest years of the church, buildings set apart solely for church use did not exist. It was commonplace for believers to congregate at a member's home. Certainly you can imagine the difficulties of hosting church in your home week after week!

We are familiar with the term *Southern hospitality*. Sadly, Christians are not as well known for Christian hospitality. For some, this may be due to ignorance. Perhaps they were never taught that Scripture requires believers to be hospitable to one another. For others, their lack of hospitality may indicate a lack of love for others. It may be that they are more concerned about personal comfort than the needs of another. And still others might not be hospitable because they do not have giving and sharing hearts. Oftentimes, hospitality requires considerable time, effort, and money. You should seek to be a cheerful giver (2 Corinthians 9:7), being willing to commit even time and finances to making hospitality possible.

Peter stated that hospitality is to be shown "without grumbling." It must be accompanied by the right heart and attitude. It is not uncommon for people to invite others into their home while, in their minds or hearts, complaining the entire time. If you show hospitality, seek to do it without murmuring.

Application

- When was the last time you were hospitable to those outside immediate family? How did you show this hospitality?

- Perhaps you know of some missionaries or other people in ministry who will arrive for a visit to your town soon. Make arrangements to have them stay at your home, a friend's home, or at a hotel.

- Jim Phillips writes, "Biblically, historically, and practically, hospitality involves a home,"[10] but it can also happen outside the home. When was the last time you took someone out for a meal or even just coffee? In what other practical ways can you show hospitality?

- Keep in mind that whether you are the visitor or the host, you are there to serve, not to be served.

Love One Another

"May the Lord make you increase and abound in love for one another and for all, as we do for you" (1 Thessalonians 3:12).

Explanation

The command to love one another is given over a dozen times in the New Testament. This command sums up all the other "one another" commands, which ultimately are an expression of this one command to love one another.

If one word could describe the Christian relationship, it would be *love*. First Corinthians 13:4-8 is a popular passage to cite at weddings, and for good reason! It provides helpful instruction on how to love God's way. One cannot help but be humbled as he reads,

> Love is patient and kind; love does not envy or boast; it is not arrogant or rude. It does not insist on its own way; it is not irritable or resentful; it does not rejoice at wrongdoing, but rejoices with the truth. Love bears all things, believes all things, hopes all things, endures all things. Love never ends.

In the original Greek text, all of these terms describing love are verbs; they denote action. In other words, they are all terms of *motion,* and not *emotion.*

In 1 Thessalonians 3:12, the phrase "increase and abound" carries a sense of something overflowing.[11] Believers are called to have overflowing love for one another. That love can even overflow toward unbelievers. Our love is to abound to all people.

Like Jesus' love for us, our love for one another should also be unconditional. Conditional love is self-seeking. It is easy to love those who can return the love. Even the most wretched unbeliever can do good to those who can return the favor. By contrast, Jesus calls us to love even those who cannot return the favor (Matthew 5:46-47). It is not easy to love this way, but we are called to do so. A true believer is enabled to love even his enemies and pray for those who harm him, because God works in the life of the regenerate person to help him obey His commands (Philippians 2:13). Loving your neighbor *and* your enemy is a distinctive feature of a Christian's life.

Application

- List three "one another" commands that, in recent weeks, have been difficult for you to implement. Explain why this is the case, and note how you will seek to obey these commands.

- List three people you need to show love to. How have you been neglecting to love them? Repent of your lack of love for them, and list specific acts of love you can show toward these individuals.

The Challenge

These "one another" commands are a great challenge to all believers, whether they are mature or new Christians. Perhaps God is helping you to see how much you struggle with these "one another" commands in your relationships with other believers. If the struggle is ongoing and significant, this may give you reason to reflect upon the sincerity of your relationship with Jesus Christ, to see if you are truly in the faith (2 Corinthians 13:5). Striving to adhere to these "one another" commands is a mark of true saving faith.

Perhaps you realize that you are having a hard time practicing these commands with a particular person in your life. This is the time to commit to obeying these commands, especially in respect toward that other believer.

Perhaps you have now realized you lack a conscious desire to pursue a truly *biblical* relationship with others. What you may have found out is that you need to actively seek to practice the "one another" commands in your life. Most believers are not seeking to be blatantly disobedient to God's Word, especially in regard to relationships. But at the same time, there are believers who aren't taking steps to *actively* implement the commands of Scripture daily and habitually. Think about how you can consciously obey these commands with regard to your spouse, children, parents, friends, others.

In Scripture, the phrase "one another," by definition, involves relationships with other believers. There are no qualifying statements to these commands. So we're to apply them far and wide, not favoring certain individuals over others.

You might find it helpful to take time to pray through each of the "one another" commands. You could pray about a different command each day for a month. This will help you to become more consciously aware of these commands and your need to pursue biblical relationships with others.

It is exciting to realize that you can grow more Christlike by practicing the "one another" commands of Scripture. Let this challenge you as you seek to love the Lord and others, and may it result in greater glory to God.

Recommended Resources

Adams, Jay E. *From Forgiven to Forgiving.* Amityville, NY: Calvary Press, 1994.

Lane, Tim, and Paul Tripp. *Relationships: A Mess Worth Making.* Greensboro, NC: New Growth Press, 2006.

Mack, Wayne A. *Your Family God's Way.* Phillipsburg, NJ: P&R Publishing, 1991.

Scott, Stuart. *The Exemplary Husband.* Bemidji, MN: Focus Publishing, 2000.

12

The Husband's Role in Leaving and Cleaving

Charles Mudd

If you have never heard the phrase *leaving and cleaving,* you're not alone. Many people have never heard this term, and even some who have heard it aren't exactly sure what it means.

Even though the phrase *leaving and cleaving* may not mean a lot to a large number of people, including Christians, the reality of what is behind this expression impacts a man's life every day. In fact, it would not be an overstatement to say that the underlying reality behind the phrase *leaving and cleaving* affects every relationship in a man's life.

While your visible life is probably filled with the hectic pace of your job (or looking for a job) and family responsibilities, the principles of leaving and cleaving are quietly working beneath the surface, influencing how you relate to the most important people in your life—your wife, children, parents, and in-laws. So what exactly is leaving and cleaving, and how does it play such an important role in your life?

Leaving and Cleaving—a Short Explanation

The idea of leaving and cleaving comes from the Bible. We are first introduced to this concept in Genesis 2:24. "Therefore shall a man *leave* his father and his mother, and shall *cleave* unto his wife: and they shall be one flesh" (Genesis 2:24 KJV). In this verse, the word "cleave" means "to be joined to."

So leaving and cleaving basically means that a man *leaves* his parents and *joins* himself to a wife; as a result, they become one flesh.

The significance of this terminology becomes clearer with further study of the Scriptures. It becomes apparent that in the biblical sense, "leave" and "cleave" mean something quite different than what we normally understand them to mean. Let's dig into a few more Bible verses to discover the meanings.

Leaving

In the Old Testament, the Hebrew word translated "leave" can simply mean "to depart," which is how we usually understand the word. However, the same Hebrew word is also translated "forsake" or "abandon." For example, Psalm 27:10 says, "My father and my mother have forsaken me, but the LORD will take me in." In this verse, the word translated "forsaken" is the same Hebrew translated "leave" in Genesis 2:24. And in 2 Chronicles 24:18 we read, "They abandoned the house of the LORD, the God of their fathers, and served the Asherim and the idols." In this verse the word translated "abandoned" is the same Hebrew word translated "leave" in Genesis 2:24. These are just a few examples of how these words are used interchangeably throughout Scripture.

This word study helps us to understand that in the Old Testament, the Hebrew word translated "leave" can mean something other than just departing. It often means to forsake or abandon someone or something. That is the sense of the meaning in Genesis 2:24. It means to give up—to abandon—certain aspects of one's relationship with a parent. Specifically, biblical leaving means to give up depending on one's parents when it is no longer necessary. It does not mean to forsake loving relationships, but only aspects of those relationships that are no longer pleasing to the Lord.

Biblical leaving takes place on the inside, not on the outside. It's an internal act of abandoning a type of relational dependence that was once appropriate, but is now inappropriate and does not honor God. Except in the case of those whose physical or mental capacity prevents them from doing so, Genesis 2:24 instructs us that it is God's plan for people to give up their dependence on their parents (or parental figures) and to replace it with a God-honoring dependence on a spouse.

Cleaving

To cleave to something means to stick closely to it, like glue or a weld. Cleaving implies a bond so strong that it cannot be separated. When husbands and wives cleave to each other, they join themselves in an inseparable union. They unite themselves in body, soul, and purpose.

When God invited Job to consider the wonders of His creation, he drew Job's attention to an ancient reptile called Leviathan, and specifically to this creature's mighty scales: "One is so near to another that no air can come between them. They are joined one to another; they clasp each other and cannot be separated" (Job 41:16-17). The word translated "joined" in this passage is the same Hebrew word translated "cleave" in Genesis 2:24. This is a great example of the meaning of "cleave" in Genesis 2, and the illustration in Job 41 illustrates perfectly the kind of bonding that takes place between a husband and wife when biblical cleaving occurs—their lives are joined so closely together that nothing can come between.

Becoming One Flesh

While cleaving emphasizes the activity, becoming one flesh emphasizes the result. As a husband and wife purpose in their hearts to unite themselves in all aspects of their shared lives, God joins them together in a sacred and profound union, second only to that between Christ and His church. "Did he not make them one, with a portion of the Spirit in their union?" (Malachi 2:15). According to Ephesians 5:31-32, the relationship Jesus Christ has with His church is a model for the one-flesh relationship of a husband and wife. This tells us that becoming one flesh is intended by God to be permanent.

Stephen Clark adds an interesting perspective on becoming one flesh, observing that an adult child who once had a type of *one-flesh* relationship with his parents forsakes this relationship by leaving and cleaving and replaces it with a *new one-flesh relationship* with his wife:

> The transition indicated by this verse can be seen most clearly by considering the social situation that it is referring to. A son is his parents' flesh and blood, and he lives as part of his parents' household. He is one with his parents, because he has come from them and lives with them. When he marries he takes on a new relationship. He

becomes more related to and more one with his wife than with his parents, He leaves the "one flesh" which is his parents and joins with a woman to create a new "one flesh." He may leave his parents behind by literally moving away and moving into a new house with his wife. If he were to move to another city, he may leave his parents behind, but he would be unlikely to leave his wife behind. In the Genesis account, this social fact is explained by the original creation of woman out of man. Something was taken out of man when woman was formed, and hence it is natural for a man to find a woman that he can join to himself, becoming one flesh as a foundation for creating a family.[1]

Putting It All Together

Now that we have a better understanding of the biblical meanings of *leave, cleave,* and *becoming one flesh,* we can summarize the principle of leaving and cleaving as follows: Leaving and cleaving is an internal act of letting go of one's dependence on a parent (leaving) and replacing it with a new and permanent dependence on one's spouse (cleaving). Leaving and cleaving is not just a change in marital status or address; it deals with giving up one type of dependence (that may or may not be pleasing to God) and *replacing* it with a new type of dependence that not only pleases God but establishes a solid foundation for a God-honoring marriage. When a man leaves and cleaves, he abandons his dependent relationship upon his parents and embraces a new dependent relationship with his wife, a "helper fit for him" (Genesis 2:18). When a woman leaves and cleaves, she abandons her dependent relationship upon her parents and embraces a new dependent relationship with her husband—her head, provider, and protector (1 Corinthians 11:3; Ephesians 5:23).

The Husband's Role in Leaving and Cleaving

The Call to Love and Lead

Having laid the foundation of the basic principles of leaving, cleaving, and becoming one flesh, we can now look at the husband's role in leaving and cleaving—a role that is unique to them. This role is defined by two responsibilities given specifically to husbands by God: Husbands are called by God to *love* and to *lead* their wives. These two responsibilities are either stated directly or implied in Ephesians chapter 5. Verse 25 says, "Husbands, love your wives, as Christ loved the church and gave himself up for her." Verse 28 adds, "Husbands should love their wives as their own bodies." And verse 33 says, "Let each one of you love his wife as himself." In these few verses, we find three clear commands for husbands to love their wives. In every case, the word "love" means a sacrificial, selfless type of love, a love that desires only to consider another person as more important than oneself.

The husband's second primary responsibility, to *lead* his wife, is implied in Ephesians 5:22-24, which says, "Wives, submit to your own husbands, as to the Lord. For the husband is the head of the wife even as Christ is the head of the church, his body, and is himself its Savior. Now as the church submits to Christ, so also wives should submit in everything to their husbands." These three verses tell us that wives are to submit themselves to their own husbands, which indicates the husband's role is to lead.

Although the word "submit" (in the singular) is not in the original Greek text of verse 22, it is carried over from Ephesians 5:21, where Christians are "submitting to one another out of reverence for Christ." Peter O'Brien notes, "At the heart of this submission is the notion of 'order.' God has established certain leadership and authority roles within the family, and submission is a humble recognition of that divine ordering."[2] By voluntarily placing herself under her husband's ordained headship, a Christian wife does so "as to the Lord." As wives have been called to place themselves under their husband's leadership, husbands have been called to lead their wives.

At this point, you may be wondering what the connection is between leaving and cleaving and the matter of a husband loving and leading his wife. We have learned that leaving and cleaving requires men and women to let go of their dependence upon parents and replace it with a new dependence upon a spouse. For most people, this is a difficult adjustment. In marriage, God calls husbands and wives to become one flesh, which is necessarily an exclusive relationship. Past parent-child dependencies must give way to a new husband-wife dependency. And it is the husband's job to lovingly lead his wife into this new priority as they embark on a life of God-honoring mutual dependence. A husband must not only demonstrate a single-minded devotion to his wife, but he must also lovingly help his wife to demonstrate a single-minded devotion to him, her God-appointed head.

The First Pledge of Allegiance

When Americans hear the words *pledge of allegiance,* their minds almost instantly start to mentally recite the first few words of the pledge to their nation's flag! Long before Francis Bellamy penned the words to the pledge in 1892, an even more solemn pledge was uttered from the lips of the first man ever created—Adam. In Genesis 2:18-23, we are given a record of God's creation of Eve and His presentation of her to Adam. Adam's response was to pledge himself to her: "This at last is bone of my bones and flesh of my flesh; she shall be called Woman, because she was taken out of Man" (verse 23). The expression "bone of my bones and flesh of my flesh" is best understood as shorthand for pledging one's allegiance to another because they are blood relatives. We see other examples of this in the Old Testament (see Genesis 29:14; Judges 9:2; 2 Samuel 5:1; 19:12-13; 1 Chronicles 11:1). Such pledges of allegiance were usually followed by the parties entering into a covenant, which bound the parties to a commitment of lifelong support. We see this, for example, in 2 Samuel 5:1-3:

> All the tribes of Israel came to David at Hebron and said, "Behold, we are your bone and flesh. In times past, when Saul was king over us, it was you who led out and brought in Israel. And the LORD said to you, 'You shall be shepherd of my people Israel, and you shall be prince over Israel.'" So all the elders of Israel came to the king at Hebron, and King David made a covenant with them at Hebron before the LORD, and they anointed David king over Israel.

Adam's pledge of allegiance to Eve is the closest thing we find in the Bible to the modern-day marriage vow. In anticipation of becoming one flesh, the bride and groom publicly and solemnly pledge mutual allegiance to each other for the rest of their lives on earth. The one-flesh relationship in a marriage speaks of a permanent unity. Because becoming one flesh is intended by God to be permanent, marriage is a sacred and unbreakable bond, an enduring lifetime commitment.

In fact, a marriage is a *covenant* (contract). Proverbs 2:16-17 speaks of "the adulteress…who forsakes the companion of her youth and forgets the *covenant* of her God." This text describes an adulteress who willingly ignores the covenant she made with her husband in the sight of God and forsakes (this is the same Hebrew word translated "leave" in Genesis 2:24) her lifelong companion so she can enjoy the fleeting pleasures of a sexually promiscuous relationship with someone else. And in Malachi 2:14 we read, "The LORD was witness between you and the wife of your youth, to whom you have been faithless, though she is your companion and your wife by *covenant*." Through the prophet Malachi, God was rebuking the people of Israel for their sinful intermarriages with idol worshippers.

These two Old Testament texts demonstrate a key aspect of a marriage: companionship. A companion is more than just a friend. A companion is an intimate friend, a person with whom one has a deep and common bond. Marriage is an agreement by a man and a woman—in the sight of God and others—to pledge themselves to be lifelong companions to each other. This pledge includes two biblical aspects of companionship: *intimacy* and *commitment*. In marriage, each partner-companion pledges to be both committed to, and intimate with, his spouse for life.

As a result, the marriage partners are thereby denied the freedom to seek intimacy outside the marriage, and they are not to inappropriately commit themselves to anyone other than their spouse. Contrary to popular thinking, because God created marriage, God and God alone has the right to determine if and when any marriage may be dissolved. Man has no right to modify or amend the design or intent of marriage as instituted and ordained by God (Matthew 19:6). In this regard, Jay Adams notes, "Neither a private individual nor the state has any competence to decide who may be married (or divorced) and on what basis."[3]

Why Leaving and Cleaving Is Important

You now have a better understanding of…

- the basic principles of leaving and cleaving
- the connection between leaving and cleaving, and loving and leading your wife

- the need to demonstrate in your life the principles of leaving and cleaving, and to encourage your wife to do the same

- the marriage covenant, in which you pledge to make your wife your lifelong companion with whom you have a unique and lasting bond

But *why* is leaving and cleaving so important? There are two reasons:

First, when Christians obey God's command to leave and cleave, they are fulfilling the function for which they were created. In doing so, they are glorifying God, which is worship.

Second, there are blessings that attend biblical leaving and cleaving. By God's grace and provision, marriages will become stronger because husbands and wives are united in their purpose for living—to glorify and honor God in their practice of living as they function in their proper roles, and in their pleasure in living as they enjoy both intimacy with and commitment to each other. A life lived in the pursuit of biblical leaving and cleaving is a blessed life indeed!

Getting Started

As important as leaving and cleaving is in helping build or strengthen a marriage, it is even more important for a person to have the ability to leave and cleave. That may sound like a strange statement—you may be thinking, *What do you mean by "ability"? Isn't this just a matter of not depending on my parents anymore, loving my wife, and showing her how it's done?* Well, not exactly. What I mean by "ability" is the unique capability that comes only through having a personal relationship with Jesus Christ. Why do I say that? Because anyone who really wants to can take steps to eliminate inappropriate parental dependence and replace it with an appropriate dependence on his/her spouse. But those are simply outward actions. Such actions may make living with your wife, parents, and in-laws a little easier, but they will do nothing for how you get along with God. For a Christian, however, it's different. With the Lord Jesus Christ's help, you'll have the power you need to make the tough choices that leaving and cleaving requires, and in the end, He will be honored by your success.

Now, to honor someone means to pay respect to that person, to esteem and appreciate him for who he is or what he has done. The Bible teaches that it is impossible for us to truly honor God, no matter how good our intentions may be, unless we first know His Son and honor Him. Jesus Himself makes this point clear. In John 5:21-27, He said:

> As the Father raises the dead and gives them life, so also the Son gives life to whom he will. The Father judges no one, but has given all judgment to the Son, that all may honor the Son, just as they honor the Father. Whoever does not honor the Son does not honor the Father who sent him. Truly, truly, I say to you, whoever hears my word and believes him who sent me has eternal life. He does not come into judgment, but has passed from death to life.
>
> Truly, truly, I say to you, an hour is coming, and is now here, when the dead will hear the voice of the Son of God, and those who hear will live. For as the Father has life in himself, so he has granted the Son also to have life in himself. And he has given him authority to execute judgment, because he is the Son of Man.

According to Jesus' own words, God the Father and God the Son are due the *same* honor. He said, "Whoever does not honor the Son does not honor the Father who sent him," and added, "Whoever hears my word and believes in him who sent me has eternal life. He does not come into judgment, but has passed from death to life."

In relation to your marriage, it is one thing to honor your wife; it is an entirely different thing to honor God. In John chapter 4 is an account of a conversation between Jesus and a Samaritan woman. Jesus said to the woman, "The hour is coming, and is now here, when the true worshipers will worship the Father in spirit and truth, for the Father is seeking such people to worship him. God is spirit, and those who worship him must worship in spirit and truth" (verses 23-24). A person cannot worship God in spirit and truth if he does not worship the Son of God. And if anyone does not worship the Son of God and honor Him, God will not be honored by anything that person does, no matter how good or right it may be. The first priority must be to love, honor, and worship the Son. If you have not honored the Son of God by believing in the Lord Jesus Christ, you can find out more about how to do so in the Appendix titled "The Gospel for Men" (see page 387). If you do have a relationship with the Lord Jesus Christ, your efforts to leave and cleave will honor Him, and the promise of Psalm 128:1-4 will be yours:

Blessed is everyone who fears the LORD, who walks in his ways! You shall eat the fruit of the labor of your hands; you shall be blessed, and it shall be well with you. Your wife will be like a fruitful vine within your house; your children will be like olive shoots around your table. Behold, thus shall the man be blessed who fears the LORD.

Practical Steps to Leaving and Cleaving

Leaving and cleaving may be difficult, but it is not impossible. It is difficult for two reasons:

First, biblical leaving and cleaving requires a person to redefine his or her closest human relationships—his relationship with his original family, and his new family relationship with his wife. Change of this sort is difficult, and is often misunderstood by affected loved ones who may not readily understand or appreciate the biblical truth that has brought this change to bear on these relationships.

Second, people are naturally inclined to seek comfort over obedience to God's Word. For most of us, there is a natural desire to return to the comfort, control, and security that has characterized our dependence upon our parents. Until a person has overcome the longings for dependence on others, he will struggle to overcome the temptation to go back to the old ways. But God's grace is sufficient to give any repentant Christian victory, for His power is perfected in our weakness (2 Corinthians 12:9).

A decision to not change our primary allegiance is rooted in things that our hearts crave—such as the above-mentioned desires for comfort, control, and security. When we give in to these cravings, we lack the strength to obey God's command to leave and cleave. In fact, to come to the place where we honor God by leaving and cleaving, these sinful cravings must be replaced with new and God-honoring desires. This will be accomplished only through diligent personal effort to obey Scripture as one relies on God's all-sufficient grace.

A method I often suggest to people who want to overcome sinful thinking and behavior is a three-step process adapted from Philippians 4:6 and Ephesians 4:22-24 that I call "The Three Rs Method." The "three Rs" stand for *Request, Renew,* and *Replace.* Here's a quick summary:

Request simply means to pray (Philippians 4:6). Ask God to show you the sinful cravings in your heart (such as cravings for recognition, approval, comfort, and control) and then confess these as sin. Ask God to give you new and holy desires that will honor Him. Ask Him to show you the way of escape when you are tempted to revert to your old ways (1 Corinthians 10:13).

Renew means to renew your mind with biblical truth (Ephesians 4:23). Meditate on Scripture passages that declare who you should be worshipping instead of what you are functionally worshipping. Memorize Bible verses that focus on God alone being worthy of your worship. Psalm 73:25-26 is a good example: "Whom have I in heaven but you? And there is nothing on earth that I desire besides you. My flesh and my heart may fail, but God is the strength of my heart and my portion forever." Memorize and meditate on Scriptures that are specific to your sinful cravings.

Replace means to replace sinful dependence in your life with nonsinful dependence (Ephesians 4:22,24). A person's first level of dependence must be on God. This applies to everyone. If a person is married, that person's second level of dependence is a God-honoring dependence on his or her spouse.

Meat on the Bones

The biblical principles for change presented thus far are a kind of theological skeleton that supports the muscle-of-life application that biblical leaving and cleaving requires. At this point you might be thinking, *I'm not exactly sure how to put these principles into practice. How can I incorporate what I've learned into my everyday life?*

With the help of three short case studies, let's look at how a husband can love and lead his wife in the way that God's Word commands him to. Each case study deals with one of the three most common types of leaving-and-cleaving problems: (1) a parent who is sinfully dependent on an adult child; (2) an adult child who is sinfully dependent on a parent; (3) a spouse who is sinfully dependent on someone other than his or her spouse. While these examples are made up, they represent typical leaving-and-cleaving problems I have seen as a biblical counselor. We'll begin with Fred's story.

Fred frequently gives unsolicited advice to his daughter and son-in law, Amy and Jack, who were married last year. The young couple doesn't mind asking for Fred's advice when they need it, but they would prefer to work through the decisions on their own. They thought that as time went on, Fred's

well-meaning suggestions would eventually stop. But now it seems he is giving
them advice every time they see him. This has become a source of irritation,
and they would like it to stop. Fred's wife, Alice, has also noticed this and has
mentioned it to Fred, but Fred doesn't think he is doing anything wrong. "After
all," he says, "isn't a father supposed to help his children make good decisions?"

Our next case study is about Andy. Andy is twenty-four and lives at home
with his parents. He graduated from high school seven years ago, and now
he spends most of his time playing computer games and working at the local
frozen yogurt store. Andy keeps all the money he earns from his job; most of
it goes for gas. Andy's parents are concerned about the way their son lives, and
think of him as an underachiever.

Finally, there's Joe and Jill. Jill has decided to put their six-year-old son,
Billy, on a vegan diet because her older sister, a vegan herself, says that it is the
healthiest way to live. Jill didn't think she needed to run this by her husband,
Joe, a meat-and-potatoes guy who doesn't know much about nutrition. Jill
often consults her sister and trusts her advice. She frequently makes decisions
without talking to Joe about them first. After learning about Billy's new diet,
Joe tells Jill that he wants Billy to go back to a "normal" diet. This leads to a
heated argument, and the couple are now in counseling.

Let's go back and take a brief second look at each case study and see how
the leaving and cleaving principles we've learned apply in each situation:

Although Fred has good intentions, he is intrusive. He sees himself as
being Amy and Jack's wise counselor. While his intentions may be good, he has
become a problem for the young couple. He is sinfully dependent on them for
recognition, and he probably also has a problem with control. Proverbs 11:29
says, "Whoever troubles his own household will inherit the wind, and the fool
will be servant to the wise of heart."

Fred, a Christian, needs to biblically leave his daughter, and forsake his
biblically inappropriate dependence on her and Jack. He needs to model a
one-flesh relationship with his wife. He should ask his daughter and son-in-
law for their forgiveness, and demonstrate to his wife and extended family that
his trust is in the Lord, not in himself or other people. It would be a blessing
to Fred if he were to memorize and meditate on Jeremiah 17:7-8, which says,
"Blessed is the man who trusts in the LORD, whose trust is the LORD. He is

like a tree planted by water, that sends out its roots by the stream, and does not fear when heat comes, for its leaves remain green, and is not anxious in the year of drought, for it does not cease to bear fruit."

Andy's problem is laziness. He's a sluggard at heart, a classic comfort-lover. Although fully capable of supporting himself, Andy is sinfully dependent on his parents for his basic needs. He's sapping them of their resources. Proverbs 28:24 says, "Whoever robs his father or his mother and says, 'That is no transgression,' is a companion to a man who destroys." It's time for Andy to biblically leave his parents.

Andy's parents, who know and love the Lord, are as much to blame in this situation as Andy. Their sinful dependence on Andy (possibly for his companionship and approval) has resulted in their failure to take any action that would help their son to become biblically independent. Proverbs 21:25 says, "The desire of the sluggard puts him to death, for his hands refuse to work," (NASB), and Proverbs 19:18 instructs parents, "Discipline your son, for there is hope; and do not set your heart on putting him to death." Biblical leaving needs to take place not only by Andy, but also by his parents.

Because Andy has clearly demonstrated a complete lack of interest in taking any meaningful initiative to become biblically independent, the long-overdue process of biblical leaving must start with Andy's parents. Together, as one flesh, Andy's mom and dad must work out a transition plan for Andy to become independent of their day-to-day practical help. Implementation, which will likely be a gradual process, will be difficult for all involved; they will need to be committed to doing what is right according to the Word of God. To help Andy's parents deal with the difficulties they will probably face in this life-changing endeavor, it would be well for them to meditate on Scriptures like Proverbs 3:5-8, which says,

> Trust in the LORD with all your heart, and do not lean on your own understanding. In all your ways acknowledge him, and he will make straight your paths. Be not wise in your own eyes; fear the LORD, and turn away from evil. It will be healing to your flesh and refreshment to your bones.

Joe and Jill are Christians who want to live according to God's Word, but they are both ignorant of the basic principles of biblical leaving and cleaving. Jill is unaware that she is so dependent on her sister that she has shut her husband out of important family decisions, allowing her sister to function as a surrogate parent. She needs to biblically leave her sister and cleave to her husband, submitting to him as her head, and enjoy her one-flesh relationship with him according to Ephesians 5:22-24.

Joe needs to take seriously his responsibility to love and lead Jill as her God-ordained head. He should demonstrate by example and instruction that his goal is not to be a dictator, but the true leader that God has called him to be. Both Joe and Jill need to spend more time in God's Word so they can develop a better understanding of what the Bible says about the biblical roles of the husband and wife in a marriage. Time would be well-spent for both of them to meditate on Ephesians 5:22-32, and particularly for Joe to commit to memory Ephesians 5:25-28, which says,

> Husbands, love your wives, as Christ loved the church and gave himself up for her, that he might sanctify her, having cleansed her by the washing of water with the word, so that he might present the church to himself in splendor, without spot or wrinkle or any such thing, that she might be holy and without blemish. In the same way husbands should love their wives as their own bodies. He who loves his wife loves himself.

The changes that Joe and Jill will have to make will not be without difficulty. Changes of this sort are difficult and often misunderstood by loved ones who may not readily understand a Christian couple's commitment to biblical teaching.

In addition, at first, Joe and Jill might not be on the same page. Therefore, Joe must make an extra effort to consistently demonstrate godly leadership in his home. This can be done by taking more initiative in general. For example, he can be proactive in his children's biblical instruction, and he can demonstrate an eagerness to hear Jill's points of view in family decisions while personally demonstrating a willingness to make decisions as the head of the family. As he does so, and in the face of difficulties that may be encountered, Joe must trust that God is at work in his family, and that whatever happens is for the honor and glory of God, and for Joe and Jill's best.

Exhortation and Encouragement

As you take into account what the Bible teaches concerning relationships, I would like to offer a word of exhortation and a word of encouragement. First, let me exhort you to take some time to evaluate your own life in terms of the principles of biblical leaving and cleaving. Consider whether you have allowed your adult children to become sinfully dependent on you and your wife, or whether you may be sinfully dependent on your own parents or other relatives. If you find your life doesn't match up with what the Bible says about these matters, you're not alone. In fact, we all have work to do! Begin by preparing yourself for the challenges you will likely face when you make the necessary changes to begin loving and leading your wife as the Bible commands. The apostle Peter said it this way: "Preparing your minds for action, and being sober-minded, set your hope fully on the grace that will be brought to you at the revelation of Jesus Christ" (1 Peter 1:13). The apostle Paul spoke of such preparation as "the readiness given by the gospel of peace" (Ephesians 6:15).

After settling the matter in your heart that you want to love and lead your wife biblically, stop and pray. Begin by asking God to forgive you for having failed to honor Him by not having properly loved and led your wife the way He has called you to do. Ask God to give you the desire and courage to begin to make things right in your home. Thank Him for having given you everything you need to begin your journey and to stay on course.

Next, remind yourself of the resources you have in Christ. These include God's own Spirit within you (1 John 4:13), who, through His Word, will embolden you and guide you in your journey. You also have the Word of God to teach you, reprove you, correct you, and train you in righteousness (2 Timothy 3:16). You also have 24/7 access to God, to whom you can pray for help and encouragement at any time. God has also given you other godly Christian men who can be examples for you—and encouragers—as they demonstrate loving leadership in their own homes.

Now you simply need to get started. And this is the most difficult part of all. Why? Because the greatest amount of determined faith is needed at this point. Starting anything new or challenging is always hard. We have envisioned the benefits and are ready to start, but then we are tempted to procrastinate. Our desire for comfort kicks in, or our faith fails and we focus on the challenge rather than on God's provision. If we keep in mind that God wants us to succeed—and He does—we will succeed. We simply have to start doing the right thing, as awkward as that might be, and trust in the grace and provision of the Lord to help us at every step.

Because this is a journey, there will be many steps and more than a few stumbles. God understands this, and that is why he has given you His Spirit, His Word, direct access to Himself, and His saints to keep you on the straight path. Even when you trip and fall, don't let that become an excuse for giving up. A wise man once said, "The righteous falls seven times and rises again" (Proverbs 24:16). As Christians, that is what we do—we get up and keep going.

Is perpetual failure an option? "No, in all these things we are more than conquerors through him who loved us" (Romans 8:37). "God is able to make all grace abound to you, so that having all sufficiency in all things at all times, you may abound in every good work" (2 Corinthians 9:8). May the Lord bless you in all that you do to honor and obey Him.

Recommended Resources

Adams, Jay E. *Marriage, Divorce, and Remarriage in the Bible: A Fresh Look at What Scripture Teaches*. Grand Rapids, MI: Zondervan, 1980.

Clark, Steven. B. *Man and Woman in Christ*. Ann Arbor, MI: Servant Books, 1980.

Liederbach, Mark. "Manliness and the Marital Vow." *The Journal of Biblical Manhood and Womanhood*, vol. 9, no. 2. Fall 2004.

Longman, Tremper, and Dan B. Allender. *The Intimate Mystery: Creating Strength and Beauty in Your Marriage*. Downers Grove, IL: InterVarsity Press, 2005.

MacArthur, John F. *What the Bible Says About Parenting: God's Plan for Rearing Your Child*. Nashville: W Publishing Group, 2000.

Mack, Wayne A. *In-Laws: Married with Parents*. Phillipsburg, NJ: P&R Publishing, 2009.

13

Parenting Young Children as a Father

Melvin Dirkse

Parenting is a daunting task! The challenge of raising well-balanced children comes with an enormous degree of responsibility. It requires wisdom, compassion, energy, and tons of patience. Many parents will readily admit to being intimidated by the weighty responsibility Scripture places on them. Understanding the gravity of one's responsibility as a parent ought to elicit a degree of fear and trepidation. After all, parents are commanded to bring their children up "in the discipline and instruction of the Lord" (Ephesians 6:4).

What makes this even more difficult is that we live in a world that is flooded with a plethora of man-centered and unbiblical parenting strategies that offer very little hope or genuine help to Christian parents. Many books, articles, and seminars that purport to be Christian are replete with secular child psychology and humanistic approaches to parenting, and the impact of these unbiblical resources has taken a toll on Christian families.

But there is hope! The Bible offers clear and practical guidelines that help parents to raise their children according to God's design. In his classic book on parenting, John MacArthur writes, "I'm convinced that if Christian parents understand and apply the simple principles Scripture sets forth, they can rise above the trends of secular society and bring up their children in a way that honors Christ, in any culture and under any circumstances."[1] With proper encouragement from the Scriptures, it is a delight for parents to raise their children in the nurture and admonition of the Lord.

Children are indeed special gifts from God. He has given them to be a blessing to their parents. Parenting these little ones should be a source of joy and fulfillment. They should not be viewed as a burden or a constant source of frustration. By God's glorious design, children are to bring parents happiness, contentment, and love. Psalm 127:3-5 says it succinctly:

> Behold, children are a gift of the LORD, the fruit of the womb is a reward. Like arrows in the hand of a warrior, so are the children of one's youth. How blessed is the man whose quiver is full of them; they will not be ashamed when they speak with their enemies in the gate (NASB).

The psalmist pointed out that God's master plan is that children are meant to be a blessing, not a hardship. However, when left to their own devices and exposed to the influences of the world, children can certainly become a source of heartache and disappointment to their parents.

This chapter is not intended to serve as an exhaustive treatise on parenting, but rather as a simple and concise guide that will help fathers make scripturally informed decisions regarding some of the most significant aspects of parenting. Neither is this a quick-fix, three-step plan to successful parenting. My hope is to encourage fathers and equip them to raise their children with God's guidelines in mind. God's ways are grounded in truth and wisdom, and as such, they are relevant for today and sufficient for every difficulty. Tedd Tripp makes this insightful statement regarding God's Word and parenting:

> The only safe guide is the Bible. It is the revelation of God who has infinite knowledge and can therefore give you absolute truth. God has given you a revelation that is robust and complete. It presents an accurate and comprehensive picture of children, parents, family life, values, training, nurture, discipline. All you need to be equipped for the task of parenting.[2]

Even though both father and mother work together in rearing their children, fathers are given a special responsibility from Scripture. This is made clear in Ephesians 6:4, where the apostle Paul directed these words to fathers:

"Fathers, do not provoke your children to anger, but bring them up in the discipline and instruction of the Lord." Fathers have a critical role when it comes to raising children. This is a natural extension of the headship of the wife in Ephesians 5:23-25. John Piper says, "Fathers should take the initiative to make sure that plans and processes and people are in place to build a vision of God and truth and holiness into the lives of the children."[3]

Parenting That Brings Children to God

In obeying God's command to bring up children in the "training and admonition of the Lord" (Ephesians 6:4 NKJV), the parents' primary task is to help their children recognize the one true God and learn that He is sovereign over everything and everyone. Parents are to help their children to develop a high view of God, and to know that He is holy and without sin.

A key way to draw children to God is to show them the hand of Creator God in every aspect of life—the flowers in the fields, the birds in the sky, the fish in the sea, the rivers that flow, the stars and the moon, the rising and setting sun, the busy insects and diverse animals, the majestic mountains, and everything else in His creation. Everything in life is to be used as a classroom to bring them to God. Sensitize your children to see the handprint of God in everything around them—everything they see has a spiritual reality that can be discovered. As Psalm 19:1 says, "The heavens declare the glory of God."

All throughout the Gospels, we see the Lord Jesus Himself using a wide variety of objects and creatures from the everyday world around Him to provide instruction about the kingdom of God. In His preaching and teaching, Jesus made use of vineyards, mustard seeds, fig trees, coins, sheep, goats, birds, flowers, foundations, children, fish, wine, servants, hidden treasures, dragnets, the rich, and the poor. Jesus consistently affirmed to His followers and listeners that the work of God is present all around us.

Cultivating a Love for God

Parents are also instructed to teach their children to love God with all their heart, with all their soul, and with all their might (Deuteronomy 6:5). Cultivating this love for God is one of the most critical responsibilities of parents. This love is developed by encouraging children to obey God's Word in every area of life, and the best way to make this happen is through your personal example to them. As you love and obey God, your children will learn what it means to do the same in their own lives. Be an example of godliness to your children, and show them that your love for the Lord dominates every facet of your life.

In order to be brought to God, our children need an accurate view of sin and a biblical understanding of their heart attitudes. What children need today is not more self-esteem, more assertiveness training, or more child psychology. These worldly approaches only drive children further away from God, for they all teach that the answers to life reside within one's self instead of in God. Unless children are taught that their sinful nature separates them from God and that they need Christ, they will grow up alienated from Him and turn to influences that shape their character in ungodly ways. They need to know that only God can change their wicked hearts through repentance and faith in the Lord Jesus Christ.

While it is true that our children's eternal destiny is a matter to be settled between them and God, still, parents are called to instruct their children in the Lord and encourage them toward saving faith. So, pray continuously for your children and impress the truths of the gospel on their hearts. Teach God's Word, and enforce it with loving and consistent discipline that helps your children to follow its precepts. William Farley, in his helpful book *Gospel-Powered Parenting*, states, "The most effective parents have a clear grasp of the cross and its implications for daily life. The implications are manifold. They include the fear of God, a marriage that preaches the gospel to its children, deeply ingrained humility, gratitude, joy, firmness coupled with affection, and consistent teaching modeled by parents daily."[4]

Shaping the Heart and Not Just Behavior

The Bible says that the human heart is the mission control center of a person's life. "Keep your heart with all vigilance, for from it flow the springs of life" (Proverbs 4:23). This theme is echoed in Luke 6:45: "The good person out of the good treasure of his heart produces good, and the evil person out of his evil treasure produces evil, for out of the abundance of the heart his mouth speaks." These passages show us that external behaviors are not the fundamental issue.

Rather, it's what happens to the heart that's critical. The words that come out of your children's mouths and the behaviors they display are direct reflections of what is in their hearts.

Too often parents get caught up in merely changing the external behavior of their children. Yet when children do wrong, it's because of sin embedded in the heart. Parents must therefore be concerned with the heart attitudes that drive a child's behavior. As one author has said, "A change in behavior that does not stem from a change in heart is not commendable; it is condemnable."[5] Because young children are unable to see how their rebellious hearts compel them toward sinful behavior, fathers need to point this out. Fathers need to explain how selfishness, self-centeredness, and wrong behavior are rooted in the heart. The goal of biblical parenting is not only to modify your children's behavior, but to facilitate heart change. Corrective discipline that is biblical will address attitudes of the heart. It shows children their sinful hearts and their need for the Lord to redeem them from their sinful ways. Help your children to understand that only repentance and faith in the Lord Jesus Christ can change their hearts.

Teaching children scriptural truth is an ongoing process, and fathers should consider it a tremendous privilege and joy to serve as a primary spiritual guide to their children. Those fathers who back away from this role out of frustration, intimidation, or neglect miss out on one of the greatest blessings of parenthood. When you abdicate your responsibility as a parent, you forfeit the rich rewards that come with seeing your children walk in the truth.

Guarding Their Hearts and Minds

A necessary aspect to bringing your children to God is the guarding of their impressionable minds. In contemporary society, children are exposed to evil and immoral value systems via television, the Internet, magazines, and secular books—much more so than in any previous generation. You can help to guard their hearts and minds by monitoring the programs your children watch on television and the content they access through the Internet.

At the same time, you can counter such negative influences by encouraging your children to memorize Scripture and to meditate on the Word of

God regularly. This will help to inform their youthful consciences. The apostle Paul encouraged the Philippian believers to guard their hearts this way: "Whatever is true, whatever is honorable, whatever is just, whatever is pure, whatever is lovely, whatever is commendable, if there is any excellence, if there is anything worthy of praise, think about these things" (Philippians 4:8). You can help your children to do the same in their lives.

Keep in mind that merely keeping your children away from immoral influences is not enough to help protect them. There is an active war going on between the sinful natures they were born with and the scriptural truths you are trying to instill. Without the intervention of the Holy Spirit in your children's lives, they will still sin—regardless of what they are sheltered from. So as you protect them from evil influences, do so with the wisdom that sees that their sinful hearts will be drawn to those influences regardless. The father who realizes the intensity of this war within will give himself over to much prayer on behalf of his beloved children.

Parenting That Understands the Value of Order and Proper Discipline

Parenting that brings glory to God is based upon a proper biblical understanding of the family structure. Looking once again at Paul's instructions regarding the family, we see that he establishes a certain order between children and parents: "Children, obey your parents in the Lord, for this is right. 'Honor your father and mother' (this is the first commandment with a promise)" (Ephesians 6:1-2). Children are to willingly submit to the authority of their parents. They are to respond to their parents as agents of the Lord, obeying them as if they were obeying the Lord Himself.

Children are to know that God Himself instructs them to obey their parents: "Hear, my son, your father's instruction, and forsake not your mother's teaching" (Proverbs 1:8). When children disobey their parents they are disobeying God's command to honor their parents, and ultimately, this means they are disobeying God.

This raises an important question: Is there ever a time when children can disobey their parents? The answer is a conditional yes. *If* parents ask their children to engage in sinful, unlawful, unethical, or immoral activities, the child is obligated to obey God's moral standard and not the demands of the parents. This is what it means to obey your parents "in the Lord"—God's moral law has precedence over the will or wishes of the parents.

Recognizing the Necessity of Discipline

A vital component of biblical parenting is consistent and corrective discipline. Proverbs 22:15 says, "Folly is bound up in the heart of a child; but the rod of discipline drives it far from him." This proverb states a principle that is generally true. However, not all parents who raise their children in solid Christian homes experience success. There are children who grow up under God's counsel in whom foolishness still abounds, and some of them even abandon the faith. This is a sad and unfortunate reality. The direction a child chooses to take in life is not always a reliable barometer of the parents' faithfulness to God. Yet as a general rule, parents who follow scriptural principles in rearing their kids will influence them for righteousness, having a meaningful and positive effect on the character and lifestyle of their children.

Children are born with a natural orientation toward foolishness, corruption, and rebellion. They have a natural inability to obey the Lord, to love Him, or to please Him. Their hearts are automatically inclined toward evil. Why? There are three main causes: The first is their innate fallenness. "None is righteous, no, not one...for all have sinned and fall short of the glory of God" (Romans 3:10,23). Second, the ever-present corruption all around our children defiles them. And third, their own childishness makes them vulnerable to many temptations. Our present-day world blatantly promotes a culture of rebellion against authority.

In our permissive and perverse culture, biblical values and morals regarding child discipline are scoffed at and ridiculed. Loving discipline, which may include the careful and measured use of spanking, is seen as child abuse and as an infringement on the human rights of the child. Some even go so far as to say it is cruel, archaic, and downright criminal. Yet the Bible clearly instructs that early childhood discipline requires both corporal (physical) punishment and loving kindness. Such discipline must have the right motivation and appropriate level of severity. Child discipline should be administered with both love and firmness. Discipline should not be punitive, but corrective. The goal is not to abuse the child, but to steer him away from folly and its resulting danger. Proverbs 13:24 says, "Whoever spares the rod hates his son, but he who loves him is diligent to discipline him." Fathers who genuinely love their children but withhold corporal punishment will produce the same kind of children as fathers who hate their children.

Ultimately, the real hope for lasting change in children rests in God's work on the children's hearts. When fathers address wrong heart attitudes and unbiblical behavior, and teach their children the ways of the Lord, the children will often respond with ready obedience. By catching defiance and rebellion at the point of the attitude, parents will be able to avert much defiant behavior. John MacArthur writes, "The Word of God must be poured into the hearts of the child so that it instructs their conscience and it constantly talks to them. When a child's heart is stoked with Scripture, the child's own conscience will often rebuke wrong attitudes. The conscience is a God-given warning system."[6]

Reviewing Key Principles of Discipline

Here are some helpful and practical steps to consider with regard to child discipline:

- Establishing house rules helps your children to understand your expectations and develop self-control. Some examples might be no television until homework is done, and no name-calling or hurtful teasing allowed.

- Decide ahead of time the consequences for certain types of disobedience, and be prepared to follow up on the consequences by enforcing the consequences. A common mistake parents make is the failure to apply discipline on a consistent basis. You cannot discipline children for name-calling one day and ignore it the next. Being consistent teaches children to respect your expectations.

- Loving discipline should be firm and implemented with the goal of steering the child away from danger.

- Discipline should be age-appropriate—a toddler should be approached differently than a ten-year-old. Be realistic and don't mete out measures that are impossible or impractical for your children to perform. For example, when you use a time-out system, do not place a three-year-old child in a room by himself for an hour or longer periods of time. This may work for an older child, but an unsupervised younger child may end up doing something that may hurt himself or put his life at risk.

- It is advisable that you avoid disciplining a child in front of others (cousins, friends, and strangers). Matthew 18:15 says matters of discipline are to be handled by the parties involved.

- Discipline should typically not be carried out in anger, frustration, or hatred. Explain to your child why he is being disciplined. Taking the time to explain the offense and the consequence will help you to keep your emotions under control.

- When you discipline your children, don't be too strict or too lenient. There is value to showing grace on occasion, as this pictures how God is toward us. However, the rule of consistency must be the norm so that children learn that consequences always follow behavior, whether good or bad.

- Clearly communicate to your children which types of behaviors are appropriate and which are not. While some behaviors might not violate a rule, it's possible they are still not appropriate. Equip your child to discern the difference—for example, it's appropriate to speak to adults with respect, and it's not appropriate to interrupt other people's conversations.

- Teach your children to watch their words—"Whoever keeps his mouth and his tongue keeps himself out of trouble" (Proverbs 21:23). "When words are many, transgression is not lacking, but whoever restrains his lips is prudent" (Proverbs 10:19).

- Provide a stable home environment for your child by applying discipline fairly, consistently, lovingly, and promptly.

Exercising Consistency in Discipline

For many fathers, disciplining with consistency is an ongoing challenge. Tiredness, lack of energy, stress, busyness, a lack of motivation, and personal problems are among the main reasons fathers struggle in this area. Yet maintaining consistency is a very big part of successful fatherhood. Because this is so important, here are some helpful guidelines:

- Be consistent in your demonstration of love and affection toward your children. Do not show loving kindness one day and demonstrate distant behavior the next day.

- Be consistent as you implement rules and consequences. Whenever your children disobey rules, deal with them.

- Make sure that you, your wife, all grandparents, and all care-givers (including teachers) are consistent when it comes to discipline. Be sure to agree on what is appropriate (acceptable) and inappropriate (unacceptable) behavior for a child. Grandma and grandpa, for example, should not tolerate behavior that is forbidden by mom and dad, as this undermines the parents' authority and encourages the child to manipulate the adults in their lives.

- Make sure you are consistent in providing positive feedback. At every opportunity, give your children constructive, helpful, and edifying feedback.

- Parent firmly, fairly, and constantly.

Providing Structure in Discipline

Structure and routine are essential to establishing a home with order and proper discipline. This is especially important when the children are younger. Without a basic structure or routine in place, children can become very difficult to work with and parent. Structure gives little ones a sense of security and stability, for it helps them to know what to expect. Make your parenting easier by establishing these things early in your children's lives.

According to *Merriam-Webster*, *structure* can mean "something arranged in a definite pattern of organization."[7] And *routine* is defined as "a regular course of procedure."[8] Parents define the structure, or how daily life will be organized. Children are then taught the routines of daily life as they grow up. Examples of routines are making one's bed every morning, keeping one's room clean, picking up one's toys, brushing one's teeth after meals, and washing one's hands after using the bathroom. As your children grow older, they will become responsible for additional routines, such as doing their homework at a set time each day.

Such routines are important because they inform children about daily expectations and motivate them to be disciplined. These routines will become habits that serve them well throughout their lives. They will help your children stay organized and get things done. In fact, if you were to take a closer look at those people who have been successful in life, you would probably find that many of them have been disciplined about following certain routines every day.

Starting your children at a young age to get used to set routines is important, especially when it comes to schoolwork. Discussing your children's daily routines with their teachers can be a very helpful exercise, as it will help to create a sense of consistency in the child's life. As an educator, I've observed that children who have a set routine for studying and doing their homework do better in their classes.

When you provide your children with a structured home and school life, they are able to know what is expected of them. Here are some of the benefits of structure:

- it encourages positive behavior and self-control
- it encourages self-responsibility
- it helps advance development
- it strengthens the parent-child relationship

Often children are frustrated when there is no clear structure at home or in school. They receive mixed messages with regard to what's expected of them, which results in tension and misunderstandings between everyone.

When fathers are overwhelmed by the responsibilities and challenges of family life, they often succumb to a parenting style called "erratic eclecticism." It is erratic in that it moves from one method of parenting to another with little or no consistency. It is eclectic in that it draws freely from many sources.

For example, a father might pick up a few parenting ideas while skimming through certain magazines; he might get some ideas from talk shows on the radio; and he might get still other ideas during casual conversations with colleagues in the workshop or office. In an effort to see whether these ideas work, he will try them out for a while. And if the results aren't immediate, he will move on to something else.

Among the ideas he might try is getting the kids to sign contracts, grounding them, using emotional appeals, resorting to bribery. Along the way, he might get frustrated and wind up yelling a lot. And the children become confused because they are not sure what dad wants. There is no clear structure or set of expectations, and the children never know what to expect next. This makes life harder for them.

Another problem is fathers who are vague in their communication: "You must be more responsible," "You must stop being naughty," or "You must obey." For many children, such broad-sweeping statements mean little. Children typically think in concrete terms—they respond better to specific instructions rather than vague statements. Clear communication may include, "Put your toys in the box after playtime," "Do your homework from 3:30 to 4:00," and "It would be helpful if you could clean the dishes after dinner."

Be clear about the rules in the home, your expectations, and the consequences for inappropriate behavior. This will go a long way toward not exasperating your children!

Parenting That Displays Love

Fathers are called to function as agents of God. And this calls for more than just providing adequate food, clothing, and shelter for your children. A father's greatest responsibility is to love his children.

How do you demonstrate Christ-honoring love to your children?

Marital Love

An essential key to good parenting is a strong and enduring marriage. One of the best things we can do as fathers is to love our wives and maintain a healthy marriage. Whereas many marriages suffer as mom and dad increasingly give themselves over to the needs (or perceived needs) of their children, Christian parents must remain first and foremost committed to one another. William Farley states,

> Marriage-centered, not child-centered, moms usually exert the greatest influence on their children for Christ and His kingdom. This means that your weekends away with your husband, alone,

might influence your children more than all your teaching and disciplining combined. Your children are watching, and it gives them great joy and security to see dad and mom loving each other.[9]

That's great advice—especially when the challenges of parenting show up.

The "Cuteness" Factor

Any parent will tell you that their children were so cute when they were little babies that they were easily loveable. However, as the kids grow older, children can become more difficult to manage. And love in terms of adoring a cute little infant is of necessity replaced with the kind of love that realizes that a reciprocal love may or may not be returned. This is when *faithful* parenting is most needed!

Fathers, loving your children can be demonstrated not by adoring your children's physical attributes, but by nurturing them, encouraging them, supporting them, showing sincere interest in their needs and concerns, genuinely paying attention to little things, spending time with them unhurriedly, playing with them regularly, listening to them attentively, attending their sports events, laughing with them, talking to them about the little things so that they will feel comfortable talking to you about the big things, praising and acknowledging their achievements, hugging and reassuring them, telling them on a regular basis that you love them, praying with them, and speaking about God with them on a daily basis. When fathers genuinely connect with their children in these ways, they develop bonds that encourage openness and truthful communication.

As you make time for your children, don't overwhelm them by "invading" their space too much. They also need time to play by themselves and to develop friendships with other children.

Empathy and Understanding

The word *empathy* means "to feel with someone from their point of view." Empathizing with your children can be very helpful, especially when they experience challenges you faced as a child. Having empathy does not mean allowing your children to get away with irresponsible and inappropriate behavior. Rather, it means fostering an open and truthful communication. As you take time to understand the difficulties and challenges your children face, you can engage with them and talk about the options that are available for resolving the problem—including options you found helpful as you were growing up.

For example, some children grow and develop more slowly than others. This may call for great patience on your part. Shepherding such a child with a tenderhearted lovingkindness and an appreciation for the child's efforts—even if those efforts fail—will cultivate a relationship built on trust and respect.

You'll want to have empathy for your children when it comes to teaching them God's Word. Even the apostle Paul exhorted Timothy to teach the Word with great patience (2 Timothy 4:2) when he worked with adults. How much more should we, as fathers, exercise patience with our little ones? Showing tolerance for spiritual ignorance on the part of our children shows patience in the process of drawing them to God. This is all part of the wonderful adventure of spiritual growth. Empathize with your children's weaknesses and shortcomings, lovingly discipline them, and be faithful to shepherd them in the direction of Christlikeness.

Loving During Times of Disagreement

Within reason, on some matters, parents can allow some room for disagreement or negotiation. As they grow older, children will develop certain personal preferences, acquiring their own manner, style, and taste in music, clothing, and food. Too often parents expect their children to be carbon copies of themselves. This is not realistic, and puts undue strain on the parent-child relationship. Understanding that children will be different and that they are unique creations of God will allow them to develop into their own persons without stifling external pressure.

Naturally, as children grow older they will have times when they make poor decisions or rebel to some degree against your established authority. As a father, you must identify with your children's struggles and then take them to the cross of Christ to find forgiveness and power to live victoriously. Fathers are not guiding their children biblically if, when they strip away all the excuses for failure and force them to see their sin as it is, they fail to point them to the well-worn path to the cross—the path of repentance and faith. In all your interaction with your children, steer them toward finding comfort and strength in knowing God. Look upon your child as a "human becoming" as well as a "human being." Look upon the task of parenting your children as a process that will take years to complete.

Parenting That Models Godliness

There is an old adage that says, "Don't worry that children never listen to you; worry that they are always watching you." This flawed statement sums up the need for parents to be sensitive to the fact that their children are constantly observing their behavior.

Your children will learn a lot from watching you. And the younger they are, the more cues they take from you. They are like sponges; they soak up everything around them and act on that which they take in. That's why it's essential for husbands to demonstrate biblical authority over their wives, and wives biblical submission to their husbands. Biblical submission can also be demonstrated by both parents to the government, employers, and the church. By being an example of submission, you will teach your children how to respectfully function under authority. The attitudes you display will teach either biblical submission or self-reliance and rebellion.

Here are some principles to keep in mind as you parent by example:

- Father and mother should demonstrate love toward each other, in appropriate ways, in front of their children. A father may express love for his wife by hugging her, kissing her, and showing interest in her needs. This will develop a sense of cohesiveness in the family which the children will pick up on.

- Before you lash out or blow up in front of your child, ask yourself: *Is this how I want my child to behave when angry?* Be conscious of the fact that your children are constantly watching you.

- Model Christ-honoring values and habits that will be helpful to your child; for example, sincerity, truthfulness, honesty, strong work ethic, unselfish behavior, benevolence (consideration for others), and integrity. Do not allow your children to develop habits such as idleness and sloth. Scripture instructs us that "slothfulness casts into a deep sleep, and an idle person will suffer hunger" (Proverbs 19:15).

- Teach your children to work hard and to be diligent. "Whatever you do, work heartily, as for the Lord" (Colossians 3:23).

- Speak the truth to your children at all times. Be truthful in all your dealings with them and teach them the value of speaking and living the truth. Nothing makes the truth more distasteful to a child than to have a hypocritical or spiritually shallow father who affirms the truth publicly but denies it in the privacy of the family home. "Lying lips are an abomination to the LORD, but those who act faithfully are his delight" (Proverbs 12:22).

- Refrain from using children as pawns to punish or get back at your wife or other family members.

- Cultivate a life of integrity through blameless personal conduct, a godly lifestyle, and exemplary character. "Whoever walks in integrity walks securely, but he who makes his ways crooked will be found out" (Proverbs 10:9).

- Model good health habits—teach and show your children the value of eating healthily and exercising regularly.

- Teach your children the value of wise and discerning decision-making, and teach them to choose their friends wisely. "Whoever walks with the wise becomes wise, but the companion of fools will suffer harm" (Proverbs 13:20).

- Teach your children how to manage their money as faithful stewards of God. Show them that the way they spend it should honor God, since He is our provider and owns everything. Teach them to be loyal managers of what the Lord gives them, since their time on earth is limited and they will one day give an account to God for how they used their time, treasures, and the talents He entrusted to them.

- Be honest enough to confess to your children when you have said or done something hurtful. Ask for their forgiveness when you sin against them. Your children will respect you more for doing this, and along the way will learn the biblical process for reconciling broken relationships.

- As the head of the home, maintain and practice daily Bible reading and study, personal times of devotion, prayer, and witnessing.

Parenting That Does Not Provoke to Anger

Fathers are exhorted in Ephesians 6:4, "Do not provoke your children to anger." What are some of the ways we can end up exasperating our children and provoking them to anger?

1. Comparing siblings—comparing one child with another communicates an unloving spirit and fosters resentment

2. Pushing achievements—fathers sometimes raise the bar so high that no achievement is ever good enough

3. Over-indulging them—when children are accustomed to getting what they want, they will become angry when we don't give them what they desire

4. Discouraging them—giving them a sense that they are useless, in the way, not needed, or a burden

5. Making them feel like an intrusion in your life—they have to figure out how to run their own lives because you can't be bothered

6. Failing to allow them to grow up—you do not allow them to make mistakes and learn from them; you overreact to small accidents; you yell or scream at them when they have a problem

7. Neglecting your children—not being attentive to their needs and being too busy for them; your commitment to other things communicates volumes about what you consider your priorities to be

8. Using hateful words and physical cruelty—you ridicule your children and use sarcasm when they make mistakes; you punish them relentlessly when they fail

9. Not giving them a sense of security and safety—you do not communicate optimism and expectancy through words or actions that show you have their interests at heart

Parenting That Sees Children as a Privilege

Indeed, fatherhood is not an easy task. Yet there is an endless supply of opportunities to influence these precious little ones for the glory of God. Be sure to make the most of the opportunities you have. Maintain an eternal perspective in your thinking and motivation. Consider it a privilege to have an active role in shaping not only the character of your children, but their perception of God.

Successful fatherhood results from faithful obedience to God's instructions for the family. There is no greater worldly blessing than rearing your children in a way that honors the Lord Jesus Christ, and then seeing them grow up to honor the heavenly Father in their own lives. As John MacArthur says, "Parents, ours is a solemn and awesome responsibility, but it's a wonderful privilege. One of the most fulfilling experiences in all the world is to have children committed to following the Lord, no matter what the cost, because they have seen the same commitment in us."[10]

May the grace of the Lord Jesus Christ be with you as you bring up your children in the discipline and instruction of the Lord!

Recommended Resources

Alcorn, Randy. *Eternal Perspectives Newsletter*. Sandy, OR: Eternal Perspective Ministries, 2011.

Dirkse, Melvin. *Bring Them Up in the Training and Admonition of the Lord* (unpublished thesis). Los Angeles, CA: The Master's College, 2007.

Farley, William. *Gospel-Powered Parenting*. Phillipsburg, NJ: P&R Publishing, 2009.

MacArthur, John. *Successful Christian Parenting*. Nashville, TN: Word Publishing, 1998.

Mack, Wayne. *Preparing for Marriage*. Tulsa, OK: Virgil Hensley Publishing, 1986.

Tripp, Tedd. *Shepherding a Child's Heart*. Wapwallopen, PA: Shepherd Press, 1995.

Parenting Adult Children as a Father[1]

Jim Newheiser

After his daughter's wedding, Ed felt a wave of emotion come over him as he recognized that an important phase of his life had come to an end. After almost thirty years of intense parenting, he and his wife Martha have an empty nest. Two of his three children are now married. Ted, the youngest, is away at college and should graduate in two years. Ed knows that he will still have relationships with his kids, but wonders what those relationships will look like. He is apprehensive because he has seen what has happened with his friends' adult kids.

For example, his good friend John still has his thirty-year-old unemployed adult son living at home. What should he do if Ted wants to move back home after college? What should he do if his grown children have financial problems? He knows that things are very tight for his oldest son, Stuart, and his wife. Should he step in and bail them out? Or should he let them learn to budget, avoid debt, and save up money on their own, perhaps learning from their mistakes?

Ed is also concerned that Ted is dating a girl who does not appear to be a believer. Martha is very upset about this and wants to lay down the law, but Ed isn't sure how much they should say. An even greater concern is that Ted hasn't been attending church regularly while going to college. Is he losing his faith?

Ed wonders whether he and Martha are prepared to deal with the challenge of parenting adult kids. When the children were young, Ed and Martha read lots of books and attended many seminars that taught the biblical principles for raising kids. And even though he is now an empty-nester, he realizes he still needs biblical wisdom on how to be a good father to his adult kids—perhaps more than ever. As one parent said, "We thought that when the children reached eighteen parenting would be pretty much over. On the contrary, we discovered that our most challenging years as parents were when they were young adults…When the children were small, parenting was simple—not easy, but simple. Now parenting has become much more complex."

The good news for Ed is that the all-sufficient Scriptures that guided him when his children were growing up also address the challenges he faces with his adult children. Some of the most important parent-child interactions in the Bible occur between parents and their grown children (consider Eli and David). There are also passages about the difficulties parents face with wayward older children (Deuteronomy 21:18-21; Ezekiel 18:1-18). And the entire book of Proverbs was written to plead with a young adult son (or daughter) to pursue wisdom instead of folly.

Be Prepared to Let Go

Unlike the marriage relationship, which is designed by God to endure until death (Romans 7:2), the relationship between parents and their children is meant to change dramatically as the children enter into adulthood. A major objective of parenting is to make our children ready to live wisely on their own. This includes training them to love and fear God (Proverbs 1:7; Matthew 22:37) and to put others above themselves (Matthew 22:39; Philippians 2:3-4). Preparing our children for maturity also includes…

- teaching them to work hard in a vocation (Proverbs 6:5-11; 12:11; 22:29),

- teaching them to manage money wisely (Proverbs 3:9-10,27-28; 6:8; 21:5; 22:7),

- teaching them God's design for sex and marriage (Proverbs 5; 6:20-35; 7; 31:10-31),

- teaching them to control their speech (Proverbs 8:13; 10:11; James 3:5-12), and

- teaching them to choose their friends carefully (Proverbs 13:20).

A wise father who wants to have significant input into the lives of his adult children would do well to engage in a study of the book of Proverbs with them.[2]

Sometimes when our kids leave home or declare their independence, we don't feel that they are as ready as they should be (or as they think they are). Even so, we are obligated to recognize the fact that they are becoming adults and that we have to relate to them as adults, albeit immature adults. One of the biggest mistakes Christian parents make is treating their adult children as if they were still young kids. Many of us have a hard time adjusting from a relationship that started with us having total control (when they were infants) to a situation that appears to be out of control. In fact, sometimes it is easier for us to respect the adulthood of our friends' children than it is to see that our own children are adults.

When do children become adults? It is generally agreed that when children get married, they leave their father and mother to be joined to their spouse (Genesis 2:24). Even if we question whether our children have married wisely and well, we must respect the integrity of their marriage and not try to exert parental control over their lives. (You can read more on this in chapter 12, "The Husband's Role in Leaving and Cleaving.")

But what about single adult children? Some claim that a child is under parental authority until the day that he or she is married. There are parents who will even try to command unquestioned obedience from a thirty- or forty-year-old adult child. Our understanding, however, is that the Bible teaches the concept of a child "coming of age" as an adult, regardless of marital status. For example, in John 9:23, the parents of a blind man who had been healed by Jesus were challenged by some religious leaders to explain what had happened, and they said, "He is of age; ask him." Jesus had to explain to his mother Mary that their relationship had changed now that He was engaged in His ministry (John 2:3-4). Paul assumed that those who had the gift of singleness would use that gift not merely to stay home and serve their parents, but to serve the Lord (1 Corinthians 7:7-8,32).[3] As we will soon see, if your adult child is a dependent or is living under your roof, you will have certain expectations of him or her, but these will be different from what you would expect of a minor child.

As your children reach adulthood, your role shifts from being an authority figure to becoming a counselor. When your children are young, you can require them to listen to you and to obey as you fulfill the responsibility of parental stewardship God has given to you. As they become men and women, however, you can only have as much of a relationship with them as you mutually agree.

While the *nature* of your relationship will change, that doesn't mean the *quality* of it will lessen. Many parents have wonderful relationships with their adult kids. As these young adults begin to face the challenges of career, finances, marriage and children, they often seek wisdom from their parents (for whom they suddenly have a growing appreciation). On the other hand, adult children are often very sensitive and insecure about receiving unsolicited advice from their parents. This can be especially true of your adult children's spouses. What you mean as helpful counsel may be taken as a meddlesome attempt to control.

You especially want to make sure any counsel you give doesn't become nagging, which can damage your relationship with your grown children. Before speaking, ask yourself, *Does she already know what I think about this? Have I said it before?* We may be inclined to think that if we stated our case in a new way, our kids will finally see our point. The problem is probably not that they don't understand you, but that they aren't persuaded. It is hard to stand back and watch our children go against our counsel, especially if it means they are acting unwisely. Sometimes the only way they will learn is by facing the consequences of foolish choices. Your bringing up certain issues repeatedly—that is, nagging—may do significant damage to your relationship and may make your children (and their spouses) less likely to seek your counsel in other situations.

Some couples are fearful of the empty nest because they have long had a child-centered home built around relationships with and activities of the children. The husband and wife may have been so busy with the kids that they haven't worked enough on the one relationship in the family that isn't supposed to change—their marriage. *When your kids leave, the nest isn't empty.* The two of you are there together, just as you were when your family began many years ago. The so-called empty nest years can be a wonderful stage in life as a couple learns anew to love, enjoy, and bless one another, and as they have more time and opportunity to serve the Lord together.[4]

What If Your Adult Children Don't Leave the Nest (or Come Back)?

In recent years the number of young adults living with their parents has multiplied[5] such that a new social phenomenon has been widely recognized.

Time magazine labeled these grown children as "Twixters";[6] Brits call them *kippers* (kids in parents' pockets eroding retirement savings); Australians say they are *boomerang kids* (you throw them out and they keep coming back); John Piper calls them *adultolescents* (stuck between adulthood and adolescence).

Now, there are some valid reasons for a single adult child to live at home. These may include completing one's education or training for a vocation, choosing to remain under parental protection while awaiting marriage, or taking care of aged or disabled family members (Matthew 15:5-6; 1 Timothy 5:4). Sometimes children move home because of extraordinary circumstances, such as a daughter with children who has been widowed or abandoned by her husband. An adult child may move back home as a last resort in economic hardship (unemployment). Some adult children are not physically or mentally able to take care of themselves. For example, we counseled a family whose adult son sustained a brain injury while at college. The parents, who had anticipated enjoying their empty-nest years, have come to realize that their son will probably need to be with them for the rest of their lives. The good news is that God is working in at least three lives through this trial (see James 1:2-4; Romans 8:28). Young adults who are living with their parents should have a clear and valid purpose for being there, and in most cases, a plan for eventually becoming independent (Proverbs 21:5).

Sadly, many young adults are living with their parents because they are sinfully postponing the responsibilities of adulthood. They are failing to gain the skills by which they can establish a career and provide for themselves (Proverbs 28:19), often spending many years as a "student" without ever making significant progress toward a degree. They expect their parents to take care of their financial needs (housing and food, and often car, clothes, and phone). They are often financially irresponsible, working only enough to pay for their discretionary spending and getting into debt (Proverbs 22:7). Even though their incomes are beneath the poverty level, they expect instant gratification, buying all the latest electronic gadgets and eating out often. Some of these adult kids have nicer phones and even take nicer vacations than their parents because mom and dad are subsidizing their lifestyle by paying for room and board. These kids aren't making the connection between hard work and the things it buys (Proverbs 14:23; 16:26), and they often have an entitlement mentality. And sadly, instead of marrying and having a family,[7] some of them indulge in uncommitted relationships and fornication.

Parents who help finance and enable such behavior only end up contributing to the problem. Like Eli, the classic biblical example of the failed parent, they fail to rein in their wayward dependent children (1 Samuel 3:13). It is significant that Eli's infamous parental failure took place when his sons were adults.[8] The Lord revealed the heart of Eli's sin, saying, "You…honor your sons above me" (1 Samuel 2:29). Eli didn't want to disturb the family peace by crossing his sons through stopping their evil practices and corrupt worship. In the same way, many parents don't want to rock the boat, so they find it easier to keep paying their kids' bills and bailing them out, rather than forcing them to face the consequences of their folly (Proverbs 10:4; 20:13).

We should also notice that Eli was not entirely passive in dealing with his sons. He nagged them about their immorality—"Why do you do such things?" (1 Samuel 2:23)—but he did not take action. In the same way, many parents today will nag their children, "Why don't you go to bed earlier instead of staying up all night playing video games or going out with your friends, and then rising in the afternoon? You need to get a job." But like Eli, these parents are afraid to take decisive action. And like Eli, these parents may face God's judgment.

What Should Be Expected of an Adult Child Living at Home?

The challenge of having an adult child living at home is that he wants to be treated as an adult (with all of the privileges and freedoms), while he is still dependent upon his parents (who often have a hard time looking upon him as a grownup). While you have no formal authority over your independent adult children, the fact they are under your roof (or otherwise economically dependent) subjects them to your rules (just as anyone else staying in your home would have to meet certain expectations). These rules should be reasonable and should recognize their adulthood, and you should communicate your expectations clearly. Sometimes conflicts occur because parents haven't made the rules and expectations clear to their adult children, and sometimes adult children will find ways to excuse noncompliance unless expectations are spelled out (usually in writing).

One important change that occurs when your children are no longer minors is that their living with you becomes mutually voluntary. You are free to kick them out if they don't meet your expectations. If they complain about your rules, they are always free to move out and go where they can find a better deal.

Expectations should include that your adult children must work as hard as the other adults in the household (Proverbs 10:1,4-5; Ephesians 4:28). This means that between work and school, they should carry out responsibilities that are the equivalent of a full-time job. In addition, they should be expected, like mom and dad, to do their fair share of work around the house. Adult children should also be expected to take financial responsibility for themselves, which includes paying for their own expenses (2 Thessalonians 3:6-12)—including car, phone, clothing, food, and household expenses (with some exceptions to be made for full-time students, who may need to use their money toward schooling). Don't make the mistake of repeatedly bailing your adult kids out of the consequences of laziness and poor planning, even giving or lending them money for discretionary items such as vacations and electronic equipment.

You can also insist that adult children living under your roof be sexually pure (Hebrews 13:4). If a young adult wants to enjoy the privileges of marriage, he or she needs to grow up enough to take on the responsibilities of marriage. In the same way, you should not tolerate substance abuse (Proverbs 23:2,30-31). Where trust has been violated, it is probably wise and necessary for you to make random drug testing a condition for living at home. Keep in mind that any rules you establish will work only if they are enforced.[9]

A Bible verse that is applicable to parenting foolish adult children is Proverbs 26:3: "A whip for the horse, a bridle for the donkey, and a rod for the back of fools." While a wise son will listen to parental wisdom (Proverbs 13:1), just as a stubborn donkey won't move unless his master whips him, an adult child who is lazy, immoral, and inebriated will only be motivated by pain. If you saw a man standing next to a donkey begging, "Please, Mr. Donkey, won't you move? It makes me want to cry when you treat me this way," you would regard the man as a fool. Yet many parents nag their wayward young adults, but do not take action. Often these parents are driven by fear. They say, "If I get tough with her, she will leave the house and live on the streets. I can't stand the thought of that."

The problem is that foolish adult children often know their parents' fears and will try to use them to manipulate their parents. Proverbs 19:18 advises,

"Discipline your son while there is hope, and do not desire his death" (NASB). Having a wayward adult child in your home may give you one final opportunity to discipline him. You may ask, "What can we do? We can't spank him." Parents must be creative when it comes to bringing consequences upon their adult children. You can start by no longer paying for their stuff, and taking away that for which you have paid, such as a phone or car. You can also require them to do extra work around the house or pay monetary fines. While there should be room for grace and forgiveness, ultimately you must be willing to kick out an adult child who is unwilling to comply with your rules. Remember that the prodigal son did not come to his senses until he was far from home and suffering the consequences of his sinful choices (Luke 15:11-21).

What if Your Adult Child Breaks Your Heart?

We have all heard stories of children from good Christian families who rebel. Some have denied the faith. Some engage in fornication through cohabiting. We have even heard of pastors' and missionaries' children who have turned to a homosexual lifestyle. Others are enslaved by substance abuse and have gotten in trouble with the law.

How can this happen? Doesn't the Bible promise that good parenting will always produce godly children? After all, Proverbs 22:6 says, "Train up a child in the way he should go; even when he is old he will not depart from it." Yet a careful study of the book of Proverbs reveals these proverbs are not unconditional promises; rather, they are maxims or principles of wisdom. (For more on this, see what chapter 2 says about properly interpreting biblical texts.) For example, it is a true principle of wisdom that "the hand of the diligent makes rich" (Proverbs 10:4). But not all diligent people are wealthy, and some sluggards get rich through gambling! In the same way, Proverbs 22:6 speaks of God's *general* blessing upon faithful parents—it's not a promise that will apply to every single child. We have to keep in mind that there are some different factors that can influence how our kids turn out.[10]

The Bible mentions at least three of these key factors:

First, parents are responsible to raise their children faithfully in the discipline and admonition of the Lord (Proverbs 23:13-14; 29:15,17).

Second, children are responsible for the choices they make (Proverbs

20:11). Not all rebellion is the fault of parents. For example, Cain and Abel were both raised by the same parents in the same environment (without external influences such as the Internet, television, or bad neighbors). Abel faithfully worshipped God, but Cain became a murderer. In Ezekiel 18:1-18 we read about a godly father who has a wicked son, and that wicked son then goes on to have a godly son. We are told that each man will be judged by his own life choices, and not on the basis of his father's choices. The entire book of Proverbs is written by a father who pleads with his son to make the right choices in life.[11] God Himself was a father to wayward Israel, and parents of ungodly children should find comfort in the fact that He sympathizes with their pain: "Children have I reared and brought up, but they have rebelled against me" (Isaiah 1:2; see also Jeremiah 2:30).

The third and most important factor in how our children turn out is the sovereign grace of God at work in them. Our children are conceived and born sinners (Psalm 51:5; Ephesians 2:1-3). Even if we were perfect parents, they— like Cain and Israel—would rebel. And we are such imperfect (sinful) parents that even if our children were blank slates, we would still ruin them. It is only the grace of God which gives our children a new birth and draws them to Christ (John 6:44; Ephesians 2:4-5).

Given these factors, we should not be shocked when children from Christian families go wayward. In fact, Jesus warned that the gospel would divide families: "From now on in one house there will be five divided, three against two and two against three. They will be divided, father against son and son against father, mother against daughter and daughter against mother" (Luke 12:52-53). So if your children are not walking with the Lord, plead with God to work in the hearts of the prodigals to bring them home. And if you have godly children, give all of the glory to the Lord for His sovereign mercy to them and to you, in spite of your sins and parenting failures.

Counsel for Parents of Wayward Children

If your children are wayward, your goal should be to show them the love and grace of Christ without enabling a sinful lifestyle. Some parents experience the heartache of children who are successful and moral in the world's eyes, but are not following Christ. Other parents have to deal with children who become involved in gross immorality, substance abuse, or crime. We have even counseled cases in which a wayward young adult has stolen from his father and physically assaulted him.

When dealing with wayward young adults, we should seek to reflect the merciful love we have received from God, in that while we were yet sinners Christ was willing to die for us (Romans 5:8). Communicate to your child that there is nothing he or she can do that will make you stop loving him or her. Don't let your disappointment over your child's unbelieving choices embitter you against him or her. Continue to express your love by working on the relationship, including him or her in family events, and being generous (so long as you are not financing sin). Even if your child is not a believer, you may still offer counsel and help. For example, I know couples who help their unbelieving children get training so that they can be successful in a vocation. A child who is in trouble may be invited to live in the home (under certain conditions, as described earlier) so that he or she can get out of debt, overcome substance abuse issues, etc.

The Bible does speak to the extreme cases of wayward adult children with whom it is impossible to have a good relationship. Deuteronomy 21:18-21 describes a rebellious young adult who is given over to sin. Under the old covenant, he was to be taken before the elders of the city to be put to death. Because we are under the new covenant in Christ, we do not execute wayward young adults. There are, however, principles to observe. One is that there is such thing as an incorrigible child—one who vehemently refuses to cooperate. Notice that such a child is held responsible for his own sin, not the parents. We also see that we are to be concerned about the influence he might have on others (verse 21). Finally, we see that sometimes drastic measures are required. The father whose son assaulted him sought help from the police and got a restraining order. He still hopes that his son will repent and will seek to restore the relationship, but this dad has to keep the rest of his family safe— hence the restraining order.

A common cause for heartache among those of us who are Christian fathers is seeing our children make unwise choices in romance. Every Christian father dreams of the day when he will walk his beautiful virgin daughter down the aisle to marry a godly young man with a good job and from an excellent family, or when he will support his son's marriage to a godly woman whose heart is to please the Lord in all that she does, including her roles as a wife and a mother. Some of us have been able to see our dreams fulfilled. Others of us, however, have had our dreams shattered and have had to entrust our hopes to the Lord.

While the ideal is that parents will be invited to give counsel and blessing to their children's romantic choices, we do not have the power to make this come to pass. If your child is making sinful romantic choices, such as dating an unbeliever or living in fornication, you must realize that the primary problem is not with the person they have chosen. Rather, your child's romantic choices reveal the state of his or her heart (Mark 7:21-23) and may even indicate that he or she is not really a believer[12] (1 John 2:3-4). While you should not finance and enable a sinful lifestyle,[13] you can still love your child and show kindness to the person with whom he or she is involved.[14] Paul tells us to make every effort to be at peace with everyone (Romans 12:18), and Jesus taught us to love even our enemies (Matthew 5:43-48). You don't need to repeatedly tell your children that you are grieved over their choices—they grew up in your home and were taught your standards. They know how you feel. Surprise them by being gracious[15] and look for opportunities to point them to Christ. Their sinful lifestyle will not be solved by mere morality. Their only hope is the life-transforming gospel.

Hope for Fathers

Many of us enjoy wonderfully fulfilling relationships with our adult children. It is exciting to watch them take on adult responsibilities in their careers and in their homes. It is a joy relating to them as fellow adults as we see the kinds of men and women they have become. And we are honored when they seek out our counsel—we now seem much wiser to a twenty-five-year-old than we did to the same child when he or she was sixteen.

Others of us will have children about whom we are deeply concerned spiritually. Our goal should be to do what we can to maintain loving relationships with such sons and daughters, and to pray that God will draw them to Himself, remembering that our heavenly Father loved us even when we were in the far country (Luke 15:11-32). We should take advantage of opportunities to demonstrate the same gospel grace. And our confidence in our good Father enables us to endure in the hope that He will give us grace and strength and ultimately work out all things for our good and His glory (Romans 8:28).

Recommended Resources

Fitzpatrick, Elyse, Jim Newheiser, and Laura Hendrickson. *When Good Kids Make Bad Choices.* Eugene, OR: Harvest House, 2005.

Newheiser, Jim. *Opening Up Proverbs.* Leominster, UK: Day One Publications, 2008.

Newheiser, Jim, and Elyse Fitzpatrick. *You Never Stop Being a Parent: Thriving in Relationships with Your Adult Children.* Phillipsburg, NJ: P&R Publishing, 2010.

Tripp, Paul David. *Age of Opportunity: A Biblical Guide to Parenting Teens.* Phillipsburg, NJ: P&R Publishing, 1997.

15

Godly Grandfathers

David Aycock

What a great gift grandchildren are from God! I have been a grandparent now for more than a decade—blessed so far with one grandson and two granddaughters. From the day my wife and I found out we were going to be grandparents, we have prayed every day that we might have an influence for godliness in the lives of our grandchildren. We have prayed that God would call them to repentance and saving faith, and that they would grow to love Jesus. It's not always easy being a grandparent, but the rewards are great. There is not a lot written about being a godly grandparent from a biblical perspective, and yet there is so much to be written on the subject. In this short chapter I will share a basic overview of some key principles we can glean from Scripture for the responsibility of being a grandparent.

The goal of every Christian is to be conformed to the image of Jesus Christ; it should also be the goal of Christian grandparents who desire to impact the lives of their grandchildren. We see the importance of this in some words of encouragement the apostle Paul wrote to Timothy: "I am reminded of your sincere faith, a faith that dwelt first in your grandmother Lois and your mother Eunice and now, I am sure, dwells in you as well" (2 Timothy 2:15). Here, Paul called to remembrance Timothy's sincere faith, and he acknowledged the influence that Timothy's mother and grandmother had on him. Timothy had a spiritual heritage that was passed down from one of his grandparents. Paul's reference to these women indicates that he must have known them personally, and it's possible Paul was instrumental in leading them to the Lord on one of his missionary journeys. Most likely Timothy's mother and grandmother were

Jews living in exile who received Christ under Paul's preaching. By the time Paul returned on his second journey, they had led their grandson and son to the Lord, and he had proved himself faithful to the Lord (Acts 16:2).

Being this kind of influence on grandchildren is an important role for grandparents to play, but this awesome responsibility requires that we have certain characteristics in our lives as we live for the glory of Christ. Together, these characteristics have to do with godliness, which author Jerry Bridges defines this way: "Godliness is devotion to God which results in a life that is pleasing to God. Godliness is more than Christian character: it is Christian character that springs from a devotion to God. Devotion to God is the mainspring of Christian character. And this devotion to God is the only motivation for Christian behavior that is pleasing to God."[1] We can then sum up godliness as walking in a pure relationship with God—it is a way of life that is based on trusting and obeying God.

Characteristics of a Godly Grandparent

A Personal Relationship with Jesus Christ

The first characteristic of a godly grandparent is that he or she has a personal relationship with Jesus Christ. The fact of the matter is that we are all sinners, and there is no hope for us in this life or the future one without Christ. Salvation is a supernatural transformation that takes place when one confesses his sin, repents of (or turns away from) all sin, and places his faith in Christ alone as His Savior. This act is in no way dependent upon the will of man, but is in response to the drawing of the Holy Spirit to salvation (John 1:12-13). The godly grandparent acknowledges this fact, repents of his sin, and by faith receives Christ as his Lord and Savior (Ephesians 2:1-9). He realizes that he does not belong to himself anymore, but belongs to Christ, and desires to live for Him (1 Corinthians 6:19-20).

This step is the most important step a person can take in life. If you try to be godly without true salvation, you are just self-righteous. This leads to greater problems in your relationships with your grandchildren—you will present to them a false hope for life and teach them how to be religious, but not how to have a relationship with God.

This brings up one of the biggest problems that grandparents face in their relationships with their children and grandchildren, especially if they became a Christian at an older age. According to Barna Research Group, "Just less than two out of three adults (63%) who attended church as children take their own children to a church."[2] So, if you were saved at an early age and you took your children to church, there is a good chance that your children will share the same core beliefs you have, as well as your grandchildren. But if you were saved at an older age and didn't take your children to church, unless your children became Christians at some point, they aren't inclined to take *their* children to church either.

Whatever your situation, saved grandparents are involved grandparents, and they have a concern for the spiritual welfare of their children and grandchildren. There are several possible ways in which you may have the opportunity to act on your concern, and the manner in which you do so will either strengthen or divide the family.

In the times of the patriarchs, the grandfather was the spiritual leader in the home. He was the one who rehearsed the promises of God to the children and grandchildren. This sharing of beliefs, customs, and traditions between grandparents and grandchildren is extremely important, and you'll want to do what you can to fulfill this role. If your children are not Christians and your grandchildren are being raised according to a different belief system—or no belief system at all—there are several things you can do to encourage them toward God, and a few things you should not do.

First, you can pray for your children and grandchildren. In 1 Timothy 2:1-4, Paul urged us to pray for the souls of all men:

> I urge that supplications, prayers, intercessions, and thanksgivings be made for all people, for kings and all who are in high positions, that we may lead a peaceful and quiet life, godly and dignified in every way. This is good, and it is pleasing in the sight of God our Savior, who desires all people to be saved and to come to the knowledge of the truth.

This is an important first step in reaching your family for Christ.

Second, be genuine in your walk with God. Matthew 5:16 says, "Let your light shine before others, so that they may see your good works and give glory to your Father who is in heaven." This is probably the most important thing you can do. Remember, you are not trying to manipulate your children or grandchildren. If they see that your faith is genuine, there is more of a chance that you'll have opportunity to dialogue with them about your beliefs.

Third, before you say or do anything, take some time to try to understand what your adult children are thinking and feeling. In their minds, they believe they have legitimate reasons for raising your grandchildren the way they are. James 1:19-20 says, "Know this, my beloved brothers: let every person be quick to hear, slow to speak, slow to anger; for the anger of man does not produce the righteousness of God."

Fourth, set up a time to meet with your children and talk to them about their decisions regarding the grandchildren. Listen to them and respect their decisions, even though you might not agree with them. You must be careful not to sabotage the relationship you are trying to build by allowing your disapproval to erode the loving communication you have established. Let your children know why you believe the way you do—this might develop into an opportunity to share Christ with them. Make sure you come alongside them in heartfelt concern, not pointing your finger at them and seeking to be confrontational. Tell them why you think it would benefit your grandchildren to be exposed to the gospel.

One thing you must never do is to act without your children's consent and usurp their authority in the home. Whether they are believers or not, God has established them as the leaders of their home. If you model respect for authority before your grandchildren, you will go far in helping the whole family observe you living out your faith. This may lead to greater openings for sharing the gospel than if you whisk the grandchildren away to Sunday school each week without getting their parents' permission.

With regard to honoring your children's authority as parents, note that in Genesis 2, man is directed to leave his parents and cleave to his wife as long as they both live. Biblical counselor Wayne Mack observes that the husband-wife relationship is the priority human relationship.[3] When our children marry, we no longer have the right to try to run their lives, and we must be careful not to overstep boundaries here. When children or grandchildren are pressured to choose one religion over another, human nature is to act in a defensive way and seek to avoid the problem, which may mean your children and grandchildren will seek to avoid you. It is better to keep our comments to a minimum and have some spiritual influence than to say too much and not be welcome at all.

Fifth, be honest with your children. Let them know that when the grandchildren spend the weekend with you, your plan is to take them to church with you. If you are going to have an impact on your grandchildren, there must be honest communication. You must be honorable in all that you do, living in accord with godly wisdom and biblical truth, and waiting upon God's timing.

Accept the Scriptures as the Authority for Life

The second characteristic of a godly grandparent is that he accepts the Scriptures as the authority for his life. A grandparent who is interested in being godly will need instruction that helps him to move toward that goal. This instruction comes from God's Word. Second Timothy 3:16-17 tells us that "all Scripture is breathed out by God and profitable for teaching, for reproof, for correction, and for training in righteousness, that the man of God may be complete, equipped for every good work." Although the context is dealing more directly with pastors, there are some helpful principles here that are applicable to all believers. The Bible is God's Word given to man for instruction on how to live. Paul said it is profitable for teaching, or divine instruction. God's Word provides the believer with everything he needs to live a life that is pleasing to God.

Be Actively Growing in Christlikeness

The third characteristic of a godly grandparent is that he is actively growing in sanctification. The work of sanctification has two steps, and the first is the *pronouncement* of sanctification. This happens when a person is saved and God declares him righteous (Ephesians 2:1-7). He is then set apart to God as a holy vessel to be used for Christ's service: "We are his workmanship, created in Christ Jesus for good works" (Ephesians 2:10). The second step is the *process* that continues until death or the return of Christ (Philippians 2:12-13). This process is empowered by the Spirit of God, who enables the believer to put off sinful habits and put on righteous ones. Paul explains in Ephesians 4:20-24 how this process works:

> That is not the way you learned Christ!—assuming that you have
> heard about him and were taught in him, as the truth is in Jesus, to
> put off your old self, which belongs to your former manner of life
> and is corrupt through deceitful desires, and to be renewed in the
> spirit of your minds, and to put on the new self, created after the
> likeness of God in true righteousness and holiness.

True progressive sanctification is the work of the Spirit through God's Word. It is not just turning over a new leaf or a reformation. If it were just a matter of reformation, we could brag and say, "Look what *I* have done." Sanctification, however, focuses not on self, but on what Christ is making us to be because of the gospel. Jesus said He is the vine and we are the branches, and we cannot do anything without Him. We are to work in cooperation with God. The Spirit enables us, but we take the action.

Serve in Your Local Church

The fourth characteristic of a godly grandparent is that he serves in the context of a local church. The church is the tool that God uses to call the lost to Himself and to nurture believers along in the sanctification process. Throughout the New Testament the church occupies a prominent place, especially in the writings of the apostle Paul. Jesus said that He would build His church, and the gates of hell would not prevail against it (Matthew 16:18).

It is a sad state of affairs when we must define what a church is. Thirty years ago, you could say the word *church* and the evangelical world, and to some degree the non-Christian world, understood what you were talking about. Today, however, a church is whatever people want it to be, and oftentimes, it seems to be very man-centered. There is less and less of an emphasis on people going to church to worship God. Instead, they are going to feel better about themselves or to be entertained. Instead of using the clear teaching of Scripture to determine what a church should be, there are many churches that are seeking direction from business and marketing consultants so that they can attract more people and make sinners feel more comfortable attending. So when I speak of a church, I am not talking about a seeker-friendly, man-centered, mass-marketed organization. I am talking about what the Bible describes in 1 Timothy 3:14-15: "I am writing these things to you so that, if I delay, you may know how one ought to behave in the household of God, which is the church of the living God, a pillar and buttress of the truth." Paul told Timothy that the church is the family of God and that it supports the truth—sound doctrine. In other words, those who belong to a church belong to God and devote themselves to Him and His Word.

That does not mean that if you are not a member of a church you will not go to heaven. Salvation comes through an individual's relationship with Jesus Christ. But it does mean that if you are not part of a church family, you are living in disobedience because God has ordained the church to make and train disciples. Going back to 1 Timothy 3:14-15, note that Paul referred to the church as "the church of the living God." That is, God is the owner of the church. It is His because He made it, designed it, and bought it with the blood of His Son before the foundation of the world. Paul then said that the church holds up the truth. The idea is implied that truth would fall if the church did not exist. And finally, Paul said the church is the foundation of truth. It is the means God has decided to use to proclaim the truth. Clearly, then, the church is of utmost importance to God. Therefore, it should be of utmost importance for Christians to be a member of a local church that is God-centered in its scope.

Being a member of a local church will do several things in your relationship with your grandchildren. First, it will show to them the importance of biblical submission. Hebrews 13:17 states, "Obey your leaders and submit to them, for they are keeping watch over your souls, as those who will have to give an account." Although the word *submission* is viewed negatively in today's society, it is biblically commanded of believers in relation to the church. In the context of grandparenting, our submission to a church shows to our grandchildren that we respect those whom God has placed as authority figures in our lives. As we submit ourselves to the teaching of God's leaders, we teach our grandchildren the importance of obedience in every area of their lives. Sometimes children think they are the only ones who must obey people in authority because they are told by their parents, teachers, and grandparents how they must act and what they must do. When they see their grandparents willingly and joyfully obeying the instructions that are given to them, it makes a lasting and invaluable impression on them.

The second way our participation in church can influence our grandchildren is through our service. Galatians 5:13 says, "You were called to freedom, brothers. Only do not use your freedom as an opportunity for the flesh, but through love serve one another." We sometimes go to church with the wrong attitude, an attitude of "I have a need that must be met, so I will go to church and look for someone who can meet that need." In other words, we want to be served. But we're to go with a heart to serve others, which, in turn, means we're also serving the Lord. No one is too good to serve; no one is too old or too young to serve. We are all called to the body of Christ to serve one another.

A third way our involvement in church can influence grandchildren is that it allows them to see us use our spiritual gifts. Dr. Wayne Mack defines spiritual gifts as "abilities that God has granted to Christians for the edification of others in the body."[4] Every true believer has received gifts from the Lord, and we all have at least one gift that is to be used to serve the body. When we do not minister our gift, we hurt the body of Christ because we are not following God's design for His church.

Unfortunately, some people today, when they reach a certain age, decide they have earned the right to sit back and let others do the work of the ministry. I have heard many different excuses: "I've paid my dues," and "It's time to let a younger person do it," and so on. But nowhere in Scripture do we find support for doing this. In fact, we find the opposite. First Corinthians 15:58 says, "My beloved brothers, be steadfast, immovable, *always* abounding in the work of the Lord, knowing that in the Lord your labor is not in vain."

Make Sure Your Marriage Honors God

The fifth characteristic of a godly grandparent is to have a marriage that is honoring to God. Tragically, many people today get divorced, even within the Christian community. As Christian grandparents, we want to do all we can to model a proper marriage before our grandchildren.

There is a perception in our culture that many older people who are married are not really in love but just tolerate each other. On some popular television shows, grandparents are portrayed as intrusive, loud, insulting, and manipulative. They lie to each other, and even say they wish their partner would leave or die—and sometimes this is said in the presence of the grandchildren. I understand that these are "just television shows," but still, the popularity of these shows shape the way people think, making them have a pervasive and often negative influence.

Children and grandchildren need to see that it is possible for two people to grow in sanctification together, remain in love, and serve Christ for their entire lives. I'm not saying you must have a perfect marriage. Whenever you have two sinners living together, there are going to be problems. But the difference in a Christian marriage is that the two sinners have come to a saving knowledge of Jesus Christ and have committed their lives to serving Him together. They understand that they have a resource in the person of the Holy Spirit, whom they must allow to control their lives. When the Spirit is not in control, the marriage is ripe for conflict and strife. They understand that God has given them a resource book that will guide them in every area of their lives as they submit to its authority in their marriage. So, Christians have many things going for them that make a marriage look very attractive—if they are willing to use the resources God has provided.

A Life Worthy of Imitation

You may have seen the bumper sticker that reads: "If I had known grandchildren were so much fun, I would have had them first!" What joy there is in being able to watch these little one come into the world and grow up! Truly, being a grandparent is wonderful. But along with the trips to the ice cream parlor and ballpark come opportunities to have a powerful influence on these precious loved ones, encouraging them to get to know God and honor Him with their lives as they grow toward adulthood. Make it your goal to live a life worthy of imitating—a life that is honorable and acceptable in the sight of God. "As for you, teach what accords with sound doctrine. Older men are to be sober-minded, dignified, self-controlled, sound in faith, in love, and in steadfastness" (Titus 2:1-2). What a heritage to pass along to the generations to come!

Recommended Resources

Adams, Jay E. *A Theology of Christian Counseling*. Grand Rapids, MI: Zondervan, 1979.

———. *Christian Living in the Home*. Phillipsburg, NJ: P&R Publishing, 1972.

————. *Solving Marriage Problems*. Phillipsburg, NJ: P&R Publishing, 1983.

Bridges, Jerry. *The Practice of Godliness*. Colorado Springs, CO: NavPress, 2001.

MacArthur, John. *The Family*. Chicago, IL: Moody Press, 1982.

Mack, Wayne A. *Your Family God's Way*. Phillipsburg, NJ: P&R Publishing, 1991.

————. *Strengthening Your Marriage*. Phillipsburg, NJ: P&R Publishing, 1997.

Scott, Stuart. *The Exemplary Husband*. Bemidji, MN: Focus Publishing, 2000.

Tripp, Tedd. *Shepherding a Child's Heart*. Wapwallopen, PA: Shepherd Press, 1995.

16

Helping Men Resolve Conflict

Ernie Baker

During the American Civil War, at the Siege of Petersburg in July of 1864, the Union Army, for the most part, had Robert E. Lee and the Confederate Army hemmed in. However, the Southern lines were so strong and Lee's maneuvering so precise that the Union Army could not break the siege. Each attack at various points along the line cost both sides dearly. By the modern standards of war, these clashes were truly massacres. For example, at one point in only four days of fighting, the Union Army alone lost 11,000 men.[1]

The Union Army wanted to break the stalemate because this would open the path to the Confederate capital, Richmond, Virginia, and it would lead to the further weakening of Lee's army. So someone came up with a plan that led to one of the most famous but horrific engagements of the Civil War—the Battle of the Crater. A group of Pennsylvania coal miners dug a tunnel that began at the Union lines, extended 500 feet under no-man's land, and ended under the Confederate line. The Confederates suspected this was happening and tried to dig countertunnels to stop the Union efforts, but to no avail. During the early morning hours of July 30, 1864, the fuse was lit to 8000 pounds of gunpowder that had been placed at the end of the tunnel.

Waiting behind the Union lines were thousands of troops under the command of General James Ledlie. After the explosion, they were to charge headlong into the Confederate position and then fan out left and right on each side of the crater.

When the lit fuse reached the four tons of gunpowder, the resulting blast blew a hole in the ground that measured 170 feet long, 80-100 feet wide, and 30 feet deep. The Union regiments surged forward as three Confederate regiments, various cannons, horses, and other equipment were hurled into the air only to land and be buried in the freshly plowed earth. The lead Union regiments, however, had not been trained precisely on the procedure to follow and, instead of going *around* the crater, they ran down *into* it. The situation was further compounded by the fact General Ledlie did not go with his men, but instead, was hiding behind the lines drinking rum.

The Confederates realized what was happening, and surrounded the hole and began returning fire at the Union soldiers trapped in the bottom. The men in the pit could not accurately and safely return fire, for they were packed so tightly together and in grave danger of hitting their own men. As you might guess, the battle quickly turned into a massacre, with almost 3800 Union casualties. What had been hailed as a brilliant idea had turned into a horrific fiasco. Later, a court of inquiry found Ledlie and a few other officers responsible for the massacre, and he was forced to leave the army.[2]

Two Wrong Responses

General Ledlie's decision to comfort himself with a bottle of rum as the battle took place is just one example of how humans respond to conflict in the wrong way. In fact, since the beginning of time, countless other men have behaved in similarly contemptible ways in the face of conflict. Even as early as Genesis 3 we see Adam *passively* neglecting his duties in the face of potential conflict with Eve and the serpent, and in Genesis 4 we see Cain *aggressively* responding to God's disapproval of his worship. General Ledlie, Adam, and Cain all responded the wrong way to pressure, and in every case, the results were disastrous. And today, men continue to respond either too passively or too aggressively when dealing with the conflicts of life—leading to bad outcomes.

What is the key to responding to conflict in a godly way? Only the gospel and progressive sanctification can help us change how we respond. When we grow in Christlikeness, the resulting maturity enables us to face conflict well and avoid the extreme responses.

Passivity: The First Wrong Response

Before we look at the disaster that we now call the Fall, let's see what the Lord's original intention was for Adam. In Genesis chapter 2, it is clear that Adam, who was created first, was to be the leader of the relationship between a husband and wife. He was the one to whom God gave the instructions for living in the Garden of Eden. Paul reinforced Adam's leadership role in 1 Corinthians 11:3 when he stated, "I want you to understand that the head of every man is Christ, the head of a wife is her husband." Adam was also designed to be in an intimate, trusting relationship with his Creator, as is implied by the fact he was made in the image of God (Genesis 1:26-27), and the rest of Scripture confirms this.

But something went radically wrong, and a lot of it had to do with Adam's erroneous response to a potential conflict. When we think about the Fall, it would be much more accurate to imagine it on the scale of the collapse of the World Trade Center on September 11 than tripping and falling over a crack in the sidewalk. And Genesis chapter 3 perfectly portrays the principle of sowing and reaping, also known as cause and effect—that is, because you did this, that happened. In the rest of this chapter we'll look at the Fall itself (verses 1-6) and its implications (verses 7-24), with a lot more emphasis on the implications, for it is vital for us to recognize the consequences that can result when we respond in the wrong way to conflict.

A Serious Consequence

Some believe that Satan's attack in Genesis 3 was a direct frontal assault on Adam's leadership in the marriage relationship, and indeed, that is emphasized in the chapter.[3] Satan attacked Adam where he was vulnerable: through relationship with his wife, who was of supreme importance to him and of whom he was to be the leader. Notice how the curses God sent upon Adam and Eve were connected to their already-assigned roles. The woman was already going to bear children, but now God says, "In pain you shall bring forth children" (verse 16). To Adam, who was put in the garden "to work it and keep it" (2:15), the Lord says, "Because you have listened to the voice of your wife...cursed is the ground because of you; in pain you shall eat of it all the days of your life" (3:17).

Raymond Ortlund Jr. summarizes what happened when he makes this observation about Genesis 3:6:

> The text does not say, "…she took some and ate it. Her husband, who was with her, also took some and ate it." What actually happened is full of meaning. Eve usurped Adam's headship and led the way into sin. And Adam, who (it seems) had stood by passively, allowing the deception to progress without decisive intervention—Adam, for his part, abandoned his post as head. Eve was deceived; Adam forsook his responsibility. Both were wrong and together they pulled the human race down into sin and death.[4]

It seems as if Adam chose his relationship with his wife over his relationship with the Lord. After all, the well-known saying applies: "If mama ain't happy, ain't nobody happy!" Being passive—or choosing to retreat from his role—got Adam in trouble, the human race in a mess, and is the reason for your relationship problems as well.

A Special Word to Church Leaders

It is obvious that some church leaders respond passively to conflict. Issues are ignored because they are uncomfortable about dealing with them. Or, there is concern about what other people might think if an attempt were made to address an issue. Such responses end up compounding the problem because problems rarely go away on their own, and left unresolved, they end up festering. In *The Leadership Opportunity*, Ken Sande states the problem and the potentially devastating results when leaders respond passively to issues in a church:

> Some conflicts smolder beneath the surface for years in the form of complaining, gossip, backbiting, resentment, or unforgiveness. These underground conflicts—the subtle things we don't take the time to get at the root of—can eventually kill a church. Other conflicts may start with a small spark, but they eventually grow into raging fires that consume marriages, pastoral careers, vital ministries, and entire congregations.[5]

If you are aware of relationship issues that need to be resolved, don't ignore them or pretend they don't exist. Instead, learn the biblical means of dealing with tensions in relationships.

Aggressiveness: The Second Wrong Response

The other extreme response to conflict is found in Genesis 4. How serious was the Fall? It was so bad that less than 25 verses later, we witness the first murder, in which one brother killed another out of jealousy.[6] Just as in chapter 3, desires were a problem. Cain's inner person was screaming out for attention (see verses 6-7). And even though our gracious Lord warned him in advance of the consequences, he fulfilled his desires and lashed out at Abel. Many men have followed suit through the years.

The Real Source of Anger

Some men have been taught that they are genetically wired to be angry or that there is some other cause of their aggressive attitudes and behavior. Robert Jones, in his excellent book *Uprooting Anger*, describes these opinions well:

> Medical-model proponents see anger arising from physiological factors—fatigue, genetic abnormalities, brain-chemical imbalances, hormone deficiencies, or bodily disabilities. Some Christians root anger in direct satanic activity within us—possession or oppression by the devil or maybe even "demons of anger."[7]

Yet James 4:1-2 makes it clear that anger doesn't have its origins in our personality or genetics. Nor can we blame demons. James asks, "What causes quarrels and what causes fights among you? Is it not this, that your passions are at war within you? You desire and do not have."

The true problem with Cain—and with us—is that something is going on inside. We have a bad case of the "I wants" and "I needs." Robert Jones insightfully states,

> In other words, sinful anger arises from the sinful beliefs and motives that reign in the unbeliever and remain in the Christian... Therefore, to change anger in your heart, you must recognize and uproot your sinful beliefs and motives, and replace them with godly ones.[8]

While counseling an angry man about his temper, I used an illustration of a tea bag in hot water to explain the source of his anger. He was blaming his temper on his daughter and his life circumstances. I explained to him that in reality, his circumstances were like hot water drawing out what was already in his heart (the tea bag). Because he was teachable and the Spirit of God was already working in his heart, he admitted this was true.

Many men are overly aggressive with their wives and children. A raised voice, a harsh tone, or irritability is what the family expects. I believe that the gospel and growth in Christlikeness can change the way men respond to their family.

A Special Word to Church Leaders

Just as some leaders can be too passive, others can be too aggressive—even pastors. I sometimes wonder what has happened to what I call "shepherd leadership." In Scripture, pastors are called to shepherd the people entrusted to their care. I find it hard to imagine a true shepherd who is abusive or unrelational. A shepherd is one who cares for those under him, which means he is to love the sheep. The apostle Paul modeled the demeanor of a shepherd well when he wrote, "We were gentle among you, like a nursing mother taking care of her own children. So, being affectionately desirous of you, we were ready to share with you not only the gospel of God but also our own selves, because you had become very dear to us" (1 Thessalonians 2:7-8).

For many years I thought I was an excellent pastor (that is, shepherd) because I diligently carried out the duties of a pastor. I visited people in the hospital, endeavored to prepare expository sermons, went to meetings, encouraged missions outreach, and so on. Yet I was accused of being unloving. I came to realize that *duty* does not necessarily equal *love*. I had no feeling for my sheep. I was very dutiful, but not relational.

Are you known for being demanding, controlling, or harsh with your flock? Or, are you known for being lovingly relational? Ask the Lord to help you emulate Christ's example as a loving, compassionate Shepherd.

The Ultimate Source of Wrong Responses

The Heart's Desires

As we have seen, Adam, Eve, and Cain had a desire problem. Scripture says, "When the woman saw that the tree was good for food, and that it was a delight to the eyes, and that the tree was to be *desired* to make one wise, she took of its fruit and ate, and she also gave some to her husband who was with her, and he ate" (Genesis 3:6). In other words, "the desires of the flesh and the desires of the eyes and pride of life" were at work in their souls (1 John 2:16). According to Scripture, when we talk about desires, passions, and appetites, we are in the realm of the heart.[9]

Proverbs 4:23 tells us that we live out of our hearts: "Keep your heart with all vigilance, for from it flow the springs of life." That is, we live out of our inner person. Actions originate in the inner person. When I read this verse, I think of the beautiful fresh water spring that's on a mountainside on our property in Virginia. After the water rises to the surface, it flows to a little man-made pond, which then overflows toward a small waterfall. From there the water goes through a creek and eventually ends up in a large pond on my neighbor's property, and this pond is stocked with fish.

Imagine what would happen if someone were to pour poison into the water at its source. The poison would flow down into our little pond, go over the waterfall, then down into my neighbor's pond, and kill the fish. When it comes to our hearts, we need to realize that the poison in our lives originates from this source. The prophet Jeremiah wrote, "The heart is deceitful above all things, and desperately sick; who can understand it?" (17:9).

When I'm counseling men in conflict situations, I want them to understand their hearts—their desires. I will ask them, "What do you want that you're not getting, and what are you getting that you don't want?" Ask yourself this question the next time you're feeling tension with your wife, children, or a member of your church. When you give the answer, you'll see what's in your heart.

What happens when we apply this to Adam and Cain? It's not hard to imagine that what Adam *didn't want* was either the possibility of losing his wife, or the possibility of tension with his wife by standing up to her and telling her that eating the fruit was wrong. For Cain, it seems that what he *wanted* (that he didn't get) was for God to accept his half-hearted sacrifice. And he *didn't want* to give God his best, as Abel had done.[10]

It's Really About Worship

Let's take all this one step further so that we can develop the proper motivation for changing the way we deal with conflict (and the rest of life, for that matter).

In Scripture, the focus of our hearts is connected with the concept of worship. This is made especially clear in Matthew 6:21, where our Lord said, "Where your treasure is, there your heart will be also." While the context here is about our view of true treasure and what we are investing in (see verses 19-20), the Lord is getting at something deeper. This becomes apparent in verse 24: "No one can serve two masters, for either he will hate the one and love the other, or he will be devoted to the one and despise the other. You cannot serve God and money." Lordship (who or what you worship) is a regular theme throughout Scripture (see also Joshua 24:14-15).

The Lord challenges us to ask ourselves, "What master am I *serving*? What do I *love*? What or who am I *devoted* to?" We realize He is not just addressing money when He broadens His challenge at the end of the verse by saying, "You cannot serve God and wealth" (NASB). The word translated "wealth" means possessions, not just money.[11] So, the Lord is challenging our belief system by asking: "Will you serve Me, or materialism?"

During conflict it is easy to value (that is, *serve* the master of) peace and quiet over resolving a conflict in a God-honoring way. It's also easy to be *devoted* to and *love* being in control. This can result in being overly aggressive as we endeavor to get what we want. Either way, it's still worship—wrongful worship that calls for repentance.

What Are You Worshipping?

When you deal with conflict either passively or aggressively, you want to take a closer look and see what it is you're worshipping, and Psalm 18 is helpful in that regard. This psalm also gives us a great example to follow when we are feeling pressure in relationships.

In Psalm 18, David testified of the many times the Lord had delivered him from various situations. In verses 4-6, we read that David was under a tremendous amount of pressure from others—so much so, that he even thought he was going to die (verse 4)! As unflattering as it is, pressure has a way of revealing character. Pressure helps us see what we are really devoted to, what we really serve, what our security is really in. In other words, what is being ultimately valued or *worshipped*.

In Psalm 18, we see what—or more precisely, whom—David worshipped when he was under pressure. In verse 2 we find numerous metaphors to describe his relationship with the Lord during these difficult times. He says, "The LORD is my rock and my fortress and my deliverer, my God, my rock, in whom I take refuge, my shield, and the horn of my salvation, my stronghold."

What do these metaphors say about David's relationship with the Lord? He described the Lord as "my rock." That is, the Lord was his stability and his security. He further said the Lord was his "fortress." He ran to the Lord for protection when he was being attacked. And he described God as the one "in whom I take refuge." The Lord was his escape. Ultimately, we see that the Lord was David's source of strength for dealing with the pressures of life.

Now, take these metaphors and apply them to your own life, especially when you experience conflict. What (or who) do you run to as your escape when there's tension with others? What (or who) is your source of security? Is God the fortress you run to? Is He your rock? Or do you tend to rely on your own ability to control a situation? I can relate to this. When things get tense or life seems to be spinning out of control, I have found myself saying, "Well, someone needs to take charge!"

Others, though, respond to tension in relationships by retreating. They find it easier to block out the tension and pretend that the conflict doesn't exist. We might call this type of response "comfort loving." Or, if you are overly concerned with what others might think about you and people become your "deliverers," then you may be worshipping people over the Lord. Scripture calls this "the fear of man" (Proverbs 29:25). Whenever we choose one of these responses, we are *not* like David in turning to the Lord for deliverance and help.

A Special Word to Church Leaders

What type of things do you tend to serve or be devoted to as a church leader? When conflicts arise, are you devoted to keeping things quiet at all costs? Do you pretend that conflicts don't exist, or just ignore them? Are you preoccupied with what others are thinking? If so, may I challenge you to consider that you may actually be devoted to people or comfort more than the Lord?

Or is your attitude, "No one is going to push me around"? Deep inside, you don't want anyone to disagree with you, and in fact, the people under your leadership might even be saying that it's not safe to disagree with you. You believe in "backdoor revivals" rather than endeavoring to work through issues with disgruntled people (see Ephesians 4:3). Perhaps you use your authoritative position or superior Bible knowledge or logic to overwhelm people rather than serve them. If so, please consider that you may be more devoted to being in control than letting the Lord be in control.

Both of these wrong responses will cultivate, in your church, an atmosphere that is conducive to wildfires rather than a culture in which people are encouraged to truly deal with conflict constructively.

The Gospel Makes a Difference

Praise God, the gospel has the power embedded within it to change the way we deal with conflict. It has the ability to balance out the extreme responses we tend to have when tensions arise in relationships.

The Gospel in General

We've already seen that humans have a significant desire problem and that things went radically wrong in Genesis 3. We've also seen that our original purpose of being a worshipper of and in relationship with our Creator was disrupted and distorted by what happened in that same chapter. This sin nature and its bad fruit of broken relationship with our Creator and others is the reason our Savior came and died in our place.

Paul wrote in 2 Corinthians 5:21, "For our sake he [God the Father] made him [Christ] to be sin who knew no sin, so that in him we might become the righteousness of God." A few verses earlier he said, "In Christ God was reconciling the world to himself, not counting their trespasses against them, and entrusting to us the message of reconciliation" (verse 19). In other words, God restored us to relationship with Himself through the death of His Son in our place. This is an amazing story of sacrificial love that should provoke heartfelt worship. It also gives us clear guidance on how to deal with tensions in our relationships.

God did His part; now what is our part? I would like to answer this by bringing up the issue of worship again. We have already seen that humans are natural worshippers. But how does that relate to the gospel? Let's consider a story in which our Lord lays the groundwork for an answer.

In Luke 18:18, a rich ruler asked Jesus, "What must I do to inherit eternal life?" Jesus, in His response, wanted to expose the ruler's value system and mentioned the Ten Commandments. The ruler then assured the Lord that he had kept these all the commandments from his youth, even though Jesus had just told him, "No one is good except God alone" (verse 19). The Lord then revealed the real motives of the ruler's heart and said, "Sell all that you have and distribute to the poor, and you will have treasure in heaven; and come, follow me" (verse 22).

This brings up some interesting questions: Why did the Lord bring up the issue of possessions when the ruler asked, "What must I do to inherit eternal life?" And, does a person have to sell everything to be a true follower of the Lord? Why didn't Jesus simply explain the gospel to the ruler, instead of talking about possessions?

To answer briefly, the Lord was seeking to reveal the motives of the ruler's heart. He was addressing the ruler's wrongful worship that would keep him from being a disciple, a true follower of the Lord. He wanted the young man to see that he was more devoted to his wealth than he was to the Lord. You see, the gospel is not just a message to believe; it is a person to follow. Our part is to commit to being a follower of Christ.

To make this more personal, allow me to ask you a question. Who or what are you serving? Earlier, we observed that things like control or love of comfort can dominate our hearts to the point that we are more devoted to those things than being a follower of Christ. Our Lord came and died not just to get us to heaven someday. He died to change the worship of our hearts and restore us to a proper worship of our Creator. Who or what are you serving? There's nothing like conflict to reveal that to us.

The Gospel as It Applies to Conflict

When you think of the word *gospel*, what other words come to mind? *Mercy* and *grace* would probably land at the top of the list. It wouldn't take long for *forgiveness* to come to mind as well. And *love* would quickly come to mind, as well as *reconciliation*. Let's take some of these words and see how they apply to conflict resolution.

Reconciliation and Love

The doctrine of reconciliation is the wonderful truth that our relationship with the Creator has been restored because of the death of our Savior, Jesus

Christ. Let's get more specific though. Romans 5:8-10 says, "God shows his love for us in that while we were still sinners, Christ died for us...For if while we were enemies we were reconciled to God by the death of his Son, much more, now that we are reconciled, shall we be saved by his life."

Because the gospel is not just a message to believe but also a person to follow, we ought to deal with conflict in relationships the same way Christ dealt with conflict in relationships. In love, He moved toward us instead of away from us. A basic principle of biblical conflict resolution is that we move toward people and not away from them. When conflict arises, your default response might be like Adam's—you may be inclined to remain passive and not say anything, or physically move away from the person who is causing tension. But that's not what God did when conflict arose with us. He moved toward us!

Grace, Mercy, and Forgiveness

Grace is a key word when it comes to the gospel. Grace is God giving us what we don't deserve and mercy is Him holding back what we do deserve. Because of God's grace and mercy, He is willing to forgive us—not based upon anything we do (Titus 3:5), but upon what our Savior did! And in Ephesians 4:32, we are admonished to extend this same type of forgiveness to others: "Be kind to one another, tenderhearted, forgiving one another, as God in Christ forgave you." This forgiveness is not based upon other people's performance; rather, it is based upon undeserved mercy and grace. Although those people may have sinned against us, we are to move toward them with the offer of forgiveness. We are to seek after reconciliation, even if they are moving away from us. True Christians eagerly repent of their sins against one another and freely extend forgiveness in the same way God has freely forgiven us.

Ken Sande, in his powerful book *The Peacemaker*, makes this incredible statement: "Christians are the most forgiven people in the world. Therefore, we should be the most forgiving people in the world."[12] We can take this same formula and ask: If Christians have been shown the most grace by God, shouldn't we be the most gracious people in the world? If we have been shown the most mercy, shouldn't we be the most merciful (see Luke 6:36)?

Maybe you don't have the Adam tendency. Instead, you are more like Cain. You agree with my statement that we should move toward people, and you do, but too aggressively. How could grace, mercy, and forgiveness change the way you deal with conflict?

Let me ask you another question: Where would you be in your relationship with God if He treated you the same way you treat others? Again, Christ is our model with regard to the grace and compassion that we are to demonstrate to others in the midst of conflict.

Growth in Christlikeness Changes Everything

At the beginning of the chapter I stated that our goal was to learn how the gospel and progressive sanctification can help us respond to conflict in more godly ways. As we grow more Christlike, we gain a maturity that enables us to handle conflict rightly and avoid responding too passively or aggressively.

So, let's finish the chapter by looking at how our growth in Christlikeness can change the way we deal with conflict. For guidance, we're going to look at what Paul said in Colossians 3. It's interesting that much of what he said about the practical outworking of being a follower of Christ is related to tensions in relationships.

For example, Paul talked about covetousness as idolatry (verse 5). Unfortunately, we're all experts at letting our covetous nature lead to tensions in relationships! In verse 8, Paul wrote that we are to put aside "anger, wrath, malice, slander." In verse 9 he said, "Do not lie to one another, seeing that you have put off the old self with its practices." These behaviors are all too common in relationships between Christians in today's churches.

Paul then goes on to say,

> ...if one has a complaint against another, forgiv[e] each other; as the Lord has forgiven you...And above all these put on love, which binds everything together in perfect harmony. And let the peace of Christ rule in your hearts, to which indeed you were called in one body" (verses 13-15).

You could almost say that Colossians 3 is all about how the gospel and growth in Christlikeness both help resolve tensions in relationships and promote harmony instead!

Our New Position in Christ

Those of us who have strong tendencies toward conflict avoidance can learn to become men who glorify God in a conflict instead of running from it. And those of us who have a history of responding to conflict with outbursts of anger can learn to "put on love which binds everything together in perfect harmony" (verse 14).

These are miraculous transformations, and they are possible because of our relationship with Jesus Christ. If you were to read from the end of Colossians 1 to the beginning of Colossians 3, you would notice that Paul's major theme here is our identity with Christ. Many would say that this is Paul's favorite doctrine—we call it the doctrine of union with Christ. In that portion of Colossians you'll find phrases like "Christ in you," "in him," and "in whom." These affirm our union with Christ, and it's because of that union—or your position in Christ—that you are capable of supernatural acts of forgiveness, mercy, and grace.

Character Traits Can Change

Paul also taught that because of your position in Christ, you are able to "put on then, as God's chosen ones, holy and beloved, compassionate hearts, kindness, humility, meekness, and patience, bearing with one another" (3:12-13). Your character traits can change! If your tendency is to be harsh, our culture would tell you that it's just a part of your personality—it's who you are. But these words from Colossians say otherwise. In Christ, you *can* put on compassion and kindness.

Think about it this way: Consider opposites of those character traits—the opposites of kindness, humility, meekness, patience, and so on. Isn't it true that these opposites *contribute* to conflict? For example, the opposite of compassion is showing a hard heart toward others. A person that is hardhearted isn't going to show concern for another person. Rather, he will have a difficult time fulfilling the commands of Philippians 2:3-4: "Do nothing from selfish ambition or conceit, but in humility count others more significant than yourselves. Let each of you look not only to his own interests, but also to the interests of others."

And then there's the opposite of humility, which is pride. Pride most definitely contributes to tensions in relationships. It wants to have the last word.

It doesn't want to admit wrong because it wants to save face. It wants to be in control.

The opposite of patience is impatience, or being irritable. This person lacks patience and is always irritable toward others. This makes people feel as if they can never do anything right around him.

As Christians, we're to put away such behaviors, and that is possible because of the gospel and our relationship with Christ. We are able to change and grow more like our Lord, who exhibited the right attitudes and responses to conflict.

Again, if we are exhibiting wrong responses to conflict, the problem is what's in our heart. We have certain desires—either we want something that we cannot get, or we're getting something we don't want. These desires of the heart reveal what we're really worshipping. If we're desiring control, it's going to affect how we talk to others. Instead of being kind, we'll be harsh. We'll be bossy instead of listening carefully to what others have to say. If we're concerned about our own comfort, we'll avoid having concern for others. If we're concerned about what others think of us, we'll be people pleasers instead of focusing on loving and serving others.

The solution to all of those wrong responses is to let the gospel and your identity in Christ change the way you respond in your relationships. Let the gospel teach you the superior worship of God instead of the inferior worship of self.

What would this look like in real life? A man who struggles with being a control freak needs to surrender all control to God instead of holding onto it himself, thus turning his worship toward God. A man who struggles with the fear of others (people pleasing) needs to grow in awe of what God thinks of him and not concern himself what others think. A man who struggles with laziness because he longs for his own comfort needs to realize that true and greater comfort is found in a relationship with the Lord and living a life of obedience to His glory.

A Final Word to Church Leaders

How would the people in your flock describe you? Remember that the qualifications of an elder require an overseer to be "self-controlled, respectable...not violent but gentle, not quarrelsome" (1 Timothy 3:2-3). Are these characteristics evident in your life? There is a demeanor that goes with being a shepherd. In what ways do you struggle with this demeanor, and when? What could you be serving in your heart that contributes to this?

If you find yourself wanting in this area, as we've already seen, real change is possible through your relationship with Christ. As you grow in Christlikeness, following His example, you'll mature in a way that helps you handle conflict correctly without going to the extremes of passivity or aggressiveness.

In light of what we've discussed in this chapter, ask yourself: What character traits do you need to work on, and what can you do to grow toward Christlikeness?

In closing, here is a prayer you can lift up to the Lord as you ask Him to help bring about change in your life:

> Father, I need help with the way I handle tensions in relationships. My human fallenness—because of what happened in Genesis 3— still impacts what I do every day. I am thankful for the cross and for the way the gospel has set me free from the extreme ways of dealing with conflict. I am also grateful for how the gospel directs my worship to You, and away from any selfish desires that are in my heart. May my character traits be more like those of the Savior. I commit my relationships to You, and ask You for the wisdom and strength to apply what I've learned about dealing with conflicts in a way that brings honor to You. In Jesus' name. Amen.

Recommended Resources

Jones, Robert D. *Uprooting Anger: Biblical Help for a Common Problem*. Phillipsburg, NJ: P&R Publishing, 2005.

Piper, John, and Wayne Grudem. *Recovering Biblical Manhood and Womanhood*. Wheaton, IL: Crossway, 1991.

Poirier, Alfred. *The Peacemaking Pastor*. Grand Rapids, MI: Baker Book House, 2006.

Sande, Ken. *The Leadership Opportunity: Living Out the Gospel Where Conflict and Leadership Intersect*. Billings, MT: Peacemaker Ministries, 2009.

————. *The Peacemaker.* Grand Rapids, MI: Baker Book House, 2004.

Sande, Ken, and Tom Raabe. *Peacemaking for Families.* Carol Stream, IL: Tyndale House Publishers, 2002.

Strauch, Alexander. *If You Bite and Devour One Another: Biblical Principles for Handling Conflict.* Littleton, CO: Lewis & Roth, 2011.

Part 4

A Man and Specific Problems

17

Manhandling Idolatrous Lust

Have you ever found yourself so obsessed by one thing in life that you are willing to do anything to get it or to hold on to it? Do you ever wonder why some things make you angry, or why other things make you worry? Have you considered why some relationships in your life are more difficult to handle than others? Or even why you find yourself disconnecting from one relationship, only to discover the same problems arising again in another? If there is a familiar ring to these questions, you are not alone. There is something going on—just beneath the surface of daily life—that is pulling at your heart and mind, and consuming you. On the surface you may relegate these issues to the "I can handle it" department, but if the truth be known, you're not able to get your mind off certain things, or you're having a hard time bringing about change you'd like to see happen in your life.

The Bible says that in our hearts—our inner being, which includes our thoughts and intentions—we treasure certain things (Luke 12:34). What we treasure determines our choices in life, which result in many of the circumstances we find ourselves in—whether good or bad. The fruit of our treasure-oriented choices is either a life characterized by stability through pursuing a growing knowledge of God and obedience to Him, or a life filled with corruption due to a preoccupation with self (Galatians 6:7-8).

When we choose not to operate with love for God and others, by default we are driven by selfish ambition. The Bible calls this walking in earthly, unspiritual, and demonic wisdom (James 3:13-16). This leads to confusion and disorder in our lives and almost always negatively impacts the lives of others. Living in this manner causes us to use this world as a means to reaching our personal goals. God's Word describes this as being friendly with the world but enemies of God (James 4:1-5). We act as enemies of God because we are consumed with His creation, yet we ignore the Creator.

All of us at one time or another have depended on and used some aspect of creation to obtain something we craved or treasured above love for God and others. All of us have given in to our selfish ambitions, using this world as a means to get what we long for. What does the Bible call this? Idolatrous lust.

Defining Idolatrous Lust

The Greek word *epithumia*, which is translated "lust," appears frequently in the New Testament and denotes a strong desire of any kind.[1] Idolatrous lust, then, is a strong desire that rules a man's heart. In my book *With All Your Heart*, I describe idolatrous lust as this:

> Bowing down to whatever you believe will bring you what you truly treasure while making what you truly treasure something you bow down to in place of the living God. It is the various aspects of life and creation we worship above the Creator as well as the basic ways we worship creation above the Creator.[2]

An idol is something we look to as our personal "god" in order to gain what we crave (lust for) above love for God and others. Another way of putting this is that our life becomes limited to our ambition (lust) while we use the world as a means (idolatry) to gain that ambition—and this results in making us a friend of the world and hostile toward God.

Idols are the aspects of creation we turn to above God as a source of satisfaction and as a solution to our problems (see Jeremiah 2:13). In our hearts, we give these idols the place that belongs to God. And we submit to these idols as we would and should submit to God (Ezekiel 14:3). We reverence these idols as we would and should reverence God (Romans 1:20-25). We use these idols to get the things we treasure most, the things we long for, the things we lust after. Any person, place, product, perspective, position, platform, or power that we depend on other than God as a source of satisfaction or a solution to our problems is an idol.

Examples of Idolatrous Lust

Consider Steve, a successful businessman in Kansas for over forty years. Steve is well-respected throughout the state for his hard work. But he is also known as one to always pursue the big bucks. Even though he has more than enough money to live comfortably without any lack for the rest of his life—and that's true about his grandchildren as well—still, he never has enough. Frequently he will tell people, "You can't be too sure with this economy. You have to stay ahead, or you could lose it all and end up with nothing to lean on!"

Steve's preoccupation with money is tied to his lust for security. The more money he has, the more secure he feels. Yet his insatiable desire for security never seems to be satisfied; therefore, he continually looks to his personal god of money to give him the security he so longs for. Can you see the idolatrous lust at play? Steve leans on money in the way he should lean on God (1 Timothy 6:17); he trusts in money in the way he should trust in God. Money is his idol; security is his lust. Steve's inordinate desire to be secure—a security he seeks apart from Jesus Christ—is resulting in sinful idolatry. He is living in direct disobedience to God's Word, which commands us to keep our lives free from the love of money and to be content with what we have, for God has promised to never leave us or forsake us (Hebrews 13:5-6).

It seems pretty simple to see this in Steve's life, but not all idolatrous behavior is as easy to notice or recognize. What about you? Can you identify times in your life during which you have allowed something other than God to be the source of your satisfaction and the solution to your problems? So much so that you have given this a place in your heart and life that you should give only to God himself? This is idolatry.

Consider how *you* have handled money. How often have you made money the source of your satisfaction and the solution to your problems? Consider how much reverence and respect you have shown to money instead of God and others. Are you preoccupied with money so that you can gain from it something you treasure or crave more than God and others? If you find that is the case, examine your heart to see if you can determine what it is that you seek. In Steve's case, it was security. What is it for you? What do you lust after? The *pleasure* of material possessions? The *approval* of others as they view your financial success? The *respect* that often accompanies wealth? The *love* of family and friends (who doesn't love a guy with a wad of cash)? Connect your idol with your lust, and you will nail down how idolatrous lust is creating havoc in your life.

Jesus told a parable that illustrates how idolatrous lust works and the consequences it can have:

> He said to them, "Take care, and be on your guard against all covetousness, for one's life does not consist in the abundance of his possessions." And he told them a parable, saying, "The land of a rich man produced plentifully, and he thought to himself, 'What shall I do, for I have nowhere to store my crops?' And he said, 'I will do this: I will tear down my barns and build larger ones, and there I will store all my grain and my goods. And I will say to my soul, "Soul, you have ample goods laid up for many years; relax, eat, drink, be merry."' But God said to him, 'Fool! This night your soul is required of you, and the things you have prepared, whose will they be?' So is the one who lays up treasure for himself and is not rich toward God" (Luke 12:15-21).

Consider how important approval is to you. What person are you willing to give control over your life in order to gain or maintain approval from him? How have you allowed that person to become a god so you can receive the approval you long for?

John is a thirty-year-old engineer employed by a large company in Houston. He is highly respected by his boss and coworkers for his hard work and dependability on the job. If you ask John to do something, he will get it done efficiently and effectively. However, John will not say no to his boss even when he has the freedom to do so. As a result, he takes on the jobs that nobody else will and misses a lot of important gatherings at church and with his family and friends due to these extra assignments at his workplace. Though John's boss gives him the option to pass the job on to others, John refuses to do so. As you spend time with him, you discover that John is afraid to say no to his boss for fear of causing his boss to dislike him.

John's fear of his boss reveals idolatry that has taken hold in his life. His preoccupation with pleasing his boss reveals his lust for approval. John's boss has become his *idol* in his pursuit of approval from him—which he *lusts* for. He craves this approval to such an extent that he fails to love God and others as he should. He demonstrates a fear of his boss that is a sinful fear. The only person to whom he should show such fear and reverence is God Himself. Proverbs 29:25 says, "The fear of man lays a snare, but whoever trusts in the LORD is safe."

In a similar way, many people are controlled by an overwhelming fear of certain individuals. They are afraid because of what they believe these individuals can give them or take away from them in relation to that aspect of creation they lust for. It is lust that drives the fear, not fear that drives the lust. If the person living in fear weren't controlled by his lust, then he would no longer fear those certain individuals. Here's another way of looking at it: The people he fears are powerful not because of who they are, but because of what he craves from them. The apostle John pointed this out in his Gospel:

> Many even of the authorities believed in him, but for *fear* of the Pharisees they did not confess it, so that they would not be put out of the synagogue; for they loved *the glory that comes from man* more than the glory that comes from God (John 12:42-43).

The idolatrous lust of the authorities was this: their idol was the Pharisees (whom they feared instead of God), and their lust was the glory that comes from man (or approval).

Are you preoccupied with always having control? You may not like to think of yourself in this way, but when you depend on control as the source of your satisfaction and the solution to your problems, you will find yourself reverencing and respecting control as you would and should reverence and respect God. What are you treasuring or craving at this time? What are you consumed with having, maintaining, and keeping control of so you can achieve some desired result?

Joe, who is in his mid-forties, is an assistant manager for a popular food chain. He is known to be on top of everything in his field. Nothing gets by Joe.

He knows about every detail of every incident and issue that arises in the day-to-day operations of the business. Joe makes sure that everything is done just the way he wants it done, and that everyone who works for him does their job exactly his way. No one who works for Joe has the freedom to think or do anything outside the box of Joe's policies and procedures, or even his preferences.

Consequently, Joe is known to be a controlling person. If you were to ask Joe about this, he would say, "I know I am a controller, but if I want to be recognized as the top manager in my company, I have got to make sure things get done in the way that I think is best." Recognition was Joe's lust, and seeking to control everyone was the means to getting that recognition. Therefore the control was Joe's idol, and recognition the lust. Joe was trusting in his own ability to control every little detail with a view toward the recognition he craved so intensely. The Bible warns against such an attitude in Jeremiah 17:5: "Cursed is the man who trusts in man and makes flesh his strength, whose heart turns away from the Lord."

If Joe had a clear understanding of the power and sovereignty of God, he would realize the foolishness of his controlling ways. "The heart of man plans his way, but the Lord establishes his steps" (Proverbs 16:9). Unfortunately, Joe's lust for recognition has driven him to make an idol of control, in direct disobedience to Scripture. He probably doesn't even see it as idolatry, so blinded is he by that which he lusts for.

The Heart of the Matter

At this point, it would be easy for us to sit back and criticize these men for their various idolatries. "Why can't they see what they're doing?" we ask. But the nature of the human heart is in play here, a nature that is clearly described in Jeremiah 17:5-10:

> Thus says the Lord: "Cursed is the man who trusts in man and makes flesh his strength, whose heart turns away from the Lord. He is like a shrub in the desert, and shall not see any good come. He shall dwell in the parched places of the wilderness, in an uninhabited salt land.
>
> "Blessed is the man who trusts in the Lord, whose trust is the Lord. He is like a tree planted by water, that sends out its roots

by the stream, and does not fear when heat comes, for its leaves remain green, and is not anxious in the year of drought, for it does not cease to bear fruit."

The heart is deceitful above all things, and desperately sick; who can understand it? I the LORD search the heart and test the mind, to give every man according to his ways, according to the fruit of his deeds.

In this passage we see that the man who trusts in himself is cursed (verses 5-6), and the man who trusts in God is blessed (verses 7-8). And because the heart is so deceitful and desperately wicked (verse 9), we are not able to clearly perceive whether we are trusting in self or in God. In fact, we will give ourselves a nice pat on the back for being a person who is trusting in the Lord. But God asks a penetrating question: "Who can understand it [the heart]?" Who can *really* know the heart of man? Man himself? No—in verse 10, God declares that it is He who searches the heart and tests the mind. Man, left to himself, will assume he is doing everything right, and he needs God's help before he can see who he really is.

We could fill up many books defining idolatrous lusts and looking at myriad of examples. But the problem is not that we don't know our definitions. Nor is the problem that we are unable to see these things in other people. The problem is that we are not quick to see our own sinful ways and repent. We desperately need the Spirit of God to use the Word of God to examine our hearts and show us where we are not trusting in Him (idolatry), and where we are making flesh our strength (lust).

The Steps That Characterize the Descent into Idolatrous Lust

People do not wake up in the morning and consciously decide, "I think I will worship the creation over the Creator today. I think I will love approval more than I love God, and I will replace God on His throne with an ungodly fear of man to get this approval." No, this is a process that takes place gradually within our hearts and our lives as we are distracted by the attractions of this world above the anticipation of the delights that are found in knowing Jesus Christ. Our hearts are subtly drawn away from love for God and others. While we may think we are doing well, often we are sliding down a slippery slope.

1. A Change of Mind-Set

Step one begins with our mind-set—what we think about God, about ourselves, and the world around us. The subtle descent into idolatrous lust often begins when we think God does not really see all that we do. Psalm 10:11 describes this mind-set, saying that this person "says in his heart, 'God has forgotten, he has hidden his face, he will never see it.'" Our deceitful hearts blind us to who we really are, as we saw in Jeremiah 17:9. The temptations of worldly things increase as we gradually set our mind more and more on the things of earth instead of the things of God (Philippians 3:17-19). The sights, sounds, and symbols of this world slowly shape and mold our thinking, leading us to dwell more on the treasures of this world than the treasures of heaven.

2. A Change of Motivation

Once our mind-set changes, our motivation changes as well. We become motivated by self-interest rather than God's will (James 3:13–4:3). We reduce the world to being about what is important to ourselves. Our priorities are self-focused instead of God-focused. We become tuned in to WIIFM (What's In It For Me). Understanding and rehearsing all we are in Christ, in contrast with the hell we deserve, is critical to a proper motivation.

3. A Change in Our Meditations

After our mind-set and motivation have changed, our meditations or thoughts become consumed with the treasures of this world, which quickly become affections of our hearts. These treasures may include security, approval, acceptance, pleasure, being viewed as competent, being understood, having our preferences accommodated, having our way, never being hurt, and so on. There is nothing wrong with most of these desires in and of themselves. The problem is that we have moved from simply liking these things to actively living for them. Suddenly we don't want to live without them. They have become the lust of our hearts (James 4:1-2). We believe we absolutely must have them. They have become the meditation of our hearts, leading us to be easily tempted into sin to gain or maintain them (James 1:13-14). Our love for God and love for others is put on hold so that we can gain or maintain these treasures (1 John 2:15-17).

4. A Change in Our Means

When we become consumed with finding a way to gain or maintain the treasures we lust after, we adopt whatever means are necessary to acquire them. We look to people, places, products, perspective, position, platform, or power as means to satisfy the wants of our hearts (Jeremiah 2:13). We bow down in adoration and submission to whatever it is that will enable us to get what we want, instead of bowing down before God Himself (Ezekiel 14:3) and trusting in the supremacy, sufficiency, and sovereignty of God to provide for us.

5. A Change in Our Master

As a result of our changed mind-set, motivations, meditations, and means, we have become mastered by our flesh (Philippians 3:17-19). We do not walk by the Spirit of God; instead, we live by the flesh (Galatians 5:16-21). We have lost our focus on pleasing God, and now only seek to please ourselves. We have become slaves to our self-serving pursuits, leading to a life of instability, trouble, disappointment, and pain as a result of pursuing the things of the flesh rather than the things of the Spirit (Galatians 6:7-8).

The Steps to Overcoming Idolatrous Lust

How can we deal with idolatrous lust? How can we protect ourselves from descending down the path toward a change in our mind-set, motivations, meditations, means, and master?

1. Identify Your Lusts

First, consider all the ways you have been walking in idolatrous lust. Write them down. Include all the people, places, perspectives, products, platforms, power, or anything you have been depending on and using apart from God as the means to achieving your goals. Look carefully at what you have been treasuring in your heart to the point of lust—such as approval, pleasure, security, and having your own way. Examine how you have been willing to sin to gain or maintain these things. And consider how unloving you have been toward God and others as a result of these idolatrous lusts.

2. Confess Your Sin

Second, confess your sinful ways to God. Tell Him everything. Do not withhold anything that comes to your mind. Call sin what it is—*sin*! You have allowed the things of this world to become your god. This must be addressed with honesty, reverence, and respect to the Almighty God who created all that exists. Recognize that you deserve God's judgment for letting the things of this world crowd Him out of your life.

3. Cry to God for Mercy

Third, cry out to God for mercy. Ask for His grace to empower you to live with Him, for Him, and through Him.

If you recognize that you have never bowed your knee to Jesus Christ as the Savior and Lord of your life, this is the time to repent and turn to Him in faith so He can save you from the penalty and power of sin and bring you into a right relationship with God. Jesus Christ was crucified for your sin; God's wrath was poured out on Him for your sin; He was buried and resurrected. This was done so that you may be rescued, redeemed, and reconciled back to God for a new life committed to knowing Him, becoming like Him, and being useful to Him. Ask God to save you from your wicked self.

If you have already become a follower of Jesus Christ, then you must examine what led you to this point. Have you become dull of hearing or lazy in applying the truth in relation to the desires of your heart? Has your heart deceived you? You must identify where you lack accountability, knowledge, support, or insight to address these matters. The same power that raised Jesus Christ from the dead is within those who belong to Jesus Christ. So the issue isn't a lack of power. Rather, it's that you weren't diligent to obey God or apply His truth in certain areas of your life. Search your heart and determine the lusts that have taken you down the wrong path, and renounce them so that you can get back in step with God.

4. Commit Yourself to Change

Finally, commit yourself to the biblical process of change that God has spelled out in Scripture. God has called us to put off thoughts, desires, motives, behaviors, relational patterns, and serving patterns that are sinful and replace them with God-honoring desires, motives, behaviors, relational patterns, and serving patterns (Ephesians 4:17-32). This is a lifestyle, not an event. For every idolatrous lust you can identify in your life, you'll want to identify the specific ways you can love God and love others in place of those idolatrous lusts.

For instance, instead of using people to satisfy your craving for approval, you can embrace the supremacy, sovereignty, and sufficiency of God in your life by accepting what He has allowed to take place in your life. You can learn to serve others for their good instead of fulfilling your own agenda. You can endure the difficult things about other people instead of seeking to please yourself. Remember, you were made to please and glorify God, not yourself. You are to live as an instrument who bears fruit for the Lord, who in turn will allow you to enjoy that fruit in this life and the life to come.

It is in God alone that all the desires of our heart can know true fulfillment. May your mind-set, motivations, meditations, and means focus solely on Him, so that He is your Master in all things.

Recommended Resources

Ellen, Nicolas. *With All Your Heart? Identifying and Dealing with Idolatrous Lust*. Mustang, OK: Dare2Dream Books, 2012.

Fitzpatrick, Elyse. *Idols of the Heart: Learning to Long for God Alone*. Phillipsburg, NJ: P&R Publishing, 2001.

Lane, Timothy S., and Paul David Tripp. *How People Change*. Greensboro, NC: New Growth Press, 2008.

Powlison, David. *Seeing with New Eyes*. Phillipsburg, NJ: P&R Publishing, 2003.

18

Struggling with Homosexuality

Daniel Kirk

The image will forever be burned into my memory. It was one of the strangest things I had ever seen. My nine-year-old twins and I were sitting in the lobby of a university building waiting for swim team practice to begin. On the television was one of those wildlife programs that children (and their dads) love to watch. This one was about snakes—big snakes! The kind that stretch up to twenty feet long and easily crush the life out of a man.

The host of the program was describing the insatiable appetite of the Burmese python and how it can eat animals larger than itself. Somehow, the jawbone of this massive creature is able to dislocate in such a way that its mouth can consume prey two or three times its size. On occasion, however, its appetite—designed to sustain the snake's life—becomes the cause of its untimely death. The images that appeared on the television screen at this point were undeniable proof. There, before our eyes, flashed stunning photographs of the tail and hindquarters of a large, dead alligator protruding from the burst belly of a large, dead snake. "Beware of your appetites," the pictures seemed to say, "left unchecked, they will kill you."

Desires Gone Wrong

I can't think of a more sobering picture to illustrate what is fundamentally wrong with the heart of man. The pathology is simple: Strong desires give birth to sin, and sin results in death (James 1:14-15). We see this as far back as the Garden of Eden, where a serpent, that living picture of pure appetite,[1] exploited man's God-given desires, seducing him to rebel against his Maker. Ever since, man's natural bent has been turned away from the rule of God in favor of the dictates of his own desires. As Russell Moore observes, "the whole of Scripture and of Christian tradition warns the church against the way of the appetites, the way of consuming oneself to death."[2]

Ministering to homosexual men in the church begins by understanding how prone humans are to being deceived by their desires. According to Scripture, "we all once lived in the passions of our flesh, carrying out the desires of the body and the mind" (Ephesians 2:3). This is particularly true of homosexual men who have wrongly concluded that their very identity is defined by their desires. Wise biblical counselors will use the profound theology of the gospel to help homosexual men find their identity in Christ and overcome the desires that consume them.

Two Case Studies

Let's consider a couple of case studies, and then think about what the gospel offers men who are consumed by homosexual desires.

Bob has been openly involved in the homosexual community for years and has been an ardent supporter of the gay-rights movement. As far back as age twelve, he remembers feeling a strong same-sex attraction, which he now describes as his sexual orientation. For five years he lived with a male lover who was ten years his senior. He hoped they could marry someday, but six months ago, that man died of AIDS. Bob doesn't consider himself a Christian. He believes, however, that there is a God who created him "gay" but demands that he lives "straight." He has asked for counsel because the loss of his lover has left him deeply depressed, and he has recently been diagnosed HIV positive.

Ryan is twenty-two years old and about to graduate from college. He has been a member of a good church his whole life. His feminine characteristics and mannerisms are obvious even to the casual onlooker, but his apparent devotion to Christ has kept questions about his sexuality at bay. On the outside, Ryan appears to be a happy young man who loves Jesus, knows God's Word, and is active in ministry. Inside, however, he is scared, lonely, and confused. As a child he often wished he had been born a girl. When he reached puberty, he became aware of his sexual attraction to boys. Four years of college life, however, have awakened temptations and desires that have rocked his world. During his first year away from home he got involved in a short-lived relationship with a young man that turned sexual. Though he confessed this sin to his pastor and has been celibate for three years since, Ryan's persistent homosexual desires are tempting him to wonder if he was born gay—if God created him gay. Ryan knows the Bible condemns homosexuality and says he wants to honor the Lord, but his unwanted desires are pulling him in the opposite direction. Ryan has come for counsel because he wants someone to make sense of it all and, if possible, help him change.

Bob and Ryan's stories are significantly different, but the cure for their souls is found at the same source. The deep, refreshing, heart-changing truths of the gospel are Bob and Ryan's only hope for experiencing the kind of change that will satisfy their souls and bring glory to God.

Because Bob is a gay-rights activist, you as a biblical counselor might find yourself intimidated by him. But gay-rights activist or not, his problem is as ancient as Eden. Like Adam, Bob has bought the serpent's lie, released the reins of his appetites, and is "consuming himself to death."[3] Bob is simply one man in a long history of sinners who prefer to obey their cravings rather than their Creator. Like Esau slurping from that bowl of stew, like Israel knee-deep in quail, like the crowds who followed Jesus merely for the food, Bob has been ruled by his cravings, and now they are killing him.

The Key to Change

As a biblical counselor, you have the amazing privilege of delivering God's message of hope to men like Bob. The shocking truth of the gospel is that God justifies the ungodly (Romans 4:5). Bob won't find the answer he's looking for by trying to live "straight" or by blaming God for making him gay. The cure for his soul is found in the gospel promise that God justifies the ungodly by the sheer power of His grace (Ephesians 2:8-9). Before addressing any other issue in Bob's life, you must first help him renounce his "right" to be ruled by his appetites. Bob needs to repent, submitting his homosexual behavior and desires to the rule of Jesus Christ.

Biblical counselors must be careful not to rush past a counselee's need for salvation, especially one whose lifestyle screams of rebellion against God. Biblical counselor John Street cautions that "many well-meaning Christians have stumbled here, trying to provide biblical help to homosexuals who were incapable of a heart-level spiritual response. This only leads to discouragement and frustration on the part of both."[4] For men like Bob, the gospel offers the transformative miracle of salvation that he desperately needs. But what about the true believer who has repented of his homosexual behavior yet still struggles with unwanted same-sex desires? What does the gospel offer men like Ryan?

Hope Found in the Gospel

Unlike Bob, Ryan has not attempted to "eat the alligator." The prospect of letting his appetites lead him into a homosexual lifestyle is frightening to him. Nevertheless, his mind is full of questions: Is it possible for a Christian to be homosexual? Is "sexual orientation" a valid concept? Is same-sex attraction the result of bad parenting, cultural conditioning, environmental influences, "gay genes," or the sovereignty of God? Is real change even possible? Ryan has serious questions. Thankfully, the gospel has sufficient answers. What's more, it offers all the resources Ryan needs to experience real and lasting change.

The first change the gospel offers is a new identity. Unfortunately, it seems in vogue these days for young men like Ryan to refer to themselves as "homosexual Christians."[5] But this betrays a heart that is looking for identity in all the wrong places. As Paul Tripp reminds us, "We are always living out of some sense of identity. You are constantly telling yourself who you are, and the identity you assign to yourself has much to do with how you respond to the difficulties of life."[6] For Christian men who are struggling with homosexual desires, it is neither biblical nor helpful to self-identify as "homosexual." If you want to lose your taste for alligator, you've got to stop thinking of yourself as a snake.

Assuming Ryan is a Christian,[7] his true identity is found in union with Christ. Before salvation, all men stand before God like Adam, naked and alone in their sin, having nothing to anticipate but the wrath of God (Ephesians 5:6). Once saved, however, we stand before God "in Christ" (Ephesians 1:3-13). This is one of those truths that drive us all into the theological deep end of the gospel. But trust me on this—there's treasure down there worth diving for, and Ryan desperately needs it.

To be "in Christ" is to be viewed by God as a completely new person. A person who has received Christ as Savior is "born again" (John 3:3). He is a "new creature" (2 Corinthians 5:17). He has been given a new Father (2 Corinthians 6:18), a new name (Revelation 2:17), and a new destiny (John 14:2). To say a person is "in Christ" is like saying he has been legally adopted by God the Father.[8] Let this truth stretch the limits of your ability to think and worship! As far as God is concerned, you are a member of His family—His child! And as His child, you have been endowed with an infinite wealth of divine blessing.

One of the blessings God gives His children is the reality that "Christ assumes all our liabilities and graciously gives us His assets."[9] This is where hope for men like Ryan (and every sinner) begins. Many men who struggle with homosexual desire secretly fear that their sin puts them beyond the reach of God's forgiveness. As biblical counselors, our job is to help Ryan wade into the deep waters of God's grace until he comprehends that the forgiveness of God is unfathomable. Let the measuring line descend into the ocean of God's grace for eternity—it will never touch bottom! The mercies of God cannot be measured.

Ryan may not realize it, but if he thinks his sin (bad as it may be) is more than God can forgive, then he is making it out to be greater than the cross, greater than the risen Christ, greater than God. He may be a Christian, but his understanding of the gospel is weak and needs to be significantly strengthened. Helping him interact with the doctrine of atonement may be a great boost to Ryan's progress.[10] Of course, it is necessary for him to see the depths of his sin. But it is equally necessary for him to learn that Christ's sacrifice was infinitely greater than all his sin. There is no sin so deep that God is not deeper still. As J.I. Packer says, "Only where these truths [of the atonement] have taken root and grow in the heart will anyone be fully alive to God."[11]

Loved by God

Absolute forgiveness is one gloriously hope-giving benefit of our union with Christ, but Ryan also needs to know that he is deeply loved by God. Being related to Christ means that we who once were God's enemies have become the objects of His infinite love. In fact, all who are in Christ are loved by God (are you ready for this?) just as much as He loves His only begotten Son. Jesus made this clear when, as He prayed to the Father, He said "...so that the world may know that you sent me and *loved them even as you loved me*" (John 17:23).

Again, this truth is liable to have a significant impact on the men you counsel. While we would never say that a poor relationship with one's father is the cause of homosexuality, it is often part of the equation. Many homosexual men will tell you that the rejection they felt from their father often tempts them to assume God's rejection. But God's love for men like Ryan is as deep as His love for Christ, as fierce as the cross, and as glorious as the resurrection! "See how great a love the Father has bestowed on us, that we would be called children of God; and *such* we are" (1 John 3:1 NASB).

Let there be no mistake. This kind of counseling requires significant effort and planning. But unpacking rich gospel truth for men like Ryan will not only help them grasp the depths of their forgiveness, but will also begin enabling them to "comprehend with all the saints what is the breadth and length and height and depth, and to know the love of Christ that surpasses knowledge, that [they] may be filled with all the fullness of God" (Ephesians 3:18-19).

The Believer's Identity

Clearly communicating the believer's identity in Christ and its resulting benefits is essential for helping men like Ryan experience real, lasting change. But with these benefits the gospel also makes corresponding demands upon the believer's life. Paul teaches us that the grace of God instructs us "to renounce ungodliness and worldly passions, and to live self-controlled, upright, and godly lives in the present age" (Titus 2:12). The privilege of becoming a child of God comes with the expectation that we will pursue a life that is worthy of our Father, the King (Colossians 1:10). He is not only our Savior and divine benefactor, He is our Lord. Moreover, He has a purpose for our lives that we are expected to joyfully pursue. What is that purpose? Simply stated, we exist to show the world what God is like (Ephesians 5:1; 1 Peter 1:15; 2:9). This has tremendous implications for the kinds of changes that need to take place in Ryan's behavior.

The effective counselor will help men like Ryan identify and put off every behavior that feeds his homosexual desires. If necessary, this will mean breaking off certain friendships, setting up an Internet filter, and avoiding certain people and places that have been a problem in the past. He must also help Ryan identify feminine mannerisms that need to change, and show him how to carry himself like a man.

On the other hand, Ryan must be taught how to put on behavior that is consistent with biblical teaching on what it means to be a godly man who models Christ. For example, Ryan might require help establishing a daily discipline of reading and meditating on Scripture. He should also be assigned other books that will introduce him to the infinite attributes of God and the glory of Christ. In addition, he may need help building male friendships that will encourage his relationship with Christ, model a life of purity, offer loving accountability, show him how to relate to women as a godly man, and perhaps one day even encourage him to marry.

Inner Change

Biblical counselors know, however, that the goal of ministry is not just behavior change. Our aim is also to bring about significant change at the deepest level of a man's secret impulses and appetites as well. God wants something more for the homosexually inclined Christian than a life of tortured celibacy. He wants him to enjoy a life that is free from slavery to sinful desires. Ryan's cravings are not a secondary issue; they are primary because behavior is always the fruit of what we worship and desire. But it is at this very point that homosexual men tend to stumble.

Men like Ryan have been told that their same-sex desires stem from their "natural" sexual orientation. "People don't choose to become homosexual" they are told, "they are born that way." At first blush, this appears plausible considering the testimony of many homosexual men. One man writes, "There was nothing, it felt, chosen or intentional about my being gay. It seemed more like noticing the blueness of my eyes than deciding I would take up skiing. There was never an option."[12] In other words, he believes he has a homosexual orientation because homosexuality feels natural.

Most Christians (and many Christian counselors) who would never condone homosexual behavior accept the idea of homosexual orientation.[13] They may disagree on its cause, but they accept the argument that some people are just born that way and have to learn to cope with it as best they can. But this misses the clear teaching of Scripture. Paul shows us that homosexuality comes from the same heart that generates greed, envy, strife, disobedience to parents, and gossip (Romans 1:29-32). Same-sex attraction feels natural to the homosexual for the same reason many other sins feel natural. Like greed, envy, and gossip, it doesn't need to be learned, nor does it need to be consciously chosen. It is one of the natural capacities of the idolatrous heart of man that craves and seeks satisfaction in things other than God. As Dr. Edward Welch points out, "Most sin works on a level where we do not feel that we self-consciously choose it. To use Old Testament language, our sin can be 'unintentional,' but that does not make us less responsible."[14]

The human heart is not born with an orientation toward homosexuality; it is born with an orientation toward sin. And we are responsible for the way we sin, even when it appears in the form of desires that we did not consciously choose. As Tim Chester writes, "The Bible's radical view of sin tells that we are responsible. We always do what we want."[15] Paul speaks of the Christian life as a battle between the desires of the flesh and the desires of the Spirit (Galatians 5:16-17). To dismiss sinful desires merely as a product of one's homosexual orientation will keep one from experiencing "the privilege of rooting out sin at the level of the imagination."[16]

Transformation and Freedom

Can desires be changed? Praise God, they can! One of the most hope-giving passages in the New Testament for men tempted by same-sex attraction comes from the apostle Paul. After specifically naming homosexuality among other life-dominating sins, he reminded his brothers in Christ, "Such *were* some of you; but you were washed, but you were sanctified, but you were justified in the name of the Lord Jesus Christ and by the Spirit of our God" (1 Corinthians 6:11). It is possible to turn away from both the practice and the desires of homosexuality. But it will not happen automatically.

Transforming our desires begins by being honest about what our hearts really want. That's what truly matters to God. Why? Because what we treasure reveals what we trust, and what we want reveals what we worship. Finding freedom from enslaving impulses begins by learning to identify these desires for what they are. They are not merely "temptations," they are inherently sinful temptations that overwhelm us because we think they can give us something that we want.

Identifying what we want will help us stand up against the temptation itself. For example, if Ryan's deep-down desire is ease and comfort, and he finds himself most comfortable in intimate relationships with other men, then his desire for comfort will drive him to pursue these kinds of relationships, regardless of his conscience and the guilt he will feel. At this point the temptation has overwhelmed him because he has not yet dealt with his desire. This is the heart struggle that precedes the fall into sinful behavior.

Jesus said, "From within, out of the heart of man, come evil thoughts, sexual immorality, theft, murder, adultery, coveting, wickedness, deceit, sensuality, envy, slander, pride, foolishness. All these evil things come from within, and they defile a person" (Mark 7:21-23). Once Ryan sees that he has allowed his desire for comfort to become more important than obedience to Christ—that he has allowed his heart to be drawn away by his idol of comfort—he will be able to repent of that idolatrous desire and really begin to work on resisting the temptations of homosexual relationships. Many temptations that arise from our own hearts' desires are inherently sinful and need to be identified, confessed, and replaced. This is how sin is cut off at the root so that we can experience the joyful freedom that purity brings.

Repentant Worship

How does a struggling believer replace sinful thoughts? First, by flooding his mind with repentant worship. "Oh, Lord," he might pray, "I confess that the thoughts coursing through my mind just now are not merely temptations, they are inherently sinful; the fruit of an idolatrous heart that secretly loves what You forbid. I bring them to the cross where my Savior suffered, bled, and died to free me from their tyranny. Father, please forgive me. Help me turn my mind to the glory of the risen Christ seated at Your right hand. I choose right now to worship Him and ask You to transform my heart until it desires only what is pleasing to Christ."

Delighting in Christ

Second, for a struggling believer to keep his heart pure requires that he overcome sinful desires with the superior pleasures of delighting in the glory of God in Christ. Puritan pastor Jeremiah Burroughs correctly observed, "As flies will not come to honey if it is boiling hot but when it is cold, so if the heart is boiling hot [for Christ] and the affections working, it will keep out vain thoughts and temptations."[17] Teaching Ryan to confess sinful desires as they arise and maintain joyful fellowship with Christ will gradually turn his heart's desires in a direction that pleases the Lord.

Change That Lasts

Though the process of change for Ryan will not be easy for him or his counselor, hope for change comes from knowing that when the gospel requires him to work out his salvation with fear and trembling, it also promises that "it is God who works in you, both to will and to work for his good pleasure" (Philippians 2:12-13). Ryan is not alone.

No Christian man has to live like a reptile enslaved by deadly desires. The gospel provides all that he needs to change—radically and permanently. In Christ he has a new identity, complete forgiveness, the unwavering love of the Father, the power of the Spirit, the fellowship of the church, and the power of true worship. All of these resources are available to every child of God and are powerful for transforming lust-driven men into holy men of God who are growing more and more into the likeness of Christ.

Recommended Resources

Chester, Tim. *You Can Change: God's Transforming Power for Our Sinful Behavior and Negative Emotions*. Wheaton, IL: Crossway, 2010.

Lane, Timothy S., and Paul David Tripp. *How People Change*. Greensboro, NC: New Growth Press, 2006.

MacArthur, John. *Right Thinking in a World Gone Wrong: A Biblical Response to Today's Most Controversial Issues*. Eugene, OR: Harvest House, 2009.

Mohler, R. Albert. *Desires and Deceit: The Real Cost of the New Sexual Tolerance*. New York, NY: Random House, 2008.

Moore, Russell. *Tempted and Tried: Temptation and the Triumph of Christ.* Wheaton, IL: Crossway, 2011.

Rose Publishing. *Straight Talk: Homosexuality, Science & the Bible.* Torrance, CA: Rose Publishing, 2005.

Sprigg, Peter. *The Top Ten Harms of Same-Sex Marriage.* http://downloads.frc .org/EF/EF11B30.pdf.

Tripp, Paul David. *Broken Down House: Living Productively in a World Gone Bad.* Wapwallopen, PA: Shepherd Press, 2009.

Welch, Edward T. *Homosexuality: Speaking the Truth in Love.* Phillipsburg, NJ: P&R Publishing, 2000.

19

Fathers and Teenage Homosexuality

Ben Marshall

Imagine, as the father of a teen son, having someone come up to you and say, "Jon, I've got something I need to talk to you about. I've been trying to figure out how to say this, but I just can't come up with a good way to do that…but I think your son is gay."

Maybe you don't have to imagine that scenario. In this day and age, there's a good chance that you have either had to say something similar to another father, or perhaps you've experienced the proverbial bomb going off as someone has said that to you. Or at the very least, you've heard of something like this happening to someone else. There are few subjects that evoke as much fear, guilt, and confusion in parents as the issue of teenage homosexuality.

"Are you telling me that my son desires intimacy with other boys? Did I do something to make him like boys instead of girls? Am I going to have to get used to him bringing his 'dates' to the house? What will family functions be like? What happens if our church finds out? What will people think about our family? Why did this happen? Did someone molest him to cause this? Is this genetic?" These questions and many more are likely to run through the mind of the father who hears that his son is gay.[1] Depending upon which Internet blogs you read, TV shows you watch, or radio stations you listen to, you could potentially hear anything from total acceptance to total rejection when it comes to this subject. So, what's a Christian father to do? How should he react?

Thankfully, God has given us clear answers in His Word. God does not react to this issue of homosexuality as though He is surprised by it. In fact,

He knew everything that would ever happen in this world before it was created. Thousands of years ago when He gave us the Bible, He wrote to us about these difficulties. If you are reading this chapter because you are facing a situation with a teenager you love who is caught up in homosexuality, or you know someone who is, you can know with certainty that God's Word has the answers—and those answers are just as true for you today as they were when the Bible was written.

Although there is not adequate space for this chapter to include a comprehensive Bible study on this subject, we can certainly address key questions and look to God's Word for answers, knowing that "all Scripture is breathed out by God and profitable for teaching, for reproof, for correction, and for training in righteousness, that the man of God may be complete, equipped for *every* good work" (2 Timothy 3:16-17).

Is This Something I Need to Be Concerned About?

In decades past, to hear that your son might be gay would have definitely been alarming and embarrassing; however, societal and peer pressure in those days would probably have discouraged your teen from moving deeper into the homosexual lifestyle. In stark contrast, the world teens live in today encourages them to live alternative lifestyles and lifts them up as heroes when they do so. Homosexuality is highlighted and celebrated in public schools, city parades, on television sitcoms, and most grievously, in some churches. With so much cultural encouragement in the direction of the gay lifestyle, it is imperative that Christian fathers be *very* concerned.

This sin, if left unchecked, may overwhelm your teenager and eventually become his perceived identity. (See chapter 18, "Struggling with Homosexuality," for biblical insight on homosexual identity.) Unlike teen couples who engage in heterosexual relations, teens caught up in homosexual activity usually begin to structure all of life around that which encourages those tendencies. By default, they isolate themselves from all who would discourage them. Romans 1:32 warns of this when it says, "Though they know God's decree that those who practice such things deserve to die, they not only do them but give approval to those who practice them."

Beyond the embarrassment and concern for your son, the most important question, of course, is this: What does God think about homosexuality? While we may tempted to change our views to lessen embarrassment and be "accepting" of a son's lifestyle choices and thereby keep peace in the family, we cannot change what God has decreed in regard to human relations. Whenever God talks about homosexuality, it's never in a favorable way. In Genesis 19, God rained down fire from heaven on the towns of Sodom and Gomorrah for the rampant homosexuality practiced by the inhabitants in those places. In Leviticus 18:22, God referred to homosexuality as an abomination. In Romans 1:18-32 we read that it is a result of exchanging the worship of God for the worship of God's creation. Those who live a lifestyle of homosexuality will not inherit the kingdom of God (1 Corinthians 6:9), and homosexuals are counted among those who are unholy, profane, godless, and disobedient (1Timothy 1:8-10). It's pretty clear that homosexuality is declared by God to be sin—sin with consequences.

God's perspective on this is serious and weighty. Because His judgment will fall on those who disobey Him, you will not be able to avoid facing severe consequences if you do not stand with Him on this issue. It will mean eternal consequences for your son if you do not teach him the ways of God. And for you it will mean living with the anguish of watching those consequences come to fruition, in addition to living with the guilt that is yours. For these reasons, it is imperative that you read on to find help for responding biblically to this difficult problem. Genuine love for your son will motivate you to do things God's way.

Who's Responsible for This?

While homosexuality isn't your temptation or struggle, you may find yourself wondering if somehow you are responsible for the decisions your teenager has made. If you were to do an Internet search on the reasons for homosexuality, you would find a plethora of articles seeking to persuade you that there are many reasons why people end up being attracted to the same sex.[2] Some will claim that biology and genetics are the primary reasons. Other will claim that the fundamental cause is a change in societal norms as to what is acceptable behavior. Still others will blame the homosexual behavior on broken or nonexistent relationships in the home.

While the world looks to place the blame on everything outside of the person struggling with homosexuality, God's Word goes in the exact opposite direction and places the blame on the person who is committing the sin of homosexuality. In the Bible, we read of a saying that younger people used to shift the blame for their sin onto their parents. The proverb[3] went something like this: "Our dads ate sour grapes, and our lips pucker." The children were saying their struggles with sin were because of things their fathers had done. God put an end to such thinking in Ezekiel 18:3-4: "As I live, declares the Lord God, this proverb shall no more be used by you in Israel. Behold, all souls are mine; the soul of the father as well as the soul of the son is mine: the soul who sins shall die." God was saying that each person is responsible for his own sin. Although no parent is perfect, according to God, you are not to blame for your son's choices. He bears that guilt himself.

Turning from who is responsible to how this came about, God describes the downward spiral into homosexuality in Romans 1. It starts when a man suppresses the truth by his unholy thoughts and actions (verse 18). The progression downward continues when God gives that person over to the lusts of his own heart (verse 24), which the Bible describes as dishonorable passions (verse 26). It is at this stage that the normal sexual desires of men toward women and women toward men are exchanged for those that are not normal—homosexuality (verses 26-27). This progression hits bottom when those who have exchanged normal passions for abnormal passions give hearty approval to everyone else who is doing the same (verse 32).

A common objection parents voice in response to Romans 1 is this: "My teen hasn't had time to make that downward spiral. He has gone to church all his life and been a good boy. He's just a kid!" Parenting your child biblically through anything, even much less devastating sins, requires you to have God's perspective on what the fall of Adam and Eve has done to all people—even to your children. Every human is born sinful (Psalm 51:5). "The soul who sins shall die" (Ezekiel 18:20). "The wages of sin is death" (Romans 6:23).

From the moment of conception, our children's hearts are turned toward wickedness and away from God—just as ours were. Who can know at what age the progression toward homosexuality begins? To know when a child starts to suppress the truth is all but impossible. Even babies show the intent of their hearts when they stiffen their bodies up in rebellion toward their parents. After 13 or 14 years of this kind of heart response, it is quite conceivable that a son could begin to show outward signs of suppressing the truth through being attracted to others of the same sex. As difficult as it is, we must let the truth of Scripture determine what indeed has happened to a child that has gone wayward.

At this point you might be asking, "Is it really the person's fault that he is gay? What about a child exposed to sexual abuse, or who grows up in a home where homosexuality is viewed as being normal, and other things like that?" Those are *influencing factors* that can impact the heart that is rebellious, but those *influences* should never be viewed as *causal* factors. After all, it would not be just of God to condemn a person for something that is not his fault. No, according to the Bible, there is only one *cause* for homosexuality, and that is the sinful human heart. God calls homosexuality sin, and so must we.

What Should I Do?

Perhaps you are already concerned for your teenager and you know he is to blame for the homosexual struggle he is facing, but you simply are not sure what to do. You're ready for help from God's Word, which you can have confidence in because "His divine power has granted to us all things that pertain to life and godliness, through the knowledge of him who called us to his own glory and excellence" (2 Peter 1:3).

Remember the Good News of the Gospel

The only hope for someone who is struggling with homosexual temptations and sin is the gospel of Jesus Christ. The gospel, or the good news, can be summed up in the life, death, and resurrection of Jesus Christ, but it's important to start at the beginning. The only reason we need a Savior—one who lived a perfect life in our place, died to take the punishment for us, and rose again to provide eternal life—is because of the magnitude of our sin. So offensive to God is our sin that He cannot overlook it. In His justice, He cannot whisk it from His view and pretend it never was. As Romans 6:23 says, the just punishment for sin is death.

God, who is perfectly holy, demands that those who live in His favor also be perfectly holy. And this we cannot do on our own merits. Sin has so stained all humans that Paul declares, "None is righteous, no, not one; no one understands; no one seeks for God. All have turned aside; together they have become worthless; no one does good, not even one" (Romans 3:10-12).

This means we would be utterly hopeless if God had not intervened in Christ. Not only did Jesus lower Himself to be born as a man and live a perfect life in our place, but when He died He took our sins upon Himself, bearing the wrath of God so that we wouldn't have to. And the good news doesn't stop there. Christ rose from the dead—defeating Satan and sin, thus promising that those who have placed their faith in Him would have the power to say no to sin, yes to righteousness, and one day live with Him forever in heaven.

This is the very truth that homosexuals seek to suppress; ironically, it is this truth that is their only hope of freedom from their sin and guilt. It is good to ponder this before you begin to work with your son, because the gospel has God's grace dripping all over the place. Consider this: If God showed His grace to you while you were a sinner and yet unsaved, then you can know He is able to show the same grace to your teenager while he is still a sinner.

Perhaps this is the first time that you have heard the good news of the gospel of Jesus Christ. The promises found in Christ's life, death, and resurrection are applicable only for those who have heard, believed, and trusted in that gospel. If you have never thought about, considered, and believed in this gospel, you need to earmark this page, put the book down, and come before God in prayer, acknowledging your need to be saved from the wrath of God by the life, death, and resurrection of Jesus. For more on this, see Appendix One, "The Gospel for Men" on page 387.

Remember that God Is Working in You

Romans 8:28 says that God is working everything together for good for those who love Him and are called according to His purpose. Because that is a promise from God Himself, you can rest assured that this present trial with your teenager is going to work for your good. In verse 29 God goes on to say that His intention through these trials is that you would be more like His Son Jesus. If you are willing to be obedient to God's Word through all of this, and rely on His Holy Spirit to empower you to do what He has called you to do, then you will think, speak, and act more like Christ. This should be the goal of every Christian.

Remember to Get the Log Out of Your Own Eye

That might seem like a silly statement, as we do not see people walking around with logs in their eyes. But it is a figure of speech used by Jesus to teach us about the need for caution when we address sin in other people's lives. In Matthew 7:1 He said, "Judge not, that you be not judged." So many people, especially those who are trying to justify the homosexual lifestyle, will say to Christians, "See, even the Bible says not to judge other people." But Jesus went on to explain that when we see some sin in someone else's life (a "speck in your brother's eye"), we are not to try to help that person if we at the same time have a major sin in our own life (which He calls "the log in your own eye"). When Jesus made that statement, He was confronting the Jewish leaders of that time, telling them that they were pointing out other people's sins while ignoring the blatant sins in their own lives. He told them to stop doing that and first repent of their own sin. Then and only then were they qualified to go to others and humbly help them out with their sin. In preparation for helping your son out with his sin, you first need to come before the Lord in prayer and in the Word to see whether there is sin in your own life.

Given the seriousness of dealing with a son who has fallen into homosexuality, it would be good for you (and your spouse, if applicable) to take a day or so to get away from work, cell phones, the Internet, and children to spend time praying and evaluating your life, using God's Word as the standard. Look to see if there are any "logs" sticking out of your eye. When you are ready to help your son, you will want to be as effective as possible, not having your own sin stand in the way. This calls for...

- *Confession of sin.* In humble prayer, ask God to open your eyes so you can see your sins against Him and others—perhaps even your son—so that you may confess those sins. To *confess* means "to say the same thing"; in this case, you will say the same thing that God says. "I have sinned in doing such and such; I say the same thing

that you do, God, about this being sinful. I have sinned before You
and my family."

- *Repentance.* God calls us to not only confess our sins, but to repent
  of them. It is God's kindness that leads us to repentance (Romans
  2:4). To *repent* means "to turn"—to turn your back on sin and live
  in obedience to God by faith in His Son.

- *Seeking forgiveness of those you have sinned against.* Nothing softens
  the heart of a child more than when his parent humbly confesses
  sin that he has repented of and asks for his forgiveness. While an
  angry, rebellious son may use your admission of sin to his advantage, you should still do this, as this is God's way for us to make
  wrongs right—to reconcile broken relationships. "If you are offering your gift at the altar and there remember that your brother has
  something against you, leave your gift there before the altar and go.
  First be reconciled to your brother, and then come and offer your
  gift" (Matthew 5:23).

- *Making a plan to change.* Having confessed your sin, repented, and
  sought forgiveness, now commit yourself to changing your ways
  and obeying God's Word. For example, if you had a habit of angry
  outbursts, live in obedience to Ephesians 4:29-32. Memorize these
  verses and ask God to help you to change. Plan ahead of time what
  kind and gracious words you will speak to others when you feel
  tempted to explode in anger. Begin to practice what the Word of
  God says, leaving behind your former ways of sinning.

This four-step process of dealing with your own sin will be just the thing
your son will need to hear when he is ready to repent.

Pray with Joy and Thanksgiving

Having made your own heart clean before the Lord, it is now time for you
to come to God and ask for the impossible to happen, humanly speaking. You
are asking for God to change the heart of your teen, which is something only He
can do. When it comes to this making request, God is specific about how you
are to come to Him—with rejoicing, without anxiety, and with thanksgiving

(Philippians 4:4-6). You may feel like asking God, "Why?" But when Job did that, he got a five-chapter response from God (Job 38–42).

You might be asking, "How can I rejoice in this painful circumstance?" There are several reasons why you can rejoice, but two rise to the forefront. First, God has providentially made it possible for you to be aware of information that could have stayed hidden for a lifetime. What's important is that you are aware your son is struggling with homosexuality. What if that information had remained hidden until eternity, when there will be no hope for change or help? In His grace, God has made it possible for this information to come to light so that you can pray for and lovingly guide your teen with regard to this issue.

Second, you can rejoice because you *know* the God of the universe who has the power and ability to do all that He purposes to do. Not only is He powerful enough to bring His great will to pass, but He is infinitely good, loving, and wise in all His dealings with His children. Not everyone can call upon the name of the Lord and expect that He will hear them. However, as God's child, you can know the peace that comes from knowing this God is your God. And, as Romans 8:31-32 says, "If God is for us, who can be against us? He who did not spare his Son but gave him up for us all, how will he not also with him graciously give us all things?" It is His delight to give good things to His children, but we have to remember that God decides what is good. He knows what outcome is the best, because He is God. There is no thwarting the plans of God—what God wants to do He will do (Psalm 33:11).

This same God who does what He wants has given you the promise that if you bring your prayers to Him, His peace will guard your heart and mind (Philippians 4:6-7). In other words, He will allow you to know peace and sleep when you would otherwise lay awake with worry trying to figure out how to change your teen. The peace that comes from God truly does surpass all human understanding, so go to Him rejoicing with thanksgiving, and ask Him to *rescue* your teen and give you peace of mind in the midst of this difficult situation.

Roll Up Your Sleeves and Get Ready to Work

Having prepared yourself through confession and repentance, reconciliation with others, and prayer, you are now at the point where you can step in and help your teen no matter how far down the path he has walked toward homosexuality. You can move toward him with a *gentle boldness* that the world knows nothing of, and with *humility*. "Clothe yourselves, all of you, with humility toward one another, for 'God opposes the proud but gives grace to the humble'" (1 Peter 5:5). Gentleness and humility are two sides of the same coin. Gently express to your teen that you want to help him, not simply condemn him. And boldly tell him—with humility—what God's Word clearly states about the sin of homosexuality and those who live in it. At the same time, offer to him the hope found in the gospel.

How Can I Help My Teen?

"You just explained how to help—with gentle boldness. Now what do I do?" It is impossible to prescribe a one-size-fits-all plan for every situation. You will need to know your son and where his heart is, where his weak spots are, whether his conscience is convicting him or he has rendered his conscience ineffective through rationalization and repeated acts of homosexual sin, and whether or not he believes God and His Word.

Here are four steps you can take to get started.

1. Listen

The book of Proverbs is filled with all kinds of practical wisdom about listening. Proverbs 18:13 is particularly noteworthy: "If one gives an answer before he hears, it is his folly and shame." Before you share your pearls of wisdom with your son, you need to hear him out. This is especially true if you heard about your son's lifestyle choices from another parent, through an email, or through any other source outside your teen. There is no "best way" for this to happen that will help take the awkwardness out of the conversation. There are some things, however, that you can do to help make your discussion go as well as it possibly can:

- Have your Bible out and turn to it often. Tell your teen that you are relying on God and His Word to help you through this talk.

- Pray aloud before you get started. This will help your son to see you have placed your dependence upon God.

- Confess any sins that you have committed against your teen. Seek his forgiveness with a humble attitude. Avoid making excuses for your sinful behavior.

- Treat your son like any other important person in your life by reminding him that you love him and want God's best for him.

- Tell him what you have heard and/or observed that has caused you to think that he might be caught in homosexuality.

- Ask good questions that require more than a simple yes or no answer. These kinds of questions will often cause a deceitful teen to stumble and eventually reveal the truth. They will also help clear up any misunderstandings. For example, perhaps your son has assumed that just because he looked at another boy in the gym shower he thinks he might be gay.

If after listening to your son you are convinced that he has fallen into the sin of homosexuality, continue to pursue helping him with gentle boldness. Is this the first time he has been called to account for this? This is the time for gentle humility—don't come down on him with harsh words of anger and say things like, "How could you do this to your mother and I?" Instead, speak with boldness and love as you say "Your mother and I love you, but we must tell you that the Bible says the path of the sinner is a difficult one, ultimately leading to judgment. We are here to let you know of our loving concern and our desire to help you."

2. Give Hope

Just as you needed hope when you found out that your teen might be struggling with homosexuality, your son needs a boatload of hope as he battles against this sin. Help him to see that this hope is found in God's Word alone. Of utmost importance in this battle is a good presentation of the gospel. Your son needs to know what the gospel is, to believe that his only hope is the gospel, and to place his trust in the gospel.[4] First Corinthians 2:14 very clearly states that as long as a person remains in his natural, unbelieving state, he will not understand the things of God. It will be impossible for your teen to pull himself up and out of this sin without the help and work of the Holy Spirit and the Word of God. Don't assume your son is already a Christian; gently ask him about his faith and listen carefully. Be ready to call him to first-time repentance if necessary.

If you are convinced that your son is a Christian, you can move on in giving him hope. Another truth that God has graciously given to us to promote hope is found in Romans 8:28-30. Take great care here because there is a condition to this promise: God works all things for good—*for those who love Him.* If your teenager does not love God and does not want to live for God, then this promise will be of no use to him. However, if your son does love God and wants help out of homosexual sin, then this passage is filled with all the hope he needs. The good that God will bring about will be his transformation into the likeness of Jesus Christ—the perfect Son of God.

Spend some time talking to your teenager about how God, in His grace, will cause everything, including the renouncing of homosexual sin, to work for his good by bringing him to look more like Christ. In other words, a true Christian finds his new identity not in his sinful state ("I am a homosexual"), but in his family ties with his perfect Savior *and Brother* (see Hebrews 2:11-12). Jesus, His Savior, predestined him to holiness, called him to be His brother, justified him so that his sins would no longer be held against him, and glorified him in being a redeemed one of God. What an amazing gift from the Lord!

Another verse that offers hope is 1 Corinthians 10:13: "No temptation has overtaken you that is not common to man. God is faithful, and he will not let you be tempted beyond your ability, but with the temptation he will also provide the way of escape, that you may be able to endure it." Your son should be encouraged to know that he is not the only one in the world who has ever struggled with this sin. Leading a sinful life results in feeling isolated from others—especially loved ones. There is a good chance your son has felt quite alone in his struggle with homosexuality. But the Bible says that all sins are common to man.

Furthermore, there is great hope because *God is faithful.* Your teen needs to understand exactly who is on his side, working in him. Our all-powerful and loving God will be faithful to your teen as he struggles against this sin. Make sure that you spend time highlighting the faithfulness and character of God. This would be a good time to open the Bible and show your son various passages that declare God's faithful character.

First Corinthians 10:13 ends by promising your teen that God will not allow homosexual temptation and sin to destroy him; rather, God will *always* provide a way of escape in every single tempting moment. Depending upon how involved your teen has been in homosexual sin, this could possibly be the most hopeful statement you make to him. There is a good chance that your teen has felt like he "had no choice." To hear that he does have a choice and that God will be faithful to provide a way of escape just might be exactly what your son needs to hear.

3. Remember the Gospel Daily

Many people think that the only use for telling the gospel is to introduce people to Christ. However, the grace and power of the gospel goes much further than that. It is by the grace of God that we are forgiven our heavy load of sin; and it is by the grace of God that He gives us the strength to say no to sin. Note this amazing truth: "The *grace* of God has appeared, bringing salvation for all people, training us to *renounce ungodliness* [say no to sin] and worldly passions, and to live self-controlled, upright, and godly lives in the present age" (Titus 2:11-12). As our minds are humbled that God would forgive such a rotten sinner, we grow in love for Him and are strengthened to live for Him, not for ourselves.

As an example of how the gospel is helpful on a day-to-day basis, you could memorize Romans 8:1, which declares what the life and death and resurrection of Jesus accomplished: "There is therefore now no condemnation for those who are in Christ Jesus." Since there is no condemnation from God for those who belong to Jesus, you can walk in the light. And even if you do fall into sin, you can still go to God because He has promised not to condemn you. Christ was condemned *for you.* That is hopeful and freeing to someone who potentially thinks that he is not allowed to mess up at all. When we sin, we know that Christ stands before God for us as our advocate, proving that all our sins have been paid for. Overwhelmed with this great love and grace, we confess our sins and humbly receive our Father's forgiveness.

A couple great resources to help you out with this task of daily reminding your teen of gospel promises are *A Gospel Primer for Christians* by Milton Vincent and *The Gospel for Real Life* by Jerry Bridges. Both of these authors go into great detail to explain that the gospel is not just for introducing the non-Christian to Christ, but for the Christian's daily walk as well. However you go about this task of daily reminding your teen about the gospel, make sure that this is a high priority on your checklist.

4. Show Him How to Change

As someone once said, "Change hasn't taken place until change has taken place."[5] The process of change is hard work and will require energy from both you and your teenager if real change is going to happen. According to Ephesians 4:22-24, this process of change consists of three parts: (1) stopping the old way of living, (2) having your mind changed, and (3) putting on a new way of living. You will need to walk alongside your teenager through each of these stages and provide as much help and support as you possibly can.

Stopping the old way of living starts by figuring out exactly what your teen's life looks like at the present moment. What music does he listen to? What friends does he have? What has he posted on his various social media websites? Where does he work? What groups does he belong to at school? What books is he reading? When does he go to bed? What does his Internet history look like? Are most of his friends guys or girls? Depending upon the answers to these and other questions, there is a good chance he will need to restructure big parts of his life. This kind of restructuring is often called *radical amputation*. This idea comes from Jesus' teaching[6] and refers to getting rid of anything that makes it easy for you to continue to sin. This part of the change process, while sometimes painful, is usually the easiest part to carry out because your teen most likely will know what influences tempt him to sin in the area of homosexuality.

The second area to consider is the renewal of your teen's mind. He will have to learn how to interpret life through the lens of Scripture. Do not be timid or shy about this second stage, even if you are not that familiar with your Bible. If necessary, confess to him that you have a lot to learn about Scripture and you are willing to have your mind renewed as his mind is being renewed. (See the Recommended Resources section at the end of this chapter for more on how to study the Bible.) The goal is not that you become an expert in the Bible, but that you simply spend time in God's Word getting to know what He says.

The final step in the change process is helping your teen to start doing what God commands him to do. This can often be one of the hardest parts in the process of change. Volumes and volumes of writing would have to be done in order to address every little nuance that might need to change in the life of your teen. The main idea you need to keep in mind is that you want to help him think of specifics and not generalities. Instead of merely exhorting him to get rid of bad influences and find good influences, you need to help him get specific and determine *which* people are having a negative influence on him, and *which* will have a positive influence. Helping your teen be specific will give him hope, because then he will know exactly what steps he needs to take—or avoid. This will also show your son that you love him and want to see God's best in his life.

Helping Your Teen

As you close this chapter and start to help your teen, remember 1 Corinthians 10:13 for yourself as well. All temptation is common to man, including having a teenage son who is struggling with the sin of homosexuality. God has been faithful and will continue to be faithful to you as you seek to be obedient to His Word. He has promised you that He will not give you more than you can handle, but with this temptation will provide the way of escape so that you can endure it. Your way of escape is to engage your teenager by listening, sharing the gospel, reminding him of the gospel, and showing him what real biblical change is all about. Most likely, showing your teen the way out will require that you work on your own life as well. This journey you take with your teen will no doubt be challenging, but God promises it will be for your good and His glory. Seek God's help daily so that you shine with the radiance of His glory and give your teen a new reason for living.

Recommended Resources

Bridges, Jerry. *The Gospel for Real Life: Turn to the Liberating Power of the Cross... Every Day*. Colorado Springs, CO: NavPress, 2002.

———. *Trusting God: Even When Life Hurts*. Colorado Springs, CO: NavPress, 2008.

MacArthur, John. *How to Study the Bible*. Chicago: Moody, 2009.

Marshall, Ben. *Help! My Teen Is Gay.* Leominster, UK: Day One Publications, 2011.

Tripp, Tedd. "A Child's Call to Conversion: As a Christian Mark." *Table Talk,* October 2010, 20-23.

Vincent, Milton. *A Gospel Primer: For Christians*. Bemidji, MN: Focus, 2008.

20

When Marriage Problems Become Legal Problems

Ed Wilde

While preparing this chapter, I met with a couple who was preparing to divorce. Certainly they had problems—serious, painful problems. However, their desire to divorce did not stem solely from their desire to rid themselves of these problems. As with many couples who divorce, their desire was to make the pain stop—and to make it stop right now.

There is a generally widespread perception that when a marriage is falling apart, getting a divorce from one's spouse will stop the pain and make it possible to be happy again. That perception, though common, is not necessarily true. The belief that one will "regain control" of his or her life after a divorce is often sorely contradicted by reality. In an effort to gain control, the parties involved will in fact lose control. In an effort to regain that elusive happiness they once had, the couple will instead encounter more frustration and despondency.

This is not what people want to hear—that their difficulties and trials can be expected to increase with the advent of divorce proceedings. Where is hope? Where is peace to be found? The only place they can be found is in a person—in the Lord Jesus Christ, who created man and woman, who created the covenant of marriage, and who can redeem people from the sin that enslaves them and from the destruction of their marriage.

Wisdom in Three Steps:
The Bad, the Good, and God

A common means of teaching wisdom in the Bible involves three elements. We can see these in Proverbs 5.

First, recognize the temptation for the danger it represents (the bad). In verses 3-14, Solomon explained that the apparent good offered by the "forbidden woman" (verse 3) will in fact...

- be bitter (verse 4),

- lead to death (verse 5),

- cause a loss of honor (verse 9),

- bring about economic loss (verse 10),

- generate anguish (verse 11),

- and result in a loss of reputation (verse 14).

While Proverbs 5 specifically addresses the temptation to sexual immorality, the pain and loss caused by divorce and other sins with devastating consequences will be similar on many points. In other words, a wise man will recognize the inevitable bitter consequences of choosing such a path.

Second, there is a means of escape (the good—1 Corinthians 10:13) provided to the one who will pursue wisdom. In Proverbs 5:15-20, Solomon wisely urges his son to delight in his wife. Again, the primary focus of the text is on sexual immorality. Yet were a man to seriously undertake the pursuit of delighting in his wife, the blessed result would be that a divorce *even in the hardest cases* could be avoided—hence the escape. While there are circumstances in which a divorce may be unavoidable, such cases are far rarer than many Christian men believe.

Third, life must be lived consciously in the sight of God (Proverbs 5:21). A great deal of sin and foolishness in marriage takes place due to the fact that we consider ourselves autonomous, thinking that we can live as if we had no Creator. In Psalm 10:11-13, the wicked and unwise man is described as one who says, "God has forgotten, he has hidden his face, he will never see it." He also says of God, "You will not call to account." Nothing could be further from the truth. Verse 14 declares, "But you do see, for you note mischief and vexation." The man who lives according to godly wisdom will recognize that God sees all he does and that he will give an account for his life to the Creator.

The bad, the good, and God—all three elements of wisdom will be considered in relation to divorce in this chapter. Harsh realities will be brought to light as we look at the dangers and damage of divorce, or the bad. But keep reading, for hope will come when we look at the good and God.

If you are playing around with the temptation to flee your problems and commitments via divorce, or if you are trying to help another man who is, I write these next paragraphs with you in mind. You must be presented with the bad—the awful details about the divorce process. With that in mind, I'll start by describing the general legal process of divorce as it appears to the man involved in a divorce proceeding.

Please note that this description cannot, in any way, substitute for actual legal counsel in a divorce proceeding. In other words, I am not providing legal advice here. In addition, note that this description of the legal process is based on my experience in the court system in the county of Los Angeles in the state of California. The rules for divorce vary from state to state, and at times from county to county. So what I share here is merely a general and typical picture of what happens with regard to the legal aspects of divorce. The laws I mention could very well change in the future. If you or a counselee would like to learn the specifics for the divorce proceedings in your state, I would recommend consulting with a family law attorney. If you'd like something more informal, many useful books have been published on the specifics of divorce proceedings.[1]

The Bad: Legal Proceedings Are Painful

Legal proceedings hurt everyone involved. French philosopher Voltaire reportedly said, "I have never been ruined but twice: once when I lost a lawsuit, and once when I won one."[2] So it is with divorce. You will be hurt, as will your children, your ex-wife, and your new wife if you remarry.

If you have children, the state will be in control of your relationships with your former spouse and your children until the children—*all your children*—reach 18 years of age. Count up the years. The state will also involve itself in your retirement, 401k, pensions, taxes, etc., for years to come. If you get a pay raise, your *former* wife might just get more of your money. If you have remarried, this will not likely result in happiness from your new wife.

Given those considerations, wisdom requires that one sit down and carefully count the cost before proceeding with a divorce. There will be a cost in terms of *money*—you will lose a lot of money no matter what; *relationships*—you will damage your relationships with your children, with your in-laws, your friends; *time*—you will need to go to court, meet with lawyers, drive across the county to pick up your children for Wednesday evening visits, etc; *witness*—"So…you're a Christian and you divorced your wife…hmmm."

Add up all these costs carefully and soberly. As you do, make sure you listen to a wise Christian, whether a pastor or a friend—someone who can and will remove any excessive hope that these losses will not affect you. Think clearly and honestly about the damage the divorce will cause, and weigh that carefully against the difficulty of reconciling with your wife. Even if you conclude that it would be better to stick your head in a pencil sharpener than to work on your marriage, I urge you to reconsider. Here are some facts about the pain the divorce process is guaranteed to bring into your life.

The Court in General

Divorces in Los Angeles County (where I live and work) are often filed in the main courthouse downtown. People who want to get to the courthouse at the time it opens have to leave early in the morning and fight the downtown rush-hour traffic. After they park, they have to make their way across the street, stand in a long line, and pass through a security inspection to make sure they are not carrying any weapons. They then walk down a long corridor and take an escalator to the second floor.

The first thing they see on the second floor is a corridor jammed with people. This is easily the most crowded area in the courthouse. There are two striking characteristics of this crowd outside the courtroom. First, there are children present. Second, many of the women are dressed as if they were seeking to seduce a man at a nightclub.

Now, imagine you're the one who is visiting the courthouse. It's very possible that you'll see your wife and children in that crowd. If your wife has already gotten involved with another man, he likely will be present with her as "moral support." This will, of course, make you feel very uncomfortable. You will not want this man near your children, yet you have no ability to stop it. This feeling of impotence will recur again and again all through the divorce proceedings, so if you go this direction, you'll need to expect this. Imagine yourself dropping off your children at 10:30 at night at your former wife's residence and watching another man hug them as they enter the house, and then driving back home to your lonely apartment. Then tell me that getting a divorce will be worth it. "Moreover, I saw under the sun that in the place of justice, even there was wickedness, and in the place of righteousness, even there was wickedness" (Ecclesiastes 3:16).

When the doors to the courthouse open, the mass of people in the corridor attempt to crowd into courtroom. Because there is not sufficient space for everyone, few are able to find a seat, and many have to stand.

The Attorney

Typically you'll have an attorney accompany you, and this will be expensive. If you make more money than your wife, you may very well find yourself paying for your attorney *and* hers. This will be frustrating and seem very unfair, but you'll have to get used to it.

The attorney's job is to help you complete the documentation in the correct manner, negotiate with the opposing side, present your case to the judge, and help you get as favorable a settlement as possible. Assuming that you have a retirement account, any sort of assets, or children, you will find that a favorable settlement typically entails keeping half of what you had to begin with. There are variations in the laws from state to state, but in the end you will end up with less property than you began with. Much of your property will be transferred from you to your attorney.

It is not uncommon to have multiple legal proceedings as you wrangle over details such as child support, alimony, visitation, etc., and it is not uncommon for the family law attorney to change over the course of time. You will likely change lawyers because you'll be so frustrated with the process, and you will hope that a different lawyer will bring more sanity to your life. This will rarely work. Moreover, you will have to pay money for the new lawyer to "get up to speed" with your case.

In many respects the lawyer is quite limited in what he or she can do. Many elements of your changed relationship will be established by statute. Other elements of your relationship with your ex-wife will be the result of negotiation involving a social worker or other court official. While there are limitations on what your lawyer can do—far less than you hoped he could do—he will be present for many of these events, and he will charge a great deal of money for his involvement. Rates for attorneys usually run hundreds of dollars per hour. And if you are paying for two lawyers—one for yourself and one for your soon-to-be ex-wife, the inadequacies of your bank account will become painfully evident.

The Court Workers

A courthouse visit is a remarkably complicated affair. The documents that you submit prior to your day in court—disclosures about property and income; information about your children, your spouse, and yourself—are filed, examined, copied, and evaluated by various persons whom you will never see. Information you hoped not to reveal to anyone will be kept in public files. While it is possible that some details may remain private, that cannot be guaranteed. Many find this uncomfortable, and the documents will remain the property of the state for perpetuity.

The Judge

As I consider this aspect of the courthouse visit, Ecclesiastes 4:1-3 comes to mind:

> I saw all the oppressions that are done under the sun. And behold, the tears of the oppressed, and they had no one to comfort them! On the side of their oppressors there was power, and there was no one to comfort them. And I thought the dead who are already dead more fortunate than the living who are still alive. But better than both is he who has not yet been and has not seen the evil deeds that are done under the sun.

The judge will hold your fate in his hands. Almost certainly, the result will be oppressive. This is not from any malice or ill will toward you personally; the judge has no idea who you are. He has so many cases to hear that he can spare only moments of his attention for you. His decisions will be quick, almost routine, and quite possibly wrong. The sheer volume of cases assigned to one judge makes careful, detailed attention to each case impossible. The system places this difficult burden on the judge, which, in turn, affects you.

In addition, the judge very likely disdains family court as much as you do. The law is not well-suited to managing the breakup of a relationship. The judges know this. I have never met a man or woman who went to law school with the hope of someday determining family outcomes in divorce court. I have, however, met judges who spoke with loathing of their time in the family court system.

To be a family law judge is a thankless occupation. Not only is the work typically dull, but it is often dangerous. Disgruntled former spouses often direct their anger toward the judicial process. Judges have told tales of physical threats, and at times actual physical violence has been directed toward them, sometimes even involving weapons. Because this job is so miserable, most judges work in the family law court only during the very beginning of their judicial career. As quickly as possible, they seek transfers to safer and more interesting appointments.

Imagine yourself to be the judge: At the end of the day, you have a stack of dozens of individual lawsuits seeking divorce. By 8:30 the next morning, you will be required to rule on them. Understandably, you are looking forward to finishing the workload so you can spend time with your family and take care of other obligations. Almost anything else will be more interesting to do. Unfortunately, many judges will yield to that pressure by giving very little careful thought to each case. *That* man or woman will be the one who makes rulings on your life!

However, I must be quick to add that not even a judge is beyond the power of God. The God who is sovereign over all is the God who is sovereign over your judge. "The king's heart is a stream of water in the hand of the Lord; he turns it wherever he will" (Proverbs 21:1). What an encouraging truth to remember in the midst of a discouraging process!

The Social Workers

You will encounter an army of facilitators who have been appointed by the government to help you divide up you and your children's lives. Imagine

Child Protective Services workers being on call to scrutinize and evaluate your parenting. Many of these men and women mean well and may be sincerely hoping to do you good. However, their idea of good may not be *your* idea of good. And, just as we can expect anywhere else in this fallen world, there will be those who determine to do mischief.

The Good: Doing Good in Difficult Situations

Divorcing the Unbeliever

One reason you may be involved in divorce proceedings is that when you and your wife got married, you were both unbelievers. Now that you are a Christian, she no longer wants to be married to you. Paul gives specific instruction on this point:

> To the rest I say (I, not the Lord) that if any brother has a wife who is an unbeliever, and she consents to live with him, he should not divorce her. If any woman has a husband who is an unbeliever, and he consents to live with her, she should not divorce him. For the unbelieving husband is made holy because of his wife, and the unbelieving wife is made holy because of her husband. Otherwise your children would be unclean, but as it is, they are holy. But if the unbelieving partner separates, let it be so. In such cases the brother or sister is not enslaved. God has called you to peace. For how do you know, wife, whether you will save your husband? Or how do you know, husband, whether you will save your wife? (1 Corinthians 7:12-16).

If the marriage cannot be reconciled, then it is your duty to make the divorce as painless and peaceful as possible: "God has called you to peace." There will be difficulties, recriminations, and bitterness, but these must not come from you.

> Bless those who persecute you; bless and do not curse them. Rejoice with those who rejoice, weep with those who weep. Live in harmony with one another. Do not be haughty, but associate with the lowly. Never be wise in your own sight. Repay no one evil for evil, but give thought to do what is honorable in the sight of all. If possible, so far as it depends on you, live peaceably with all (Romans 12:14-18).

In this situation, where one party is not a Christian, God has specifically designated the government to resolve controversies that take place outside of the church and to mete out whatever justice must be given (Romans 12:19; 13:1-5). This you must willingly submit to out of obedience to Scripture. Consider your specific circumstance and resolve to act peaceably in it. Clarity in how to make this happen will come about with much wise counsel, study, and prayer.

Lawsuits and Believers

Scripture clearly teaches that one Christian must not take another Christian to court, and this would include two Christians involved in a divorce. See Paul's instructions here regarding this matter:

> When one of you has a grievance against another, does he dare go to law before the unrighteous instead of the saints? Or do you not know that the saints will judge the world? And if the world is to be judged by you, are you incompetent to try trivial cases? Do you not know that we are to judge angels? How much more, then, matters pertaining to this life! So if you have such cases, why do you lay them before those who have no standing in the church? I say this to your shame. Can it be that there is no one among you wise enough to settle a dispute between the brothers, but brother goes to law against brother, and that before unbelievers? (1 Corinthians 6:1-6).

Let's assume that your circumstance entails an appropriate biblical divorce (perhaps a divorce based on repeated, unrepentant adultery on the part of your wife).[3] In such an instance, the primary work of "trying the case" should take place in the confines of the church. That means the parties agree to work out a resolution of support, property division, child rearing, and living arrangements privately with some wise men in the church. Typically this will be the elders of the congregation, although Paul does not require that the elders alone perform such service. The parties would then work out the details of their divorce and, upon completion of the arrangements, they would take the papers to court to have the resolution entered as an order of the court. A private negotiation that the court later approves is not uncommon. If the parties can find a Christian family law attorney, then the attorney can help complete the paperwork. This will significantly decrease the cost, limit the damage to the family, and best of all, protect the honor of Christ and his church.

Doing Good to Your Wife

With all that in mind, let's look at what Scripture says to husbands about their wives:

> Husbands, love your wives, as Christ loved the church and gave himself up for her, that he might sanctify her, having cleansed her by the washing of water with the word, so that he might present the church to himself in splendor, without spot or wrinkle or any such thing, that she might be holy and without blemish. In the same way husbands should love their wives as their own bodies. He who loves his wife loves himself (Ephesians 5:25-28).

Until your divorce is final (which takes a minimum of six months in California), this woman is still your wife. Your duty to her is independent of her cooperation. Certainly it will be substantially more difficult to fulfill this duty once you are separated, but you undertook an oath to God to fulfill this task. You must carry out your calling to the best of your ability.

The point I want you to consider is this: The purpose of a husband is to *love his wife* so that she may be *sanctified, cleansed,* and *be holy and without blemish.* When you consider the matter carefully, the only complaint that you can rightly lodge against your wife (and I say "rightly" with serious limitations) is that she is ungodly in her life. Paul said that a husband is to love his wife with the aim of encouraging her toward godliness. Yet you likely complain that you cannot love your wife, because she is not godly. Yet you need to realize that any lack of godliness on her part is the reason—the motivation—to love her. God tells you to give yourself for the sake of your wife's godliness, which is precisely what Jesus did for His bride, the church.

Therefore, realize that even if you decide to divorce your wife, you still have to love her!

Moreover, you must love her even if she is the one divorcing you. That's because she will continue to be your "neighbor" in the biblical sense: "The second [greatest commandment] is this: 'You shall love your neighbor as yourself.' There is no other commandment greater than these" (Mark 12:31). Even after you have been divorced for five years, you have spent $80,000 settling the terms of the divorce, and see your kids only four days a month, you will still have to love her because even though she is no longer your wife, she *is* your neighbor.

And what if she is your enemy?

> You have heard that it was said, "You shall love your neighbor and hate your enemy." But I say to you, Love your enemies and pray for those who persecute you, so that you may be sons of your Father who is in heaven. For he makes his sun rise on the evil and on the good, and sends rain on the just and on the unjust. For if you love those who love you, what reward do you have? Do not even the tax collectors do the same? And if you greet only your brothers, what more are you doing than others? Do not even the Gentiles do the same? You therefore must be perfect, as your heavenly Father is perfect (Matthew 5:43-48).

And so you must love her. If you find this difficult, your study of Christ's love for His enemies will encourage you in this challenge.

Doing Good to Your Children

Easily the greatest difficulty of the divorce will be in your changed role as a parent. The most likely outcome is that your children will not live with you. It is customary, even now, for the mother to be the primary caretaker and for the father to have visitation rights. However, that custom does nothing to lessen the responsibility God has placed upon you as their father. There are 1855 uses of "father" (or some related word, such as "fathered") in the ESV translation of the Bible. While not every single usage bears directly upon how to be a good father, the sheer volume of usage demonstrates that the concept of "father" is fundamental to the Bible. The first father your children will know is you. And thus, to make sure that the concept of father is rightly understood by your children, God has given you the profound, though difficult, task of being a father to the human beings He has entrusted to your care.

When God spoke to His people long ago, fathers were expressly given the task of training and raising their children:

> Hear, O Israel: The LORD our God, the LORD is one. You shall love
> the LORD your God with all your heart and with all your soul and
> with all your might. And these words that I command you today
> shall be on your heart. You shall teach them diligently to your chil-
> dren, and shall talk of them when you sit in your house, and when
> you walk by the way, and when you lie down, and when you rise.
> You shall bind them as a sign on your hand, and they shall be as
> frontlets between your eyes. You shall write them on the door-
> posts of your house and on your gates (Deuteronomy 6:4-9).

While the old covenant was replaced with a new and better covenant
(Hebrews 10:1-4), this model of childrearing should not be disregarded. In
the New Testament, the apostle Paul instructed men to bring up their children in the fear of the Lord, even quoting the fifth commandment in the context of instructing fathers:

> Children, obey your parents in the Lord, for this is right. "Honor
> your father and mother" (this is the first commandment with a
> promise), "that it may go well with you and that you may live long
> in the land." Fathers, do not provoke your children to anger, but
> bring them up in the discipline and instruction of the Lord (Ephe-
> sians 6:1-4).

This duty does not cease because you are divorced from your children's
mother. In fact, you will need to demonstrate even greater diligence in training
as a result of the divorce. You will not be able to train your children every day
because you will not be with them each day. But still, you are to provide instruction to them as you are able.

Moreover, if your wife remarries, another man will be in the home with
your children. While you may gain some cooperation from him and your ex-
wife with regard to visiting your children, you will have limited ability to train
and influence them.

Consider this example of the parenting struggles that can ensue when a
couple divorces: "A Shelby County mother is facing contempt-of-court charges
and possible jail time for baptizing her two children without the knowledge
or consent of her ex-husband."[4] Both parents professed to be Christians, but
she was Presbyterian and believed in infant baptism. He was a Methodist and
did not want the children baptized until they were older. The point is that if

you have divorced your wife, your control over your children's religious education will likely be limited. So it's important to make your few opportunities count. At the very least you should teach your children the gospel and the wisdom of Proverbs (a book written specifically to fathers who desire to train their sons). These topics merely begin your duties of training; they do not exhaust your duty.

If you have not yet divorced, make sure you realize the serious consequences you'll face if you proceed. You're still obligated to carry out your responsibilities as a father to whatever extent you're able, and it will likely be very limited.

God: Living Your Life Before Him

The third element of wisdom is to realize your entire life is to be lived before God. Scripture calls all believers to live for God's glory. "Whether you eat or drink, or whatever you do, do all to the glory of God" (1 Corinthians 10:31). "A man's ways are before the eyes of the LORD, and he ponders all his paths" (Proverbs 5:21).

Many of us live as though we can make choices that are completely our own, and that God has no say-so in these matters. Unfortunately, marriage difficulties often fall into this category of thought. But the God who created marriage from the very beginning also has the solutions to the problems of marriage.

These solutions, of course, can only work in the life of a person who has given himself completely over to the Lord Jesus Christ in true repentance and faith. If this is not true of you, I urge you to read Appendix One, "The Gospel for Men" (see page 387).

If you are a Christian, I want to assure you that no matter what has transpired between you and your wife, real hope can be found in the pages of God's Word. Every believer has been forgiven their sins at the cross of Jesus Christ, and you can learn to forgive your spouse as well. Your commitment to living in obedience to Scripture is the start of being the man that God not only desires you to be, but also equips you to be. I am always encouraged when I read this great promise from the apostle Peter: "His divine power has granted to us all things that pertain to life and godliness, through the knowledge of him who called us to his own glory and excellence" (2 Peter 1:3). That is, you have *everything you need* to live godly in this life![5]

As you seek to make changes in your life and marriage, including turning away from divorce (if it's up to you), you'll find it necessary to implement many truths from the Bible. Confession of your own sins and seeking your wife's forgiveness is imperative. You also must learn how to love your wife sacrificially. Study 1 Corinthians 13:4-8 and Romans 12:9-21, and put these passages into practice every day. If your wife has wronged you, you must learn to forgive her. This is the one biblical teaching that is most often rejected by husbands and wives when it comes to restoring broken relationships. It seems that many people want to be forgiven by God and others, but are not willing to extend that same forgiveness to others.

Because forgiveness is such a crucial point of reconciliation, I want you to consider its definition and benefits.

If you were to ask a couple why they must move ahead with getting a divorce, they would likely tell you that reconciliation is impossible. The truth, however, is not that they *cannot* forgive. Rather, it is that they *will not* forgive.

For those who profess faith in Christ, forgiveness is not an optional matter—it is an absolute requirement. We are called to forgive others in the same manner and upon the basis of God's forgiveness of us in Christ (Ephesians 4:32). Thus, failing to forgive is a sin. In fact, failing to forgive is a sin that comes with a stated penalty: "If you forgive others their trespasses, your heavenly Father will also forgive you, but if you do not forgive others their trespasses, neither will your Father forgive your trespasses" (Matthew 6:14-15).

Let's back up a bit and make sure we understand exactly what biblical forgiveness is. Through the prophet Jeremiah, God promised His people a new covenant—one of forgiveness (Jeremiah 31:31-34). This covenant was not put into place for many years. When it was, it came by way of the gospel—the good news of Jesus Christ as the once-for-all sacrifice for all sin for all time (Hebrews 10:11-18). Based upon the sufficiency of that sacrifice, those who repent and believe in His name now have forgiveness of sins. In both Jeremiah 31:34 and Hebrews 10:17, God said He will remember their sins no more. As each believer lives in obedience to Ephesians 4:32—"forgiving one another, as God in Christ forgave you"—they do so by promising to others what God promised to them. They promise not to remember another person's sin. This goes far beyond merely forgetting what the offense was. Rather, it is a choice *not to remember* the offender's sin—choosing not to hold it against him or her any longer, based on his or her repentance.

Bible teacher John MacArthur defines forgiveness functionally in this way: "The person who chooses to forgive resolves not to remember the offense, refuses to hold a grudge, relinquishes any claim on recompense, and resists the temptation to brood or retaliate."[6] That last bit about brooding and retaliation is the key to forgiveness in a marriage.

Assume a catastrophic breakdown of the marriage, such as a matter of adultery. In such a circumstance, the offended spouse will often refuse forgiveness without some sort of recompense from the offending spouse. There will be a demand for justice because an injustice has occurred. This is a moment for both parties to reflect deeply upon the promise of forgiveness as grounded in the gospel. Every sin ever committed will be punished to the fullest. However, because of God's forgiveness in Christ, not every sinner will feel the pain of that punishment. For those who refuse to repent and trust in Christ alone, the punishment will indeed fall on them personally. For Christians, the punishment has already fallen upon Jesus Christ, who stood in their place as their substitute. "He is the propitiation [atoning sacrifice] for our sins, and not for ours only but also for the sins of the whole world" (1 John 2:2). The offended spouse who continues to demand retribution is directly attacking the validity and sufficiency of Jesus' death. The spouse who continues to demand recompense says, in effect, that Jesus did not pay sufficiently *for this sin*.

In the case of your marriage, if your wife has sinned against you and repents, you are obligated—by reason that you have been forgiven all your sins by God—to forgive her those sins and to not hold those sins against her any longer. If your wife has sinned against you and does not repent, you must stand ready to forgive when she does. This will require a humble and compassionate heart on your part—the same heart God has for His children, whom He freely forgives when they cry out to Him for mercy from a repentant heart.[7]

If you are a marriage counselor, your job is to help both the husband and the wife to see the enormity of their sin in contrast with the great mercy of Christ—the surpassing value of His death, burial, and resurrection—so that they might recognize their need to extend true forgiveness to each other.

By the way, it's vital to note that forgiveness is not a matter of personal emotion. Rather, it is a commitment of the will: It is a determination to forgive, not a feeling that "I am ready to forgive." Jay Adams, in his book on forgiveness, notes the objection that extending forgiveness in some circumstances is inhumanly difficult.[8] MacArthur makes a similar point when he discusses the blessing of forgiveness, in that forgiveness entails a loss of pride and an extension of mercy beyond normal human limits.[9] Adams also strikes at the excuses people might use to avoid forgiving someone else, and reminds us of Jesus' own responses to such excuses:

- "I don't have sufficient faith," to which Jesus responds, "If you had the smallest amount of faith you could do tremendous things" (Luke 17:6).

- "If I see a proper response that shows the fruit of true repentance, then I will forgive," to which Jesus responds, "If he sins 490 times a day, forgive him" (Luke 17:4)

- "I don't feel like forgiving," to which Jesus gives the parable of the unprofitable slave. We must aim for godliness, irrespective of everything else (Luke 17:7-10).[10]

The Route to Blessing

There is far more that could be said in relation to the legal aspects of divorce and what is necessary to help bring healing and reconciliation to a marriage. But by now this much should be clear: Divorce is painfully hard work, and its consequences devastating even to the most stalwart of heart. It takes years of sustained effort to get and remain divorced. In many ways, divorce is more difficult than marriage. I propose the following: that the man who is contemplating divorce take all that effort, money, time, and emotional energy and pour it into living like a Christian man who honors God, loves his wife, and raises his children in the fear of the Lord. Both choices involve much work, but the results of doing things God's way will bring blessing upon blessing.

I have personally counseled with couples whom I "knew" were ready to divorce when they sat down in my office. They had endured years of bitterness, adultery, lying, general unkindness—a complete lack of the love that should characterize a marriage. Yet with a steady application of God's Word to their lives, I've seen some of those very same couples completely change their marriages—which resulted in a tremendous witness and blessing to their children, families, and friends.

If God can change their hearts, He can change yours too.

Recommended Resources

Adams, Jay E. *From Forgiven to Forgiving*. Amityville, NY: Calvary Press, 1994.

———. *Solving Marriage Problems: Biblical Solutions for Christian Counselors*. Grand Rapids, MI: Zondervan, 1983.

———. *The Case of the Hopeless Marriage*. Stanley, NC: Timeless Texts, 2007.

Harvey, Dave. *When Sinners Say "I Do": Discovering the Power of the Gospel for Marriage*. Wapwallopen, PA: Shepherd Press, 2007.

Mack, Wayne A. *Your Family God's Way: Developing and Sustaining Relationships in the Home*. Phillipsburg, NJ: Presbyterian & Reformed Publishing, 1991.

———. *Strengthening Your Marriage*. Phillipsburg, NJ: Presbyterian & Reformed Publishing, 1999.

Priolo, Lou. *The Complete Husband: A Practical Guide to Complete Husbanding*. Amityville, NY: Calvary Press Publishing, 1999.

Sande, Ken, and Tom Raabe. *Peacemaking for Families*. Carol Stream, IL: Tyndale House, 2002.

Scott, Stuart. *The Exemplary Husband*. Bemidji, MN: Focus Publishing, 2000.

Strauch, Alexander. *If You Bite and Devour One Another: Biblical Principles for Handling Conflict*. Littleton, CO: Lewis & Roth, 2011.

Tripp, Paul David. *What Did You Expect? Redeeming the Realities of Marriage*. Wheaton, IL: Crossway, 2010.

Rebuilding a Marriage After Adultery

Wayne Mack

I'm sure that I don't have to convince you that the subject of this chapter is one that deserves a place in a Christian book on men's issues. I wish it were not so, but several major surveys reveal that about 4 out of 10 married men engage in sexual relations outside their marriage.[1] Other surveys indicate that the number of men who break their marriage vows may be as high as two out of every three men.[2] One man who had counseled in many marital situations after adultery writes that "some reports suggest that 50 to 65 percent of husbands have had extramarital affairs by the time they are forty."[3] These surveys, of course, were taken among men who were not necessarily professing Christians, but every pastor and biblical counselor knows that this phenomenon does occur among people—and even pastors—who are very much involved in the church.

I doubt that there is a church anywhere in the world in which none of its people have been involved in some type of marital infidelity. I suspect that there is hardly a pastor who has not been called upon to counsel in homes where unfaithfulness has occurred. So many Christian men either have been tempted or have fallen in this area, or know someone who has. This subject matter is not unheard of in Christian circles.

My intention in this chapter is twofold: to provide help for men who want to rebuild their marriage after having broken their marriage vows, and to provide biblical direction for those who are providing counsel to a friend or fellow Christian who has been unfaithful to his wife.

Because of space limitations, I will primarily focus on just a few key issues that need to be addressed for a marriage to be restored. In other words, this chapter is only a starter program for putting a broken marriage back together again.[4] Moreover, while I recognize that fixing a marriage that has suffered the train wreck of adultery requires that help be given to the nonadulterous person, in this chapter, I will limit my discussion to marital rebuilding counsel for the offender.

Contributing Factors

While it is true that no one is forced into committing adultery, there are circumstantial factors that definitely contribute to a person's fall into sexual unfaithfulness. Often these factors are given as the reasons for adultery. We must understand that from a biblical point of view, these factors are not the real causes for sexual impurity, nor are they determinative. In other words, they do not make a person commit adultery, but even so, it is helpful to know what they are for preventative or cautionary purposes. I mention them with the hope that being forewarned will motivate men to be especially watchful and prayerful in case any of them or a constellation of them are present in their lives.

Here are some of the warning signs:

- unsatisfactory/disappointing/unfulfilling sex relations in their marriage

- a lack of spousal support, respect, and cooperation

- a family background with a history of sexual immorality

- no close accountability relationship with another godly person

- dissatisfaction and boredom about life in general or their marriage

- acceptance of promiscuity as normal, expected, and unavoidable through the influence of the media and Internet

- a background of early adolescent sexual activity

- a propensity to enjoy testing the limits or living on the edge

- a bent for seeing what one can get away with without being caught

In earlier generations, many of the sexually suggestive influences that are now commonplace weren't even mentioned publicly, and pornographic or suggestive material was largely frowned upon. Much of this can be attributed to a breakdown of the nuclear and extended family. When I grew up, most people cared about what their families thought about their behavior. Even many non-Christians didn't engage in certain behaviors because of what their parents—who also weren't Christians—would think or say. But that is not nearly as true anymore today. And this has had an enormous effect on how people behave.

Men rationalize their infidelity by saying they're bored with the "same old, same old" and seek to get their kicks out of conquering new territories—including new romantic interests. Perhaps they're trying to prove their worth and desirability by winning the interest of someone else. The fact that they can get someone else to participate in sexual activities may be a way of convincing themselves that they still "have what it takes."

For some men, the catalyst is a major life transition point or a severe crisis. The normal circumstances of life have suddenly been thrown out of order, causing them to lose their sense of security, safety, and satisfaction. What used to bring pleasure and stability is gone, so they look for "that certain something" that will provide some comfort and pleasure. For some men, the "something" they choose is sexual immorality.

A man is particularly vulnerable when there are conflicts with his marriage partner that remain unresolved. When this happens, frustration and unhappiness set in, and the man looks for escape and relief from his misery. The prospect of pleasurable sexual relations with a woman with whom he has no conflicts becomes very appealing. Because of the unresolved conflicts with his wife, this man may no longer desire or enjoy sexual relations with his spouse and therefore become vulnerable to finding that satisfaction elsewhere.

These men often give up hope that their unmet desires and expectations will ever be fulfilled in their marital relationship. Scripture warns of this when it says that "hope deferred makes the heart sick" (Proverbs 13:12). Other men allow their desires to become demands; they perceive their wants as needs. "I would like to have this" becomes "I must have this" or "I can't be satisfied until I do have this." The result is often bitterness and anger accompanied with a desire to hurt or punish the mate for what she has or hasn't done—and unfaithfulness is practiced as a means of coercing the other person to change.

These are some of the most common circumstantial factors that unfaithful men have shared with me when they came for counseling. Please remember that—as stated earlier—none of these factors constitute the basic *cause* of their adultery. If the marriage is to be restored, every man who has had an extra-marital sexual relationship must understand that though these factors may be present and very real, they are not the primary causes of the adultery.

A Biblical Understanding of the Primary Causes of Adultery

Let's turn now to what the Bible teaches about the primary causes of adultery. I've read many resources about rebuilding a marriage after adultery, and frequently they ignore what Scripture teaches on this crucial subject. This oversight hinders any real resolution of the problem. To rightly solve the problem of adultery requires rightly identifying and dealing with the fundamental causes.

The Heart of the Adultery Problem

In Matthew 15:19, Jesus said that adultery comes out of the heart. In Matthew 12:33-35, Jesus changed the illustration a bit, but said essentially the same thing. If the tree is good, the fruit will be good; conversely, if the fruit is bad, it's because the tree is bad. Even so, the good man out of the good treasure of his heart brings forth what is good, but the evil man out of the evil treasure of his heart brings forth what is evil.

James 1:13-16 puts it this way: A man is led into sin by the wicked desires of his heart. James 4:8 makes adultery and every other sin a heart matter when it says that to overcome sin of any sort we must cleanse our hearts. Certainly this passage would label adultery as sin, a sin that is committed because something is wrong in the heart.

Galatians 5:16-19 makes it clear that our wicked deeds, which include immorality, are the manifestations of wicked desires. In other words, we do bad things because in our hearts, we want (desire) bad things. The bad things we do are manifestations of what is going on in our hearts.

Romans 1:24 teaches that it is "the lusts of their hearts" that lead people to commit immorality. More specifically, they commit immorality because the restraints are removed and they do what their hearts want them to do.

The book of Proverbs frequently reiterates this same point. For example, Proverbs 4:23 informs us that the issues of life flow from our hearts and are a revelation of what is already in the heart. Proverbs 6:25 tells us that if men commit adultery it is because of their heart's desire. Proverbs 7:25 states that if a man commits immorality it is because he has allowed his heart to turn aside to the person with whom he commits adultery.

Often when I am counseling with a man who has committed adultery he will say to me, "I don't know why I do it."

I respond, "Do you really want to know why?"

"Yes."

"Do you want to know what the Bible says about why you do it?"

"Yes."

Then together we read these passages.

Some men come with their minds already made up as to why they committed adultery. As they explain their reason, they will mention some of the circumstantial factors we looked at earlier. When they do that, I will say, "So you think that's why you did it?"

"Yes."

"What do you think God would say about why you did it?"

"I don't know."

Then I will say, "Do you want to know?"

Usually the answer is yes—and we turn to what the Bible says. Then I ask them to tell me what God says is the cause of their adultery.

Next I turn to Deuteronomy 8:1-14, where God explains that the circumstances we encounter—the wildernesses (circumstantial factors) we experience—are simply the context in which we discover what is going on in our hearts. This truth is aptly confirmed in an illustration I share with the counselee: "Suppose I squeezed a sponge, and ink came out. Why would ink come out of the sponge?" Inevitably they respond, "Because there is ink in the sponge." Then I point out that according to God's Word, if nasty, sinful stuff comes out of us, the problem is not with our actions, but rather with our hearts. If adultery comes out of the heart, it's because our heart is not clean. Adultery comes out because adultery is inside (see Matthew 5:27-28).

So to overcome adulterous actions, a person must first clean up his heart. And he will never overcome adultery in a lasting fashion unless he applies the biblical solution to his heart problem.

The Idolatry of the Adultery Problem

Colossians 3:5 lists five specific sins that the Christian is to "put to death." Three of them undoubtedly refer mainly to sexual sins (immorality, impurity, and passion). The other two are covetousness and evil desire, and both of them are often a part of sexual immorality as well. After mentioning these five sins, Paul then stated that they are that "which is idolatry," indicating that all of them constitute idolatry. The text is saying that men commit sexual immorality because they are idolaters.

Ephesians 5:5 also describes the nature and cause of sexual immorality, stating that the immoral, impure, or covetous man is an idolater. First Corinthians 10:6-8 identifies sexual immorality with idolatry as well. Verse 7 sounds out the warning to us that we should not be idolaters as the Israelites were when they were in the wilderness going from Egypt to Canaan. Verse 8 specifies that part of the idolatry in which they were involved—and from which we are admonished to stay away—was making an idol out of sexual immorality. At this point, the desire for and practice of sex ruled their lives and controlled them. And it is from this form of idolatry that we are admonished to stay away.

Thus, the Bible makes it clear that when we commit immorality, we are bowing down—at least internally—at the idol of sex and doing what the "god" of sexual desire wants us to do. At that point, we are more concerned about fulfilling our personal sexual desire than we are about pleasing God, even though fulfilling that desire outside of marriage is contrary to the Lord's will. We are worshipping the "god" of sex rather than the true and living God.

Romans 1 speaks of sexual immorality in the same way. Verse 25 speaks of people who exchange the worship of God for the worship of created things. That, of course, means that they become worshippers of a false god, which, according to God's Word, is the essence of idolatry. And then verses 26 and 27 inform us that one of the ways this idolatrous worship manifests itself is in the form of sexual immorality. Whenever we allow our sexual desires to motivate and control us to be fulfilled in ways that are not prescribed by God in His Word (marriage), we do so because fulfilling our desires is more important to us than fulfilling God's will. That is idolatry.

So according to Scripture, one cause for sexual immorality is that it's a heart problem; another cause is idolatry. That idolatry is said to be a cause may be hard for some people to accept and difficult to understand. But the reason idolatry is considered a cause is because the person involved in sexual immorality is more concerned about pleasing self than pleasing God. It is idolatry because this person is being ruled by his passions rather than by God. This person is worshipping at the altar of pleasure instead of the throne of God. He is being motivated purely by his own fleshly desires rather than God's desires. This person is focused on satisfying and serving his own passions rather than on serving the living God. And functioning that way amounts to the very serious sin of idolatry.

In the course of counseling men who have been unfaithful to their wives, some of them have attempted to diminish the seriousness of their sin by blaming circumstantial factors. But when we look to God's Word, we see that God leaves the adulterer with no excuse or justification on the basis of circumstances. Instead, God shows us that the primary cause is not *outside* of the person in terms of what happens to the person or around the person, but rather, it is *inside* the person in terms of his relationship with God. From a biblical point of view, sexual immorality is not merely a horizontal or behavioral issue; it is a vertical and internal issue because it has everything to do with the state of a person's relationship with God, what is going on in his heart, and who is really ruling his life. If we leave these dimensions out of our thinking, we will never really understand the dynamic that propels people into idolatry. The wrong diagnosis of a problem and its cause will inevitably lead to wrong solutions.

Understanding the causes of sexual unfaithfulness in this biblical way will inevitably lead us to the conclusion that the only real solution to infidelity is as follows: (1) a genuine and continuous repentance from the heart; (2) a genuine 1 John 1:9 and Proverbs 28:13 confession of sin; (3) an understanding of and faith in the redemption that comes only through Jesus Christ (John 8:32,36;

Romans 8:1-2; 1 Corinthians 6:9-11; Titus 2:14); (4) a renewed commitment to the lordship of Christ (Luke 9:23; Romans 10:9-10; Colossians 2:6-10); and (5) a daily, vital relationship with Jesus Christ through which a person will receive the power to put off sinful desires, thoughts, and actions and put on godly desires, thoughts, and actions (John 15:1-5; Romans 6:5-14; 13:14; Ephesians 4:17-24; Philippians 4:13; Colossians 3:5-17).[5]

Florence Littauer has rightly written, "No good Christian man…gets up in the morning and says, 'My, this is a lovely day! I guess I'll go out and commit adultery.' Yet many do it anyway."[6] And the question is this: Why is it true that many do it anyway? Because they have not continuously (by the power of the indwelling Holy Spirit and through the cleansing blood of Jesus Christ) purified their hearts and filled them with godly thoughts and godly desires, and because the desires and cravings of their hearts have become idolatrous.

Other Issues Related to Putting the Marriage Back Together

Now that we've examined the most important foundational issues that an immoral spouse must deal with, let's consider some additional restorative issues that relate to overcoming the damage the adulterer has done to his own personal life and to his marriage relationship.

Confession of Sin and Forgiveness Issues

After a man comes to see the primary causes of his adultery in a biblical manner and experiences genuine conviction and repentance, one of the first restorative issues he needs to address is that of disclosing the adulterous affair. Now, to whom should he confess his transgression? King David's words in Psalm 51—which were spoken after his transgression with Bathsheba—indicate that the most important confession an adulterer can make is to God, who is the primary party he has sinned against. "Wash me thoroughly from my iniquity, and cleanse me from my sin…Against you, you only, I have sinned and done what is evil in your sight…Purge me…and I shall be clean; wash me, and I shall be whiter than snow…Blot out all my iniquities. Create in me a clean heart, O God, and renew a right spirit within me" (Psalm 51:2,4,7,9-10).

Psalm 32 also extols the virtue of confessing sin to God and mentions the blessing we experience in the midst of God's forgiveness. This psalm, which Bible scholars believe was associated with David's sin of adultery, also warns against the danger of hiding and refusing to acknowledge and confess our sin.

The significance and method of confession to God is clearly seen in 1 John 1:7–2:1. Note carefully the words in this passage, and as you read them, apply them specifically to the sin of sexual immorality. This passage assures us that

> the blood of Jesus his Son cleanses us from all sin. If we say we have no sin, we deceive ourselves, and the truth is not in us. If we confess our sins, he is faithful and just to forgive us our sins and to cleanse us from all unrighteousness. If we say we have not sinned, we make him a liar, and his word is not in us...if anyone does sin, we have an advocate with the Father, Jesus Christ the righteous.

Proverbs 28:13 also warns against covering or hiding our sin, and mentions the assurance of forgiveness when we confess and forsake our sin. God's mercy is extended to those who openly acknowledge their sin, and if we refuse to be honest about our sin, we will not prosper.

So dealing properly with the sin of adultery requires an honest and forthright confession of that sin to God. Without that confession, any restoration of that person's relationship with God and the spouse will be hindered.[7]

However, fully answering the "to whom" question goes beyond a person's honest and open confession to God. Psalm 51, which gives us much help in this matter of confessing sin to God, was written "to the choirmaster," which means it was to be sung by God's people in their worship services. That means David was not only confessing his sin to God, but also to God's people. Similarly, in Luke 15, when the prodigal son came to understand that he had sinned grievously against God, he also recognized he had sinned against his earthly father. When the prodigal was convicted of his sin, he came back to his father acknowledging that he had sinned against God *and* against his father (Luke 15:18-19; see also James 5:16).

Matthew 5:23-25 clearly teaches us that if another person has something against us, we should go and be reconciled to that person. Being reconciled would certainly require acknowledging any sin to the person who has something against us, asking for his or her forgiveness and also seeking to correct whatever wrong we had done. The basic principle that should be observed here is that the confession of sin and request for forgiveness should be as broad as the people who have been hurt by the sin.

Bible teacher R.C. Sproul insists that when two people commit adultery, a lot of people suffer from their infidelity. Therefore, confessions should be made and forgiveness sought from all who were wounded by what happened. Sproul writes, "The affair was not a private thing. Marriage involves many more people than simply the husband and wife. The marriage is contracted not only in the presence of God, but in the presence of human witnesses who are called to testify or bear witness to the truth."[8] This confession certainly would include the man's spouse, his children, his and her parents, his and her friends, fellow church members, and the other person with whom the adultery was committed.

Operative guidelines for confession to people would include that secret sins known only to the person and God should be made to God only. Private sins of which only the injured person is aware should be made to the injured person privately, whereas public sins which are known by many people should be acknowledged to all who have been offended by them. A request for forgiveness should also be included with each confession of sin.

Elimination of Barriers

Appropriately and honestly making confession and seeking forgiveness is fundamentally important for rebuilding the marriage in that, if the shattered marriage is to be rebuilt, it must be built on the foundation of truth and honesty. Ephesians 4:25 states that if we want to have godly relationships with people, we must put away every form of falsehood and speak truth with our neighbors, for we are members one of another. In terms of intimate human relationships, there is no relationship that God intends to be closer than two people in marriage. Hence, all barriers caused by hidden sins must be eliminated if the couple is to put their marriage back together again.

A husband's confession to his wife should include specific confession—not only of the sin of infidelity, but of all other attendant sins associated with the sin of adultery. As in the case of David in 2 Samuel 11–12 and Psalm 32, adultery is almost always accompanied by other sins. David was deceitful, hypocritical, selfish, inconsiderate of others, and a poor example to his children, to others who followed God, and to the people over whom he had authority and responsibility. So it is in most cases when a man breaks his marital vows. In addition to the sins just specified, the man who commits adultery may also be guilty of misusing family finances and neglecting his marital, parental, social, occupational, and spiritual responsibilities. He may even end up exposing his mate to sexually transmitted diseases, including AIDS. It has been said that when a person has sexual relations with another person, there is a sense in which he is having sex with every person with whom that person has had sex.

Honesty in Confession

Another reason confession of sin and seeking forgiveness is essential is because without honest confession, it is almost impossible to work on other deficiencies in the marriage. In a marriage where infidelity occurs, you can be sure that prior to the unfaithfulness there were marital deficiencies that provided the context in which the sexual immorality took place. It then follows that those pre-adultery deficiencies cannot be corrected unless there is honest confession and identification of all those areas in which changes must be made. In addition, honest and appropriate confession of sin to all who have been hurt by the transgression is also indispensable because it gives evidence of genuine repentance. This assures the offended parties of the genuineness of the offender's conviction of sin and desire to change.

In relation to the issue of confession, an important question men often ask is this: "How much detail should I give about what transpired between me and this other woman?" When we turn to the Bible, we find God's altogether trustworthy and appropriate answer to this question. Ephesians 5:4 instructs us that filthy talk and crude joking are not fitting for us as believers. Ephesians 4:29 informs us that our conversation should be wholesome and designed to minister grace. Psalm 19:14 prescribes that the words of our mouths be acceptable in God's sight. Colossians 3 forbids malicious, abusive, slanderous, immoral, impure, unkind, unloving speech. In the book of Proverbs, many verses provide guidelines we should observe in terms of how much detail should be given. A study of my book *Your Family God's Way* will also give biblical direction about what could be called constructive, edifying, God-honoring speech.[9]

One of the finest examples of the proper method of confession is found in what the prodigal said in Luke 15:18-19. When he decided to confess his sin and seek forgiveness, he carefully thought through what he would say. He determined that he would go to his father and declare a well-prepared confession. In his confession, he avoided any rationalization or justification of his sin. He did not engage in any blame-shifting, nor did he attempt to minimize his sin or evade personal responsibility. Rather, he specifically acknowledged his sin, requested forgiveness, and expressed a willingness to accept whatever consequences the father would prescribe for him.

When a man makes confession and asks for forgiveness of his infidelity— or any other sin—he should be painfully accurate in his words about himself, even if it embarrasses or condemns him (Proverbs 12:22). In making confession, he should include sins of *commission*—what he did that he should not have done toward his wife in word or actions. And he should confess sins of *omission*—what he failed to do that he should have done. Then after he identifies the specific ways he sinned in word or action, he should go on to specifically ask his wife for forgiveness, saying something like, "Will you please forgive me for _____ or for not _____?" In his confession, he should avoid accusing or even pointing out to his wife her sins or failures. And he should not imply that he did what he did because of anything she did or did not do. Rather, he should determine to let God deal with and convict his wife of her own sins and failures.

In his book *The Peacemaker*, Ken Sande wisely suggests that a biblically based request for forgiveness will involve what he calls practicing the seven A's, which I've adapted here: (1) addressing everyone involved; (2) avoiding all ifs, buts, and maybes; (3) admitting your own sin specifically; (4) acknowledging sorrow for the way your sin has offended God and hurt the other person; (5) accepting the fact there may be consequences because of your sin and being willing to accept what those consequences may be as part of the Romans 8:28 process; (6) altering your sinful behavior to godly behavior and thinking; and (7) asking specifically for forgiveness from everyone who has been hurt by your sin, focusing especially on your wife.[10]

Timing and Sensitivity

What about the proper timing for a confession of sin and a request for forgiveness? Here are a few considerations: Proverbs 15:28 indicates that a man should speak on important issues only after he has done some serious thinking and some fervent praying about what God would have him say. This verse also indicates that when he speaks, he should not just pour out words—he should control his speech and be sensitive to his wife's receptivity and feelings. Ephesians 4:29 says, "Let no corrupting talk come out of your mouths, but only such as is good for building up, as fits the occasion, that it may give grace to those who hear." This of course means giving serious consideration to the needs of one's wife. Does she need reassurance, comfort, encouragement, a listening ear? Does she need for her husband to remain silent and allow her to express sympathy, affirmation, or sorrow over the way he has hurt her? Does she need a word of hope or of commitment, a word of assurance that the illicit relationship has definitively been brought to an end?

Finally, it would be wise for a man to seek wise counsel from godly people before he makes his confession and asks for forgiveness. "Without counsel plans fail, but with many advisers they succeed" (Proverbs 15:22). Godly and biblically wise people may help him to speak that which is good and useful as he says what needs to be said—in a truthful manner and yet in a way that is appropriate and sensitive (Proverbs 15: 2,7; 12:15; 18:1,6-7).

Genuine Repentance: A Key to Rebuilding

Wayne Grudem, in his book *Systematic Theology*, defines *repentance* as "a heartfelt sorrow for sin, a renouncing of it, and a sincere commitment to forsake it and walk in obedience."[11] Another way of looking at this key term is to see it as a change of mind so complete that it results in a change of life (actively turning from sin to obedience to Christ). All efforts to rebuild a marriage will be in vain unless the adulterous man has genuinely repented. Without repentance, there may be some temporary improvement, but there will not be any lasting change. In John Bunyan's classic allegory *The Pilgrim's Progress*, two main characters, Christian and Hopeful, discuss why people don't persevere in turning from their sin. In essence, the answer is that if a person lacks genuine repentance, he will never really change.[12]

Likewise, before a marriage can be rebuilt, the adulterer must experience genuine repentance. And that brings up an important question: How can a person be relatively certain that he has repented? It's vital that he manifests the following:

- He is willing to call the adultery what God calls it—sin.

- He is willing to accept personal responsibility for all his sinful and unbiblical thoughts, choices, and actions.

- He understands the seriousness and horrendous nature of his sin.

- He shows a concern about heart sins (his attitudes, desires, motivations) as well as behavioral sins (Matthew 5:27-32; James 4:8).

- He is willing to turn to Christ for the forgiveness of his sins and is willing to be saved by the grace of God alone.

- He displays a sincere desire to be free from sin itself, not just the problems caused by sin.

- He is willing to commit himself to obeying and serving God rather than self, and he takes the lordship of Christ seriously.

- He is willing to work on changing the things in his life and marriage that are displeasing to God (Luke 3:7-14; 2 Corinthians 7:9 -11; 1 Thessalonians 1:9-10).[13]

More to Consider

As I conclude this brief look at restoring a marriage damaged by adultery, I want to leave with you a list of some additional important issues that need to be dealt with. There is much more that could be said about rebuilding a marriage than is presented in this chapter:

- The need for the adulterer to break off relations with the person with whom he has been committing adultery, and to close off the means for carrying out the adultery.

- The need for the adulterer to change the positive feelings he has for the person with whom he has been practicing immorality and change any negative feelings he might have toward his wife.

- The need to determine how much he should tell his children.

- The need to figure out what is necessary to rebuild trust on the part of the wife and others, including parents, in-laws, close friends, and other Christians.

- The need for the adulterer to effectively deal with the emotions of self-pity, anger, resentment, discouragement, and impatience, which might arise when people seem to keep him on trial and be suspicious of his trustworthiness.

- The need to properly handle any unrealistic expectations he might have of others and that others might have of him.

- The need to understand that behavioral adultery is usually preceded by a chain of events that lead up to it. People don't usually fall into adultery right away. It's vital for the adulterer to recognize the kinds of events that could lead to his downfall so he can break this chain of events at the earliest possible opportunity.

- The need to develop close discipleship and accountability relationships with other men and how to do it.

- The need to learn how to develop a deep friendship/intimacy relationship with his wife so they can cultivate a strong marriage and thus truly be sweethearts for a lifetime.[14]

Let me also reiterate that if one of the marriage partners has committed adultery, the marriage will need to be rebuilt. It is unrealistic to think that there will be no need for some hard work if infidelity has occurred. Diligence and perseverance will be required because there is hardly anything more devastating to the well-being of a marriage than infidelity.

I have encountered some couples who think they can just pretend the immorality didn't happen, and therefore they won't have to do any serious evaluation or renovation of their marriage. When I perceive such an attitude is present, my hope that the marriage will survive or improve ends up diminishing. From experience, I have seen that marriages damaged by adultery require major and sometimes painful efforts to restore. And though adultery may be and usually is extremely devastating to a marriage, still, *it is definitely possible for the couple to rebuild their marriage relationship.* They can have hope, even though the process of bringing about restoration won't be easy.

With God's Help

It may be true of Humpty Dumpty in the well-known nursery rhyme that when he was broken by a fall, all the king's horses and all the king's men couldn't put Humpty Dumpty back together again. But the hopeless message of the Humpty Dumpty rhyme is not true of marriages that have been broken by the tornado of adultery. With God's help, a marriage that has been ravished and broken by the sin of adultery can be "unbroken" and healed and restored. If the husband and wife are willing and determined to trust God and follow the directives found in His Word, their marriage can be rebuilt and made stronger and better than ever before.

It may be that you yourself have experienced or are experiencing the brokenness that adultery can bring to a marriage. If that's true of you, I encourage you to reflect on the directives from God's Word for rebuilding and apply them to your marriage relationship. These principles, when applied, will help you to re-establish and restore your marriage.

And if your marriage has not experienced the brokenness associated with adultery, I hope you will use the biblical information found within these pages to take preventative measures that will help protect your marriage, keep it on track, and make it even better. In addition, I hope you are now better equipped to understand and provide assistance (counsel) to men who have fallen into the sin of adultery and need some clear direction for putting their marriages back together again.

Recommended Resources

Ferguson, Sinclair. *The Christian Life*. Edinburgh: The Banner of Truth Trust, 1989.

Mack, Wayne A. *Strengthening Your Marriage*. Phillipsburg, NJ: P&R Publishing, 1997.

————. *Sweethearts for a Lifetime*. Phillipsburg, NJ: P&R Publishing, 2006.

Sande, Ken. *The Peacemaker.* Grand Rapids, MI: Baker Book House, 2004.

Sproul, R.C. *The Intimate Marriage: A Practical Guide to Building a Great Marriage*. Phillipsburg, NJ: P&R Publishing, 1975.

Tripp, Paul David. *A Quest for More: Living for Something Bigger Than You.* Greensboro, NC: New Growth Press, 2008.

22
Using Psychotropic Drugs

Geoffrey V. Drew, MD

P*eace* I leave with you; my *peace* I give to you. Not as the world gives do I give to you. Let not your hearts be troubled, neither let them be afraid" (John 14:27).

Peace is defined as "total well-being, prosperity, and security associated with God's presence among his people," according to the *Tyndale Bible Dictionary*.[1] Peace is not the absence of trouble; rather, it is the soul at rest, whether in times of prosperity or difficulty.

Does the trouble you are in today call for using psychotropic drugs? Would this chemical alteration of your mind offer you the peace you long for—the peace of God?

Peace, but There Is No Peace... by Means of Drug Usage

I've been told by those who have been addicted to psychotropic drugs that what they were pursuing in the drug experience was peace and release. They desired freedom from pain, want, and fear. They were looking for safety; they wanted their present predicament to end and for a return to happy days and smiles in every direction. A few decades ago, this was pursued as the psychedelic experience.[2] Drugs, however, don't deliver. They do something sarcastically off the mark so as to mock and ridicule our pitiable estate in this mortal existence.

Andrew was not a happy camper. When this forty-seven-year-old father of three children came to my office, he was in fear of his health. I had not seen him for more than two years. His youngest daughter was now eighteen months old. Headaches and heartburn had become more frequent. He was experiencing aches and pains all over his body, as well as heaviness in his chest. He had lost his appetite and desire for socializing. Because of a family history of heart attacks, he feared he might be having one himself now.

Two years earlier, Andrew had some transient white-coat hypertension. His masked face and clenched fists told a grim story of futile determination. Fatigue and debilitation had become his daily mountain to climb, a complaint that was now even worse than when I had seen him before. Desperately he blurted out. "Doctor, I can't sleep, and I can't concentrate. Am I losing my mind? I can't go on like this! I may lose my job! What is wrong with me?" A physical examination, blood tests, and EKG revealed that all was normal. Something else was going on.

Then Andrew told me about his home life. His wife was an angry woman. As he headed home from work each day, he was filled with dread. To him, entering his home was like walking into a hornet's nest. "We always fight and argue. There is constant discord. We can't talk. I have no patience for her anymore. It is so bad I asked my sixteen-year-old daughter [from his previous marriage] to move back to her mother. My eighteen-year-old son keeps to himself in his room and I haven't seen him for days. This can't be good for my eighteen-month-old baby daughter. She cries when she sees me. What can I do?" Andrew had no peace. His heart was troubled and afraid. He did not feel good, to say the least. He wanted relief!

Previously he had come to me, his physician, because he had experienced some mild jet-lag insomnia and I had prescribed a short course of sleeping tablets. That solved the problem. He had not since requested a repeat prescription. Now he was back, wondering if there was some other similar medication that could help relieve his current predicament.

What's a Christian man to do? Is medicine the only answer? The question is not "What can help this man?" but "*Who* can help this man?" I suggested to Andrew that we needed to pray. I asked his permission to do so, and he agreed. We then turned to the one source for true peace, Jesus Himself: "I have said these things to you, that in me you may have peace. In the world you will have tribulation. But take heart; I have overcome the world" (John 16:33). We prayed.[3] This is the biblical approach; the Bible instructs us, "Rejoice always, pray without ceasing, give thanks in all circumstances; for this is the will of God in Christ Jesus for you" (1 Thessalonians 5:16-18). Andrew joined me in a pleading "Amen."

After our prayer, I explained to Andrew that his sleep was extremely important. I offered to prescribe a mild sedative once again.[4] In addition to this short-term sleeping aid, I began to give him biblical help—a prescription right from God's Word so that he could begin to make the necessary changes in his day-to-day living. I carefully challenged him from Scripture to be humble with his wife. He was especially to speak softly and gently. "A soft answer turns away wrath, but a harsh word stirs up anger" (Proverbs 15:1). He was not to respond to her in anger, but rather to obey Ephesians 4:32 and be kind and tender-hearted. I encouraged him to be kind and helpful with the baby. Fortunately, by God's grace, the child was a good nighttime sleeper, and Andrew would soon gain his rest. We were to meet again a week later, and he was to feel free to call me at any time.

A few days later, Andrew called to say he was going to church for the first time since he was a young man. His mother had invited him, and he was very uplifted by the pastor's preaching. In regard to his health, while he was still not sleeping as well as he would like, he was able to enjoy an improved onset of sleep. He had a little more energy and was able to concentrate better at work. I explained that he should not expect good natural sleep from the sedative, or become dependent on the medication to make everything better. Such chemical therapies are temporary and imperfect. This drug was not a *cure*, but a mere mitigation of the symptoms. In fact, Andrew might even begin to experience *more* daytime anxiety if he used the drug for longer than intended. No, he would need to gain a little sleep from the medication, but at the same time utilize the spiritual prescription through obedience to God's Word. The elements here side-by-side are chemical (as the world gives) and spiritual (as Jesus gives, by His Word). It often seems there is an arm-wrestling match between the two!

To *merely* give Andrew medication at this point would have been to apply a band aid to his wounds, which were not physical, but spiritual in nature. Drugs would only mask his true feelings and emotions, and not solve or cure anything. Psychotropic medication or drugs, by definition, are capable of affecting the mind, emotions, and behavior, which in turn can alter a man's attitude toward his tasks, projects, and duties. Ultimately they can influence all the disciplines of a godly man.[5] For instance, some medications, such as Lithium, which may be used to treat depression, are psychotropic. The word *psychotropic* comes from the Greek *psycho* ("the mind') + *trop* ("a turning") = capable of turning the mind. Sleep loss, among other ailments, however, can also prove to be psychotropic—that is, they can lead to a change in thinking and behavior.[6] So I elected to treat Andrew's insomnia through medication, but under close management, hoping to orient him toward biblical thinking and responding in regard to his difficult circumstances.

Those who seek after drug therapy for life's struggles crave good feelings. They want peace at any cost. Peace and feeling good have become the idols of their hearts. They have placed their confidence in the vain belief that a drug will deliver these idols to them. Men who are desperate to feel better will often deviously circumvent the medical purposes of the physician in prescribing these drugs. The Christian man, however, will follow the physician's instructions exactly. He will not allow a drug to dominate his mind so as to allow an idol to occupy and disrupt his walk with God. He realizes the illness-experience can directly affect his worship, his praise, and his devotion to Christ.

Therefore, the use of psychotropic drugs—if at all—should be short term, for a specific medical purpose, and always supervised by a physician. *A Christian man should search for a physician who is likeminded in terms of solutions— one who will use medication only as needed for medical diagnoses, not one who prescribes drugs to merely mask the pain of life.*

Psychotropic Substances…of All Kinds

The range of psychotropic substances available for use is huge. They are encased in a world of feelings and effects and include such substances as alcohol and food in addition to medicine. When you realize that the definition of *psychotropic* is "capable of turning the mind," it's easy to see that this love affair that people have with feeling good often manifests itself in substances far beyond drugs. It includes food (habitual overeating) and alcohol (out-of-control consumption), among other things. Think about it: even your daily Starbucks fix could become a serious problem if you get to the place where you can't live without it—or if you find yourself knocking bystanders out of the way to get to the front of the line! In my experience, I have seen patients who demonstrate that overindulging in chocolate has a somewhat psychotropic effect— and this extravagance is making a strong comeback, especially among women. In my medical practice I treat men who are addicted to sugar, arguably the most abused addictive substance on the face of the planet. Donut gorging can be just as harmful to your body as winebibbing. More than 70 percent of men today need to admit to and deal with their sugar addition.[7]

Ingestion, inhalation, injection, and absorption are all medical routes of drug administration that can be abused. People snort, sniff, eat, drink, and inject themselves for special mental effects. The escapism is obvious. This is done against the advice of medical doctors who have been licensed and trained to administer these otherwise dangerous chemicals safely and for particular therapeutic purposes, not for a mere pleasure trip. Those who circumvent the physician's management of these substances are playing with fire, and the consequences are often disastrous. No Christian man should be knocking on his physician's door looking for a medicinal high to escape life's difficulties. Note this important principle taught by the apostle Paul in 1 Corinthians 6:12-13:

> "All things are lawful for me," but not all things are helpful. "All things are lawful for me," but I will not be dominated by anything. "Food is meant for the stomach and the stomach for food"—and God will destroy both one and the other. The body is not meant for sexual immorality, but for the Lord, and the Lord for the body.

However, the real problem is not which substance is used or which sin is committed, but rather, it is the fact people have become feeling-oriented and believe that comfort or pleasure or escapism are rights to be pursued. The Christian man has this warning from Paul: Don't mess with it. "Do not get drunk with wine, for that is debauchery, but be filled with the Spirit" (Ephesians 5:18). Truth will not be found by continually giving in to your feelings. If you want to find the peace that only God can give, you must have *self-control.* "The fruit of the Spirit is love, joy, peace, patience, kindness, goodness, faithfulness, gentleness, *self-control*; against such things there is no law" (Galatians 5:22-23).

Test yourself: can you say no to something without a little panic rising in your heart? If you cannot, then you should ask whether you are able to keep your body under control. "Every athlete exercises self-control in all things. They do it to receive a perishable wreath, but we an imperishable. So I do not run aimlessly; I do not box as one beating the air. But I discipline my body and keep it under control, lest after preaching to others I myself should be disqualified" (1 Corinthians 9:25-27). Much like the athlete, you must maintain control over yourself because you are in the race for your life. As John MacArthur has observed,

> *Only* the disciplined Christian will consistently read and study God's Word and then diligently apply it as he allows God's power to conform him more and more to the image of Christ. None other than the disciplined Christian can truly evaluate and effectively challenge the world's culture and value system in the light of Scripture. Simply stated, self-discipline is the willingness to subordinate personal and selfish interests to God's eternal interests.[8]

Self-control will keep you from giving in to your feelings—from reaching for that food or drink or drug that you use in an attempt to escape painful realities.

The psychotropic drugs at the doctor's disposal have a wide variety of applications in modern medicine. There is a long list of them.[9] Most physicians will write prescriptions for them out of sheer habit from years of practice. From simple nausea and runny noses through mental illness to major pain—there is a drug for every concern. Most of them have psychotropic side effects. Who said all medicines are supposed to make you feel good? To medically treat simple, nonmedical complaints is a primal folly of our time. It is a distinct wisdom-deficiency in our culture that leaves behind a litany of tragic tales.

It is this arena of simple minor complaints that the naïve one (or simple one) will dabble with and attempt to deal with his anxiety and the blues and relieve his situation according to his own understanding. "The simple are killed by their turning away, and the complacency of fools destroys them" (Proverbs 1:32). Some stay foolish for a long time; Andrew was like an overgrown school kid, failing to know things he should have learned long ago. "The simple inherit folly, but the prudent are crowned with knowledge" (Proverbs 14:18). It is hard for the wayward to learn to depend on God. "Trust in the LORD with all your heart, and do not lean on your own understanding" (Proverbs 3:5). But there is hope for men like Andrew!

Only Scripture Is Sufficient

The sufficiency of Scripture is assumed in every chapter of this book, and I wish to testify to its supremacy here over drugs. There is nothing superlative— nothing outstanding—that can be said about psychotropic drugs. For though I prescribe them carefully and strategically, there are some patients who don't demand them and yet do well; and then there are those who have the chemical expectation, demand the drug, but still don't do well. Medication is not a final solution. It is my art and privilege to work from both medical and spiritual perspectives toward the goal of a medication-free status. Medical practice today is what I call a fluctuating animal—a changing science. Only the Word of God is rock-solid—truth that *never* changes. It is the most scientific instrument we have, telling us exactly who we are and where we are going. "His divine power has granted to us all things that pertain to life and godliness, through the knowledge of him who called us to his own glory and excellence" (2 Peter 1:3).

In contemplating the deficiencies of psychotropic medications, it is important to understand what medication *cannot* do.

- Medicine can't teach us to think on God's truth, which leads to peace and happiness instead of thoughts leading to anxiety or depression.

- Medicine can't show us how to make godly lifestyle choices that will help keep our bodies healthy.

- Medicine can't reveal how to respond to physical limitations with spiritual attitudes that build us up instead of tearing us down.[10]

Having considered all this as I was working with Andrew, I was keen now to see that Scripture must inform and bring structure to his *conscience*.[11] The insufficiency of medication over against the sufficiency of God's Word must be brought to bear upon Andrew's thinking, thereby informing his conscience. He will be most helped *not* by turning to mind-altering substances, but by turning to the only One who can solve his life problems. Once Andrew places his faith in God's truth, which is sufficient for his difficulties, his newly-trained conscience will help him to turn from the world's empty claims.

It is the Christian's high and holy duty to guard the purity of his regenerated conscience. Paul had much to say about this. Note how he spoke of the conscience in the following verses: "I always take pains to have *a clear conscience* toward both God and man" (Acts 24:16), and "The aim of our charge is love that issues from a pure heart and *a good conscience* and a sincere faith" (1 Timothy 1:5).

To aid Andrew in this endeavor, I pointed out his need to meditate on God's truth. He must let Scripture control his *mind*. He must think about that which will please God, not that which will bring escape from his troubles. True peace belongs to the character of God and is one of His gifts, and Andrew must look for peace where it will be found!

The *mind* is a subset of the soul—an integral part of the totality of man. The whole of the man, including his mind, is bought by costly blood—"you were ransomed...not with perishable things such as silver or gold, but with the precious blood of Christ" (1 Peter 1:18-19). The mind is where we worship and praise our God. I beseech you: Don't lose your mind to a psychotropic experience. It is now clearer than ever—as the saying goes, "A mind is a terrible thing to waste."

The fourteen billion cells of your brain are extremely delicate. It is surmised that in the brain there are more than 10,000 connections and 1000 switchboards with a huge, complex capacity. The neurochemistry of this network baffles neurologists, neurosurgeons, neuropathologists, and neurophysiologists. Inside this complex organic machine, *your mind* functions. This is a mystery between our ears where the battle for good or evil is waged by supernatural spiritual means. "The weapons of our warfare are not of the flesh but have divine power to destroy strongholds. We destroy arguments and every lofty opinion raised against the knowledge of God, and take every thought captive to obey Christ" (2 Corinthians 10:4-5). Guard your reason; gird your *mind*. "Preparing your minds for action, and being sober-minded, set your hope fully on the grace that will be brought to you at the revelation of Jesus Christ" (1 Peter 1:13). Devote your mind completely to Jesus Christ and His sustaining, delivering grace.

I knew the Scriptures would be sufficient for Andrew's present trial, so my plan was to follow up and see the power of God's Word on display. I called Andrew to check up on him. His voice was bright and cheerful—even joyful. He sounded less urgent and frantic and more at peace. "You keep him in perfect peace whose mind is stayed on you, because he trusts in you" (Isaiah 26:3). Things were going better for him. There was more peace and harmony at home. I exhorted him to go to church the following weekend.[12] He would again be going with his mother. His wife was not yet willing to join him. His mother's influence in getting him back to church had been a great help and encouragement. Andrew could rejoice in that and enjoy her company until his wife would be ready to come as well.

Like Andrew, we too can draw strength and hope from Jesus, the Lover of our souls. He is a sympathetic Savior who endured much difficulty from the hands of sinful men and is indeed with us in our trials. "Consider Him who endured from sinners such hostility against Himself, so that you may not grow weary or fainthearted" (Hebrews 12:3; see also 1 Corinthians 10:13). In addition to these Scripture passages, I encouraged Andrew with truth from John 14:16 regarding the presence of the Holy Spirit, who is our Helper. When I read these verses to Andrew, he said he was already familiar with them because his pastor had preached on them. Also, some men in Andrew's Bible study had affirmed that they were studying the precious truths and promises in John 14. Andrew was excited about what he was learning and was sharing these things with his wife.

So that was how Andrew conquered insomnia and found help in God's Word for the desperate situation in his house. The Bible led him to the truth regarding our great salvation in Christ. He understood much better now that he would not need medication to live as the spiritual head of his family.

Key Areas of Drug Use

A Biblical View of Recreational Drugs

So what about *recreational drugs*—chemical substances consumed for the sheer thrill and supposed pleasure that results from taking them? This is madness! For the Christian man, there can be no such consideration. It is understandable that those without the hope of Christ cannot deal with the raging clamor of their thinking and want to escape their desperate lives. The wise king Solomon spoke to this in Ecclesiastes 9:3: "The hearts of the children of man are full of evil, and madness is in their hearts while they live, and after that they go to the dead." In other words, insanity, madness, and craziness are the heritage of the ungodly. None of us in this world are completely sound-minded, and from time to time we all can relate to the intense desire for thrill and pleasure. I suppose some would even say that we are all a little bit crazy in some way. From a worldly perspective, each of us could wear a label as derived from the "bible of psychiatry," the *DSM IVR* (the current *Diagnostic and Statistical Manual of Mental Disorders*). But to know the full truth about ourselves is to be diagnosed by the real Bible and get into the grip of God and His truth to be sanctified (John 17:17). Christians are to be in full command of their God-given faculties. We must learn to use them better and better.

The most common and popular recreational drug today is marijuana. Yet to use it is to merely exchange whatever madness we might have for the chemical madness of a drug that has absolutely no benefit. As for those who have been prescribed marijuana as a medical treatment, there is nothing medically wise about "medical marijuana." To be perfectly frank, frequent users of marijuana lack motivation and discernment and the use of such should not even be of mention in the ranks of men who claim to be devout followers of Christ. Those who use marijuana and other recreational drugs are not in full command of their minds.

What About Drugs for PTSD?

Psychotropic drugs are often overused and misused in mental health situations. We have a whole generation of servicemen and women coming back from war with not only physical injuries but *spiritual wounds*. Their minds are trying to grapple with the monstrous evils they have witnessed. Military psychiatrists will almost certainly administer a variety of psychotropic medications to them. Some of these individuals will be labeled with posttraumatic stress disorder (PTSD). When these individuals return to our Christian fellowship, we must guide them into the more invigorating truths and thoughts of Christ and His grace as found in His Word.

Nothing is new under the sun, and so from the shell-shocked veterans of World Wars I and II to the PTSD of our modern era, men are struggling to regain their sober minds. Paul was a supreme soldier of Christ, and we can see the measure of his afflictions in 2 Corinthians 1:8-9:

> We do not want you to be unaware, brothers, of the affliction we experienced in Asia. For we were so utterly burdened beyond our strength that we despaired of life itself. Indeed, we felt that we had received the sentence of death. But that was to make us rely not on ourselves but on God who raises the dead.

And again in 2 Corinthians 11:24-27:

> Five times I received at the hands of the Jews the forty lashes less one. Three times I was beaten with rods. Once I was stoned. Three times I was shipwrecked; a night and a day I was adrift at sea; on frequent journeys, in danger from rivers, danger from robbers, danger from my own people, danger from Gentiles, danger in the city, danger in the wilderness, danger at sea, danger from false brothers; in toil and hardship, through many a sleepless night, in hunger and thirst, often without food, in cold and exposure.

Paul shared his perspective on these severe difficulties in 2 Corinthians 12:9-10:

> [God] said to me, "My grace is sufficient for you, for my power is made perfect in weakness." Therefore I will boast all the more gladly of my weaknesses, so that the power of Christ may rest upon me. For the sake of Christ, then, I am content with weaknesses, insults, hardships, persecutions, and calamities. For when I am weak, then I am strong.

This is a good beginning point for the returning veteran. It is the very best news and word that can be given. The Word of God and the power of Christ have greater intrinsic power than any drug to encourage the downcast heart. God Himself is at work in their suffering, which they incurred for our benefit. Having suffered affliction to an extent that we can hardly imagine, we can only continually thank these men from the bottom of our hearts. To call what these dear men have endured *stress* is an understatement. They were tested beyond ordinary life skills. It is not surprising that so many become depressed and suicidal, despairing to find a way out.

There is a way up and out, as Andrew discovered. God is in the business of restoring the soul (Psalm 23). These individuals can join the ranks of those who experience PTGD—Post Traumatic Growth Development.

They can do so by following in the footsteps of the apostle Paul. They can study God's Word to discover the power of Christ in their moment of greatest weakness. They can find that God desires to help them in their despair and bring them hope.

Are Drugs Needed for ADHD?

The same conclusion can be made even for those diagnosed with attention deficit hyperactivity disorder, or ADHD. For this condition, amphetamines like Ritalin are popular. Now I am certain that when I was a boy I was inattentive in many ways. A recurring remark on my report cards was "He is careless." I had difficulty sustaining attention in tasks and at play. I was very easily distracted and often forgetful. I don't think I was very organized. I know I was very envious of my peers for their gifts and abilities. To be sure, I was restless and fidgety. I loved to climb trees and anything climbable. It was hard for me to sit and study.

As I look back on my childhood, I don't think my brain was broken in some way—only untrained. Oh yes, I was impulsive, and even to this day must still check myself in that way. Manners and courtesy instilled in me by my mother took care of rudeness and pushiness, and I am grateful to her for teaching me those essential skills. But I could have done better sooner. I was the naive one—par excellence! I needed to be drilled in the lessons found in the book of Proverbs.

This problem—this theoretical diagnosis of ADHD—is not a disease, but a character deficit. No drug is going to change such things as inattention to detail and work. The success that is seen in high school when students are better able to concentrate and succeed academically is offset by their crippling dependence on these drugs without benefit in later life. Clearly spiritual nurture has been neglected, but this must not remain so.

My advice as a physician is that the medications prescribed for ADHD are to be an absolute last resort. Make quite sure through a medical doctor that there is no other complicating medical condition present. Pay close attention to eating habits and nutrition.[13] Consult with your pastor to see if he knows of any biblical helps for children other than medications. A good place to seek biblical help online for this challenge is at the website of the National Association of Nouthetic Counselors, www.nanc.org. Don't give up on these kids, and proceed with caution, for we don't know yet what the long-term effects of ADHD drugs are.

Finding True Peace

Finally, when it comes to dealing with issues in our lives, let us consider carefully the example of Jesus Christ, whom we seek to emulate at all times. Christ was tempted just as we are. "We do not have a high priest who is unable to sympathize with our weaknesses, but one who in every respect has been tempted as we are, yet without sin" (Hebrews 4:15). Jesus, in His greatest hour of distress, pain, and physical weakness, did not accept the "drug" of the day that was offered to Him. "They offered him wine mixed with myrrh, but he did not take it" (Mark 15:23). Myrrh was a narcotic of Jesus' day. The Jews had a custom, based on Proverbs 31:6, of administering a pain-deadening medication mixed with wine to victims of crucifixion to help deaden the pain they were experiencing. Tasting what it was, Christ, though thirsty and suffering, would not drink, lest it dull His senses before He completed His work. The lessening of physical pain would probably not have diminished the efficacy of His atoning work. But He needed His full mental faculties for the hours yet to come. It was necessary for Him to be awake and fully conscious, for example, to minister to the dying thief (Luke 23:39-43).

When Christ was faced with His cross and a drug option, He did not take it. Clearly it is crucial for us to respond as He did to the drug option. We should *recognize that the answers of life come from God* (Psalm 62). "All Scripture is breathed out by God and profitable for teaching, for reproof, for correction, and for training in righteousness, that the man of God may be competent, equipped for every good work" (2 Timothy 3:16-17). And trusting in this all-sufficient Word—which produces such good works—will enable us in the fight against discouragement, despair, and depression. "His divine power has granted to us all things that pertain to life and godliness, through the true knowledge of Him who called us to His own glory and excellence" (2 Peter 1:3). Only in the Scriptures do we find true hope and encouragement. For Peter this was the more sure word of prophecy—precious and magnificent promises that have enabled us to become partakers of the divine nature and escape the corruption that is in the world by lust.

We can change our thinking by recognizing that true hope comes only from God (Romans 8:28-29; 1 Corinthians 10:13; Philippians 4:13). We can change our thinking about feelings by moving from mere reacting and feeling to action (John 13:17; James 1:25). We can change our heart and our thinking through Scripture: "Being no hearer who forgets but a doer who acts, he will be blessed in his doing" (James 1:25). We can change our thinking about problems (Romans 6:11; 8:28-29), viewing ourselves as alive to God and to Jesus Christ in eternal realities, for eternity is written in our hearts. "So you also must consider yourselves dead to sin and alive to God in Christ Jesus" (Romans 6:11).

When we pursue biblical responses to life's problems, we equip ourselves to fight against discouragement and depression and are strengthened without medication. We are called to do well with the time allotted to us on this earth, and we can do that by giving ourselves fully to the praise and worship of God with thanksgiving (Philippians 4).

This is how we find true peace.

Recommended Resources

Busenitz, Nathan, ed. *Men of the Word: Insights for Life from Men Who Walked with God.* Eugene, OR: Harvest House, 2011.

Fitzpatrick, Elyse, and Laura Hendrickson, M.D. *Will Medicine Stop the Pain?* Chicago, IL: Moody Publishers, 2006.

Hughes, R. Kent. *Disciplines of a Godly Man.* Wheaton, IL: Crossway, 1991.

MacArthur, John F. *The Power of Integrity: Building a Life without Compromise.* Wheaton, IL: Crossway, 1997.

———. *The Vanishing Conscience* (elec. ed.). Logos Library Systems (43). Dallas, TX: Word, 1994.

———. *Think Biblically! Recovering a Christian Worldview.* Wheaton, IL: Crossway, 2003.

Appendices

Appendix One:

The Gospel for Men

John D. Street

According to international statistics, women generally tend to have higher rates of emotional instability than men.[1] Yet, men are still prone to high rates of emotional problems during their lifetime as well. Whereas women generally outpace men with regard to anxiety and mood disorders, men greatly exceed women with regard to substance abuse and dependence issues. For example, approximately one in five men—compared to one in twelve women—tend to develop a heavy dependence on alcohol at some time during their life.[2] So men will often resort to some type of chemical abuse in order to deal with their problems. It is much easier in our culture for men to turn to substance abuse in dealing with their problems, because the perception is that real men are tough. We are told that "real men" can handle hard drugs and drink. The reality, however, is that hard drugs and drink are often a man's way of attempting to escape his problems.

It is also interesting to note that a woman will often seek formal counsel for her problem long before a man will. There is a general reluctance among men to admit to a problem and be viewed as weak. In fact, society considers it is shameful for a man to acknowledge weakness. This is why the gospel is an insult to every man's pride. It shows him his utter inability and helplessness before a holy God. And if a man does not understand his own helplessness, then he will not see his need for Christ. Because of this fact, counseling a man with the gospel in this culture will often prove to be a significant challenge.

In order for a man to receive biblical counsel, he *must* be a Christian. You cannot truly offer biblical counsel to a person who rejects Jesus Christ and the Bible as his authority. Even if you were the most persuasive counselor in the world and were able to get your unbelieving counselee to follow biblical counsel, he could only, at best, make external changes to his life. He might have a new coat of paint on the exterior of the house of his life, but the rotten wood under the paint would still be there. You will have, in effect, turned him into a good Pharisee—proud of his own proper behavior, but not yielded in his heart to God. Even worse, he may even take pride in his own "ability" to fulfill the commands of God. As a result, he will end up further away from the dependent grace of the gospel and will sink even deeper in his own self-righteousness.

There is a place for "pre-counseling" sessions with an unbelieving man. Galatians 6:10 encourages every Christian counselor, "So then, as we have opportunity, let us do good to *everyone*, and especially to those who are of the household of faith." The good we can do for the unbelieving man who is struggling with some type of chemical abuse is to give him physical and medical help with his enslavement. If he is having financial or marriage difficulties, we can provide assistance as much as godly wisdom will permit. But at the same time, always look for opportunities to talk with him about the gospel, because the immediate problems he faces are only symptomatic of a greater and more serious problem: his rebellion against God and his need of repentance. The old saying among Christian counselors still holds true, "All counseling is pre-counseling until a person comes to Christ."

You will also encounter men who seek biblical counsel and are convinced they are already Christians, but after a number of counseling sessions it becomes apparent to you that they are not. Their problems have brought to the surface an underlying spiritual deficiency. The Lord Jesus Christ is not their Lord and Savior. As they seek help for their depression, anger, fear, severe forms of dissociative identity disorder, schizophrenia, and more, they may adamantly insist they are Christians. Yet you'll notice indicators in the counseling process that suggest their profession of Christ is false.

Some may even reach the point that they walk out of counseling and refuse to follow biblical guidance. In such cases, even though you cannot see your counselee's heart and know with certainty his ultimate spiritual condition, if he is acting in disobedience to the Lord as a non-Christian would, you must view him as a non-Christian (1 John 2:19) and seek to bring him to repentance. But for those who remain in counseling—for those who do not walk out or refuse God's counsel—how can a counselor know whether his counselee's faith is authentic? Below is a brief biblical criterion of authentic Christianity that can and should be applied with wise discernment.

The True Christian Counselee

Characteristic	Biblical Reference
Love for God (concerned for God's glory in the midst of difficulty)	Psalm 42; 73:25; 105:3; 115:1; Isaiah 43:7; 48:10-11; Jeremiah 9:23-24; Matthew 22:37-38; Romans 8:7; 1 Corinthians 10:31
Love for others (selfless)	Psalm 15:3-4; Matthew 7:12; 22:39; Philippians 2:1-11; 1 John 2:9-10; 3:14; 4:7-8
Sorrow over sin (leads to real repentance)	Psalm 32:5; Proverbs 28:13; Romans 7:14-20; 2 Corinthians 7:10; 1 John 1:8-10
Motivated by the grace of the gospel for change	2 Corinthians 5:17-19; Titus 2:11-12; Hebrews 4:14-16
Humble (teachable)	Psalm 51:17; Proverbs 1:5; 9:9; 18:15; Matthew 5:1-12; James 4:6-10.
Separated from the world (attitude and activity)	Genesis 14:21-24; 1 Corinthians 2:12; James 4:4-10; 1 John 2:15-17; 5:5; 3 John 7
Desires God's Word for change and growth	Matthew 5:6; 2 Timothy 3:14-17; Hebrews 4:12-13; 1 Peter 2:1-3;
Persistent in prayer (dependent upon God)	Luke 18:1; Ephesians 6:18-20; Philippians 4:6-7; 1 Timothy 2:1-4; James 5:16-18

When a counselor becomes convinced the counselee is not a Christian, then it is important to see that the problem that brought him into counseling is the opportunity that God has provided for sharing the gospel with him—but not immediately. This means you must resist the powerful temptation to jump straight into the gospel. It is easy for a counselor to inadvertently communicate insincerity when the counselee's devastating problem is so quickly dismissed and a rush to judgment is made about his spiritual state. Genuine Christian love will show deep concern for the counselee by probing every aspect of the difficulty he faces (Proverbs 18:13).

This could mean taking the time to go through several pre-counseling sessions with this man—sessions full of data-gathering and the building of a solid, caring friendship (Proverbs 17:17). When the counselee is convinced that you fully understand his problem and have his long-term welfare in mind, he is more likely to trust you and be ready to hear the gospel. An effective biblical counselor will not cram the gospel down the throat of an unwilling counselee (Proverbs 9:7-8; 23:9; Matthew 7:6). This will only embitter his heart. A patient counselor will always wait to allow for the efficacious work of the Holy Spirit in the man's heart before the gospel is presented (1 Corinthians 12:6; Philippians 2:13).

Pre-Counseling Outline for Sharing the Gospel

1. Be sure you understand the person and the problem.

    a. Collect good data (Proverbs 18:13).

        i) What is he experiencing with this problem?

        ii) What are his feelings and emotions at this time?

        iii) What is he thinking?

            (1) What is his evaluation of the problem?

            (2) What is his evaluation of God in this problem?

            (3) What is his evaluation of himself and his responsibility?

            (4) What is his evaluation of others and their responsibility?

        iv) What is his behavior? How is he reacting and responding?

    b. Build a caring friendship (Proverbs 27:9).

        i) Communicate concern and care for what he is experiencing.

        ii) Communicate that you have confidence God has answers.

        iii) Provide practical assistance and help where it is needed.

        iv) Be loyal, though circumstances may be desperate (Proverbs 17:17).

        v) Pray openly and frequently for him and his experiences.

c. Communicate God's care for him and for what he is experiencing.

    i) God is aware of everything (Proverbs 5:21; 15:3).

    ii) God is near and cares (Exodus 34:6-7; Psalm 119:64,151).

    iii) Tough times focus our thoughts on God (Psalm 119:67,71,75).

2. Be sure the gospel is seen as the answer to a more serious spiritual problem and not as a quick fix for the more immediate problem.

    a. Diagnostic questions for the gospel[3]

        i) Are you at a place in your spiritual life where you are ready to handle your problems God's way?

            (1) *If the answer is no:* What are the barriers that are preventing you from making this critical change? Proceed to the next question (ii).

            (2) *If the answer is yes:* What reasons can you give for desiring this change? Proceed to the next question.

        ii) Suppose for a moment all your problems were resolved, and you died happy, but after death God asked you, "Why should I let you into My heaven?" What would you say to Him?

            (1) Listen carefully to the counselee's response then repeat it back to him.

            (2) This will help you to identify where his ultimate trust lies.

        iii) Self-righteous answers are common instead of complete trust in Christ alone for forgiveness and eternal life—this is where the good news of the gospel is life-transforming.

    b. Discussing the gospel

        i) Eternal life is unearned and undeserved because it is a free gift of God (Romans 6:23; Ephesians 2:8-9).

        ii) Every man is a sinner and a wicked rebel against God deserving of eternal punishment, death, and hell (Proverbs 14:12; Luke 12:5; Romans 3:23; 5:12; 2 Peter 2:4-9).

iii) Even though God is gracious and merciful, He is also holy and cannot ignore sin (Exodus 34:6-7; Numbers 14:18). He resolves this by sending His Son, Jesus Christ (Romans 5:8; 6:23).

iv) Essential atonement for sin is achieved by God, who sent the infinite God-man, the Lord Jesus Christ, to earth to live a perfect life in the flesh and die a substitutionary death on behalf of believers to provide the gift of eternal life (John 1:1,12,14; 2 Corinthians 5:21; 1 Peter 2:24). God's acceptance and approval of Christ's atoning death is seen the resurrection of Jesus from the dead (Romans 1:4; 6:5; 1 Peter 1:3).

v) Embracing this gift by faith involves, first, repenting of one's sinful condition (Acts 3:19; 20:21), and second, placing one's faith and full trust in Jesus Christ alone as Lord and Savior (Romans 10:9; Ephesians 2:8-10).

Once a man has realized his helpless condition and repented of his sin, trusting the amazing grace of the Lord Jesus Christ, he is now a true counselee ready to receive biblical counsel. This does not mean his problems will automatically go away. In fact, in some cases, his problems may get worse. For example, his unbelieving wife may not like the change that has occurred in his life and may make things more difficult for him around the home. But now he has a reliable resource for handling his problems that he never had before. There is a new peace and confidence that takes over his soul in the midst of his problems—not to mention the overwhelming relief of having been freed from guilt. For the first time, he has a totally clear conscience because Jesus Christ has paid for his sins, once for all (Hebrews 10:14,18). And he is receptive to the truth of God's Word.

Because the counselee now marches under a new authority, he can begin to study the Bible for answers to his problems. His heart is ready to respond to its truths. Counseling sessions are more meaningful and exciting because the counselee is viewing the words of Scripture through new, redeemed eyes of faith. Furthermore, the grace of the gospel now invigorates his sanctification and growth. He realizes that he has been released from the terrible bondage of his masculine pride and redeemed by the true Man, Jesus Christ.

Quick Reference Guide for Men's Problems

John D. Street

This guide is intended to provide the male counselor with quick biblical references to some of the more common problems of men. It is highly recommended that the second chapter in this book, "Counseling Men with the Bible," first be read and completely understood before using any of the biblical references in this guide. This will help you to more faithfully interpret the passages that are listed on the following pages as they apply to serious counseling problems. Always check the context of the verses you use for counseling—the careful application of good hermeneutics (principles of biblical interpretation) makes a good biblical counselor.

Modern psychological titles are often labels that are not used in the Bible. For example, the Bible doesn't talk about phobias, but it does address a variety of fears. It does not talk about peer pressure, but it does deal with the fear of man. The following list makes use of some psychological terms only because they have become commonly used "handles" in today's society to describe certain conditions. The biblical information in each scriptural reference, however, uses the biblical terminology that rightly describes the condition the counselee is dealing with. It is this biblical terminology that should be emphasized and used in the discussions between counselor and counselee.

Finally, this quick-reference list is not intended to serve as an exhaustive guide for each problem listed. The biblical references are only key beginning points for the counselor's further theological study on that particular topic in the Bible. Some references describe the condition; other references are listed to give spiritual insight and guidance. And some references do not speak directly to the issue but are helpful to know because they supply theological truth that is applicable to a specific problem. Remember as well that sometimes the Bible will record a sinful activity or event without comment or commentary. This does not mean that this activity or event is condoned by God; rather, it is recorded in the Word simply to serve as an example of the sinfulness of man.

Whatever the case, these references should be of help in the development of how you, as a Christian counselor, should think about and label the counselee's problem. When a counselee's problem is properly diagnosed with biblical labels, then you are able to guide him to the right biblical solutions.

Counselor's Reference Guide

Abuse

Physical Abuse

Proverbs 3:31; 4:17; 16:29; 22:3; 24:1-2
2 Corinthians 11:32-33
1 Peter 2:11–3:16; 4:1-2,19

Sexual Abuse

Deuteronomy 22:25
Judges 19:25; 20:3-4,12
2 Samuel 13:11-15
Proverbs 3:29-30
Habakkuk 2:15-16
Ephesians 5:3-5

ADD and ADHD

Proverbs 1:8; 25:28
1 Corinthians 9:25
Galatians 5:23
Titus 2:2
1 Peter 1:13
2 Peter 1:5-6

Adultery

Psalm 51; cf. 2 Samuel 12:1-7
Proverbs 4:13-27; 6:20-35; 7:1-27; 22:14
Matthew 15:19
Romans 7:2-3
1 Corinthians 6:9-10
Hebrews 13:4

Alcohol Abuse

Genesis 9:20-23; 19:30-38
Proverbs 20:1; 21:17; 23:19-20,29-35
Isaiah 28:1-8
Luke 21:34
Ephesians 5:15-18
1 Corinthians 5:11; 6:9-11

Anger

Genesis 4:5-7
Proverbs 10:12; 12:16; 14:17,29; 15:1,18; 17:19; 19:11
Ephesians 4:26

Antisocial Personality Disorder (sociopath or psychopathy)

Genesis 4:5-13
Proverbs 1:11-15; 3:29-31; 4:17; 10:6,11; 16:29; 19:26; 24:2
Romans 2:14-16
Ephesians 2:1-3

Bestiality

Exodus 22:19
Leviticus 18:23
Deuteronomy 27:21
Ephesians 5:3

Bipolar Disorder

Genesis 4:1-14
1 Samuel 18:7-11
1 Kings 18:36–19:18
Psalm 32; 38; 42; 43
John 14:27
Colossians 3:15
1 Timothy 6:6
James 1:8; 4:8

Bitterness

Genesis 37
Leviticus 19:17
Proverbs 26:24-26
Galatians 5:15,19-20
Ephesians 4:31
Hebrews 12:15-17
1 John 2:9-11; 3:11-20

Blame-Shifting

Genesis 3:12-13
Proverbs 19:3
Matthew 7:1-5

Conscience

Acts 24:16
Romans 2:14-16
1 Corinthians 4:4; 8:7,10,12
1 Timothy 3:9
Hebrews 9:14
1 Peter 3:16

Decision Making

Deuteronomy 29:29
Joshua 24:14-27
1 Kings 18:21
Daniel 4:25,35
Romans 9:15-23; 14:23
1 Timothy 6:15
2 Timothy 2:15
2 Peter 1:3

Demons

1 Samuel 16:14-15
Job 1:6–2:10
John 13:27
Ephesians 6:10-17
James 4:7
1 Peter 5:9

Depression

Genesis 4:6-7
Psalm 32:1-5; 42; 51
Isaiah 40
2 Corinthians 4:8-9

Dissociative Identity Disorder (multiple personality disorder)

1 Samuel 21:13
Proverbs 26:24-26
Luke 4:41; 8:26-39; 20:20
John 17:17
2 Corinthians 5:17; 11:15
James 1:8; 4:8

Divorce

Deuteronomy 24:1-4
Malachi 2:13-16
Matthew 5:23-32; 18:15-18; 19:3-9
Romans 7:1-3; 12:18
1 Corinthians 7:10-16

Drug Abuse

Psalm 4:7
Proverbs 20:1; 23:20-21,29-35
Romans 6:6
1 Corinthians 10:31; 14:7-8
Galatians 4:3,8
2 Timothy 3:1-5
2 Peter 2:19

Eating Disorders

Job 23:12
John 4:34
1 Corinthians 10:5-14
1 Peter 4:1-5

Anorexia Nervosa

Genesis 1:29-30; 2:9
1 Corinthians 8:8
Colossians 2:16
1 Timothy 4:3-5

Bulimia Nervosa

Proverbs 23:1-3,8; 25:16

Gluttony

Deuteronomy 21:20
Proverbs 23:12
1 Corinthians 11:18-22

Exhibitionism (flashing)

Genesis 3:7,10-11; 9:22
1 Samuel 16:7
Matthew 25:36-46
Romans 13:14
1 Timothy 6:8

Fear

Psalm 27:1; 56:10-11
Proverbs 14:26-27
Matthew 10:28-30
Romans 8:15
2 Timothy 1:7
Hebrews 13:5-6
1 John 4:18

Fetishism

Romans 1:32
Ephesians 5:3-5
Philippians 2:3-5; 4:8
1 John 2:15-17

Forgiveness

Forgiveness of others

Matthew 6:12-15; 18:21-22
Mark 11:25
Luke 15:20-24; 17:3-4
1 Corinthians 13:4-5
Ephesians 4:32–5:2
1 Peter 4:8

Forgiveness of sins

Psalm 32:1-5; 51:1-17; 86:4-7; 103:12; 130:3-4
Proverbs 28:13-14

Isaiah 1:18; 55:6-7
Matthew 6:12; 11:28-30
Luke 7:36-50; 15:11-24; 23:42-43
Romans 5:1; 8:1
1 John 1:7-9

Gossip

Proverbs 10:19-20; 12:18-19; 15:2,4; 17:4,20; 18:8,21
2 Corinthians 12:20
James 1:26; 3:5-6,8
1 Peter 3:10

Guilt

Genesis 3:7-11; 4:13
Leviticus 5:1-19; 7:1
Job 4:12-17; 33:14-18
Psalm 5:10; 18:23; 25:11
Proverbs 14:9
Isaiah 53:10
Hebrews 9:9,14; 10:22; 13:18
1 Peter 3:16

Hate

Psalm 5:5; 81:15; 109:3
Proverbs 1:22; 8:13; 9:8; 19:7; 29:10
Amos 5:15
Matthew 5:43-48
Luke 6:22,27

Homosexuality

Genesis 18:20-21; 19:4-5,24-25
Romans 1:18-32
1 Corinthians 6:9-11

2 Peter 2:4-10

Jude 6-7

Hot Temper

Psalm 37:8

Proverbs 14:29; 15:1,18; 16:32; 19:11; 22:24; 29:22

Ecclesiastes 7:9

2 Corinthians 12:20

Galatians 5:29-20

Ephesians 4:26,31

Colossians 3:8

James 1:19-20

Husband

Proverbs 12:4; 31:11,23,28

Romans 7:2-3

1 Corinthians 7:2-5,10-11,13-16,33-39; 11:3

Ephesians 5:21-33

Colossians 3:19

1 Peter 3:7

Incest

Genesis 19:31-36; cf. 2 Peter 2:7-8

Leviticus 18:6; 20:11-12,17

Deuteronomy 27:20,22-23

2 Samuel 13:1-22

Matthew 18:6; 25:45

Mark 6:17-29; 9:42

1 Corinthians 5:1

Insomnia

Esther 6:1

Job 4:12-17; 33:14-18

Psalm 4:8; 121:4; 127:2

Proverbs 3:24; 4:16

Ecclesiastes 5:12; 8:16

Isaiah 29:10

Philippians 4:6-8

Laziness

Proverbs 6:6-11; 10:4,26; 12:24,27; 13:4; 15:19; 19:15,24; 20:4; 21:5,25; 22:13; 24:30; 26:13-16

Ecclesiastes 10:18

1 Timothy 5:8

Titus 1:16

2 Peter 1:10; 3:14

Jude 4

Leadership

Genesis 18:19

Exodus 18:17-27

Deuteronomy 6:7; 11:19-21

Proverbs 13:22; 20:7; 29:17

Matthew 20:25-28

Ephesians 5:23-33; 6:4-9

Colossians 3:19–4:6

1 Timothy 3:1-13; 5:8

2 Timothy 2:24-26

Titus 1:5-9

1 Peter 5:1-5

Lust

General Passion

Psalm 68:30; 140:8

Proverbs 11:6; 21:10

Galatians 5:16-24

Ephesians 2:3; 4:22
2 Timothy 2:22
1 Peter 2:11-12
1 John 2:16-17
Jude 16

Sexual Lust

Proverbs 5; 6:23-35; 7:5-27
Isaiah 57:4-5
Ezekiel 16:36-42
Matthew 5:27-30
1 Corinthians 6:12-20; 7:1-5
1 Thessalonians 4:3-5
Hebrews 13:4
2 Peter 2:4-10

Lying

Psalm 15:4; 31:18; 52:3; 120:2
Proverbs 6:17; 10:18; 12:19,22; 17:4; 19:22; 21:6; 26:28; 30:5-8
John 8:44
Romans 3:4
Ephesians 4:15,25
1 John 2:22; 4:20

Marriage

Genesis 2:18-25; 3:6
Matthew 5:31-32; 19:4-6,9
Mark 10:6-12
Luke 16:18
Ephesians 5:31-33
1 Timothy 4:1-5
Hebrews 13:4

Marriage to an Unbeliever

Genesis 6:1-4
Exodus 34:16
Joshua 23:12-13
Ezra 9
Nehemiah 13:23-27
Amos 3:3
2 Corinthians 6:14-16

Masculinity

Genesis 1:26-27,31
1 Samuel 4:9
2 Samuel 10:12; 17:10
Isaiah 19:16
Jeremiah 50:37; 51:30
1 Corinthians 16:13
Ephesians 5:28-29

Masturbation (autoeroticism)

Proverbs 4:23; 5:21-23; 6:25; 7:25
Ecclesiastes 2:1; 7:26
Matthew 5:28-30
1 Corinthians 7:3-4
Ephesians 5:3-5
1 Thessalonians 4:3-5
James 3:14-16

Obsessive-Compulsive Disorder

Psalm 33:8,18; 49:5; 118:6
Proverbs 3:5-6; 4:23-27; 12:25; 14:30; 29:25
Ecclesiastes 8:12; 12:13
Matthew 6:25-34

Luke 12:25-26
Ephesians 4:22-24
Philippians 4:6-8
Colossians 3:1-4
Hebrews 10:11-13

Overcoming Evil

Exodus 23:4-5
Proverbs 17:13; 20:22; 24:17-18,28-29; 25:21-22
Matthew 5:43-47; 18:15-17
Romans 12:14,17-21
1 Thessalonians 5:15
1 Peter 2:18-23; 3:8-16

Parenting

Deuteronomy 6:6-7; 11:18-21
Psalm 34:11; 103:13; 127:3-4
Proverbs 3:12; 4:3-10; 13:22,24; 15:20; 17:6,21,25; 19:13,18,26;
    20:20; 22:15; 23:13,22-25; 29:15-17
1 Corinthians 7:14
Ephesians 6:4
1 Timothy 3:4

Peace .

Psalm 4:8; 85:8
Isaiah 9:6; 26:3-4; 53:5
Matthew 11:28-30
Luke 7:36-50
Romans 5:1; 8:6
Galatians 5:22-23
Philippians 4:6-8

Pedophilia (child-love)

Leviticus 18:6-18
Deuteronomy 1:39
Psalm 127:3
Proverbs 3:29-30; 14:22; 21:10
Jeremiah 19:4
Matthew 18:6,10,14
Luke 17:2
Romans 1:24-25
1 Corinthians 5:1
1 Peter 4:3-6

Peer Pressure (fear of man)

Deuteronomy 2:25; 3:2
Joshua 10:8
Proverbs 29:25
Isaiah 2:22
Matthew 10:28
Mark 14:66-72
John 7:13

Phobias (fears)

Psalm 2:11; 4:4; 19:9; 27:1,14; 31:24; 49:5; 56:10-11; 91:5
Proverbs 14:26-27
Matthew 10:28-30
Romans 8:15
2 Corinthians 5:6,8
Philippians 1:20
Hebrews 13:5-6
1 John 4:18

Pornography (voyeurism)

2 Samuel 11:2; 13:1-19
Psalm 51
Proverbs 4:23,25; 5:21-23; 6:25; 7:25
Matthew 5:28-29
Ephesians 5:3-5
1 Thessalonians 4:3-5

Prayer

Nehemiah 4:9
Psalm 32; 34:15-18; 50:15; 51; 66:13-20; 105:1-4
Proverbs 3:5-6
Isaiah 55:6
Matthew 6:9-13; 11:28-30
Philippians 4:6-7
1 Thessalonians 5:17-18
Hebrews 4:14-16
James 1:6; 5:13-18
1 Peter 5:5-7

Priorities

Proverbs 10:5; 13:16; 14:8; 16:1,9; 20:18; 24:27
Matthew 22:37-40
Romans 1:9-13
1 Corinthians 10:31
2 Corinthians 5:9
Ephesians 1:17; 3:14
Colossians 1:28

Prostitution

Genesis 34:31; 38:15-22
Leviticus 19:29; 21:7

Deuteronomy 23:17-18
Proverbs 7:10; 23:27
1 Corinthians 6:15-16

Purity

Psalm 12:6; 24:4; 73:1; 119:9
Proverbs 15:26; 16:2; 20:9,11; 22:11
Matthew 5:8
2 Corinthians 6:6
Philippians 1:10
1 Timothy 4:12; 5:2
2 Timothy 2:22
Titus 1:15; 2:5
James 1:17; 3:17
1 John 3:3

Rape

Genesis 19:1-29
Deuteronomy 22:23-30
Judges 19:25; 20:3-4,12
2 Samuel 13:11-15
Lamentations 5:11
Habakkuk 2:15-16
Zechariah 14:2

Repentance

1 Kings 8:47-48
2 Chronicles 6:37-38
Psalm 7:12; 32; 51
Matthew 4:17; 11:20
Luke 13:3,5; 15:7; 24:47
2 Corinthians 7:10

Sadomasochism (e.g., paraphilia sadomasochist)

Proverbs 17:15
Ecclesiastes 11:10
Isaiah 5:20
Mark 7:21-23
Romans 1:24-25
2 Corinthians 12:21
Galatians 5:13
Ephesians 4:19
Philippians 2:3-4
1 Peter 4:3
2 Peter 2:10,12

Self-Centeredness

Genesis 4:3-8
Psalm 119:36
Matthew 20:20-28
Luke 9:23-25
Romans 15:2-3
1 Corinthians 10:24; 13:4-5
Philippians 1:17; 2:3
James 3:14-16

Self-Control or Self-Discipline

Genesis 39:9-10
Proverbs 20:19; 23:2; 25:28; 29:11,19
Acts 24:25
1 Corinthians 7:5,9; 9:25
Galatians 5:22-23
2 Timothy 1:7; 3:3
Titus 1:8; 2:2-6
Hebrews 12:9-10
1 Peter 1:13
2 Peter 1:5-6

Self-Pity or Brooding

Genesis 4:13
1 Kings 19:1-18
Psalm 37; 73
Proverbs 15:13
Jonah 4:10-11

Sex

Proverbs 5:18-20
Ecclesiastes 9:9
Song of Solomon
1 Corinthians 7:2-5
Hebrews 13:4

Sexual Immorality

Proverbs 4:23-27; 6:29
Matthew 5:27-30; 15:19-20
Romans 6:15-23
1 Corinthians 6:12-20; 7:1
Galatians 5:16-18
Ephesians 5:3-5
Colossians 3:5-7
1 Thessalonians 4:3-6
Revelation 17:2; 18:3

Singleness

Matthew 19:10-12; 22:30
1 Corinthians 6:19-20; 7:6-9,26-38
2 Corinthians 5:9

Substance Abuse

Genesis 9:20-23; 19:30-38
Deuteronomy 29:6

Proverbs 20:1; 21:17; 23:19-20,32-35
Isaiah 28:1-8; 29:9
Luke 21:34
1 Corinthians 5:11; 6:9-11
Ephesians 5:15-18

Suicide

Judges 9:52-54
1 Samuel 31:4-5
2 Samuel 17:23
1 Kings 16:15-20
Psalm 33:20-22
Matthew 11:28; 27:3-5
John 8:44; 10:10
Romans 14:7-8
1 Corinthians 6:19-20

Tongue

Psalm 15:3-4; 34:13; 35:28; 119:172; 120:2-3
Proverbs 6:17,24; 10:20,31; 12:18-19; 15:2,4; 16:1; 17:4,20; 18:21;
    21:6,23; 25:15,23; 26:28; 28:23
Romans 14:11
Philippians 2:11
James 1:26; 3:5-6

Transsexual

Genesis 1:26-31
Deuteronomy 23:1
Philippians 4:11
1 Timothy 6:8

Transvestitism

Deuteronomy 22:5

Video Game Addiction

Matthew 22:39
Romans 6:6
1 Corinthians 6:12; 13:4-7
Galatians 4:3,8
Ephesians 5:28-29
2 Peter 2:19

Violence

Psalm 140:1,4,11
Proverbs 1:16-19; 3:11; 4:17; 10:6,11; 13:2; 16:29; 19:26; 21:7;
    24:2,15; 26:6
Matthew 11:12
Acts 21:35
1 Timothy 3:2-3
Titus 1:7

Work

Genesis 2:15
Exodus 20:9-11
Deuteronomy 5:13
Proverbs 6:6-11; 10:5; 12:11; 14:23; 15:19; 19:15; 20:4,13; 24:30-34;
    26:13-16
Ecclesiastes 5:12
Matthew 25:14-30
1 Corinthians 10:31
Colossians 3:17
1 Thessalonians 4:11-12
2 Thessalonians 3:6-15

Worry

Psalm 37:3-7
Proverbs 12:25; 14:30; 17:22
Matthew 6:25-34
Philippians 4:6-8
1 Peter 5:6-7

Youth

Genesis 39:9-10 (cf. 1 Thessalonians 4:3-5)
Exodus 20:12
Proverbs 1:7–9:18; 3:1-4; 4:1-4; 9:10-11; 13:24; 15:33
Ecclesiastes 11:9-10; 12:1-7
Daniel 1:8-10; 3:16-18
Ephesians 6:1-3
Colossians 3:20
Hebrews 12:5-11

Appendix Three:
Biblical Counseling Organizations and Resources

Following is a list of training centers where you can receive formal or informal training in the practice of consistently biblical counseling:

The Master's College, www.masters.edu

The Biblical Counseling and Discipleship Association of Southern California, www.bcda-socal.org

The Institute for Biblical Counseling and Discipleship, www.ibcd.org

The National Association of Nouthetic Counselors, www.nanc.org

The Association of Biblical Counseling and Discipleship for Asia-Pacific, www.abcd-apac.org

European Bible Training Center, www.ebtc-online.org

Brazilian Association of Biblical Counselors, www.abcb.org.br

Biblical Counseling Center of Sonoma County, CA, www.counselfromthebible.org

Valley Bible Church Biblical Counseling Center, www.livetheword.squarespace.com

Biblical Counseling and Education Center, Visalia, CA, www.bcecvisalia.net

Grace Community Church, Sun Valley, CA, www.gracechurch.org/ministries/logos

Faith Biblical Counseling Center, Sharpsburg, GA, www.faithbiblechurch.us

Biblical Counseling Center, Arlington Heights, IL,
www.biblicalcounselingcenter.org

Clearcreek Chapel Counseling Ministries, www.clearcreekchapel.org

Crossroads Bible College, Indianapolis, IN, www.crossroads.edu

Faith Biblical Counseling Ministries, Lafayette, IN, www.fbcmlafayette.org

Redeeming Grace Biblical Counseling Center, Overland Park, KS,
www.redeemer-pca.org

Southern Baptist Theological Seminary, www.sbts.edu

Biblical Counseling Center, Jenison, MI, www.bccmi.org

Biblical Counseling Center of Southeast Michigan, Ypsilanti, MI,
www.bcceastmi.com

Mt. Carmel Ministries, Grandview, MO, www.mtcarmelmin.org

Southeastern Baptist Theological Seminary, www.sebts.edu

Biblical Counseling Center of Grand Island, NY, www.biblepres.org

Faith Fellowship Biblical Counseling Center, Clarence, NY,
www.faithfellowship.us

Wheelersburg Baptist Church, Wheelersburg, OH,
www.wheelersburgbaptist.com

Beamsville Counseling and Discipleship Center, Greenville, OH,
www.beamsvillechurch.com

Biblical Counseling Institute, Garrettsville, OH, www.bciohio.com

The Fountain Counseling Ministries, Medina, OH,
www.thefountainofgrace.org

Christian Counseling and Educational Foundation, Glenside, PA,
www.ccef.org

The Institute for Nouthetic Studies, Greenville, SC, www.nouthetic.org

Counseling

If you're looking for a counselor in your area, please visit www.nanc.org,
where you'll find a list of certified counselors by state.

Audio Recordings

If you are looking for audio recordings of teaching by well-known biblical counselors, please visit www.soundword.com and peruse their library. Look especially at the conferences sponsored by NANC, IBCD, or The Wayne Mack Library.

Annual Conferences (open to all)

If you would like to attend a conference on biblical counseling, please visit the following websites:

The National Association of Nouthetic Counselors: During the first week of October, NANC sponsors a national biblical counseling conference. This conference's location moves around the country from year to year. NANC also holds regional training conferences. Information on all these conferences can be accessed at www.nanc.org.

The Institute for Biblical Counseling and Discipleship: Annually in June, IBCD sponsors a biblical counseling conference in the suburbs of San Diego, California. See www.ibcd.org for more information.

The Christian Counseling and Educational Foundation: Every year in November, CCEF sponsors a conference in Pennsylvania. For more information, see www.ccef.org.

Faith Baptist Counseling Ministries: Annually in February, FBCM sponsors a week-long training course in biblical counseling on six different levels. For more details about the conference, held in Lafayette, Indiana, see www.faithlafayette.org/counseling.

Appendix Four:

The "One Another" Commands

Be Devoted to One Another and Outdo (Prefer) One Another
Romans 12:10—"Love one another with brotherly affection. Outdo one another in showing honor."

Live in Harmony (Be of the Same Mind) with One Another
Romans 12:16—"Live in harmony with one another."

Judge Not and Build Up One Another
Romans 14:13—"Let us not pass judgment on one another any longer."

Romans 14:19—"Let us pursue what makes for peace and for mutual upbuilding."

Accept One Another
Romans 15:7—"Welcome one another as Christ has welcomed you."

Admonish One Another
Romans 15:14—"I myself am satisfied about you, my brothers, that you yourselves are full of goodness, filled with all knowledge and able to instruct one another."

Sue Not One Another
1 Corinthians 6:7—"To have lawsuits at all with one another is already a defeat for you. Why not rather suffer wrong? Why not rather be defrauded?"

Deprive Not One Another
1 Corinthians 7:5—"Do not deprive one another."

Wait for One Another

1 Corinthians 11:33—"When you come together to eat, wait for one another."

Care for One Another

1 Corinthians 12:25—"Have the same care for one another."

Provoke Not and Envy Not One Another

Galatians 5:26—"Let us not become conceited, provoking one another, envying one another."

Bear One Another's Burdens

Galatians 6:2—"Bear one another's burdens, and so fulfill the law of Christ."

Speak Truthfully to One Another

Ephesians 4:25—"Let each one of you speak the truth with his neighbor, for we are members one of another."

Be Kind to One Another

Ephesians 4:32—"Be kind to one another."

Be Subject to One Another

Ephesians 5:21—"Submitting to one another out of reverence for Christ."

Regard One Another

Philippians 2:3—"Do nothing from selfishness or empty conceit, but with humility of mind regard one another as more important than yourselves" (NASB).

Lie Not to One Another

Colossians 3:9—"Do not lie to one another."

Bear with One Another

Colossians 3:13—"Bearing with one another."

Forgive One Another

Colossians 3:13—"Bearing with one another and, if one has a complaint against another, forgiving each other."

Teach One Another

Colossians 3:16—"Let the word of Christ dwell in you richly, teaching and admonishing one another in all wisdom."

Love One Another

> 1 Thessalonians 3:12—"May the Lord make you increase and abound in love for one another."

Comfort One Another

> 1 Thessalonians 4:18—"Comfort one another with these words" (NASB).

Encourage One Another

> 1 Thessalonians 5:11—"Encourage one another and build one another up."

Peace with One Another

> 1 Thessalonians 5:13—"Be at peace among yourselves."

Seek Good for One Another

> 1 Thessalonians 5:15—"Always seek to do good to one another and to everyone."

Pray for One Another

> 1 Timothy 2:1—"I urge that supplications, prayers, intercessions, and thanksgivings be made for all people."

Stimulate One Another

> Hebrews 10:24—"Stimulate one another to love and good deeds" (NASB).

Speak Not Against One Another

> James 4:11—"Do not speak evil against one another."

Complain Not Against One Another

> James 5:9—"Do not complain, brethren, against one another" (NASB).

Confess to One Another

> James 5:16—"Confess your sins to one another and pray for one another."

Be Hospitable to One Another

> 1 Peter 4:9—"Show hospitality to one another without grumbling."

Serve One Another

> 1 Peter 4:10—"As each has received a gift, use it to serve one another."

Be Humble Toward One Another

> 1 Peter 5:5—"Clothe yourselves, all of you, with humility toward one another."

Greet One Another

　　1 Peter 5:14—"Greet one another with the kiss of love."

Fellowship with One Another

　　1 John 1:7—"If we walk in the light, as he is in the light, we have fellowship with one another."

Appendix Five:

About the Contributors

David Aycock was born and raised in the city of Chicago. He came to know the Lord at the age of eight at a vacation Bible school at Messiah Baptist Church in Addison, IL, where he has been the pastor for twenty-three years. He holds a BA from Baptist Bible College in Springfield, MO, and the MABC from The Master's College. David has worked in inner-city Chicago with teens for twelve years. He has been married to his wife, Jill, for more than forty years. They have two married sons and three grandchildren. He enjoys spending time with his grandkids and riding his motorcycle, and hopes the Cubs win a World Series before the Lord comes!

Ernie Baker joined the faculty of the Biblical Counseling Department at The Master's College in 2005. He received his MDiv from Capital Bible Seminary, and his DMin in counseling from Westminster Theological Seminary. Dr. Baker has been in ministry since 1980 with extensive experience of twenty-five years as a pastor and in training and equipping pastors and laymen in the skills of biblical counseling and conciliation. He is a certified conciliator with Peacemaker Ministries, teaching a number of conflict-resolution courses and doing conciliation work. He is certified as a biblical counselor with NANC and a council board member of the Biblical Counseling Coalition (BCC). He is a frequent speaker nationally and internationally at conferences, churches, and retreats, addressing issues related to marriage and counseling. He is married to Rose, and they have three sons and three daughters and three grandchildren. Ernie enjoys reading, hunting, and gardening.

Nathan Busenitz (ThM, MDiv) has written or edited several books, including *Reasons We Believe* (Crossway, 2008) and *Men of the Word* (Harvest House, 2011). From 2003 to 2009, Nathan served as a full-time member of the pastoral staff at Grace Community Church. During this time, he worked as the director of the Shepherds' Fellowship, the managing editor of *Pulpit* magazine, and also as the personal assistant to John MacArthur. In 2008, Nathan began teaching Historical Theology at The Master's Seminary, and joined the full-time faculty in 2009. He is currently working to complete his ThD in historical theology. He and his wife, Beth, have four children.

Mark C. Chin, MD was born in Toronto, Canada. He did his premed studies at the University of Western Ontario, medical school at the University of Ottawa, and family practice residency at the University of Toronto. Mark worked as a family practice physician in Culver City from 1994 to 2006. He has also served as a pastoral care intern at Grace Community Church, Sun Valley, CA. Mark began his studies in biblical counseling at The Master's College in the early 2000s. Soon after, he turned his attention to preparing for full-time ministry at The Master's Seminary. He earned his MDiv and ThM degrees at the seminary between 2006 and 2012. Mark is married to Julie, and they have one son, Athan.

Joshua Clutterham grew up in Santa Clarita, CA, where he attended and graduated from The Master's College with a BA in biblical languages and the MABC. He also holds MDiv and ThM degrees from Southern Baptist Theological Seminary. He has been employed by both alma maters as a graduate teaching assistant, serving under Drs. John Street, Robert Somerville, and Ernie Baker at The Master's College, and Drs. Stuart Scott and Heath Lambert at Boyce College and Southern Baptist Theological Seminary. Joshua is a certified biblical counselor with NANC. He is married to Meredith and has two sons, Samuel and Benjamin. He loves spending time with his family, studying God's Word, traveling, camping, and ice hockey.

Melvin Dirkse lives in Cape Town, South Africa, where he completed his undergraduate degree in psychology at a South African university. Afterward he graduated from the MABC program at The Master's College. He is a special education instructor, counselor, and Bible teacher—teaching in both mainstream and special schools over the past fifteen years. He currently works for the Western Cape Provincial Legislature (Cape Town) in the Public Education and Outreach Section. Melvin is a translator with Gospel Translations International, translating biblical educational material from English to Afrikaans (an official language of South Africa). He enjoys hiking, kayaking, mountain biking, camping, and sandboarding in the breathtakingly beautiful mountains of the Western Cape. He is an avid reader and writes tracts and educational articles on Christian-related matters. He has been a deacon at his home church over the last ten years.

Geoffrey V. Drew, MD, a native South African, has served as a family physician in Thousand Oaks, CA, since 1987, and a member and a deacon at Grace Community Church, Sun Valley, CA, since 1990. Active in his family practice, he loves his daily encounters with patients who are downcast of soul and whom he can lead to Christ in prayer and biblical counseling. He and his wife, Holly, both hold the MABC from The Master's College and she is his very able helpmate in all these endeavors. Their son, Donovan, and his family run a church-based home for orphans in South Africa. Their daughter also lives in South Africa, working as a teacher and vocational counselor. Geoff and Holly will soon join them in South Africa as biblical counselors at the Sasolburg Grace Fellowship, Free State, South Africa to partner in the ministry with pastor Tony McCracken.

Nicolas Ellen is the senior pastor of Community of Faith Bible Church in Houston, TX, and an instructor of biblical counseling at the College of Biblical Studies. Dr. Ellen has also developed a biblical counseling training center called the Expository Counseling Center. He holds a BA from the University of Houston, his MA in Christian Education from Dallas Theological Seminary, the MABC from The Master's College, and his DMin in biblical counseling from Southern Baptist Theological Seminary. Dr. Ellen is a certified biblical counselor with NANC and travels nationwide with the organization teaching biblical counseling principles. He is also a senior member of the Biblical Counseling Framework Association. Nicolas and his wife, Venessa, have two children and two grandchildren.

Dwight D. Ham has been in the business world for over thirty-five years, effecting positive change, taking organizations to the next level, and expanding business and financial operations across diverse industries. He spent fourteen years in banking and is currently serving on the board of directors of the Bank of Santa Clarita. He has served on several nonprofit Christian ministry boards of directors, including Pregnancy Resource Center, World Opportunities, Encouragement International, and El Camino Ministries. Dwight holds a BS in Business Administration from California State University Northridge, an MBA from Pepperdine University, and the MABC from The Master's College. He serves as an elder in his church and has taught in the adult singles ministry. Dwight has been married to Kathy for nearly 40 years, and they have two married sons and three grandchildren.

S. Andrew Jin came to saving faith in the Lord Jesus Christ during his final year at the University of Virginia. Upon graduation, he worked as a CPA at the Washington, DC office of Price Waterhouse, which he later left to attend The Master's Seminary in Los Angeles. After graduating from the MDiv program, Andrew realized the importance of the application of God's Word in a believer's life for biblical change and so obtained the MABC from The Master's College and certification from NANC. Andrew has participated in domestic mission trips as well as international trips to Japan, Bolivia, and Hong Kong/China. Andrew previously served as the first MABC graduate teaching assistant. He currently works as a CPA for an investment fund manager in Los Angeles and is an elder at Immanuel Bible Church in Santa Monica, CA. Andrew resides in Stevenson Ranch, CA, with his wife, Esther, and their three children.

Wayne Erick Johnston serves Valley Bible Church in Lancaster, CA, as a deacon and founding director of the Valley Bible Counseling Center. This center provides biblical counseling, a biblical counselor training program, and many unique counseling resources. Wayne is the director of training center certification for NANC and president of the Biblical Counseling and Discipleship Association of Southern California (BCDA SoCal). Wayne holds a BA in Bible and the MABC, both from The Master's College, where is he also an adjunct professor. He coauthored *A Christian Growth and Discipleship Manual* with

Wayne Mack in 2005. Wayne is married to Julie, and they have two grown children. He enjoys running in the desert and welding.

Daniel Kirk is senior pastor of Calvary Bible Church in Fort Worth, TX. He graduated from Word of Life Bible Institute, Schroon Lake, NY; Tennessee Temple University, Chattanooga, TN; and Dallas Theological Seminary in Texas. He is currently nearing completion of the MABC degree at The Master's College. He is also a certified counselor with NANC. Daniel has been married to his wife, Christine, for twenty-five years, and they have seven children. Daniel enjoys rock climbing, camping, hunting, helping lead a Boy Scout troop, and all things outdoors.

Chris Kropf is a graduate of The Master's College and Seminary. He currently serves The Master's College as the director of the MABC program. He enjoys counseling and does so on a volunteer basis both for the college and his local church. He and his wife, Brooke, met while she was a student in the MABC program. They have three children. Chris and his wife enjoy "team counseling" (counseling together) and watching the St. Louis Cardinals.

Jeff Lair lives in Wheaton, IL. He serves on the leadership team of Grace Church of Dupage Biblical Counseling Ministries. He has a passion for discipleship and helping believers grow in their walk with Jesus Christ. He earned the MABC degree from The Master's College, an MA in biblical studies from the Moody Bible Institute, Chicago, IL, and a BS in business from Messiah College. In his spare time Jeff enjoys swimming, biking, golfing, and watching college sports.

Wayne Mack has a love for the local church and spends most of his time strengthening and equipping it through his writing (more than 24 books and many articles), teaching, and conference speaking. Wayne started his ministry as a pastor; later he taught college and graduate courses in biblical counseling at several schools and seminaries. In 1992 he established the MABC program of study at The Master's College, in which over 200 students are currently enrolled. Wayne holds a BA from Wheaton College, MDiv from Philadelphia Seminary, and a DMin from Westminster Theological Seminary. He is a charter member of NANC, also holding the elite position as a member of the NANC Academy. Wayne and his wife, Carol, have been married since 1957 and have four children and twenty grandchildren.

Ben Marshall grew up the son of a navy chaplain, Captain Robert Marshall. He has been in full-time ministry since 1997, and was ordained in 2000. Currently he is the pastor of counseling at Canyon Hills Community Church in Bothell, WA. Ben holds a BA in psychology from St. Martin's College and the MABC from The Master's College. He has authored a helpful booklet entitled, *Help! My Teen Is Gay.* Ben loves being a devoted husband to his wife, Cory, and father to their five children.

Charles Mudd is a deacon at Grace Community Church in Sun Valley, CA, where he has served as a lay counselor for more than ten years. Currently he serves as a counselor and coordinator of counseling for the church's prayer room. Charles is a NANC-certified biblical counselor and holds the MABC degree from The Master's College. He is employed as a full-time commercial real estate appraiser. Charles and his wife, Cindy, have been married for nearly 40 years. They have been blessed with one daughter and three grandchildren.

Jim Newheiser finds great joy in combining pastoral ministry with training men for ministry, both in his local church and abroad. He is currently the pastor of Grace Bible Church of North San Diego County. He is the director of the Institute for Biblical Counseling and Discipleship (IBCD), an adjunct professor for the MABC program at The Master's College, and has taught Bible training courses in Korea, India, Spain, Qatar, Oman, Nigeria, and the Philippines. He has written several books, booklets, and discipleship courses, one of which is *You Never Stop Being a Parent.* He is a Fellow with NANC, certified counselor with IBCD, cofounder and board member for FIRE, and a board member for the Biblical Counseling Coalition (BCC). He holds a BA from Baylor University in business administration, and MA and DMin degrees from Westminster Seminary. He and his wife, Caroline, have been married since 1979 and have three adult sons.

Andrew D. Rogers serves as the pastor of soul care at College Park Church in Indianapolis, IN. He earned his BS in business administration and marketing from California State University, Fresno, the MABC at The Master's College, and his MDiv from The Master's Seminary. He was ordained by the EFCA and is certified by NANC. He has had the privilege of pastoring for seventeen years in California and Northeast Florida as a pastor to youth, college students, and young adults, a pastor of counseling, and most recently as a senior pastor. He has served as an adjunct professor at The Master's College and occasionally teaches for NANC. Andrew has been married to his lovely bride, Jenny, for eighteen years. They enjoy their four children and reside in Carmel, IN.

Robert B. Somerville has served as a pastor-teacher in the Evangelical Free Church since 1970 and as a professor of biblical counseling at The Master's College since 2005. He holds a BA from The King's College, MDiv from Trinity Evangelical Divinity School, and DMin from Westminster Theological Seminary. While pastoring in the greater New York area, he handled the crisis telephone calls for the family radio station and out of that ministry wrote the book *Help for Hotliners: A Manual to Train Telephone Crisis Counselors*. In 1980 he accepted the call to a church-planting ministry in Visalia, CA, and while serving that church for twenty-five years he established the Biblical Counseling and Educational Center, equipping laymen and pastors in the field of biblical counseling. He has spoken widely on the subject of biblical counseling, teaching seminars in the United States as well as speaking to missionaries in Europe, Central and South Africa, Mexico, and Japan. Dr. Somerville is a fellow and member of the Board of NANC. Bob and his wife, Mary, have two married children and seven grandchildren.

John D. Street is the chair and professor of the MABC graduate program at The Master's College and Seminary. His education includes a BA from Cedarville University, MDiv from Grand Rapids Theological Seminary, and DMin from Westminster Theological Seminary. Along with his ministry at The Master's College, he is an elder and lay pastor at Grace Community Church in Sun Valley, CA. Prior to coming to the college, John was the founding pastor of Clearcreek Chapel in Springboro, OH, where he built a strong counseling program and training center with a special emphasis in training pastors. John is a contributing editor of *The Journal of Modern Ministry* and a fellow and the president of NANC. He serves as chief advisor to ABCD-APAC, a fellowship of pastors and lay leaders committed to the sufficiency of Scripture in the Asia-Pacific countries of Australia and New Zealand, among others. He is cofounder and instructor of BCDA SoCal. John is married to Janie, his wife of more than thirty-five years, and they have four children and four grandchildren.

Ed Wilde graduated from UCLA with a BA in English literature in 1985 and from the University of San Diego in 1989 with a JD. He has been licensed to practice law in the state of California since 1989. Ed was in full-time practice of law from 1989 through December 2007, at times arguing before the California Supreme Court. He published law review articles for *The Whittier Law Review, The UCLA Entertainment Law Journal,* and *The Intellectual Property Law Journal*; and articles on the law for the state bar of California, the ABA, the journalism department of USC, and the *Los Angeles Daily Journal*. Ed is currently completing his thesis to conclude the MABC program from The Master's College. Since December 2007, he has served as the adult ministries pastor at Calvary Bible Church in Burbank, CA. He is also an adjunct professor at The Master's College, where he teaches "Business Law, Discipleship and the Local Church" and is an instructor for the online course "Introduction to Biblical Counseling."

Notes

Preface

1. The Greek term translated "men" can generally refer to both men and women. However, because Paul is dealing with leadership issues, and males were the main teachers in the church (1 Timothy 2:12), within this context it is possible his primary reference is solely the masculine gender.

Chapter 1—Understanding Biblical Counseling

1. David Powlison, *Seeing with New Eyes* (Phillipsburg, NJ: P&R Publishing, 2003), 1. On this point, also consider E. Bradley Beevers, "Watch Your Language!" *The Journal of Biblical Counseling*, vol. 12, no. 3 (Spring 1994): 24-30.

2. Anne Smith, "Speaking Is No Small Task," The Stuttering Foundation, http://www.stuttering help.org/Default.aspx?tabid=417 (accessed May 18, 2012). Anne Smith, "Development of Neural Control of Orofacial Movements of Speech," in *The Handbook of Phonetic Sciences*, 2d ed., eds. William J. Hardcastle, John Laver, and Fiona E. Gibbon (Malden, MA: Blackwell, 2010), 251-52.

3. The apostle Paul's example of counseling ministry is pictured in Acts 20:31-32 as incessant, night and day, lasting three years, and accompanied by tears. His example alone is sufficient to strike down all claims that biblical counseling is shallow and not deeply invested. (Again, Jesus' example—the governing presentation of biblical counseling—was far more profound, involving His own willingness to die; however, Paul's example as one who was transformed by Jesus and then counseled in a biblical way breaks down the objections.)

4. The recent publication *Counseling the Hard Cases: True Stories Illustrating the Sufficiency of God's Resources in Scripture* (Nashville, TN: B&H Academic, 2012), edited by Stuart Scott and Heath Lambert, is a testimony of God's transforming work in the lives of people encountering some of the most difficult problems in the human experience.

5. *Merriam-Webster's Collegiate Dictionary*, 11th ed., s.v. "Psychology."

6. On this point, consider David Powlison's chapter in *Psychology & Christianity: Five Views*, ed. Eric L. Johnson (Downers Grove, IL: IVP Academic, 2010), and Edward T. Welch's article, "A Discussion Among Clergy: Pastoral Counseling Talks with Secular Psychology," *The Journal of Biblical Counseling* 13, no. 2 (Winter 1995): 23-34.

7. "Psychology is not a uniform body of scientific knowledge like thermodynamics or organic chemistry. When we speak of psychology, we refer to the complex menagerie of ideas and theories, many of which are contradictory...It is a pseudo-science, the most recent of several human inventions designed to explain, diagnose, and treat behavioral problems without dealing with moral and spiritual issues." John MacArthur, *Counseling: How to Counsel Biblically* (Nashville, TN: Thomas Nelson, 2005), 10.

8. Johnson, *Psychology & Christianity*, 256.

9. Welch, "Discussion," 28-35.

10. Jay Adams uses the expression "God is man's environment" to describe this concept. Jay Adams, *A Theology of Christian Counseling* (Grand Rapids, MI: Zondervan, 1979), 38-56. This thought dominated the perspective of the theology of Jonathan Edwards, exemplified in his *Dissertation on the End for Which God Created the World*. John Piper has called his perspective a "God-entranced vision of all things"—John Piper, and Justin Taylor, eds., *A God Entranced Vision of All Things: The Legacy of Jonathan Edwards* (Wheaton, IL: Crossway, 2004)—and carried on his legacy through his own preaching and writing ministry. John Piper's *Desiring God* (Sisters, OR: Multnomah, 2003) advances Edwards's thesis in a fresh way.

11. Consider John Owen, "Of the Mortification of Sin in Believers," in *The Works of John Owen*, Vol. 6 (1656; repr., Edinburgh: The Banner of Truth Trust, 1974).

12. See John Calvin's *Institutes of the Christian Religion* 1.6.1 (1559); The Belgic Confession, Article 7 (1619); and The Westminster Confession of Faith 1.1 (1646).

13. *Merriam-Webster's Collegiate Dictionary*, 11th ed., s.v. "Sufficient."

14. Romans 10:18 is another place where Paul alludes to Psalm 19. In that text, God confirms that He has made the good news of His glory known to Israel. He proves this not with a list of every Israelite to whom He has explained the gospel, but by turning the focus to His character of making His glory known. He quotes Psalm 19:4, "Their voice goes out through all the earth, and their words to the end of the world," to make the point that He is one who proclaims His glory night and day to all creation. So also He has made the good news of His glory known to them through Scripture.

15. Consider Heath Lambert's description of salvation being a process in the introduction of his recent publication: Stuart Scott and Heath Lambert, *Counseling the Hard Cases* (Nashville, TN: B&H Academic, 2012), 10-12.

Chapter 2—Counseling Men with the Bible

1. For additional reading, consult Jay Adams, "Biblical Interpretation & Counseling," *Journal of Biblical Counseling*, 16, no. 3 (Spring 1998): 5-9; Jay Adams, "Biblical Interpretation & Counseling, Part 2," *Journal of Biblical Counseling*, 17, no. 1 (Fall 1998): 23-30.

2. For example, the New Testament books (27) were written in a Greek dialect known as Koine Greek, or Common Greek. They were authored in the common trade language of the near-Eastern people of the first century and thus were read by both Jews and Gentiles. The Old Testament books (39) constitute Judaism's Torah. They are best represented in the Masoretic Hebrew texts. The Roman Catholic Church, at a later time, added an unreliable group of intertestament texts known as the Apocrypha (cf. *Apocrypha of the Old Testament*, ed. Robert Henry Charles, Bellingham, WA: Logos Research Systems, Inc., 2004). Both Jewish and Protestant scholars deemed these unacceptable for inclusion into the inspired canon due to their highly questionable authorship and content.

3. A review by the United Bible Society recently reported that the Bible had been translated in whole or in part into over 2287 languages out of 6900 languages in the world. Many of the languages without any Bible translation are obscure dialects, for 98 percent of the world's population now has some form of Bible translation available in an understood language.

4. For additional reading the counselor should consult Leland Ryken's book *The Word of God in English* (Wheaton, IL: Crossway, 2002).

5. For example, Jay E. Adam's *The Christian Counselor's New Testament* (Grand Rapids, MI: Baker Book House, 1980) is a very helpful translation for counselors who seek a good translation from a counseling perspective.

6. For additional reading, see Carl F.H. Henry, *God, Revelation and Authority* (Wheaton, IL: Crossway, 1976).

7. On occasion a New Testament author may use quotes from the Septuagint (LXX, translated during the third century BC) and when this is done, under the inspiration of the Holy Spirit, then the Greek rendering of the Hebrew Old Testament text should be seen as an accurate and authoritative rendering of the text.

8. A *Textus Receptus* manuscript of the New Testament is marginally sufficient but tends to be built upon later Greek manuscripts and not the earliest and most reliable ones. It is the basis of the *King James* (KJV) and *New King James* Versions (NKJV) of the Bible.

9. "Two facts also become apparent: 1. Counselors cannot avoid dealing with doctrine because 2. Doctrine influences life. Those are reasons why every counselor not only must be a good exegete, but also must know doctrine (the systematic understanding of what the Bible teaches on various subjects)." Jay Edward Adams, *A Theology of Christian Counseling: More Than Redemption* (Grand Rapids, MI: Ministry Resource Library, 1986), 269.

10. Kevin J. Vanhoozer, *Is There a Meaning in This Text? The Bible, the Reader, and the Morality of Literary Knowledge* (Grand Rapids, MI: Zondervan, 1998), 462. This text is primarily written to challenge the destructive approach of deconstructionism to biblical hermeneutics and relies on the speech-act theory of J.L. Austin in the communicative act.

11. For a condensed discussion of each book of the Bible see Norman L. Geisler and William E. Nix, *A General Introduction to the Bible, Revised and Expanded* (Grand Rapids, MI: Eerdmans, 1986).

12. Wisdom literature in the Bible is a distinctive type of revelation that included naturalistic observations and conclusions about the common experiences of life, often formulated in a proverbial fashion and uniquely inspired by the Holy Spirit (for example, Proverbs 24:30-34). For this reason it is good resource material for biblical counselors.

13. Proverbs 25:1–29:27, King Hezekiah's men assembled many proverbs authored by Solomon; 22:17–24:34, certain wise men (cf. 1 Kings 4:31; 12:6); 30:1-33, Agur son of Jakeh; 31:1-31, King Lemuel.

14. "Heart, understanding, mind (also used in idioms such as 'to set the heart upon' meaning 'to think about' or 'to want')." Robert Laird Harris, Gleason Leonard Archer, and Bruce K. Waltke, *Theological Wordbook of the Old Testament*, elec. ed. (Chicago, IL: Moody Press, 1999), 466.

15. For additional study on genre and general hermeneutics, see R.C. Sproul, *Knowing Scripture* (Downers Grove, IL: InterVarsity Press, 2009); J. Scott Duvall and J. Daniel Hays, *Grasping God's Word* (Grand Rapids, MI: Zondervan, 2012); and Roy B. Zuck, *Basic Bible Interpretation: A Practical Guide to Discovering Biblical Truth* (Colorado Springs, CO: David C. Cook, 1991).

16. John MacArthur, *How to Study the Bible* (Chicago, IL: Moody Press, 2009).

17. Positional sanctification in Christ is the central motivating factor in providing the passion for a believer's obedience, but practical sanctification will also often involve surrendering of the will to God's will in genuine repentance along with putting on deliberate deeds and desires of righteousness. To believe otherwise would lead the Christian into the dangers of antinomianism (against the law of Christ), which the apostle Peter warns against with regard to false teachers (2 Peter 2:17-22).

18. The Bible is "living and active" (Hebrews 4:12) as it convicts "the thoughts and intentions of the heart," but it will not vocally argue with its reader. It will not actively change, disguise or be dishonest with its meaning like a counselee will often do.

19. John MacArthur and Wayne Mack, eds. *Counseling: How to Counsel Biblically* (Nashville, TN: Thomas Nelson, 2005), chapters 8-10.

Chapter 3—Hope for Men in Despair

1. National Institute of Mental Health, "Anxiety Orders: Introduction," U.S. Department of Health and Human Services, 2009. Online at http://www.nimh.nih.gov/health/publications/anxiety disorders/introduction.shtml (accessed May 2012).
2. American Foundation for Suicide Prevention, "Facts and Figures: Special Populations" and "Facts and Figures: National Statistics," articles accessed online at http://www.afsp.org (accessed May 2012).
3. Dan G. Blazer, "The Depression Epidemic," *Christianity Today* (March 2009), http://www.christianitytoday.com/ct/2009/march/15.22.html?start=2 (accessed May 2012).
4. Andrew Murray, cited by Amy Carmichael, *Though the Mountains Shake* (New York: Loizeaux Bros., 1946), 12.
5. Jerry Bridges, *The Pursuit of Holiness* (Colorado Springs, CO: NavPress, 1978), 145.
6. John Gill, *Exposition of the Entire Bible* (Philadelphia: W.W. Woodward, 1811), comment on Hebrews 10:23.

Chapter 4—Man and the Meaning of Life

1. M. James Sawyer, "The Theology of Ecclesiastes," http://www.bible.org/page.asp?page_id=1632.
2. Jeffrey Forrey, "The Concept of 'Glory' as it Relates to the Christian's Self-Image," *The Journal of Pastoral Practice,* 10 no. 4, 34.

Chapter 5—Developing Discernment as a Counselor of Men

1. John Eldredge, *Wild at Heart* (Nashville, TN: Thomas Nelson, 2001).
2. For an excellent critique of how the love cup model makes sinners into victims, read chapter 14, "Love Speaks Many Languages Fluently" in David Powlison, *Seeing with New Eyes* (Phillipsburg, NJ: P&R Publishing, 2003).
3. For guidance on being approachable and learning to build trust, see "Approachability: The Passport to Real Ministry and Leadership" by Ken Sande at http://www.peacemaker.net/site/c.aqKFLTOBIpH/b.1172255/apps/s/content.asp?ct=6869375.
4. For additional help thinking through what wise love in action looks like, I highly recommend David Powlison, *Speaking Truth in Love* (Greensboro, NC: New Growth Press, 2005).
5. For a more exhaustive list of God's purposes in suffering, see Appendix B in Joni Eareckson Tada and Steven Estes, *When God Weeps* (Grand Rapids, MI: Zondervan, 1997).

Chapter 6—Men and Depression

1. American Psychiatric Association, *Diagnostic and Statistical Manual of Mental Disorders, Fourth Edition* (Washington, DC: American Psychiatric Association, 1994), 327.
2. Julie Scelfo, "Men and Depression: Facing the Darkness," *Newsweek* (February 25, 2007), www.thedailybeast.com/.../02/.../men-depression-facing-darkness (accessed July 5, 2012).
3. John Piper, *When the Darkness Will Not Lift: Doing What We Can While We Wait for God—and Joy* (Wheaton, IL: Crossway, 2006), 25.
4. Edward T. Welch, *Blame It on the Brain* (Phillipsburg, N.J., P&R Publishing, 1989), 212.
5. Arthur Bennett, ed., *The Valley of Vision: A Collection of Puritan Prayers and Devotions* (Edinburgh, Scotland: The Banner of Truth, 1975), 158.

Chapter 7—When a Man Gets Angry

1. Jerry Bridges, *Respectable Sins* (Colorado Springs, CO: NavPress, 2007), 122.
2. Robert D. Jones, *Uprooting Anger* (Phillipsburg, NJ: P&R Publishing, 2005), 15-16.
3. Our lives and transformations are described in 1 Corinthians 1:26-31.
4. Scott, Stuart. *Anger, Anxiety, and Fear* (Bemidji, MN: Focus Publishing, 2009), 10.
5. Bridges, *Respectable Sins*, 126.

Chapter 8—Handling Emotional Extremes

1. *Forbes* magazine in 2007 estimated that Americans spend at least 13.5 billion dollars a year on prescription medications for depression and anxiety and in 2004, they spent close to 9 billion dollars on therapy. Robert Langreth, "Patient Fix Thyself: A Therapy Revolution," *Forbes* (April 9, 2007), 83.
2. Of the present-day treatments and causes of major depression, a review article on major depressive disorder in the *New England Journal of Medicine* concluded the following: "Depression is a heterogenous disorder with a highly variable course, an inconsistent response to treatment, and no established mechanism." R.H. Belmaker, M.D., and Galila Agam, Ph.D., "Major Depressive Disorder: Mechanisms of Disease," *The New England Journal of Medicine,* 358:1 (January 3, 2008), 55. It is critical that we distinguish, both scientifically and biblically, between influences, associations, and causes. Without a doubt, our environment, our circumstances, and our physical bodies can influence our emotions. However, to assert that such factors have an influence is distinctly different from attributing to them causal authority.
3. Jonathan Edwards, *The Religious Affections* (Carlisle, PA: The Banner of Truth Trust, 2004), 24.

Chapter 9—Living with Severe Physical Affliction

1. The source(s) of one's affliction or suffering may have occurred prior, during, or after his or her birth or any combination thereof. These sources might include genetic disorders, accidents, infections, illness, and intentional physical injury caused by others.
2. J.I. Packer, *Knowing God* (Downers Grove, IL: InterVarsity Press, 1973), 19.
3. Packer, *Knowing God*, 19.
4. Jay E. Adams, *Christ and Your Problems* (Phillipsburg, NJ: P&R Publishing, 1971), 22.
5. Adams, *Christ and Your Problems*, 22.
6. Jerry Bridges, *Trusting God: Even When Life Hurts* (Colorado Springs, CO: NavPress, 1996), 22.
7. Packer, *Knowing God*, 37.
8. Bridges, *Trusting God*, 138.
9. A.W. Pink, *The Sovereignty of God* (Carlisle, PA: The Banner of Truth Trust), 79.

Chapter 10—Contentment for Men

1. Burroughs, Jeremiah, *The Rare Jewel of Christian Contentment* (Carlisle, PA: The Banner of Truth Trust, 1998), 163-68.
2. Wilhelmus Á. Brakel, *The Christian's Reasonable Service, Vol. 3, Contentment* (Pittsburgh, PA: Soli Deo Gloria Publications, 1994), 379.
3. Brakel, *The Christian's Reasonable Service*, 380.
4. *Evangelical Dictionary of Theology* (Grand Rapids, MI: Baker Books, 1984), 280.

5. Wilhelmus Å. Brakel, *The Christian's Reasonable Service, Vol. 3, The Tenth Commandment* (Pittsburgh, PA: Soli Deo Gloria Publications, 1994), 239.

6. Lawrence O. Richards, *Expository Dictionary of Bible Words* (Grand Rapids, MI: Zondervan, 1985), 200.

7. Thomas Watson, *The Art of Divine Contentment* (Morgan, PA: Soli Deo Gloria Publications, reprint of the 1835 edition published in London by the Religious Tract Society), 24-25.

8. Richard Sibbes, *The Complete Works of Richard Sibbes, Vol. 5, The Art of Contentment* (Carlisle, PA: The Banner of Truth Trust, 1977), 178.

9. Burroughs, *The Rare Jewel of Christian Contentment*, 28.

Chapter 11—How to Develop Biblical Relationships

1. Stuart Scott, *The Exemplary Husband* (Bemidji, MN: Focus Publishing, 2000), 47.

2. Douglas Moo, *The Epistle to the Romans*, NICNT, eds. Ned. B. Stonehouse, F.F. Bruce, and Gordon D. Fee (Grand Rapids MI: Eerdmans, 1996), 777-78.

3. A. Skevington Wood, "Ephesians," *The Expositor's Bible Commentary*, vol. 11, gen. ed. Frank E. Gaebelein (Grand Rapids, MI: Zondervan, 1978), 66.

4. Jay Adams, *From Forgiven to Forgiving* (Amityville, NY: Calvary Press, 1994), 82.

5. Readers should consult Jay Adams' book *From Forgiven to Forgiving* for a more detailed discussion of forgiveness.

6. Curtis Vaughan, "Colossians," *The Expositor's Bible Commentary*, vol. 11, gen. ed. Frank E. Gaebelein (Grand Rapids, MI: Zondervan, 1978), 215.

7. It is important to distinguish that this command is not referring to tolerating a person's *sin*. Matthew 18:15-17 clearly shows how sin should be confronted in love.

8. Philip Edgcumbe Hughes, *A Commentary on the Epistle to the Hebrews* (Grand Rapids, MI: Eerdmans, 1977), 415.

9. Edmond D. Hiebert, *I Peter*, rev. ed. (Chicago, IL: Moody Press, 1992), 273.

10. Jim Phillips, *One Another* (Nashville, TN: Broadman Press, 1981), p. 90.

11. William Hendriksen, *The New Testament Commentary, I & II Thessalonians* (Grand Rapids, MI: Baker Book House, 1975), 91.

Chapter 12—The Husband's Role in Leaving and Cleaving

1. Stephen B. Clark, *Man and Woman in Christ: An Examination of the Roles of Men and Women in Light of Scripture and the Social Sciences* (Ann Arbor, MI: Servant Books, 1980), 20.

2. Peter T. O'Brien, *The Letter to the Ephesians* (Grand Rapids, MI: Eerdmans, 1999), 411.

3. Jay E. Adams, *Marriage, Divorce, and Remarriage in the Bible* (Grand Rapids, MI: Zondervan, 1980), 4.

Chapter 13—Parenting Young Children as a Father

1. John MacArthur, *Successful Christian Parenting: Raising Your Child with Care, Compassion, and Common Sense* (Nashville, TN: Word, 1998), xi.

2. Tedd Tripp, *Shepherding a Child's Heart* (Wapwallopen, PA: Shepherd Press, 1995), xvii.

3. John Piper, Gospel Translations, http://gospeltranslations.org/wiki/More_Thoughts_for_Fathers_on_Ephesians_6:4.

4. William Farley, *Gospel-Powered Parenting: How the Gospel Shapes and Transforms Parenting* (Phillipsburg, NJ: P&R Publishing, 2009), 15.

5. Tripp, *Shepherding a Child's Heart*, 4-5.

6. MacArthur, *Successful Christian Parenting*, 124.

7. See at http://www.merriam-webster.com/dictionary/structure.

8. See at http://www.merriam-webster.com/dictionary/routine.

9. Farley, *Gospel-Powered Parenting*, 113.

10. MacArthur, *Successful Christian Parenting*, 233.

Chapter 14—Parenting Adult Children as a Father

1. The content of this chapter is greatly expanded in Jim Newheiser and Elyse Fitzpatrick's book *You Never Stop Being a Parent: Thriving in Relationships with Your Adult Children* (Phillipsburg, NJ: P&R Publishing, 2010).

2. See Jim Newheiser, *Opening Up Proverbs* (Leominster, UK: Day One Publications, 2008).

3. Paul himself was a single man who was using his singleness to serve God, apparently without any parental control.

4. After our children grew up my wife was able to engage in a much more extensive ministry of hospitality and of counseling women. She received her NANC counseling certification and now works with me as we counsel couples together.

5. As of 2011, approximately 20 percent of young men from ages 25-34 live with their parents, which is twice the percentage recorded in 1980. Over half of those from ages 18-24 are still living with their parents. Approximately two-thirds of college graduates return to their parents' home after graduation. Many young married couples are also choosing to live with one set of their parents (in possible tension with Genesis 2:24). See http://www.census.gov/newsroom/releases/archives/families_households/cb11-183.html.

6. Lev Grossman, *Time Frames* (January 16, 2005), http://www.time.com/time/magazine/article/0,9171,1018089,00.html.

7. Over the past generation, the median age of first marriage has significantly risen for both women and men.

8. Eli had authority over his sons because they were working in the family priest business, in which they were blaspheming God, stealing sacrifices, and engaging in sexual immorality.

9. Some parents have wondered if they should require their young adult children to attend church with them (or at least to regularly attend some evangelical church). I regard this as a matter of parental choice. You are free to require church attendance as an expectation of a child living under your roof. You are also free to conclude that forcing a young adult, who is probably not a believer, to attend a worship service may not result in the gospel becoming more attractive to him or her.

10. These factors are discussed in more detail in the book by Elyse Fitzpatrick and Jim Newheiser, *When Good Kids Make Bad Choices* (Eugene, OR: Harvest House, 2005).

11. Given that Solomon is the author of Proverbs and that Rehoboam was his son, it appears that neither father nor son did very well in heeding the wisdom of Proverbs.

12. If your child professes to be a Christian and is living in a clearly sinful situation, the church of which he or she is a member will have to deal with this as a matter of church discipline (Matthew 18:15-20 and 1 Corinthians 5).

13. For example, if your child is living with someone to whom they are not married, I believe that you are free to have them in your home for a meal, or if they are from out of town, to let them stay with you (but in separate rooms).

14. Some parents choose to shun a child of whose lifestyle they disapprove. While they think they are making a stand for righteousness, we do not believe that Scripture requires such shunning. It appears that such parents often do this because they are angry that their dreams have been shattered (James 4:1-2).

15. One question I am often asked is whether parents should attend the wedding of their child if they disapprove of their child's marital choice. Unless the marriage itself is clearly in violation of Scripture, I strongly advise parents to attend the wedding and to show kindness. Your child will already know of your disappointment. The decision to shun your child's wedding could have negative implications in future relationships (including those with grandchildren) for years to come.

Chapter 15—Godly Grandfathers

1. Jerry Bridges, *The Practice of Godliness* (Colorado Springs, CO: NavPress, 2001), 20.

2. Barna Research Organization, www.barna.org.

3. Wayne Mack, *Strengthening Your Marriage* (Phillipsburg, NJ: P&R Publishing, 1997), 2.

4. Wayne A. Mack and David Swavely, *Life in the Father's House* (Phillipsburg, NJ: P&R Publishing, 1996), 117.

Chapter 16—Helping Men Resolve Conflict

1. Jeffry Wert, "Petersburg Campaign," *Historical Times Illustrated History of the Civil War,* ed. Patricia Faust (New York: Harper & Row, 1986), 578.

2. Wert, "Petersburg Campaign," 190.

3. Raymond C. Ortlund, "Male-Female Equality and Male Headship: Genesis 1–3," *Recovering Biblical Manhood and Womanhood: A Response to Evangelical Feminism,* eds. John Piper and Wayne Grudem (Wheaton, IL: Crossway, 2006), 108.

4. Ortlund, "Male-Female Equality," 107.

5. Ken Sande, *The Leadership Opportunity, Living Out the Gospel Where Conflict and Leadership Intersect* (Billings, MT: Peacemaker Ministries, 2009), 8.

6. Leupold writes, "It should be pointed out more directly that Cain's sin in reference to his brother was primarily jealousy culminating in hatred…" H.C. Leupold, *Exposition of Genesis* (Grand Rapids, MI: Baker Book House, 1942), 1:202.

7. Robert D. Jones, *Uprooting Anger: Biblical Help for a Common Problem* (Phillipsburg, NJ: P&R Publishing, 2005), 46.

8. Jones, *Uprooting Anger,* 48.

9. See F. Brown, S.R. Driver, and C.A. Briggs, *A Hebrew and English Lexicon of the Old Testament* (Oxford, United Kingdom: Oxford University Press, 1953), 523-5 (227) for definitions of the heart. Three of the words used to describe the heart are "appetites, passions, desires."

10. The text clearly emphasizes the quality of Abel's gift by stating he brought "the firstborn" and "their fat portions" (verse 4).

11. Marginal note and footnote on verse 24 in John MacArthur, *The MacArthur Study Bible,* NASB (Nashville, TN: Thomas Nelson, 2006), 1371.

12. Ken Sande, *The Peacemaker: A Biblical Guide to Resolving Personal Conflict,* 3d ed. (Grand Rapids, MI: Baker Books, 2004), 204.

Chapter 17—Manhandling Idolatrous Lust

1. W.E. Vine, *Vine's Expository Dictionary of Old and New Testament Words.* F.F. Bruce ed. (Iowa Falls, IA: World Bible Publishers, 1981), Vol. 3, 25.

2. Dr. Nicolas Ellen, *With All Your Heart? Identifying and Dealing with Idolatrous Lust* (Mustang, OK: Dare2Dream Books, 2012), 18.

Chapter 18—Struggling with Homosexuality

1. Russell Moore, *Tempted and Tried: Temptation and the Triumph of Christ* (Wheaton, IL: Crossway, 2011), 64.

2. Moore, *Tempted and Tried*, 64.

3. Moore, *Tempted and Tried*, 64.

4. John D. Street, "Hope, Holiness, and Homosexuality," in John MacArthur, *Right Thinking in a World Gone Wrong: A Biblical Response to Today's Most Controversial Issues* (Eugene, OR: Harvest House, 2009), 99.

5. Wesley Hill, *Washed and Waiting: Reflections on Christian Faithfulness and Homosexuality* (Grand Rapids, MI: Zondervan, 2010), 21.

6. Paul David Tripp, *Broken Down House: Living Productively in a World Gone Bad* (Wapwallopen, PA: Shepherd Press, 2009), 35.

7. Once again, be careful not to draw conclusions about a counselee's salvation prematurely. For more on this see Appendix One, "The Gospel for Men."

8. Timothy S. Lane and Paul David Tripp, *How People Change* (Greensboro, NC: New Growth Press, 2008), 53.

9. Timothy Lane and Paul Tripp, *How People Change* (Greensboro, NC: New Growth, 2006), 55.

10. A good systematic theology book will offer an extended treatment of the atonement. Here's one I recommend: Wayne Grudem, *Systematic Theology: An Introduction to Biblical Doctrine* (Leicester, England: InterVarsity Press, 1994).

11. J.I. Packer and Mark Dever, *In My Place Condemned He Stood: Celebrating the Glory of the Atonement* (Wheaton, IL: Crossway, 2007), 26.

12. Hill, *Washed and Waiting*, 29.

13. R. Albert Mohler, *Desires and Deceit: The Real Cost of the New Sexual Tolerance* (New York: Random House, 2008). This book has an excellent treatment on the origin of the concept of homosexual orientation.

14. Edward T. Welch, *Homosexuality: Speaking the Truth in Love* (Phillipsburg, NJ: P&R Publishing, 2000), 13.

15. Tim Chester, *You Can Change: God's Transforming Power for Our Sinful Behavior and Negative Emotions* (Wheaton, IL: Crossway, 2010), 103.

16. Chester, *You Can Change*, 10.

17. Jeremiah Burroughs, *Gospel Worship* (Orlando, FL: Soli Deo Gloria Publications, 1997), 132.

Chapter 19—Fathers and Teenage Homosexuality

1. For our purposes, this chapter will focus on a father-son situation. The father who faces this issue with his daughter will also find much help here for his relationship with her as well.

2. For more information on these issues, read Ben Marshall, *Help! My Teen Is Gay* (Leominster, UK: Day One Publications, 2011).

3. Ezekiel 18:1-4.

4. Tedd Tripp, "A Child's Call to Conversion: As a Christian Mark," *Table Talk* (October 2010), 20-23.

5. Paul David Tripp and David Powlison, *Changing Hearts Changing Lives: Session 8* DVD (Greensboro, NC: New Growth Press, 2006).

6. Matthew 5:29-30.

Chapter 20—When Marriage Problems Become Legal Problems

1. An introduction to family law at the state of California can be found here: *California Courts: The Judicial Branch of California*, http://www.courts.ca.gov/selfhelp-family.htm. Another online resource can be found here: *Nolo: Law For All*, http://www.nolo.com/legal-encyclopedia/family-law-divorce.

2. When looking for the source of this quotation, I found it quoted in a book on divorce, which included this statement: "The outcome of a divorce trial can only define the extent of your loss. It cannot define victory, because victory has never been in the cards." J. Richard Kulerski, *Divorce Buddy System* (Bloomington, IN: AuthorHouse, 2008), 13.

3. For clear biblical teaching on divorce, read Jay E. Adams, *Marriage, Divorce, and Remarriage in the Bible: A Fresh Look at What Scripture Teaches* (Grand Rapids, MI: Zondervan, 1980).

4. Associated Press, http://charlotte.cbslocal.com/2012/03/30/tennessee-mother-faces-possible-jail-time-for-baptizing-children/ (accessed March 31, 2012).

5. Institute for Biblical Counseling and Discipleship, www.ibcd.org, has many excellent counseling resources, including materials on marriage. Grace Community Church in Sun Valley, California, has many sermons and other resources on marriage. The sermons on the husband and wife as discussed in Ephesians 5 are a particular favorite of mine: http://www.gty.org/resources/sermons/scripture/ephesians. Calvary Bible Church in Burbank, California, has a series of classes on marriage, along with written materials. These can be found as follows: "Marriage Tune-up": http://calvarybiblechurch.org/site/cpage.asp?cpage_id=180023487&sec_id=180007745. "Marriage Workshop": http://calvarybiblechurch.org/site/cpage.asp?cpage_id=180023488&sec_id=180007745. "Why Can't We Just Get Along?": http://calvarybiblechurch.org/site/cpage.asp?cpage_id=180023503&sec_id=180007745. "Forgive, Forgive, and Forgive Again!" (November 2009): http://calvarybiblechurch.org/site/cpage.asp?sec_id=180007650&cpage_id+180020121&secure=&dlyear=2009&dlcat=0.

6. John F. MacArthur, *The Freedom and Power of Forgiveness* (Wheaton, IL: Crossway, 1998), 111.

7. Jay E. Adams, *From Forgiven to Forgiving* (Amityville, NY: Calvary Press, 1994). This is suggested reading for a more in-depth treatment of the Bible's teaching on forgiveness.

8. Adams, *From Forgiven to Forgiving*, 19-21.

9. John MacArthur develops this point at length in John F. MacArthur, *The Freedom and Power of Forgiveness* (Wheaton, IL: Crossway, 1998), 166-70.

10. Adapted from content found in Jay Adams, *From Forgiven to Forgiving* (Amityville, NY: Calvary Press, 1994), 20-22.

Chapter 21—Rebuilding a Marriage After Adultery

1. Les Carter, *The Prodigal Spouse: How to Survive Infidelity* (Nashville, TN: Thomas Nelson, 1990), 14.

2. J. Alan Peterson, *The Myth of Greener Grass* (Wheaton, IL: Tyndale House, 1991), 8.

3. Dave Carder, *Torn Asunder: Recovering from an Extramarital Affair* (Chicago, IL: Moody Press, 2008), 26.

4. DVD presentations covering much more information about rebuilding a marriage after adultery are available from www.noutheticmedia.com.

5. To help you more fully understand the importance and the nature of the biblical change dynamic I have briefly described here, I recommend four books: Paul David Tripp, *A Quest for More* (Greensboro, NC: New Growth Press, 2007); Paul David Tripp and Timothy Lane, *How People Change* (Greensboro, NC: New Growth Press, 2006); Wayne Mack and Joshua Mack, *God's Solutions to Life's Problems* (Tulsa, OK: Hensley Publications, 2002); Wayne Mack, *A Fight to the Death* (Phillipsburg, NJ: P&R Publishing, 2006).

6. Petersen, *The Myth of Greener Grass*, 15.

7. For a fuller explanation of the importance and meaning of confession and the freedom that comes through God's forgiveness, I suggest you read C.J. Mahaney, *The Cross-Centered Life* (Portland, OR: Multnomah Press, 2002). See also Jay Adams, *More Than Redemption* (Phillipsburg, NJ: P&R Publishing, 1979), 184-232.

8. R.C. Sproul, *The Intimate Marriage* (Phillipsburg, NJ: P&R Publishing, 2003), 128-129.

9. Wayne Mack, *Your Family God's Way* (Phillipsburg, NJ: P& R Publishing, 1991). This book explores a variety of biblical communication principles. Chapters 6-10 provide specific information on the "How much should be told?" issue.

10. Ken Sande, *The Peacemaker* (Grand Rapids, MI: Baker Books, 2004).

11. Wayne Grudem. *Systematic Theology: An Introduction to Biblical Doctrine* (Grand Rapids, MI: Zondervan, 1994), 713.

12. John Bunyan, *The Pilgrim's Progress*, trans. Cheryl Ford (Pretoria: Word of the Cross, 2007), 203-8.

13. Wayne Mack, "Faith's Siamese Twin: Repentance" (CD) can be found at http://www.nouthetic media.com/index.php?p=catalog&parent=7&pg=1 . Wayne Mack, "Repentance: Turning Point in Counseling" (CD) can be found at http://www.noutheticmedia.com/index.php?p=catalog& mode=catalog&parent=7&mid=0&search_in=all&search_str=&pg=4. Wayne Mack, "Am I Stuck or Can I Really Change?" (CD) can be found at http://www.noutheticmedia.com/index.php?p= catalog&mode=catalog&parent=7&mid=0&search_in=all&search_str=&pg=1. Also, read chapter 8 on "True Repentance" in Sinclair Ferguson's *The Christian Life* (Edinburgh: The Banner of Truth Trust, 1989).

14. Much help can be gained from studying and applying the truths about marriage found in the books Wayne Mack and Carol Mack, *Sweethearts for a Lifetime* (Phillipsburg, NJ: P&R Publishing, 2006) and Wayne Mack, *Strengthening Your Marriage* (Phillipsburg, NJ: P&R Publishing, 1977).

Chapter 22—Using Psychotropic Drugs

1. Walter A. Elwell and Philip Wesley Comfort, *Tyndale Bible Dictionary* (Wheaton, IL: Tyndale House, 2001), 1004.

2. See http://www.erowid.org/library/books_online/psychedelic_experience/psychedelic_experience .shtml.

3. Justin McKitterick, "Real Men Pray with Boldness," in Nathan Busenitz, *Men of the Word: Insights for Life from Men Who Walked with God* (Eugene, OR: Harvest House, 2009), 47.

4. Temazepam is a drug that is used for treating anxiety. It is in the benzodiazepine class of drugs, the same family that includes diazepam (Valium), alprazolam (Xanax), clonazepam (Klonopin), flurazepam (Dalmane), lorazepam (Ativan), and others. Temazepam and other benzodiazepines act by enhancing the effects of gamma-aminobutyric acid (GABA) in the brain. GABA is a neurotransmitter (a chemical messenger that nerve cells use to communicate with each other) that

inhibits many of the activities of the brain. It is believed that excessive activity in the brain may lead to anxiety or other psychiatric disorders and that Temazepam reduces the activity. Temazepam increases the user's total sleep time. The FDA approved Temazepam in February 1981. See http://www.medicinenet.com/temazepam/article.htm.

5. Kent R. Hughes, *Disciplines of a Godly Man* (Wheaton, IL: Crossway, 1991).

6. Any amount of sleep deprivation will diminish mental performance, cautions Mark Mahowald, a professor of neurology at the University of Minnesota Medical School. "One complete night of sleep deprivation is as impairing in simulated driving tests as a legally intoxicating blood-alcohol level." See http://www.fi.edu/learn/brain/sleep.html.

7. According to the CDC (Center for Disease Control) nearly 40 percent of men are now considered obese. Then there are those who may not be considered obese by CDC standards, yet are about 10-20 pounds overweight due to excessive ingestion of sugar-filled foods and drinks—this has been my personal observation as I've noticed patients' lifestyle eating habits over the course of 20 years of medical practice in the US. My estimate is this would include about another 30 percent of all men. For more information about what the CDC says about obesity statistics, see http://www.cdc.gov/obesity/adult.html.

8. John F. MacArthur, *The Power of Integrity: Building a Life Without Compromise* (Wheaton, IL: Crossway, 1997), 112-13.

9. See http://www.reference.com/browse/List_of_psychotropic_medications.

10. Elyse Fitzpatrick and Laura Hendrickson, MD, *Will Medicine Stop the Pain?* (Chicago, IL: Moody Publishers, 2006), 55.

11. On this matter a valuable resource is John MacArthur, *The Vanishing Conscience*, elec. ed., Logos Library Systems (43). Dallas, TX: Word, 1994.

12. Brent Small, "Real Men Love the Church" in Nathan Busenitz, *Men of the Word: Insights for Life from Men Who Walked with God* (Eugene, OR: Harvest House, 2009), 177.

13. Before you try medication, do your homework. Read this helpful pamphlet: Edward T. Welch, *A.D.D: Wandering Minds and Wired Bodies* (Phillipsburg, NJ: P&R Publishing, 1999).

Appendix One: The Gospel for Men

1. "Depression is not only the most common women's mental health problem but may be more persistent in women than men…Men are more likely than women to disclose problems with alcohol use to their health care provider." World Health Organization English website: www.who.int/mental_health/preventions/genderwomen/en/.

2. See www.who.int/mental_health/preventions/genderwomen/en/.

3. Adapted for precounseling purposes from questions developed by D. James Kennedy in *Evangelism Explosion* (Carol Stream, IL: Tyndale House, 1996).